To

Dad

with love and good wishes

from

Bill and Lorraine,

Christmas, 1978.

W. B. Graham
2 PARK DRIVE
NEWPORT
GWENT

# THE NAVAL SIDE OF
# KING WILLIAM'S WAR

*The author died in February 1968. It has, therefore, been my privilege to read the proofs and watch over publication. Accordingly, I would like to thank Miss E. Jacklin for her share in proof correction and all her help. Mr D. Kidd of the Publishers has been especially kind and patient in reading proofs and giving advice. Finally, I am sure it will be appreciated that a book so detailed as this needs its master's critical eye. I hope any errors due to this lack will be forgiven.*

IRIS POMEROY

# BY THE SAME AUTHOR

*The English Navy in the Revolution of 1688* (with Foreword by Admiral of the Fleet EARL JELLICOE, G.C.B., O.M.). Cambridge University Press, 1928.

*Vicisti Galilaee? or Religion in England* in 'Today and To-morrow Series'. Kegan Paul, 1929.

*A Hundred Years of English Poetry* (the Cambridge continuation of Palgrave's *Golden Treasury*). Cambridge University Press, 1931 and 1940. Macmillan, Canada (in 'The St. Martin's Classics'), 1937.

*The Laurel Bough—an Anthology of Verse, 1380–1932, excluding Lyric and Dramatic.* Bell, 1934.

*The House of de la Pomerai . . . from the Conquest to 1548 . . . with Appendix: 1720 onwards.* Liverpool University Press, 1943.

*Poems 1914–1950.* Muller, 1950.

*Catalogue.* The Cromwell Museum, Huntingdon, 1965.

Koning Stadhouder Willem III (artist unknown).

# THE NAVAL SIDE

## OF

# KING WILLIAM'S WAR

16th/26th November 1688–14th June 1690

## Edward B. Powley

*B.A.(Lond.), M.A.(L'pool), B.Litt., D.Phil.(Oxon.), F.R.Hist.S.,
Temporarily R.N., Sometime Assistant Master
in Merchant Taylors' School, Crosby.*

FOREWORD

## Sir Arthur Bryant

*C.H., C.B.E., LL.D.*

5 ROYAL OPERA ARCADE
PALL MALL LONDON SW1

©

1972 E. B. Powley

*First published in 1972 by*
*John Baker Publishers, Ltd.,*
*5 Royal Opera Arcade*
*Pall Mall, London*
*S.W.1.*

ISBN 0 212 98363 6

*The publication of this book has been assisted*
*by a grant from the Marc Fitch Fund*

Printed in Great Britain
at
The Curwen Press Ltd.
Plaistow, London

# Contents

# Illustrations

The Owners of Portraits and Institutions allowing reproductions to be made are asked to accept grateful acknowledgement.

7

# Foreword

## Sir Arthur Bryant

In *The Naval Side of King William's War* the late Dr Edward Powley
has left us a work of scholarship of the highest quality on a subject – or
rather two subjects – which have much relevance at the present time.
One, though incidental to his main theme, is the story of Northern
Ireland's classic ordeal of survival when its brave people, apparently –
though only apparently and temporarily – abandoned by England
and her new Dutch king, saved themselves from what in the words of a
famous Orange toast they regarded, with whatever prejudice, as
'Rogues and Roguery, Slaves and Slavery, Knaves and Knavery, Popes
and Popery.' The siege and relief of Londonderry is still for the
Protestant people of Ulster the supreme moment of their history – the
epic of self-help and courage by virtue of which their continuance as a
separate people was assured. For the non-Protestant people of Ulster
– today a deprived or supposedly deprived, minority – the significance of all this is, of course, very different, as it is also for the Catholic
people of independent Eire. Yet wherever one's sympathies may lie in
the confrontation now occurring – not for the first time – in the 'distress-
ful island's' story, history is the inescapable record of what happened
and how it happened, and here, in Dr Powley's pages, simply and
clearly, and with the authority of meticulous scholarship, is a relation
of certain events in time which help to explain what is now occurring
nearly three hundred years later. Though his account of the siege and
relief of Londonderry may not match Macaulay's in eloquence, it
is even more effective by virtue of its objectivity and the cumulative
industry with which a great scholar has marshalled the contemporary
evidence of a past age to enable us to see and feel what the men and
women of that time experienced. 'We beseech and obtest you, honoured
Sir, in the Bowells of Our Lord Jesus Christ that ye faile not to hasten
to our relief with provisions at least,' ran the appeal from the besieged,
which the valiant McGimpsey carried in a shot-weighted bladder tied
round his neck, as he attempted to swim the long sea-miles to Colonel
Kirke and the relieving squadron beyond the boom. The message never
got through. 'At the close of the 30th,' Dr Powley writes, as the starving,
fever-stricken city, reduced to its last rat and mouse, awaited the
seemingly inevitable end, its heroic commander 'lay dead; across the
river McGimpsey's proclaimed body dangled on a gallows; de Rosen,
not Kirke, had read the letters from the shot-weighted bladder that
the swimmer had not been able to sink; and the rumour of the special

barbarity de Rosen would apply should capitulation be withheld beyond 6 p.m. the next day spread through the mourning rain-soaked city;
that no quarter should be granted, no respect shown for age or sex.'
I found the author's account of how the unexpected deliverance came
almost breathlessly exciting. 'Since I was born,' wrote tough Colonel
Kirke, 'I navar saw a town of so little strength to rout an army with so
many generals against it.'

Yet if this remarkable book enlarges our knowledge of Ulster's
history–reminding us of what a reluctant 'Liberator' Dutch William,
with his eyes on wider horizons, was and how long he left a 'poor
people' at the mercy of merciless foes–its principal service to our knowledge of the past is the light it throws on the beginning of that long sea-
duel for command of the oceans between Great Britain and France
which, with half a dozen brief intervals continued from 1789 till 1815
and reached its culmination in the unchallengeable naval supremacy
of the globe won by Nelson and his fellow admirals. In these pages,
covering twenty crowded months between William's landing at Torbay
and the eve of his–and England's–shaming and unnecessary defeat
at sea under the cliffs of Beachy Head and of his own victory at the
Boyne, the scene is set for all the Royal Navy's struggles, hardships and
achievements to follow–storm and scurvy, tempest-torn and foundered
ships, stinking victuals and arrears of pay, adverse winds, press-gang
and mutiny, as its hard-used admirals, officers and men, building on
the great legacy of the thirty new ships-of-the-line and the administrative rules and discipline with which Mr Secretary-of-the-Admiralty
Pepys had endowed his country, contended with almost inconceivable
difficulties to guard the trade-routes, blockade the enemy's ports,
convey the merchantmen who for ever criss-crossed the perilous seas,
and maintain, in the face of royal, ministerial and parliamentary ignorance and folly, the indispensable touchstone of all–a Fleet in Being. 'It
may be now said to England,' wrote the great Lord Halifax in the dark
hour so brilliantly foreshadowed in this revealing, germinative book,
'Martha, Martha, thou art busy about many things, but one thing is
necessary. To the question, "What shall we do to be saved in the
world?" there is no other answer but this, "Look to your Moat." The
first article of an Englishman's political creed must be, that he believeth
in the sea . . . We are in an island, confined to it by God Almighty, not
as a Penalty but a Grace and one of the greatest that can be given to
Mankind. Happy Confinement that hath made us free, rich and quiet:
a fair portion in this World and very well worth the preserving.' The
late Dr Powley's scholarly masterpiece tells with what pains we first
learnt to do so.

ARTHUR BRYANT

# Preface

The pages following deal with *King William's War—Naval Affairs 16th November 1688–14th June 1690*. The intentions of a Franco-phobe King, originating naval policy and planning treaties to effect it; the moves of the Privy Council and the Secretary of State forwarding that policy; the deliberations of Parliament granting support and supply; the attitude of the House of Commons, supervisory and critical—to the extent, on occasion, of ordering naval officials and combatant officers to account at the bar of the House for their actions—these are handled side by side with the day-to-day conduct of the business of Admiralty and the course of operations at sea.

James's descent on Ireland, the battle of Bantry Bay, the 1689 first cruise of an Anglo-Dutch fleet, successful in establishing military command of the Channel and adjoining Irish and North Seas, but unfortunate in its failure to intercept the squadron which Tourville, two months out from Toulon, led into Brest, receive, for the first time from the English side, critical treatment. A like claim holds good for the naval operations culminating in the relief of Londonderry; Schomberg's passage to Carrickfergus; the return of the 1689 Grand Fleet, stricken with scurvy, to Torbay; the detachment of Lord Berkeley to cruise in the Soundings; the preparation of the Mediterranean and West Indies squadrons for convoy of trade and the first stage of the passage of the proxy-married Queen of Spain from Flushing to Coruña—to all English seamen 'The Groyne'. The sailing of Russell with his Queen, belated from Spithead, delayed from Torbay, Killigrew and Van Almonde in company, with 400 merchantmen to dispose of Oporto to Lisbon or from Cadiz into the Mediterranean (Malaga to Scanderoon) has attracted Dutch but not English attention. Dutch authority supplements Burchett's outline of the two admirals' abortive attempt to trap, in the Gibraltar strait Chateaurenault bound from Toulon to reinforce Tourville in Brest. Repetition, by d'Amfréville, across Russell's wake, of

Chateaurenault's earlier Bantry exploit (this time 'Cork' for
'Bantry' and no battle for d'Amfreville to fight) has received no
English notice. The present narrative discusses these neglected
matters and leads on to the day, the 14th June 1690, on which
King William has landed in Ireland, Torrington rides off St
Helens, commander-in-chief of the second, the 1690, Allied Grand
Fleet, and Tourville has just emerged from Brest with overwhelm-
ing force. But the Admiral designate of Torrington's Blue squad-
ron, Killigrew, with his dozen English and Dutch warships, is a
thousand miles distant–off Cadiz; and his Rear Admiral designate
of the Blue, with his six, half as far away–in Carrickfergus!
Neither will be with the Union flag when, shortly, the issue
Beachy-Bévéziers is joined.

The exercise of command for the protection of Allied trade, the
destruction of enemy trade and the prevention of neutral contraband traffic with France, are of course topics to receive attention.

Naval, even more than military historians, are prone to complain that what they write is but slowly absorbed and used
by the 'general' historian, who can often fairly retort that, if
there were 'world enough and time' and were naval monographs
less specialized, he would do better. In writing Naval History
specialization is, of course, intended and inevitable; but, in these
pages, some attempt has been made to avoid arbitrary disconnec-
tion of maritime narration from the broader history of the time.

Each Chapter of this work is preceded by its 'Argument'.
Additional to annotation there are Appendices, some of illustra-
tive, some of reference value–among them signals not hitherto
published. A list of Authorities follows. Charts are provided. There
are many illustrations. An Index ends the work. Throughout this
study, the technical term 'command' is used in the sense indicated
in an Appendix (A).

                *             *             *

Acknowledgements for permission to reproduce certain Plates and
Charts have already been made (pp. 7, 8). Mr T. W. H. Talbot
assisted with cartographic detail and Mr G. W. Rawlings, of the
University of Cambridge Library, solved intractable problems in
map photography. My publisher added to acceptance of the MS

welcome guidance. To my wife I owe deep gratitude for day to day encouragement and continuous scholastic help; and to Miss Eileen Jacklin, who typed my MS, read the proofs, and constructed the Index, I am particularly indebted. The Trustees of the Marc Fitch Fund have my especial thanks; for it is their generosity which makes the appearance of this research possible. Lastly, recommendation by Sir Arthur Bryant–fellow Pepysian and outstanding man of letters–is an honour which I very greatly appreciate.

Edward B. Powley
The Old Rectory
Grafham
Huntingdon

# CHAPTER I

# Francophobe King

### ARGUMENT

The dynastic settlement of 1688 decided by the refusal of the Prince of Orange to consider regency—His threat to return to Holland—Assessment of William's reason for invasion—The English, in domestic revolution, blind to the consequence of rule by a Francophobe King—King William's War already begun.

'THAT WILLIAM and Mary, Prince and Princess of Orange be, and be declared, King and Queen of England, France and Ireland and the Dominions thereunto belonging: to hold the Crown and Royal Dignity of the said King James and Dominions to them the said Prince and Princess during their Lives and the Life of the Survivor of them: And that the sole and full Exercise of the Regal Power be only in and executed by the said Prince of Orange in the Names of the said Prince and Princess during their joint lives: and after their Deceases, the said Crowns and Royal Dignity of the said Kingdoms and Dominions be to the Heirs of the Body of the said Princess: And, for Default of such Issue, the Princess Ann of Denmark and the Heirs of her Body: And for default of such Issue, to the Body of the said Prince of Orange.'[1]

Such was the agreed formula with which, upon Shrove Tuesday, 12th February 1688/9, the debates of the Lords and Commons, sitting as a 'Convention', concluded; and, next day, Lords and Commons, waiting upon the Prince and Princess in the Banqueting House of Whitehall, the Declaration of Right first being read, the Marquis of Halifax, acting Speaker of the Lords, tendered to the Prince and Princess the crown. The ceremony, followed in London and elsewhere by the customary proclamations, invested William and Mary, in English eyes, with the fullest measure of legal sovereignty that the Convention could claim to bestow.

Dynastically and executively the settlement thus effected was that which, indicated on the last day but one of December to Halifax,[2] had been 'required' by the Prince when, early in

February he had summoned before him Halifax, Danby, Shrewsbury and other leaders and broken his hitherto politic silence with
intimation of his own particular terms.

Some, he had heard, purposed to settle the government in the
hands of a regent, during the King's life. He had no objection:
It might be a wise project: But, if he was the person intended for
the office, he thought proper to let them know, he would accept
no dignity dependent on the life of another. Others, he understood, proposed to settle the Princess alone on the throne, and
admit him to a participation of power through her courtesy.
Her rights he would not oppose: Her virtues he respected: No
one knew them better than he did: Crowns to others had
charms: To him they had none. But he thought it proper also
to let them know, that he would hold no power dependent upon
the will of a woman. Therefore, if either of these schemes were
adopted, he could give them no assistance in the settlement of the
nation; but would return to his own country, happy in the
consciousness of the services he had endeavoured, though in
vain, to do to theirs.

The smooth diction of the foregoing quotation, does not pretend to
*ipsissima verba*; but the statement will serve.[3] Whether, at any
time or under any circumstances, the liberator would have
accepted regency is much to be doubted.[4] On this day, at this
conference, William left no uncertainty as to his personal standpoint—he rejected regency. *Aut Caesar aut—nihil!* Moreover, the
Prince had just received letters from the Princess in which she told
of her resentment at the solicitation of Danby to be allowed to
advance her claims to sole regality—or in any way 'divide her
interests from her husband's';[5] and, she said, she had acquainted
Danby with her resolution. Plainly, if William would not be
regent and Mary would neither be regent nor queen without a
king, little choice was left to the caballing senators. And if William
concluded his *démarche* with polite reference to the possibility of
regretful, unfruitful return to Holland, to be sure he did so with
suppressed ironic humour!

Whig historians are notoriously naïve in their apparent credence
of their hero's declarations. The Prince, general of an army of

fifteen thousand mercenaries, stood upon English soil, much of the disrupted military, the mobilized and reserve naval forces of the realm at his bidding. The realm's king was fugitive; himself, his queen and heir pawns at the court of the Prince's arch-enemy Louis. Whig to High Tory the English peerage were largely compromised in a rebellious cause; the newly elected Commons and the great mercantile capital stood the Prince's committed supporters. Who, indeed, can be persuaded that the Prince, at this climacteric stage, would have been prepared to go back to the Hague, either leaving Mary (if she had been willing) to cope with inevitable faction, likely risings, and probable invasion, her worsening needs clamouring for his intervention anew, or, alternatively, not even calling her from Honslaerdyk, himself return, discredited in the eyes of the Provinces and all Europe? Should he relinquish the enterprise, the mutual antagonisms of the Dutch and English must triumph, the merchants of Amsterdam be given ample cause to lament the cost of an abortive expedition unrepaid in English gold, all diplomatic initiative in European affairs be negatived, the prayers of Protestants, with which had mingled the officially ordered petitions of Catholic Austria, fail.[6] That Louis, during the Prince's expeditionary sojourn in England, should have seized the opportunity to declare open war against the States General (the declaration had been made within ten days of the Torbay disembarkation) can scarcely have been, for the aspirant, an unforeseen contingency – the event no cause whatever for withdrawal. No, useful as the threat of retirement might be, such 'tragical, comical, historical' dénouement can never have ranked as a serious possibility in William's personal plans.

Why had the Prince intervened in England?

William was thirty-eight. For over sixteen years, as Stadholder, Captain and Admiral-General of the United Provinces, the integrity of the republic, menaced by le Roi Très Chrétien, Louis le Grand, had been his care. No certitude had ensued upon his efforts. The indecisive battle of Senef, the defeats of Maestricht, Montcassel and Charleroi rankled; the treaty of Nimeguen, made in 1678, sealing an armed truce and strengthened, for a time, by

the Prince's first serious essay in the building of an anti-French
continental alliance, had, in great measure, been negatived by the
conclusion, in 1684, of the twenty years' truce of Ratisbon made
between France and her non-Dutch opponents, an agreement
which left Luxembourg and Strasbourg added to Louis' rule. The
league of Augsburg had cut no teeth. Stalemate obtained. Across
all Europe–in England, France, Savoy, Hungary, the Palatinate–
the fortunes of Protestantism darkened and the Protestant Stadholder of the tolerant Provinces[7] found himself the acknowledged
leader of a cause. To him, in that capacity, none looked more
hopefully than the English opposition to a Catholicizing king; and
the Prince, if for no other reason than that his wife was heiress-in-
tail to the English crown, was bound to reciprocate their concern.
Probably before the close of 1686 the suggestion of armed intervention in England had been mooted to the Prince, whose dispatch
of Dykvelt to the court of St James in the Spring of 1687 was
indubitably a mission 'not to the government but to the opposition'.[8] Whig and Tory alike corresponded with William. Nottingham, for example, declared:

> he [Dyckvelt] has so fully informed himself . . . that he can give
> you a very exact account . . . and of one thing especially he may
> assure you, and that is, the universal concurrence of all Protes-
> tants in paying their utmost respect and duty to your Highness,
> for you are the person on whom they found their hopes, as
> having already seen you a refuge to the miserable, and a most
> eminent defender of their religion.

And Danby expressed the view that, could personal conference be
arranged, 'some overtures might be made which would be of use
to the Prince's service'.[9] Answering his father-in-law, the Prince
explicitly told his disapproval of the abrogation of the 'Tests'. He
went to the length of allowing Pensionary Fagel's letter to circulate
to encourage the recalcitrancy of James's subjects. All this is the
commonplace of History; no less so our knowledge of the English
domestic events of the opening months of 1688 reaching their
climax in June with the birth of an heir to the throne, the acquittal
of the Seven Bishops and the sending, the self-same day, of the
celebrated cipher-signed invitation to the Prince to do that for
which he had been stealthily preparing ever since the news of the

Queen's pregnancy had been noised abroad. The invitation received, William took decision to invade. Four months later, on 1st November, after a false start, the expedition sailed. 'His flag was English colours; the motto impaled thereon was "The Protestant Religion and Liberty of England"; and underneath, instead of "Dieu et Mon Droit" was "And I will maintain it".'[10] It is not to derogate from the sincerity of the Prince's unemotional Calvinistic Protestantism, his distaste for persecution, to affirm that the proud blazon which flapped from the mast-head of *den Briel*, the Prince's frigate leading the van, and the similar insistence upon the theme of 'Protestantism and Liberty' in the language of the Prince's printed declarations, published the ostensible but concealed the fundamental motive of intervention. Not Protestantism as such, certainly not the 'liberties of England' as expressed in her 'parliamentary' system, not pique at a birth which robbed his wife of the expectations of an heiress-in-tail, but simple desire to wield the power of the English throne launched the winter venture. True, the wearing of 'the round and top of sovereignty' made to William but limited appeal; but not to conclude that the Prince, before he sailed, had determined to acquire authority to command the great economic and naval strength of a realm, secure (as the Provinces were not) from frontal attack, a western bastion from which to harass, possibly invade his foe, is to make nonsense of the interpretation of History. '*Guillaume, confiant dans sa destinée . . . impassible au milieu du mouvement universel . . .*'[11] had dared the fate of Medina Sidonia to range England, the Provinces, such German states as faced or watched the arms of France with apprehension, the Emperor's Austria, against a Catholic and a King with whom no 'good correspondence' was possible. For Louis rejected all comity, persecuted at home and devastated abroad as ruthlessly as his heathen helper the Turk; would bestride the Rhine, revive the Europe of Charlemagne without partnership with the Pope and, core of his policy, acquire, soon or late, family legatee interests in the empire of Spain–the Iberian peninsula, the Sicilies, the Netherlands and the lands beyond the Atlantic line. And it has been somewhat severely but justly observed that, the crown obtained: 'The destinies of England, her internal development had for him [William] no interest save as they rendered her a factor more or less conducive to the Great Design.'[12] Did the inclusion of the word 'France' ('King and Queen of England, *France* and Ireland . . .') in the Whitehall recitation of the royal style and dignities wring a wry smile from the impassive visage? Presumably not. William left even moderate elation to the recently arrived Princess Mary or countenanced its expression in metallurgic art. A medal, struck at this very time, displays large the new-made King in a readily recognizable biblical rôle; it bears the circumscription *Iosua cursum solis retinet*![13]

From the day of the landing of the Prince to that of his and the Princess's accession, Englishmen, occupied with domestic revolution, gave limited thought to European happenings, little or none to what must be the immediate and contingent consequences of rule by the Francophobe Stadholder they had made King. Few in England then realized how surely the nation had been led into the conflict which their descendants were to call *King William's War*.[14] True, the official declaration of that war lay almost three months in the future; but, for practical purposes, on the 13th February 1688/9, the issue was already three months joined–that is to say from the date on which Louis had declared war on the United Provinces, the 16th/26th November 1688. It is the purpose of this work, as has been indicated in the Preface, to examine the naval side of the confrontation from that date to the 14th June 1690. On that day William landed at Carrickfergus to face the Irish campaign he had avoided. That day Torrington, commander-in-chief of the second, the 1690, Allied English-Dutch Main Fleet, reached St Helens from his preliminary rendezvous in the Downs; and his opponent Tourville, out from Brest with superior force, left behind Iles d'Ouessant–and his galleys. A fortnight ahead– the engagement Beachy-Bévéziers!

### REFERENCES

1 *Journals of the House of Commons from 12th December 1688 to 26th October 1693*, vol. X.

2 Foxcroft, H. C., *The Life and Letters of Sir George Savile, Bart., First Marquis of Halifax* . . . 2 vols. 1898, vol. I, p. 46.

    A note by Dartmouth to Burnet's *History* . . . implies that the Marquis, in conversation with the Prince on the occasion of the first night of the

Prince's residence in St. James's, ventured the remark that he, the Prince: might be what he pleased himself . . . for, as nobody knew what to do with him, so nobody knew what to do without him.

Burnet, Gilbert (Bishop of Salisbury), *Bishop Burnet's History of his Own Times* (*with Notes by the Earls of Dartmouth and Hardwick, etc.*) ed. Routh, M. J., 6 vols, Oxford, 1833, vol. III, p. 396.

3 Dalrymple (Sir )John, *Memoirs of Great Britain and Ireland, from the Dissolution of the last Parliament of Charles II until the Sea-battle off La Hogue*, 2 vols, London and Edinburgh, 1771 (2 edn.), vol. I, i, p. 269.

4 Foxcroft, *op. cit.*, vol. I, p. 46. Miss Foxcroft considers that, before James's flight, William did not expect to be more than Regent.

5 Dalrymple, *op. cit.*, vol. I, p. 269.

6 *Négociations de M. le Comte d'Avaux en Irlande 1689–90*, ed. Hogan, J., Dublin 1934, p. 171 (Projet de Lettre by James).

7 . . . *Amsterdam, Turk–Christian–Pagan–Jew*,
Staple of Sects and Mint of Schisme grew;
That *Bank of Conscience*, where not one so strange
Opinion but finds Credit, and Exchange.
In vain for *Catholicks* our selves we bear;
The *universal church* is onely there.

Marvell, Andrew (the younger) *The Character of Holland* (1681), v. Margoliouth, H. M., *The Poems and Letters of Andrew Marvell*, Oxford, 1952, p. 95.

8 Macaulay, T. B. (Baron), *History of England from the Accession of James II*, 5 vols., 1856, vol. II, p. 245.

9 Dalrymple, *op. cit.*, App. I, pp. 192, 195, 18th and 30th May 1687.

10 *Expedition of the Prince of Orange to England 1688*. Signed N. N. [= Burnet] *The Harleian Miscellany*. . . vol. I, p. 449; *Somers Tracts* . . . vol. IX, p. 276.

11 Mazure, F. A. J., *Histoire de la Révolution de 1688 en Angleterre*, 3 t. Paris 1848. vol. III, p. 301.

12 Foxcroft, *op. cit.* vol. I, p. 64.

13 A medal (very rare—the British Museum has an example) struck in 1689 pictures the new-made King in the biblical role *Iosua cursum solis retinet. v. Histoire métallique des XVII Provinces des Pays Bas* . . ., Loon, G. Van. vol. IV, la Haye, 1736, p. 7. For illustration—*Metallic Illustrations of British History*, vol. I, 1885, p. 684, or *Medallic Illustrations of the History of Great Britain and Ireland*. Plates LXXI–LXXX, Oxford, 1908 (for B.M.).

14 Sir G. N. Clark, in *The Later Stuarts 1660–1714*, Oxford 1934, p. 143, expresses this view with much emphasis:
The aspect of his intervention in England which had all along been most important to him had hardly occupied the attention of the English for a moment.

# CHAPTER II

# This Side the Channel

## *16th/26th November 1688 – 13th February 1688/9*

*ARGUMENT*

I

*Louis declares war on the States General, 16th/26th November–On which date the English Admiral Dartmouth resumes from the Downs his pursuit of the invasion fleet under Herbert, riding in Torbay–Herbert quits Torbay for Plymouth and Dartmouth falls back on Portsmouth–In spite of permission to attempt to blockade Dartmouth's ships, Herbert takes no action–Dartmouth, 2nd December, required by James to spirit away from Portsmouth to France the infant Prince of Wales, refuses; learns, by the 11th, that the Queen, with the baby (returned to London) is in flight and that the King intends to follow–The English admiral then, in response to an invitation from William, surreptitiously delivered, surrenders, 12th December, the royal fleet–Dartmouth, concerned lest depredatory raids on England occur, Herbert, ordered to attack alike French corsairs and trade, share a common anti-French outlook–But the two fleets are not joined; Dartmouth is instructed to leave a squadron in Portsmouth and sail for the Nore–The Prince, Admiral-General of the United Provinces, now also, 16th December, in control of the Admiralty of England–Decision, 26th December, to lay up Dartmouth's ships suddenly reversed–The City's loan–Dartmouth's ships reach the Nore and the Dutch pass homeward–Mobilization into Mediterranean, Channel and Irish squadrons and a reserve–A Pepysian régime continues–Anglo-Dutch treaty relations.*

*Tyrconnel's vice-royalty enters a new phase and the siege of Londonderry begins.*

II

*Wisdom and neglect in William's naval policy to date.*

I

IN DECLARING WAR on the States General of the United Provinces, on Friday, 16th/26th November, Louis XIV asserted that it was the Dutch, who had desired the treaty of Nimeguen but had not kept it. Witness their *'levées et armements extraordinaires'* and engagements made with princes of the Empire: *'pour traverser par toutes voyes l'établissement du Cardinal du Furstemberg.'* They, the document alleged, had caused to assemble under the Prince de Waldeck an army *'actuellement joint'* with the forces leagued against the cardinal. War must follow *'tant par Mer que par Terre'*, communication, commerce, intelligences between the respective countries cease. *'Monsieur l'Admiral'*, the marshals of France and all royal officers within the limits of their authorities must act to enforce the declaration. In all towns, '*tant Maritimes qu'autres et en tous Ports, Havres* . . .', the broadsheet must be exhibited.[1] Though the proclamation made no mention of the passage, less than a fortnight earlier, of the Dutch Stadholder to England, it is difficult not to regard that descent as the proximate irritation productive of the drafting of this formal display. November is scarcely the month for beginning land–or sea–warfare! Whatever his troop dispositions Louis had no fleet at sea.

There were, however, on the day in question, two fleets in the Channel waters–less than 150 sea miles apart–those of the invading Dutch and the pursuing English.

How that conjuncture had happened has elsewhere been told in documented detail.[2] The invading fleet, heading first for a landing on the eastern coast of England had slipped past the English fleet immobilized by wind and tide in the Thames estuary. [Intent, after ill-fortune and enforced delay, to attack the Dutch fleet and transports in the Devonshire waters, the English commander, Lord Dartmouth, in the *Resolution*, his fleet in three squadrons (Sir Roger Strickland and Sir William Berry respectively Vice and Rear Admirals), late on the night of Friday the 16th, put Dungeness astern. At noon on Saturday the 17th Dartmouth was passing the Wight; on the morning of Sunday the 18th Alderney bore south-eastward, some estimated seven leagues. Shortly 'a very great storm' arose, battering and scattering the fleet so seriously that when, on Monday the 19th, the remnant looked into Torbay, twenty-two only of Friday's effective strength of thirty-three rates (with fourteen fireships) rode in the admiral's view. Nor was foul weather spent. At night followed 'a violent storm at W.S.W.', which, next morning, Tuesday the 20th, 'continuing very hard' swept the three ill-cohering English squadrons into St Helens Road. Two days later the fleet anchored in the Spithead, the King's Bedchamber.

On the initial day, Friday the 16th November, Lieutenant-General Admiral Herbert, in the *Leyden*, commanding fifty or fewer Dutch ships of war, which by no means overwhelmingly outmatched in gun power the English armament, ten fireships and miscellaneous warcraft, the whole organized in three squadrons

(Lieutenant-Admirals Cornelis Evertzen and Van Almonde, Herbert's subordinates), hovered in or off Torbay shepherding over 200 transports. These, by the terms of Herbert's original instructions of the 27th/17th October, were overdue of return to the Maas and Texel; for the frigates expected to sail from Holland to accept them had not arrived. The Prince, at Exeter, had just given Herbert an asked-for permission to seek the English fleet and drive it into port—saluting, attempting pourparler, and only at necessity resorting to force. The English accounted for, Lieutenant-Admiral Bastiaensze was to convoy the transports and Lieutenant-Admiral Evertzen take home the fleet. Herbert, however, made no specific move against Dartmouth; and, on the 17th, the Prince commiserated: '*je suis bien marry que le vent contraire vous oblige d'y rester.*'

By the 21st, the *Gazette* reported that the Dutch fleet was not in Torbay. In need of provisions it had coasted round to Plymouth making it at much the same time as the battered English fleet, itself immobilized off Portsmouth. Neither fleet neglected scouting; both showed awareness of the presence of French privateers in the Channel.

The last week of November alike for Dartmouth, refitting, and for Herbert, in much better case, each well informed of the other's whereabouts and strength, was a period of waiting upon land events. Then, as against France, their interests suddenly converged.

On Sunday 2nd December Dartmouth received a request from James to spirit across the water the baby Prince Charles—already sent down to Portsmouth for conveyance. The request, even when turned to an order, met with refusal. Dartmouth wrote James: 'that sending away the Prince of Wales without the consent of the nation [would be] at no time advisable.' It would yield 'fatal consequence'; inducing subjects to 'throw off their bounden allegiance'; it would entail: 'a perpetuall warre . . . giving France alwayes a temptation to molest, invade, nay hazard the conquest of England.' No man in England had a clearer right to speak. Treason against himself as King *and* the nation James might not rightly require. Lord Dartmouth took no risks. Certain ships received orders to prevent egress from the harbour and armed boats watched the waterfront. The baby was returned to London and, by Tuesday the 12th December, the Admiral is found replying to an invitation from the Prince of Orange to place his fleet under the Prince's protection. The solicitation of the Prince by certain officers of the fleet 'well-inclined' towards him, the verbal delivery of their message by Lieutenant Byng, cleverly on leave from his ship, the manner in which the young man brought the invitation from Sherbourne to the fleet ('he thought it best to quilt it in the rowlers of his breeches'), and how adventurously it was laid upon the Admiral's toilet table is a story of absorbing interest. Dartmouth, as he wrote, was well aware that the Queen with her infant was already making from the Kingdom; and he possessed information that James himself was resolved upon flight. A Parliament and the Prince should, Dartmouth conceded, consult to save the Protestant religion and the laws. Meanwhile he promised a Papist purge and his 'utmost to prevent any French forces landing, or making any descent, on these Kingdomes.' The two fleets, he said, must be merged: 'no distaists . . . given that either may be liable to.' Captain Aylmer carried to the Prince this surrender. Meanwhile Vice-Admiral Strickland and other Catholics laid down their commissions, Berry succeeding Strickland as Vice and Lord Berkeley Berry as Rear-Admiral of the fleet.

That Herbert, as befitted the English commander of a three-squadron Dutch fleet hampered by responsibility for the empty transports, should, on the 8th December, have requested the Prince for specific guidance as to the proper attitude towards the French, is not a matter for surprise. His questionnaire was returned, with marginal comments, on the 10th, from Newbury. The main directive was brief: '*Attaque tous les armateurs françois. Et prendre tous les vaisseaus marchands et les mainer en Flandre.*'[3] English ships or forts coming over to the Prince's side were not to be required to change flag; they too should, if opportunity arose, seize French vessels; it would be permissible for their crews and soldiers to receive a month's pay in advance.

Thus, ere mid December, there were no longer in the Channel a Dutch and an English fleet in opposition but two armaments both commanded by Englishmen, who professed, though not as friends, and in varying degree, a common domestic cause and a like anti-French outlook. While to the mind of Dartmouth occurred the possibility of depredatory raids and descents, St Malo and Dunkirk privateers troubled the Prince's imagination. Each commander assumed that he held a substantial measure of command of the Channel and one had been specifically bidden to exercise it in the destruction of privateers and of French trade.

Captain Aylmer returned from Windsor to the English fleet on Wednesday the 19th December. He brought the Admiral a letter of acknowledgement and approbation from the Prince, its main purport an instruction to lead the fleet to the 'Boy of the North' (Nore) and thereafter wait upon the Prince with advice. The missive bore the date the 16th December and was signed 'Your affectionate Friend, Prince d'Orange'. Certain enclosed orders had, however, the effect of subtracting thirteen men of war and two fireships from Dartmouth's total fleet, a compact squadron of vessels to be placed under the command of Vice-Admiral Sir John Berry, and left based on Portsmouth. Dartmouth's ships were to empty surplus provisions for Berry's benefit. To the squadron's Admiral was assigned the task of countering any 'affront' by the French and the prevention of the sailing of suspects from the port. Sir Richard Beach, the local Navy Board Commissioner, was to be told not to fit out further ships.

News of Dartmouth's surrender was, of course, duly dispatched to Herbert at Plymouth and the arrangements for the disposal of the invading fleet and transports, made before the expedition sailed, were not substantially varied.

Thus the Prince, two days before his entry into London on the 18th and before the second flight of the King, a few hours earlier, had, in effect, added to his Admiral-Generalship of the naval forces of the United Provinces the ultimate attribute of a Lord High Admiral of England – the direction of an English fleet. From this point onwards the machine of Admiralty, its Secretariat, the Navy Office, Victualling Office and Yards were at the Prince's direction and, on and after the 19th, the Secretary for the Affairs of Admiralty of England, Mr Samuel Pepys, was in close attendance upon William. It must also be remembered that at the Prince's side stood Edward Russell. A scion of a great house, he was three years younger than William and had served eleven years at sea under Narborough and Herbert. He was one of those Englishmen who had crossed to Holland to throw in his lot with

William, accompanied him to Torbay, and, at this juncture, acted, it seems, as his secretary.

Dartmouth's assumption that the Prince would join the fleets had not been realized! So, on the 20th, the day after receiving the Prince's letter and order, the English admiral made ready to sail for the Nore; but the wind, as he told the Prince, hung easterly and provisions would, he said, be needed should the wind not change. He urgently advised the Prince to order ships to cruise off the Guernsey banks and to 'put good garrisons in Jersey and Guernsey'. Of the latter island he commented: 'If it should be possessed by the French [it would be] a thorne in England's sides for ever.' Dartmouth touched also upon affairs of the Ordnance Office, of which he was Master. Ten days were to elapse before the fleet could fill sails; and consequently the shortage of victuals was progressively felt.

A communication from Pepys, speaking as mouthpiece of the Prince, went forth on Christmas Day. (James on that day made a fugitive's landfall at Ambleteuse and close on his heels followed the French ambassador, le Sieur Barillon d'Amancourt, who, ordered on the Prince's sole responsibility to be clear of the country within forty-eight hours, quitted the capital on the 24th.) Dartmouth's advice concerning Jersey and Guernsey would be acted on and steps taken to stop the annoyance which French privateers were causing the Holland packets. Special services were to be provided for St George's Channel (111–156).]

Next day, the 26th, Pepys wrote again to Dartmouth revealing the Prince's mind. He spoke of the Prince as 'intending with all the speed he conveniently [could] to retrench the present extra-ordinary charge of the Navy [but only] as farr as the state whereto the affairs of this Kingdom [would] admitt.' And, on the 29th, Pepys informed the Admiral that the Prince had: 'in generall concluded upon laying up and paying off all the 3d rates, and all the larger fourths, and of the lesser fourths and shipps and vessells below them all but what he [had] determined to keep out the remainder of the winter.' Dartmouth's views on retrenchment were conveyed in a dispatch of the 29th, which appears not to be ex-tant; but, from Pepys's reply, made upon New Year's day, the Admiral's convictions and advice can be readily inferred.

For his Highness has, upon great deliberation and time taken in it, determined upon putting in practise what I lately made some mention of to your Lordshipp, in relation to the retrenching the greater part of the present charge of the fleet: and this not without haveing had laid before him all the considerations that have occurred on one side or other concerning it, and particularly what your Lordshipp offers in your letter to me of the 29th of the last, which came to my hand yesterday, and has been since communicated to me by his Highness. Who was pleased thereupon to give me this for answer, that the charge of soe great a fleet is too great, and otherwise inconvenient to be unnecessarily borne at this season of the year for soe many months, as the remainder of this winter containes, and therefore thought not fitt to make any alteration in the disposall he had made thereof.[4]

It is plain that Dartmouth, who had earlier assumed that the two fleets would be combined, was contending strongly, on the 29th, for keeping at sea a force appreciably larger than William wished to employ. Pepys passed on orders for two small frigates to be based without delay on Chester, for eight companies of troops to be taken to Guernsey and Jersey, others to be brought back and 1500 disbanded Irish troops to be transferred to the Isle of Wight.[5] What ships precisely were to be paid off, what limited few left at sea Dartmouth in due course learned—probably by the 4th January. Forty-nine vessels were to be laid up in the yards of Chatham, Deptford and Woolwich, seven third rates with fireships to be left at Portsmouth, one fourth to be detached to guard the Dutch packets.[6] But, even before he read, the retrenchment decision had been superseded and the day ended with the Secretary informing Dartmouth that 'His Highness was come to some fresh resolutions' and that it was not now proposed that *any* of Dartmouth's command should be laid up.[7] It can only be supposed that the Prince had yielded to advice—Russell was still at his side, and, a possibility which must not be overlooked, Herbert by this time may have travelled from the West and reached London.[8]

[Lieutenant-Admiral-General Herbert with his transports and fleet had spent Christmas in or off Plymouth Sound. By orders of the 26th December he had been required to dispatch Vice-Admiral Almonde with thirteen warships to '*l'embouchure de mer nommée 't veersche Gat*'[9] to be employed by the States General for the convoy of Mediterranean trade; five or six others were to sail under Van der Putten '*à Spit Head*', thence to cruise in the Channel to prevent the depredations of '*Corsaires François dans cette mer*'; Lieutenant-Admiral Evertzen was to be detailed to bring the rest of the fleet about '*dans cette Rivière*' and Lieutenant-Admiral Bastiaensze required to escort 'hither' as many transports as would be needed to convey to Holland 1000 horse and 6000 fantassins, which task performed, he would, with the rest of the transports return to Holland according to preceding orders. It was a postscript to these orders which had given Herbert authority to make his way as soon as possible to St James's (159).][10]

Two recent writers[11] attribute the change of policy concerning laying up the English fleet to the fact that the Prince was assured of a loan of £200,000 from the City of London. Though the City's 'Maior Aldermen and Comõns . . . in common Councell assemb^d' had as early as the 17th December stated that they would 'not spare to expose . . . lives and estates' in gratitude for deliverance, no formal approach to their generosity was made before the 8th day of January. The very business-like arrangements beginning with agreement upon the conditions on which the loan should be secured upon the Excise were expeditiously effected; but several days necessarily elapsed before the large subscriptions came in.[12]

[The anchors of that portion of the English fleet directed from the Spithead to the Buoy of the Nore (see p. 26) were weighed on Sunday, the 30th December; Beachy was passed by midnight, Dover reached by Monday at dusk. Next day, the fleet but little advanced, a cold fog fell. The new fourth rate *Sedgemore*[13] went ashore under the Foreland and the weatherbound Admiral sought permission to travel overland to London, a request which William, hinting that he could not well trust a deputy, would not entertain.[14] Tuesday, the 8th January, witnessed the fleet clearing the Strait. The Buoy of the Nore was made on Friday the 11th and, with anchorage, the struggle to sail victuallers out of the Thames against an east wind to the delayed incoming fleet also ended.

Orders awaited Dartmouth to hand over his charge to his second in command and hasten to audience with the Prince.[15]

At the end of the month Dartmouth was attending the House of Lords. He cast his vote for a regency. For a while he retained the post of Master of the Ordnance; but he was not to be allowed to fill any naval office and received no further commission. Once only was he to be called by the Commissioners of Admiralty to meet 'with Severall Flagg Officers and other Commanders . . . to conferre on some affairs'.[16] With Herbert for rival and personal enemy and with Russell ill-disposed, Dartmouth disappeared from the public stage. 'It will be an act so commendable that it will not only oblidge me for ever to be your friend but even to study which way I may shew my kindnesse to you in the most particular manner.'[17] The words of the note laid upon the toilet table of the *Resolution* upon the 29th November must have been remembered hollowly two years later in a spell of imprisonment ended with death in the Tower! (157–8)]

The Prince, Herbert, Mr Secretary Pepys, and possibly Russell met on the night of Saturday, the 12th January, took up and settled the problem of limited or wider mobilization.[18] The personal relations of the group might well prove a topic of speculation. The Prince aloof, with cause to lean upon Herbert's advice, Russell, if present, in all probability critical of Herbert, Herbert and the Secretary estranged, the latter correct and unadulatory – his sole concern England and the service which was his proper pride! The presence of Herbert at this most important conference is not to be taken as evidence that he proposed or was a party to fixing the ratios of or allocation to the squadrons, though he was largely responsible for decisions concerning manning and victualling the same.

Four third rates, the *Elizabeth, Plymouth, Yorke, Warspight*, and eight fourths, *St Albans, Assurance, St. David, Diamond, Foresight, Portland, Woolwich, Deptford*, and three fireships were detailed for the Streights (Mediterranean), one third rate *Defiance* and five fourth rates, *Antelope, Ruby, Tyger, Phoenix, Greenwich*, for the Channel; six fourths, *Advice, Bonadventure, Dover, Jersey, Mordaunt, Swallow*, and two sixths, *Lark* and *Saudadoes* for Ireland. Dartmouth's October 1688 fleet had consisted of over sixty vessels. All

not allocated for the above services or otherwise 'counted out' were
to be kept in pay 'in readiness for future services'. This reserve
included the nine third rates, *Cambridge*, *Dreadnought*, *Edgar*,
*Hampton Court*, *Henrietta*, *Mary*, *Kent*, *Pendennis* and *Resolution*, the
seven fourths, *Bristoll*, *Centurion*, *Constant Warwick*, *Crowne*, *Newcastle*, *Portsmouth*, *Tyger Prize*, the two sixths, *Firedrake* and *Quaker
Ketch* and seventeen fireships. The Streights squadron would carry
middle complement of men, the Irish and Channel vessels muster
full crews. Victuals for the south-bound ships were to be supplied
four months wet, six months dry; for the Irish on a three months'
calculation; for the Channel contingent as much as possible and
not less than for two months should be taken aboard. The non-
allocated vessels were to retain minimum complements.[19] These
arrangements represented an employment of ten thousand men
'after all abatements of number yet in view'. The names of all
except three of the thirty-five thirds and fourths mentioned in a
table which, on 14th October, Dartmouth sent to James, may be
found duplicated in the above lists, and also those of a further
eight which were ordered to reinforce him. The four sixth rates
known to have been with the Admiral are named above. Dartmouth had with him at least twelve fireships and up to nineteen
at call; for the new groupings twenty are stipulated.[20]

It was from the dozen or so ships left in the Spithead under
Vice-Admiral Berry that a few ships required for immediate
duties off the Channel Islands and in the St George's Channel were
provided, *Swallow* and *Jersey* being ordered to Chester.[21] [On the
15th January, Berry, leaving Captain Ashby as Commodore,
brought five of the thirds and fourths, convoying smaller vessels,
to the Downs (158)[22]] and later dispatched four to overhaul
Herbert who had sailed on the 18th with yachts to Goree to fetch
the Princess.[23] Berry, chosen for the command of the Mediterranean squadron,[24] quickly raised with Pepys the question of
manning and victualling his fleet. He received reply:

As to the V$^c$ [Victualling] of Shipps appointed for ye Streights
Squadron and ye Complem$^{ts}$ of men allowd them, both ye one
and ye other was proposed to and adjusted w$^h$ ye Prince by
Adm$^{ll}$ Herbert who I doubt not did it with good deliberačon as

to the Shipps & must be tho[t] a very good Judge as to their Manning.[25]

In the Downs the Vice-Admiral picked up three more frigates and sailed just after mid-day on the 30th January. An entry in the log kept by the Captain of the *Ruby* which, with another fourth rate, the *Portland*, was standing by the wrecked *Sedgemore* (see p. 29) to take off 'geare' indicates the manner in which part of the morning had been spent: 'This day being ye Anniversary of King Charles's ye first Marterdome I lowered my Colours hafe Staff downe & fired 20 gunns in the Commemoration of his Murder & rest of ye Shipps doeing the same . . .'[26] Berry reached the Nore by the 5th February[27] and on about the 7th brought his vessels, what and such as they were, into the Swayle: 'for scrubbing of the s[d]shipps and ye giving them Boat-hose-topps.'[28] The Navy Board was ordered to add to the Mediterranean contingents' victuals an additional allowance, which, enough for 700 men, constituting 'this year's supply' was to be delivered to Gibraltar where, for some years, an agent had been allowed to function. Berry was now given[29] the leave which, like Dartmouth, he had unsuccessfully sought while passing through the Downs.[30] Pepys fought hard, at this juncture, to prevent all absence of officers from their posts.[31] To Captain Graydon, up in town instead of on the deck of the *Saudadoes*, and he might 'take it in good or ill part!' the martinet promised a court-martial – the offence: 'such a peice of Liberty as [he Pepys] had never before mett w[t] in neere 30 yeares Service [a default which] would not now be adventured by any Comander in the Fleet.'[32] Graydon replied, as he conceived, suitably; but Pepys had the last word: 'nor shall you find me less Solicitous for the Support of good Discipline in any Other Case (be it who it will or the number as great as it will) then I am in yours.'[33]

At this time the Secretary was particularly incensed with Lord Berkeley. It was to that Rear-Admiral's squadron that the *Sedgemore* (see p. 29), run aground off the South Foreland, belonged. Pepys, who had, on the 9th, expressed to his Lordship expectation that the customary enquiry would follow,[34] learned with horror that Berkeley had gone so far as to order the breaking up of the third rate's hull. Whereupon he wrote to the Navy

Board, observing that not even the Lord High Admiral James
would have acted without initial consultation with the Board and
intimated that he had no doubt the Board would know how to
proceed. It at once ordered a survey.[35]

Commanding officers in this transitional time, undoubtedly experienced difficulty in convincing some of the crews that their
wages 'for their service in the late fleet' would be paid. Pepys, on
the 18th January, alarmed at reports of 'disorders', 'p'ticularly in
ye *Ruby* where it proceeded to a downeright Mutiny'[36], sent the
Navy Board, for suitable distribution, a 'Piele of Printed Copies'
of a Declaration which the Prince had issued in order to remove
the 'Jealousie . . . lately . . . raised (how and by whom is not
known) among the seamen.'[37] The Declaration dated 16th
January promised:

> as well as the Arrears due . . . the growing Wages of all and
> every Officer and seaman serving in the . . . Fleet . . . according
> to the known methods of the Navy, so soon as the Ships whereon
> they shall respectively Earn the same, shall be brought in and
> laid up.[38]

It extended 'pardon' to deserters who returned within fifteen days
with reminder of the existent penalties if they did not. Pepys had
already dispatched bundles of the broadsheet to Harwich,
Portsmouth, the Downs and the Naze and the Nore where
command had been taken over by Rear-Admiral Davis.[39] Pressing,
William would not on any consideration allow.[40]

One hears little of the dispersal of the Dutch fleet and transports
from English waters. The log of the *Ruby*, quite silent as to 'open
mutiny', makes reference on the 13th January:

> *Jan. 13* Amsterdam squadron passed by. Admirall of Amsterdam
> and ye Dutch rere-admirall all past close by us and took in
> their fflaggs 14 saile of Dutch men-of warr and fireshipps in
> Company all from Plymouth Bound for Holland.
> *Jan. 14* Ye Zeeland squadron consisting of 4 fflaggs several men
> of warr and Hake boates, and ffly boates in all about 12 saile
> bound to London.[41]

Captain Ackerman of the *Dreadnought* reported to Pepys this same
passage—but only to cavil at the fact that, though the flags were
struck in salute, they were run up again and so continued during

B

the Dutch stay. The Secretary's reply to Ackerman was a model
of the acknowledgement non-committal:

> they being now gone there is noe occasion nor roome left for my
> pres$^t$ saying any thing to you more then to desire your letting
> me know as pticular as ye can to what Fflaggs they were that is
> to say whether ye Ordinary Dutch Flagg, or the Prince's
> p'ticular Flagg, or any other. Upon my knowledge of w$^{ch}$ I
> shall be better able to judge what is reasonable to be observed
> therefrom.[42]

Some Dutch sailors 'in great want of health' were confided to the
care of the Chirurgeon-General, John Pearce.[43]

On or just before the 29th December the arrival of three
important Dutchmen had been noted in London.[44] Everard Van
Weede Dijkvelt, the special emissary of 1687 to the court of James,
Willem van Nassau van Odjik, of Zeeland, and Nicholas Witsen, of
Amsterdam, were visiting England as a deputation from the
States General to their Stadholder.[45] He, William, had asked for
two of them by name and indicated that the third should be able
to speak for the powerful city. They had arrived to discuss the
problem of Anglo-Dutch co-operation.

A treaty of defensive alliance effected between the King of
England and the States General, 3rd/13th March 1677/8, at
Westminster,[46] had provided for military and naval assistance
against an aggressor, England to the extent of 10,000 infantry and
twenty warships. The aid was to be given at once; but diplomatic
relations between the assisting power and the offender could per-
sist for a further two months in which time the assisting power
might be expected to attempt to heal the breach. Two months
having elapsed, the attacked partner might opt for the continuance
of the aid or demand that the helper break with the enemy. All
assistance was qualified by the proviso 'le tout pourtant dans
l'estenduë de l'Europe seulement'. The assistant forces were to
accept the command and orders of the aided authority. Neither
state was free to make a separate peace.[47] This Westminster
agreement had been modified almost immediately. On 26th/16th
July, at the Hague,[48] by a new Treaty of Alliance England engaged 'un tiers plus sur mer, et un tiers moins par terre'[49] and, on
17th/27th August 1685 James II in a Treaty of Windsor,[50] which

gathered up six preceding agreements, confirmed the 1678 commitment.

In Holland the Raadpensionaris Antoine Heinsius, 'William's most constant correspondent', occupied the centre of naval affairs. Late in January the Prince named further emissaries he would welcome for the purpose particularly of handling the naval aspects of co-operation. Of those by far the most important was Hiob de Wildt, Secretary to the Amsterdam College of Admiralty. But the new advisers were not in session with their forerunners before the new reign began.[51]

In so far as the Treaty of 1678 could be considered alive and in so far as the Prince assumed the authority of Kingship, he was, from the 26th November, bound to assist the States General with twenty ships and 10,000 men though not compelled to break diplomatic relations with Louis. To the date of his accession as King, the States had no cause to complain of his attitude. At least English ships were mobilized and, if 10,000 Englishmen had not been shipped, diplomatic relations with France were non-existent. At the landing of the Prince of Orange, the notorious deputy-lordship-viceroyalty of Tyrconnel in Ireland entered upon a more violent stage,[52] the Viceroy's unfulfilled aims the reversal of the Cromwellian confiscations confirmed by Charles II, the elimination of all Protestants from administration and, in spite of a Declaration of Indulgence, their virtual proscription from the island – in brief a Catholic absolutism under James or under the French King. By promiscuously granted commissions a host of captains were turned into avaricious recruiting agents, through whom Tyrconnel hoped to make good, or more than good, the loss of that half of the Irish standing army sent to James's assistance but now enduring banishment in the Isle of Wight. To arm these sturdy recruits Tyrconnel, who had boasted two years previously that, whether he became a viceroy or not, he could, at will, hand over the island to Louis, turned as ever towards France – and, upon James's safe arrival at Saint-Germain, to James as the protégé of the French king.

By the beginning of December the Protestants of the north began to look towards Londonderry, whose apprentices slammed the Ferry Gate in the face of Antrim's 'Redshanks' on the morning of the 7th. Coleraine, by the sea, and Enniskillen, were lesser refuges in Ulster. At Sligo in Connaught and, bordering the coast of Munster at Dungannon (by Waterford) as well as at Kinsale and Bandon, there were foci of resistance to Tyrconnel. But while among Protestants the scattered acquiesced and the militant stood guard, scores of the timorous and sufficiently wealthy obtained passages to England, especially from Dublin and the eastern ports. Present in England, from whatever cause, fear or policy, the Anglo-Irish refugees were numerous and influential enough to place before the Prince, by mid December arrived in the capital, the plight of their fellows and their own views on the merits of attempted discussion or challenge.[53] Captain Shaw's *Proposals of December 31st*, personally passed on to Lord Coote 'to be communicated to those in power' urged 'conquest rather than compact'–seven or eight nimble frigates off Munster and troops to Ulster.[54] Sir Robert Southwell's paper from Kinsale (the seat of the family), *Twenty Eight Aphorisms relating to the Kingdom of Ireland, Humbly submitted to the Most Noble Assembly of Lords and Commons at the Great Convocation of Westminster 12th January 1688/9* gave unequivocal advice:

> Without the subjugation of Ireland England cannot flourish and perhaps not subsist. For every harbour in Munster would be more prejudicial to the Trade of England than either Sally or Algiers ever was that island be so situated that England cannot trade with Spain, the Levant, Africa, the East Indies or West without sailing in view of the Old Head of Kinsale.

A simultaneous descent on Ulster and Munster would, Southwell argued, militarily distract Ireland. From 'private undertakings in this matter of Ireland' no good, he said, could come. The cited lessons of the past were conclusive! Therefore let a well planned expedition be put at once in train.[55]

But, in spite of the number and force of such recommendations, to employ the words of Lord Coote on handling Shaw's Proposals, 'things proposed of that nature would not take'.[56] The Prince, as is well known, influenced by John Temple, whose uncle, Sir William, had received from Chief Justice Keating in Dublin a letter suggesting that Tyrconnel would, if approached, show a conciliatory spirit, allowed Richard Hamilton, young Temple's nominee, one of the officers sequestered in the Isle of Wight, to travel to Dublin to present to Tyrconnel terms. Hamilton did not return within the stipulated three weeks and, by the end of January, the Prince had no cause to hope for a peaceful settlement of Irish affairs.[57]

On the 10th February Captain Beverley of the *Jersey*, off Chester, was commanded, with the *Swallow* whose captain was to act under Beverley's orders, to follow Captain James Hamilton's instructions for receiving all the arms and ammunition the vessels could 'conveniently stow' and, being so provided, accept from Chester, Liverpool, Whitehaven or Carlisle, one or more merchant ships similarly laden and sail for Derry. In the event of inability to approach Derry, the cargoes were to be put ashore at some other port in County Down or returned to England. By customary formula, 'in ye execution of all & every part' of this duty Beverley was bidden use his 'best Circumspection & Diligence'. Authority for the production of the arms and ammunition had previously been served upon Dartmouth as Master of the Ordnance and Sir John Lowther at Carlisle.[58]

## II

If the events of the initial months of the hostilities, 26th/16th November to the 13th February 1688/9 be fairly surveyed, is it reasonable to suggest that, navally, William, in his passage to Kingship, failed, either by omission or commission, in his conduct of the war?

He, willy-nilly a Lord High Admiral, Herbert and Pepys at hand, had accepted and retained the 'James-Pepys' administration of Admiralty, which, in matters small[59] as well as great, had continued to function, allowance made for revolution, wind and weather, with surprising surety. The Prince had wisely refused all suits for professional advancement;[60] he had used available forces defensively (in respect of the Channel Islands and protection of trade); he had, in spite of a temporary vacillation of judgment, kept potentially intact Dartmouth's original fleet and, from it, allocated three squadrons to special services. Though the projected

Streights squadron could—on the 13th February—be regarded as adequate for trade-convoying tasks, no such sufficiency could be claimed for the Channel and Irish designations. The Prince, as would-be King, had, wisely or unwisely, allowed the flight of the frightened James into the land of the arch-enemy. If, attempted negotiation with Tyrconnel having failed ere February began, he did not envisage a likelihood that Louis would try to place James in Ireland and assist him with all possible troops and supplies, he must have been singularly blind to an obvious probability against the execution of which, as 'Lord High Admiral', he took—as time would prove—no adequate naval precautions. The later part of the interval had witnessed the first steps towards making real the naval factor in the co-operation of England and the United Provinces.

## REFERENCES

1 Du Mont, J. (baron de Carels Croon), *Corps universel diplomatique du droit des gens* . . . 8 t. in 15 vols., Amsterdam, 1726–31, t. VII, vol. ii, p. 212.

2 Powley, E. B., *The English Navy in the Revolution of 1688* (Foreword Admiral Earl Jellicoe). Cambridge, 1928. The passages enclosed between square brackets on pp. 23–27, pp. 28–29, pp. 29–30 and a sentence on p. 31 of this chapter are also based on the detailed narrative of the 1928 book, the contributing pages of that work are indicated at the end of each bracketing. It has not been thought necessary to supply annotation of the bracketed matter—except in a few instances in which repetition might be held to assist the reader or a completely new authentication is made available. Nor has biographical data, readily accessible in the *Dictionary of National Biography*, Oxford, 1925, concerning the English fleet officers who figure in this chapter been added. For Dutch admirals Almonde and Evertzen *v.* Chapter VIII.

3 *Journal du Corsaire Jean Doublet de Honfleur* . . . ed. Bréard, C., provides an amazing picture of contemporary Corsair activity.

4 *H.M.C. XI, v. The MSS of the Earl of Dartmouth*, pp. 241, 242, 246.

5 *Ibid.* op. 246, Jan. 1.

6 Bodleian MSS. Rawlinson, A. 186, f. 112, 3rd Jan.

7 *H.M.C. XI, v. Dartmouth*, p. 249, 4th Jan.

8 *v. infra.* order of 26th Dec.

9 Passage between Schowen and N. Beverland.

10 B.M. MSS. Egerton 2621.

11 Bryant, A. (Sir), *Samuel Pepys* 3 v. 1938, III, p. 361. Ehrman, J. *The Navy in the War of William III, 1689–1697.* Cambridge, 1953, p. 248.

12 City of London Records, Misc. MSS. 133.25. Returns of subscriptions made or promised by the inhabitants of the Wards, to the loan to William of Orange Jan. 1688/9. The entry for *Portsoken Ward* specifically mentions 'for . . . paying the Fleet and Souldiers'.

For difficulties with Tally Court officers who demanded, unsuccessfully, fees from 'dispatches [dispatches of business] on levying tallies of loan and tallies of pro for the repayment' *v*. Shaw, W. A., *Calendar of Treasury Books 1685–1689 preserved in the Public Record Office*, vol. VIII, Part iv, p. 2156, 19th Jan. Luttrell, N., *Brief Relation of State Affairs from September 1678 to April 1714*, 6 v. Oxford 1857, I, p. 495, takes note of the borrowing and reports over £200,000 in before 22nd Jan., p. 496.

13 A court-martial, interesting as a specimen of routine enquiry on the loss of a ship, followed, 13th April 1689, on board the *Mary* yacht, Captain Wm Davis President, with nine other captains, Henry Croome Judge Advocate. P.R.O. Adm.1/5253. Reports of Courts Martial 1680–July 1698.

14 Bibliotheca Pepysiana MSS. Adm'ty Letters XV, f.508, 8th Jan., 'rather (to give it you in his own words) because when you are gone there will be noe body to lead it'.
Reference to these letters is made only where they supplement MSS Rawlinson or Dartmouth.

15 Rawl. A. 186, f.120, 10th Jan.

16 The summons to the meeting–for the consideration of what particular matter is not revealed–went out on 4th April 1689. P.R.O. Minutes of Commission of Admiralty, Adm. 3/1.
Nottingham, 28th September, enquired of Dartmouth of 'a shipwright of great reputation in Denmark, named Shelton who has built some excellent bomb vessels and ships for transporting horse'. Nottingham asked to see 'models' in the possession of Dartmouth and for observations on the character of Shelton, believed to be known to his lordship. *H.M.C. The MSS of the late Allen George Finch*, vol. II, p. 250.

17 Powley, *loc. cit.* p. 143.

18 Bib. Pepysiana, Adm'ty Letters, XV, f.527, 14th Jan. (Pepys–Victualling Board). *v*. also pp. 31–32 and note (25).

19 'The Streights'–to retain the usual naval 17th-century and earlier spelling (*var*. 'Straights', 'Straits')–is a plural used in a singular sense to signify Strait of Gibraltar and, by implication, the Mediterranean entered past Gibraltar. 'Streights' and 'Mediterranean' become interchangeable labels for the same squadron or fleet. *Cf. Straits Settlements* the name the British possession in the Malay Peninsula took in 1884, from proximity to the Straits of Malacca. Rawl, A. 186, ff.122, 3. 12th Jan.
Two orders to Dartmouth as Master of the Ordnance, another to the Navy Board.

20 As note (18) for number of men.
For data used to check ship names *v*. Powley, *op. cit.* Dartmouth's table, 14th Oct., pp. 57–9. The three ships in that list later 'counted-out' are *Nonsuch, Montagu*, and *Rupert*; for reinforcements some of which joined– *Tyger* (p. 59 n), *Portland, Tyger Prize, Phoenix, Hampton Court, Kent, Warspight, Edgar* (pp. 109, 139.)

21 Rawl. A. 186, f.120, 12th Jan.

22 *Ibid.* and Powley, *loc. cit.* p. 158. (This is possibly the first mention of 'commodore' as an English naval rank. The *N.E.D.* has an example for 1695.)

23 Bib. Pepysiana, Adm'ty Letters XV. f.543, 17th Jan. (Pepys-Berry).

24 *Ibid.* f.547, 18th Jan. (Pepys-Berry).
25 *Ibid.* f.554, 21st Jan.
26 P.R.O. Adm. 51/4322. Log of the *Ruby*. (See the *Book of Common Prayer* of
   that period for the service appropriate to the day—one of 'Three Forms of
   Prayer and Service made for the Fifth of November the Thirtieth of
   January and the Twenty Ninth of May . . .' and enjoined for use by Charles
   II.)
27 Bib. Pepysiana, Adm'ty Letters XV, f.575, 5th Feb. (Pepys-Berry).
28 Rawl. A. 186, f.134, 7th Feb., and as note (27) for 'boat-hose-topping'.
       Boat Hose Tops—'Are laid on about three Strakes of Plank below the
   Water's Edge with Tallow and generally given Ships when ordered on a
   Cruize' *A Naval Expositor*, 1750. After breaming, the burning off of the
   accretions of barnacles, weed and filth adhering to the tarred bottom of the
   ship, 'boot-hose' topping with tallow and sulphur was resorted to in order
   to assist passage through the water.
29 Bib. Pepysiana, Adm'ty Letters, f.576, 7th Feb. (Pepys-Berry).
30 *Ibid.* f.513, 9th Jan. and f.547, 18th Jan. (Pepys-Berry).
31 *Ibid.* passim.
32 *Ibid.* f.526, 14th Jan.
33 *Ibid.* f.548, 19th Jan.
34 *Ibid.* f.513, 9th Jan.
35 *Ibid.* f.536, 16th Jan. P.R.O. Adm. 1/3557 Board to Secretary 20th Jan. for
   text of the survey.
36 *Ibid.* f.544, 18th Jan.
37 The case of the *Ruby* is of interest. Her log (*v.* note (26)) is silent as to any
   trouble. Evidently her captain measured up to the emergency. As has been
   noted, with the *Portland*, *Ruby* was engaged, at the end of the month of
   January, taking gear off the wrecked *Sedgemore*.
       The following suggests a busy prize-seeking and not a mutinous ship:
       *4th Feb.* Took an 'owler' . . . a small Boate off Rye, Ma^r William Goodier,
       that had been at Callis with wooll & brought 2½ hoggsheads of Brandy
       from Callis.
   (The captain called a notary aboard. He took evidence before the captain
   and lieutenant. '17 paques of wool' had been carried. The brandy was
   freight for his work!)
       *11th Feb.* Took 3 prizes to Mr Emms who received them into his dock.
   (The sails and gear also went into store and the wool aboard into the
   King's storehouse at Dover.)
       The earliest example of the use of the word 'owler' recorded in the *N.E.D.*
   is for 1696 (Luttrell).
38 Rawl., A. 186, f.126.
39 Bib. Pepysiana, Adm'ty Letters, f.544, 18th Jan., and f.540, 17th Jan. *v.*
   also f.545, 19th Jan.
40 *Ibid.* f.547, 19th Jan. (Pepys-Berry).
41 As note (26).
42 Bib. Pepysiana, Adm'ty Letters, f.539, 17th Jan. The ordinary Dutch or
   States flag bore horizontally, named downward on the halyard, orange,
   white, blue; but sometimes three lower bands were added making a six
   stripe flag.

The Prince's 'p'ticular Flagg' might have been

(a) red with device—a lion rampant or, langued sable and argent, holding in his dexter paw a scimitar, in his sinister a sheaf of arrows,

or (b) a rectangle segmented equally from the centre in eight, four of the segments forming a white Maltese cross erect; the segments touching the halyard, named downwards, orange, white, blue and so oppositely,

or (c) a rectangle quartered, each of which rectangles was segmented from the centre of the flag in three—twelve segments in all. Named downward along the halyard the colours exhibited were orange, white, blue, repeated in that order round to the halyard again.

The Admiralty of Amsterdam, the Maas (Rotterdam), Zeeland, Friesland and North Holland had their own flags. For an incomparable series of coloured representations of these and, apparently, of all maritime flags of the late 17th century *v. Le Neptune François ou Atlas Noveau des Cartes Marines*, Jaillot, Paris, 1693. But Bib. Pepysiana, MS.1608, a fine small square MS volume of painted illustrations of naval flags, dated 1686, may be the earliest preserved like record?

43 Rawl., A. 186, f.134, 2nd Feb.

44 Luttrell, *op. cit.* vol. I, p. 492.

45 Clark, G. N. (Sir), *The Dutch Alliance and the War against French Trade*, Manchester 1923, provides, Ch. II, guidance concerning this and later missions of 1689.

46 *Actes et Mémoires des Négociations de la Paix de Nimègue*, t. ii, 3ᵉ edn. La Haye, 1697, p. 354 *et seq.*

47 *Ibid.* pp. 356–361.

48 *Ibid.* p. 553 *et seq.*

49 *Ibid.* p. 556.

50 Du Mont, *op. cit.* VII, ii, p. 110.

51 Clark, *op. cit.* p. 16 'Torck, de Wildt, Godijn and the deputy of the town of Hoorn to the college of Friesland and the Noorderquartier; these, with others, came over and conferred with the first mission . . . from the middle of March till the middle of April.' For the significance of de Wildt *v.* de Jonge, *Geschiedenis van het Nederlandsche Zeewezen* 5 dln en Register (2ᵉ druk) Haarlem 1858–62, III, p. 194. de Jonge refers to Heinsius as 'de ziel en de leven van het Zeewezen', III, p. 175, *v.* also Clark *op. cit.* App. I.

52 For Irish Affairs in general:
Bagwell, R., *Ireland under the Stuarts and during the Interregnum*, 1916 and Murray, R. H., *Revolutionary Ireland and its Settlement*, 1911. For Tyrconnel—Richard Talbot, earl and titular duke (1630–1691) see *D.N.B.*

53 *H.M.C.*, *XII, App. pt. vi, The MSS of the House of Lords, 1689–1690*, 'The Miscarriages in Ireland', pp. 136–144, at this point becomes an authority, with evidence given before Committee of the House reported pp. 136–192.
*v.* also note (2), Ch. IV of this work.
*v.* also Luttrell, 16th and 21st Dec. 1688 and 2nd–7th Jan. 1688/9.

54 *H.M.C. XII, App. pt. vi, H. of L.*, p. 183.

55 Murray, *op. cit.* p. 57 makes use of Trinity College Dublin, Southwell MSS, I, 6, ii. Southwell, a year later, will be found saying 'One harbour in

Munster, say Kinsale, will be more useful than half the province of Ulster can be' *Calendar of State Papers Domestic, William & Mary, 1689–1690*, p. 440.

56  *v.* note (54).

57  For the career to date of Richard Hamilton, who had served with distinction in the French army but been banished from France for aspiring to the hand of the Princesse de Conte, see *D.N.B.*

58  Rawl., A. 186, f.137, 10th Feb.

59  See Pepys Adm'ty Letters and Rawl. MSS. There was no 'let-up' in the running of Pepys's office!

60  Bib. Pepysiana, Adm'ty Letters, XV, f.563, 26th Jan.

Berry, seeking to recommend his brother, is told that the Prince has 'not yet thought fitt to dispose of any Employments in ye Navy'.

# CHAPTER III

# With James—Ambleteuse to Kinsale

### 25th December/4th January – 12th/22nd March 1688/9

---

*ARGUMENT*

*James at the court of Louis; his use to the French king. The mission of de Pointis to Tyrconnel—de Pointis' report to Seignelay—Résumé de raisons for establishing a French pied-à-terre in Ireland: in chief the facilitation of the passage of James into Scotland as a step to the undoing of the Prince—The outspoken advice of a viceroy to his sovereign—Preparations for Gabaret to transport James, his entourage and military assistance to Ireland. The delayed but picturesque sailing—James, 12th March, lands at Kinsale.*

---

JAMES, reunited with Queen and heir, accorded by the Most Christian King dignified residence at St Germains and, withal, an allowance ample to support his state, was not long in France, declares Mme de la Fayette, before he became known for what he was—'*un homme entêté de sa religion*' (had he not given up three Kingdoms for a Mass?), a weak prince, surrendered to the Jesuits, supporting ill-fortune through lack of feeling rather than by courage.[1] To the Grand Duke of Tuscany the Abbé Melani wrote of His Exalted Majesty . . . '*così tranquilla e così insensibile*'; he saw him as a man who would be resigned to remain in France solely occupied with the exercises of devotion and the chase.[2] For Mme de Sévigné the English Queen were the better king! James appeared '*content*' and, she added, '*c'est pour cela qu'il est là*'.[3] Louis, for all his courtesy, had no intention of harbouring an idle king; he determined to make use of him—in Ireland.

So, as early as 12th/2nd January,[4] the French Secrétaire d'État de la Marine, Seignelay,[5] instructed M. de Pointis, an officer of marine artillery,[6] to visit Ireland to confer with Tyrconnel and view the land. de Pointis was allowed to promise arms and powder but ordered to inform Tyrconnel no men could be sent. Especially he was commissioned to discover whether the Catholics, aided only in respect of arms and ammunition, would be able to win the north and hold the island.[7] With the Frenchman went Captain

Routh, an Irishman, carrying from James to Tyrconnel a letter promising muskets and expressing the hope that Ireland would hold out till the summer at least.[8] Upon his return, de Pointis reported to Seignelay; and the French view of the Irish situation took official shape.

The Protestants of Ulster were believed to equal in numbers the Catholics of that Province and, elsewhere, the Catholics were said to outnumber the heretics by twenty to one. A couple of thousand cavalry and rather more infantry of the old army were still at Tyrconnel's side; for the forty thousand raw recruits raised by the gentry, arms, ammunition, officers and pay all were lacking. It was not to be expected that Londonderry and Sligo could be taken without the aid of artillery, which Tyrconnel did not possess; compensatingly the rest of the island's towns lay, to all appearance, open. Kinsale fort had just been wrested from Protestant hands; Dungannon and Waterford had not . . .[9] Arms, ammunition and money provided, the prospects of successful intervention were indeed good. A '*Résumé de raisons* . . .',[10] based no doubt on de Pointis' report to Seignelay, stressed the consort of Ireland's circumstance and France's opportunity. The whole enterprise might be financed through the continuance of His Most Christian Majesty's grant to the deposed King, the profits of the captured Irish wool trade and some sale of plate. France should not delay to acquire a pied-à-terre in the island '*où il peut le plus nuire à Angleterre*' and facilitate the passage of James to Scotland where 25,000 Highlanders awaited the Stuart call. Such venture dared, must not the Prince of Orange maintain one army in Scotland, another in England, consume his means, risk revolt? At last, a lucky battle might yield to James the opportunity of invasion of his own Kingdom of England and force the Prince to re-cross to Holland '*plus vite qu'il n'en est venu*'.

de Pointis, returning to France, carried not only information to Seignelay but bore[11] a long letter in two parts from Tyrconnel to James, dated the 29th January [8 Fév[12]]—surely one of the most outspoken utterances ever intended by a Viceroy for the eyes of his monarch. Taking for granted a supply of arms and ammunition from France, Tyrconnel demanded 500,000 crowns, in cash, before the middle of March, to clothe and subsist his raw Irish thousands who, otherwise, would break loose and ruin the country. He catalogued his requirements in arms but stressed, equally, the need for officers to drill and lead the levies. James's presence he invited, putting forward the view that the monthly allowance of 200,000 livres, which (so he had heard) the royal exile already received from the French King, would, if applied in Ireland, prove sufficient for the waging of war. With the sentence:

I beg you to consider whether you can with honour continue where you are

Tyrconnel flung down his challenge. Then, by way of a survey of conditions in Leinster, Munster, Connaught and Ulster, he came to a roll call of his troops, old and new, and a list of the forts and ports of the island. Galway and Waterford 'or any other ports' he would willingly 'putt into the King of France's hands for Security of repaying him his money', even though the pledge implied fortification and permanent cession. Let 'three or four light Frigatts' be sent; for, without them Ireland could not 'live'. Above all—speed in succour; for delay would spell destruction. This letter was followed by another no less urgent. If the Prince of Orange should land in Ireland before French help arrived, Tyrconnel would not answer for the consequence![13]

At much the same time as the new reign in England began, then report of de Pointis having been appraised by the French King and Council and the necessary stimuli applied by Tyrconnel and Louis to the hesitant James, naval preparations were put in train. On the 24th/14th February an instruction was sent by Louis from Versailles to Gabaret[14] at Brest, informing him of selection to take command of a projected squadron to convey James and an entourage to Ireland. He should accept from James orders as to port of landfall and, service performed, return as quickly as possible to Brest to receive for Ireland troops which, by that time, would be collected at that base. Louis remarked that the King of England had asked that the squadron should wear English colours. He, Louis, had consented; he gave the admiral details.[15] On the same day Seignelay communicated with Desclouzeaux, the Intendant-de-Marine at Brest, indicating the vessels, about fourteen in number, to compose Gabaret's squadron; to which were to be added some eight light frigates and three fireships. He repeated his

King's flag instructions with a wealth of explanatory detail and enclosed drawings which left nothing by default to imagination.[16]

While the vessels assembled and, as a precaution against delay in fulfilling further missions after return to Brest, took in four months' victuals, James pursued his appeals to the Emperor, the Papacy and states of Italy;[17] and Louvois, for Louis, worked out the limits of intended aid.[18]

The nature and extent of the assistance supplied by Louis are well known. The Count de Rosen, as lieutenant-general, Maumont, as 'mareschal-de-camp', the three brigadiers, Léry-Giraudin (of cavalry), Pusignan (of infantry) and Boisselau–these, with de Pointis the naval artillery expert, and a whole corps of inferior officers to train and lead Tyrconnel's levies, were induced to offer their swords in service. A very full purse rested in the keeping of the Comte d'Avaux (Jean-Antoine de Mesmes), who, under fifty years of age, because of the success of his services in Holland, was preferred before Barillon 'en qualité d'Ambassadeur Extraordinaire de Sa Majesté' to accompany James to Dublin. Equally well known are the romantic details of the royal leave-takings, the ill humour of the disappointed Lauzan, recently pampered by James with the grant of the Garter, the last religious observances and the accidents of the passage from Saint Germain-en-Laye to the sea.[19] Of the sailing of the expedition nothing, it would appear, has been written.[20]

d'Avaux arrived with Rosen at Brest in the late afternoon of Saturday the 5th March/23rd February and the King with his entourage at nightfall.[21] With the wind in the wrong quarter there could be no question of the squadron's departure. The morning of Sunday was given up to inspection.[22] At five o'clock on Monday afternoon, the wind 'un peu favorable', James went aboard the flagship Le Saint Michel expecting that Gabaret would be able to weigh at 4 a.m. on Tuesday–well before the first breaking light, presumably on a morning tide.[23,24] But, till the following Saturday, the 12th/2nd, sails could not be set, and the ambassador, handing on the news to Louis, forecast that, if the wind didn't veer by next day, it would sit in the same quarter for the rest of that moon. On the 13th/3rd Sunday, a show of activity–happily foiled! For the wind swung back and a battering tempest followed, which, the landsman reflected, could better be ridden out in harbour than in the Iroise.[25] Whilst the storm spent itself and the captains complained that their vessels were so laden that it was to be hoped it would not be necessary to fight Dutch or English, *Le Soleil d'Afrique* ran in from Ireland, having deposited there Lord Dungan.[26] Her captain, de la Clocheterie, as far back as 24th/14th February was under orders from Louis immediately to take to Ireland officers selected by the Duke of Berwick. They constituted valuable freight! For that reason and because of the lading of powder the ship had accepted at Rochelle, her captain was peremptorily instructed to avoid enemy vessels and to return promptly to report to Gabaret.[27] At mid-day on Tuesday the 15th/5th up came the anchors once more; but, meeting, at the narrowing harbour mouth, a head wind and a high-running sea, the squadron was driven '*bord-sur-bord*' and de Rosmadek's vessel, *Le Fort?*, threatened by another which he tried to avoid, bore down on the flagship. Vainly de Rosmadek trimmed his sails to come about. In the concourse of vessels, with a ship robbed of wind and known to be somewhat unready at any time to answer the helm, he could not prevent the collision which, but for an anticipating tactic by Gabaret, would have had serious consequences. As it was, not even the *éperons* were damaged; at worst broken anchors and rent cordage resulted. James and all the marine officers agreed that de Rosmadek could not have avoided the accident.[28] A week's delay followed. Thus it was not until the morning of Monday 21st/11th March[29] that Gabaret's squadron, *Le Saint Michel, L'Apollon, Le Comte* (de Relingue), *Le Soleil d'Afrique, Les Yeux* and others—*Le Courageux, Le Furieux, Le François, Le Fort, L'Entreprennant, Le Sage, Le Duc, Le Faucon, Le Neptune*—to the number of perhaps fourteen, accompanied by the light frigates *La Mutine, La Jolie, La Bien Aimée, La Legère, La Friponne, La Tempête, La Railleuse, La Mignonne* and three fireships made the open and much-subsided sea—an imposing and surely a lovely sight. For, at the main of *Le Saint Michel* spread the royal standard of England, not less ample of folds than that which the admiral of France breaks at the grand mast, while, at the bowsprit and poop of the flagship, the flags she would have worn had she been an English warship took the breeze. At the bowsprit and poop of every other ship flapped the same fore and aft ensigns; and, from the ends of all the ships' yard-arms, streamed 'flammes' of red, blue and white with a 'chief' of red with a white cross within–those of the King's vessel so long their tips trailed to the morning sea. The passage was fair and smooth; and, except that a Bristol trader was intercepted and questioned, quite without incident. During the afternoon of Tuesday, 22nd/12th March the Old Head of Kinsale hove in view and by five o'clock the anchors sank to the shingle in Kinsale harbour.[30]

## REFERENCES

1  la Fayette, M-M (Comtesse de), *Mémoires de la Cour de France pour les années 1688 et 1689*, in *Mémoires de Mme de la Fayette*, ed. Asse E., Paris, 1890, pp. 209, 230.

2  Campana di Cavelli [Emilia] (Marchesa), *Les derniers Stuarts à Saint Germain en Laye*, 2 t. Paris etc., 1871, t. ii. DCCLXVIII, p. 528. *v.* also DCCLIV, p. 504 for James's apathy and DCCXXVIII, p. 471 for public disappointment at his bearing. Cavelli references–Archives de Medicis à Florence, L'Abbé Melani–Secrétaire d'État du Grand Duc de Toscane, Liasse 4802.

3  Sévigné, M. R-B (Marquise de), *Lettres de Madame de Sévigné de sa famille et de ses amis*, ed. Monmerqué M., Paris, 16 t. 1862–6, viii, p. 448.

4  Archives du Ministère de la Marine de France: Instructions, *v.* Campana di Cavelli, DCCLXX, p. 529.

5  Seignelay, Jean Baptiste, Colbert (Marquis de), (1651–1690), son of the 'grand Colbert', was, by his father, destined and, as far as possible through travel acquaintance with administration and experience afloat, fitted for reversion of the office of Secrétaire d'État de la Marine, which office he acquired in 1683. He was present at the bombardment of Genoa in 1684. By 1689 he was at the height of his career, consistently favoured by Mme de Maintenon against Louvois. For a critical notice of his career see the Introduction to Clément, P., *L'Italie en 1671 Relation d'un Voyage du Marquis de Seignelay*, Paris 1867, pp. 3–92 ('Etude Historique'); for a contrast of father and son *v.* Sue, E., *Histoire de la Marine Française*, t. iv, Paris 1836, p. 389.

6  de Pointis, Jean Bernard Louis Desjean (1645–1707) saw service in the Mediterranean against Algiers, Spain and Genoa; present at the great bombardment of Genoa 1684. Biographies (Larousse, *La Grande* and Hoefer) overlook de Pointis' presence with James in Ireland but note that he commanded *Le Courtesan* at Bévéziers (Beachy Head), 1690. He continued his naval career–with d'Estrées in the Mediterranean and was promoted chef-d'escadre 1691. He captured *La Neuva Carthagena* 1697; in 1704 commanded *Le Magnanime* at Velez-Malaga, and later suffered the loss of four ships in attempt to retake Gibraltar.
   Archives du Ministère de la Guerre de France; 'Campagne d'Irlande 1689', f.177. *v.* Campana di Cavelli, DCCLXXVII, p. 546.

7  *v.* note (4).

8 Clarke, J., *The Life of James II, King of England, collected out of Memoirs writ of his own hand* . . . 2 v. 1816, ii, p. 319. '. . . all I [James] can get this King to doe, is to send 7 or 8000 muskets he not being willing to venter more drms or any men till he knows the condition you are in.'

9 Archives . . . Marine: de Pointis' report, *v.* Campana di Cavelli, DCCLXXIII, p. 537.

10 Archives . . . Marine. *Ibid.* DCCLXVII, p. 524.

11 Archives . . . Guerre: Fév. 1689. *v. Ibid.* DCCLXXII, p. 535.

12 B.M. MSS Additional, 28053, Leeds correspondence, f.386, is the copy from which Campana di Cavelli, DCCLXXI, p. 530 is taken–but with wrong folio reference.

13 *v.* note (11). The letter mentions *en passant* the sailing of several vessels for France with letters to a cover address in Paris and the dispatch, five days prior to de Pointis' arrival, of Chief Baron Rice with Viscount Mountjoy, the latter by this time in the Bastille. James, from the first, should have been well informed of the state of Ireland.

14 Gabaret, Jean de (le Grand Gabaret), (1620 or 1627–1697) born in l'Île de Rhé of a naval family, reached captaincy before or by 1672 when he fought at the battle of Southwold at which he was wounded and maimed for life. With his younger brother, Louis, he distinguished himself next year in the fight at Walcheren; in the Sicilian expedition commanded the rear and took part in the battles of Stromboli, d'Agosta and Palermo (1676). Under d'Estrées he was the first to enter the port of besieged Tobago (1677). Though beyond his sixtieth year he yet, at this date 1688/9, had extensive service before him. He fought (as will shortly be seen) at Bantry, was promoted 'lieutenant-général des armées navales', assisted, by his determined opposition to Ashby, Tourville's retreat at La Hougue (1692) and excelled in the defence of Martinique, of which, in 1693 he became governor. Though he received the order of St Louis a year before his death in 1697 (Larousse)

comme Jean Bart, il eut tort de ne pas naître gentilhomme: ce qui empêcha Louis XIV de ne pas toujours le récompenser selon son mérite (Hoefer).

(Larousse, *La Grande* and Hoefer).

15 Archives . . . Marine: Louis–Gabaret. 24 Fév, *v.* Campana di Cavelli, DCCLXXIV, p. 540.

16 Archives . . . Marine: 24 Fév. *Ibid.* DCCLXXV.

17 *Ibid.* Index, p. 596.

18 Archives . . . Guerre: Instructions Secrètes, Louis–Maumont, 16 Fév. *Ibid.* DCCLXXVII, p. 544. It is difficult to reconcile these with the instructions to d'Avaux for which see Archives . . . Guerre, v. 896, f.193. *v.* DCCLXXX, p. 557, or *Négociations . . . d'Avaux*, p. 1; 11 Fév. Failure to reconcile does not affect discussion of the naval happenings.

Louvois, François Michel le Tellier (Marquis de), (1639–1691), son of le Tellier (Chancelier), obtained survivance from 1665 as Secrétaire d'État de la Guerre, gathered to himself the 'surintendance' of posts, building, arts and manufacture and completely reorganized the army of Louis. He was of the King's inner council. He suggested the Dragonnades and the devastation of the Palatinate (Larousse, etc.).

19  The career of the irascible Rosen is worth a note! Rosen, Conrad (Marquis de) (1628–1715), born in Alsace, soldiered from boyhood. He joined his uncle, a lieutenant general in service of the Swedes but, condemned to death for a duel, fled to France to serve in the cavalry. He distinguished himself at Arras, 1654 and Senef, 1674. Brigadier 1675, maréchal de camp 1678, he defeated Brandenberg troops at Minden and on the Weser 1679 and reached the rank of lieutenant-général in 1688. Rosen was entitled marshal by James; and, when returned discountenanced by James to Louis, 1689, was found continued employ. He was present at Nerwinden, Charleroï and Nimègue and received his bâton of Louis in 1703. He died in 1715 at his seat, Bollweiler, Haute-Alsace.

The career of the equally ungovernable Gascon, Lauzun, Antonin Nompar de Caumont (Comte, puis Duc de) (1633–1723), is better known— especially from the time that the favourite, who had become colonel-général of dragoons, broke his sword before a King who revoked his intention of making the courtier 'grand-maître de l'artillerie' and caused that monarch to hurl his own cane through the window rather than strike a gentleman! From the Bastille to favour, captaincy in the guards and courtship (possibly secret marriage) of Mlle de Montpensier, he found his way to command of Louis' troops in Flanders; but, falling foul of Madame de Montespan, paid for his temerity by five years' imprisonment in the fortress of Pignerol and four in exile in Angers. Rescued from obloquy by Mlle de Montpensier he served James in England and, as is common knowledge, escorted the English Queen and baby Prince to France. He was destined to retain James' favour but not to regain the trust of Louis. Yet Louis did, in 1692, make him a duke! Dezobry, C., Bachelet, T., Darsy, M. E., *Dictionnaire Général de Biographie et d'Histoire*. . ., Paris (édition d'après guerre).

*v.* note (17). Sévigné, *op. cit.* p. 503; de la Fayette, *op. cit.* pp. 225–228. Campana di Cavelli, DCCLXXVIII, p. 550 and DCCLXXXIX, p. 571. Cavelli references—Archives d'Este à Modène, l'Abbé Rienzi–Duc de Modène and Archives de Medicis–l'Abbé Melani–Secrétaire d'Etat du Grand-duc de Toscane.

20  de la Roncière, C. B., *Histoire de la Marine Française*, Paris, 1932, has p. 46 a single sentence. Similarly Guérin, L., *L'Histoire maritime de France* . . ., 6 t. Paris, 1859–63. *v.* t. III, p. 438–with an incorrect date! Sue, E., *op. cit.* ch. vii, gives no notice.

21  Archives du Ministère des Affaires étrangères de France: d'Avaux–Louis, *v.* Campana di Cavelli, DCCLXXXI, p. 561.

The entourage of at least a hundred included, apart from the ambassador designate and the six officers mentioned on the preceding page, James Fitz James, duke of Berwick, and Henry Fitz-James (Grand Prior!), two of James's natural sons by Arabella Churchill, the duke of Powis, Cartwright, bishop of Chester, the earl of Melfort, lord Thomas Howard, chief Baron Rice, lady Melfort. *A Jacobite Narrative of the War in Ireland 1688–1691*, ed. by Gilbert, J. T., Dublin 1892, p. 46, and also pp. 315–6 for a paper endorsed: 'Mareschal d'Estrées order–What ships King James and his train should go upon to Ireland, 12th March 1688/9 landed at Kinsale?' (The original appears to be in the Royal Academy, Dublin, collection.) (Eleven ships (*v.* note (30)) and over eighty persons are named.)

22 Archives . . . Guerre (892): de Maumont–Louvois, *v.* Campana di Cavelli, DCCLXXXIII, p. 562.

23 Archives. . . Affaires étrangères?: d'Avaux–Louis, 7 Mars, *v. Ibid.* DCCLXXXVI, p. 567. For ship's name *v.* DCCXC, p. 572, Cavelli reference–Archives d'Este, l'abbé Ronci–duc de Modène and Gilbert *op. cit.* p. 315.

24 *Négociations* . . . *d'Avaux*, p. 16. d'Avaux wrongly speaks of 'lundi . . . huitième'. Monday was the 7th.

25 *Ibid.* p. 18. d'Avaux–Louis, 14 Mars.

26 *Ibid.* p. 19. d'Avaux–Seignelay, 14 Mars. Dungan=Dungannon. Presumably Lewis Trevor, 2nd Viscount (–1692) of whom little is known.

27 Archives . . . Marine: *v.* Campana di Cavelli, DCCLXXVI, p. 543. Though still under twenty years of age Berwick the son of James and Arabella Churchill had distinguished himself in Hungary against the Turks and a remarkable career lay before him. See *D.N.B.* James Fitz-James 1st Duke of Berwick (1670–1734).

28 *Négociations* . . . *d'Avaux*, p. 20, d'Avaux–Louis (also in Campana di Cavelli, DCCLXXXVII, p. 567).

'*Bord-sur-bord*': 'Bordée courte, succédant à une autre bordée qui a peu de durée; route de peu d'instants sur un rhumb de vent, succédant à une route faite sur un autre rhumb de vent pendant un temps assez court.' [rhumb v. rum: 'C'est le trait en droite ligne d'un vent à l'autre, soit du vent entier, ou demy-vent.']

'*éperons*': ornamental curvilinear protuberances forming part of the bow and carrying figureheads.

Jal. A., *Glossaire Nautique–Répertoire polyglotte de termes de marine anciens et modernes*, Paris 1848, pp. 312, 1299, 640.

'trimmed, etc.': 'il mit toutes les voiles pour arriver' (d'Avaux).

29 *Négociations d'Avaux*, p. 23, d'Avaux–Louis, 23 Mars.

30 *v.* notes (15) and (16) and Campana di Cavelli, DCCXC, p. 572, Cavelli references Archives . . . d'Este, l'Abbé Ronci–duc de Modène.

Gilbert, *op. cit.* pp. 315–16 lists *Le Saint Michel, Le Courageux, Le Furieux, Le François, L'Appollon, Le Fort, L'Entreprennant, Le Sage, Le Duc, Le Faucon, Le Neptune.*

To gather a vivid impression of the probable appearance of *Le Saint Michel* see the plate, hand-coloured?, 'Vaisseau royal d'Angleterre' in *Le Neptune François*–previously referred to (*v.* p. 34, note (42)). Some thirty 'flammes' flutter to the wind–some even trail to the sea.

For time of arrival–note (29).

# CHAPTER IV

# Mediterranean or Channel
# and Irish Strategy

*14th February-13th March 1688/9*

---

*ARGUMENT*

I

*The King to his first Parliament, 18th February—An Irish Committee of the Privy Council, just formed, takes cognizance of the dispatch of Captain James Hamilton, with arms and stores to Colonel Lundy, commanding Londonderry, and arranges instructions be sent him—A royal declaration to the Irish people.*

*The official retirement of Mr Secretary Pepys, 20th February—Two further days of caretaker interest—The appointment of a Commission of Admiralty with Admiral Herbert as First Commissioner—Men as well as stores to be sent to Ireland—Herbert given authority to issue all necessary naval orders until the Commissioners' patent be engrossed—Sir Richard Haddock presents to the Irish Committee 'a list of the squadrons intended for the Streights, Ireland and the Channel and the day when they will be ready'—The various naval orders issued by Herbert.*

*The King again, 8th March, receives the Lords and Commons in Parliament, repeating his plea of the 18th for assistance to Holland, declaring that he need not 'tell . . . of the deplorable condition of Ireland' and asking for 'such a fleet as [might] in conjunction with the States [be] entirely master of the sea'—Rumours of James's design to land in Ireland. Shrewsbury stresses to Lundy the King's concern for Londonderry, affirms that two regiments are ready for embarkation and that more men will follow.*

*The activities of the Irish Committee and Herbert on the 8th and 9th instant; the reception by the former of news of Captain James Hamilton.*

*The Commission of Admiralty now meets, 9th March; the letters-patent are read; their contents; Phineas Bowles made Secretary; the first day's business.*

*The tedious task of negotiating an Anglo-Dutch naval convention—The States reciprocate, 27th February/9th March, Louis' earlier declaration of war.*

*The unremitting efforts of the Irish Committee and Admiralty to hasten the regiments of Colonels John Cunningham and Solomon Richards to Ireland and to effect the rendezvous of a fleet at Spithead.*

*Nottingham transmits to Herbert his instructions as 'Admirall & Com̃ander of . . . Ships in ye Narrow Seas' and a sealed order to be opened if the admiral encounter James on the sea—Herbert's strength at this juncture, 12th March.*

*A note on naval finance during the month ended 12th March.*

II

*In mid-March 1688/9 the prospects of William abroad supported sober satisfaction; in England and Scotland sorted well enough with 'predestination'; in Ireland gave cause for apprehension—Neglect to guard against French intervention in Ireland, whether or no headed by James, a serious charge against the King; concerning which a contemporary pamphleteer is eloquent, maintaining that a Channel command might and should have been exercised to forestall intervention; the fact that the pamphleteer overlooked the extent to which Dartmouth's fleet returned damaged not invalidatory of his contention – The hypothesis which alone explains the omission: – William regarded France from the Hague rather than London, attached undue importance to the provision and rôle of a Mediterranean squadron, and too late ordered that squadron and other ships to the Channel to close the 'Irish back door' – While the English authorities were not blind to William's neglect to put out in time a Channel squadron, they found in William a King whose opinions were decisions – The burden of repair, re-equipment and victualling thrown upon the yards mid-January to mid-March, and a degree of unrest existing among seamen concerning pay, not factors in William's failure to act against James's landing.*

---

## I

I think it necessary to acquaint you That the Condition of our Allies abroad, and particularly that of Holland, is such, that, unless some speedy care be taken of them, they will run a greater hazard than you would have them exposed to.

You yourselves must be sensible that the Posture of affairs here require your serious consideration . . .

And particularly the state of Ireland is such That the Dangers are grown too great to be obviated by any slow Methods.

I must leave it to you . . . to judge what Forms may be most proper to bring these things to pass.

Thus, upon Monday the 18th February, the King, six days regnant, to his first Parliament.[1]

Four days previously, by an Order in Council, 'A Committee for the Affairs of Ireland' had been appointed and ordered to meet at 4 o'clock in the afternoon. Its members were the Lord President of the Council (Thomas, Earl of Danby), the Lord Privy Seal (George, Marquis of Halifax), the Lord Steward (William, Earl of Devonshire), the Secretary of State (Charles, Earl of Shrewsbury), Thomas, Viscount Fauconberg, Charles, Viscount Mordaunt, John, Baron Churchill, the Marshal Schomberg and Mr William Harbord.[2] Mordaunt was shortly to attain to first rank in the Commission of Treasury, Churchill to the Lieutenancy of the Forces, Schomberg to the Ordnance Office. Danby (far from satisfiedly), Fauconberg, Mordaunt and Churchill were soon all to receive elevation in the peerage; Schomberg awaited the 'naturalization' of his ducal dignity; for Mr Harbord the office of Paymaster was in store.

This Committee, which might well have been regarded as a veritable repository of the political wisdom of the hour, met on the 15th, 17th and 18th, listened to the advice of a 'Committee of the Irish Lords and Commons', the views of 'several of the Nobility and Gentry of Munster' and presented, on Wednesday the 20th February, to the King in Council, its first report.[3] The Committee noted that Captain James Hamilton, under orders from the King to take supplies of arms, ammunition and stores of war into Ireland, had arrived in Chester. It was held that he ought to hasten his mission, additionally receiving and conveying to Lieutenant Colonel Lundy, 'Commission and Instructions to command the town of Londonderry. And . . . likewise carry . . . 1000 l in money and deliver it to Lieut. Col. Lundy for the necessary occasions of the garrison.' But, before handing over supplies, commission or money, Hamilton should, while on ship-board and before the chief magistrate of Londonderry, cause Lundy to swear the recently approved oath to their Majesties William and Mary. Mr Anderton and Mr Frith, respectively the Officers of Customs and Excise at Chester, could be expected to supply the money. Anderton would attend to ship hire. It was assumed that the convoying frigate already rode in Chester water.

Next day Lundy's instructions were drawn; those of Hamilton the day after; but, as will later appear (see p. 63), a letter of the 21st February from Shrewsbury (Secretary of State) to Hamilton preceded or accompanied these instructions and was calculated to leave in Hamilton's mind doubt as to the urgency of setting out for Londonderry, under frigate convoy, in the Chester vessel at his disposal. Authorization to Anderton and Frith went out as a matter of course. And, as a matter of form, if not with high hope that displayed proclamations and scattered broadsheets would effect any useful purpose, a Declaration was drafted for exhibition in Ireland generally. In it William and Mary promised such of 'their' loving subjects as had rebelled against them indemnity, if, before the tenth day of April, they would lay down their arms and turn again homeward. To all such, freedom privately to exercise their Romish religion was assured; and, indeed, an even more general indulgence might be expected from that Irish Parliament which their Majesties were minded 'speedily' to call. Recalcitrance would entail land and property confiscation.[4]

Wednesday the 20th February, was the day and date which Pepys always regarded as setting a period to the official tenure of his Secretaryship of Admiralty.[5] The 'cessation' which the King had placed upon the holding of all offices – until such time as old appointments should be confirmed or new ones made – called forth from the Secretary at least a technically voluntary retirement. In laying down his lifework three days before his fifty-sixth birthday, Pepys avoided all pettiness and show of ill-will.[6] The orders which he had transmitted during the six elapsed days of the new reign possess no particular naval significance; and, in one matter only, did Admiralty business touch upon Irish affairs. It so happened that, on the 18th instant, the Clerk to the Privy Council, Sir John Nicholas, wished to discover whether Captain Collins had made 'Plotts of ye Coasts of that Kingdom' [Ireland]. Pepys replied that he thought not; but believed that Collins, the year before, had executed charts of the shores of England and Wales opposite to Ireland and left his sheets with the correspondent. He, Pepys, would send Collins to Sir John.[7]

But, in spite of 'retirement', Pepys's Admiralty copy-folio of 'out letters' continued to show evidence of 'caretaker' interest. On Friday the 22nd, for example, though Pepys hesitated at handling matters no longer officially under his control, he appealed to the Navy Board to expedite the fitting out of every ship against the King's obvious need.[8] The same day went out to Captain Tyrrell of the *Mordaunt* an answer to his complaint that Captain Shovell wore, in the Downs, the 'distinctive pennant' of senior captain of the station. An easy problem! 'I have always understood it to be ye known Law & Practice in the Downes, for ye Eldest Comandr (and him alone) to wear ye Distinction Pendant.' Would he, Tyrrell, take himself to be senior to Shovell? Evidence of such seniority 'did not appear in any of the Records' at Pepys's hand. As a retired Secretary speaking out of 'friendship', he might venture to advise though not to order. 'I cannot but think [he declared] that it will be well taken by the King and those to whom he shall commit the administration of the Admiralty that you should forbear.' He wrote, he said, as one concerned for the good order and discipline of the Navy and the prevention of the 'several inconveniences which may otherwise happen thereto' and rested in the assurance that a friend would not disregard his explicit guidance.[9]

As Pepys sent off his letter, the names of those to whom the King had decided to commit the routine business of Admiralty were published. The warrant was out to appoint Arthur Herbert, John, Earl of Carbery, Sir Michael Wharton, Sir Thomas Lee, Sir John Chicheley, Sir John Lowther of Whitehaven and William Sacheverell, Commissioners for exercising the affairs of the ancient office of Lord High Admiral of England.[10] This office, the late King James, assisted by 'that most expert gentleman Mr Samuel Pepys, Secretary of the Admiralty'[11] (in all but name, James's 'Minister of Marine'–an English Colbert) had filled and exercised with skill. For the last two months, William, not unaided by Pepys, but, relying mainly (so it appears) on the executive guidance of Herbert, had perforce taken James's place. He could, of course, have decided openly to double his Dutch rôle of Admiral-General, openly to reserve in himself the integrity of the office of Lord High Admiral. He could have made a bid to retain the Secretary or have appointed another. To ask whether the conscience of the retiring Pepys would have allowed him to respond to an indicated royal wish or accept from William a clear order to continuance of duty is to pose an unanswerable problem– Speculation is not History.[12] It must suffice to record that the office was placed in commission–with consequence which events were shortly to show. If we are to credit Burnet, Herbert was ill-pleased with the appointment of a Commission of Admiralty: 'it was thought that he hoped to have been advanced to that high trust the Lord High Admiralty alone'. But, at his swearing in as a member of the Privy Council, on Monday 26th, Herbert gained, for what it was worth, the satisfaction of being regarded as 'First Commissioner'.[13] And the dignity of 'Vice-Admiral of England' was soon to follow (see p. 102).

By the 26th the Committee for Irish affairs had met on three further occasions[14] and, next day, for the first time, the King in Council faced the problem of sending more than arms and ammunition to Londonderry. As a preliminary, two battalions, their needs to be supplied from Exeter, were talked of and, because their despatch would require the provision of frigate-convoyed transport from Liverpool and frigate-protected conveyance of the military stores in ships of burthen from Exeter's port, Topsham, the Commissioners for Executing the Office of Lord High Admiral were told forthwith to attend to the business. And they were enjoined to select fifteen or sixteen ships of war of suitable rates to guard the Irish coast, 'according to such instructions as should be given . . . on their behalf'.[15] But the Commission did not exist! Its patent was not yet engrossed and no meeting could be held. Consequently, on Thursday 28th, Herbert was invested with a temporary executive authority which placed squarely upon him the responsibility for carrying out the directions of King or Council and, particularly and mainly, of insuring effective liaison between the Committee for Irish Affairs and the Principal Officers and Commissioners of the Navy.[16]

On Friday the 1st March, and Saturday 2nd, the Irish Committee was again in session, tackling, in a manner typical of the times, the problem of providing soldiery for Ireland, searching for a dozen colonels, willing, upon stipulated conditions of engagement and pay, to raise 10,000 troops for expedition.[17] Down to Hampton Court went the members on Sunday 3rd, reported progress, and, with the King, took decision to move the regiments of Colonels Cunningham and Richards to the sea in anticipation of transport to Londonderry. Principally, however, the occasion was used to cross-examine Sir Richard Haddock the Comptroller of the Navy[18] on the readiness or otherwise of the contingents of the three projected fleets.[19] Sir Richard, who had been warned on the 1st of the impending ordeal, produced a paper headed: 'The squadrons intended for the Streights, Ireland and the Channel and the day when they will be ready'. It is set forth overleaf.[20]

Almost two months previously, on the 12th January (see p. 30 *ante*), fifteen had been allocated to service in the Streights, eight to Ireland, six to the Channel, thirty-five placed in reserve. Of the fifteen, four named thirds, eight named fourths and three fireships, designed for the Streights, two thirds, six fourths and three fireships are shown unready for sea; nor is there mention of any

| *Streights Squadron* | *2nd March 1688* |
|---|---|
| 3 Elizabeth | 12 days |
| 3 Plymouth | 10 days |
| 4 Advice | 6 days |
| 4 Assurance | 8 days |
| 4 Deptford | 12 days |
| 4 Foresight | 6 days |
| 4 Portland | 6 days |
| 4 Woolwich | 12 days |
| 5, 3 Fire Ships | 8 days |
| *Irish Squadron* | |
| 4 St Albans | 12 days |
| 4 Bonadventure | 8 days |
| 4 Dover, now in the Downs. | |
| 4 Jersey, on the coast of Ireland. | |
| 4 Mordant, in the Downs. | |
| 4 Swallow, on the coast of Ireland. | |
| *Channel Squadron* | |
| 4 Antelope, in the Downs | |
| 4 Greenwich | 10 days |
| 4 Ruby, in the Downs | |
| 5 Dartmouth | 6 days |
| 5 Garland | 8 days |

preparedness of two other thirds and two other fourths to supply the balance. The designated Irish squadron had consisted of six fourths and two sixths; two fourths were on station, two in the Downs, two unready and, as no doubt the Committee were supposed to be aware, the proposed sixths, *Lark* and *Saudadoes* were on special service in the North Sea. One third rate and five fourth rates had been intended for the Channel and Herbert's command. The Committee might be expected to recall that the third rate *Defiance* had been left, in December, in Spithead by Berry sailing for the Nore; they now learned that two fourth rates of this Channel grouping were in the Downs, yet another fourth and two fifths, apparently replacements for fourths (one of which, *Phoenix*, was on duty in the North Sea) were not yet effective. Whether discussion proceeded to review of the condition of the great reserve of nine thirds, seven fourths, two sixths and seventeen fireships is not revealed. It is unlikely that Haddock could have pointed to more than two of those near or at Portsmouth–the thirds *Dreadnought* and *Edgar*–in approximate readiness. He could not have reported encouragingly on the rest. A decision was reached that ships as they became ready were to sail speedily for the Downs.

Between this Sunday 3rd and Friday 8th–a date of significance –the Committee met again thrice, pursued with vigour its work begun, twice received reports from Ireland and sent back by one of the bearers a message of encouragement to Londonderry.[21] Among those attending, on 5th March, the Committee's proceedings for the first time was Daniel Finch, Earl of Winchelsea and Nottingham,[22] that day appointed a Principal Secretary of State and destined–perhaps already personally determined–to play a leading part in naval affairs.

In spite of indisposition, Herbert addressed himself to the task of giving such naval orders as the decisions of the Committee, the requirements of the King and routine needs of the service demanded. He called to his side on Friday 1st Mr Phineas Bowles (Bowles had been Admiral's Secretary and Muster Master in Dartmouth's fleet) who took down 'his thoughts' which were transmitted next day to the Navy Board for action.[23] Twenty-four orders went out in the week to the following Friday. Of those to Thursday 7th some related to the transport to be taken up at Liverpool (victualling requirements not to be overlooked) for the troops intended for Ireland; some to the necessity to secure east-coast shipping to move 4,000 men from the River to Holland, 2,000 from Harwich to the same destination, and 2,000 from Gravesend to Scotland. Ammunition and stores at Exeter awaited loading at Topsham for Londonderry; ships preparing for sea were to be regarded as sufficiently victualled with but two months' provision on board.[24] The Ordnance Office, supplied with lists of the ships fitting out, was asked to be ready to provide without delay gunners' stores. To a few captains special orders were sent, in particular, after Herbert had consulted Shrewsbury,[25] to Killigrew of the *Dragon*, who, riding off Cadiz with Hosier of the *Sapphire*, had reported fourteen French warships of forty guns and upwards at Malaga. Killigrew was to bring home the Streights trade; he was given permission to accept plate and jewels for carriage (see p. 151).

At the Banqueting House, on the morning of Friday the 8th March, the King once again received the Lords and Commons in Parliament, accepting and acknowledging a loyal address which owed its inception, on Monday the 4th March, to the Commons, which House, if we are to believe a contemporary historian, had, on the 27th February, been advised by William–quite wrongly– of the sailing of James from Brest. The royal speech was, in effect, an expansion of that of the 13th February. 'When' said the King, he spoke to them last, he 'told them of the necessity of assisting the Allies, and, more especially the States of Holland' which had 'exhausted themselves' to a degree not easily to be imagined. Therefore, he asked to be enabled to keep 'the treaty with them', to 'make good' what the States had 'actually laid out on this occasion'. The ruin of Holland would, he reminded Parliament, be but 'a step to England's destruction'. He also knew that he needed not: 'take pains to tell . . . of the deplorable condition of Ireland . . . it [was] not [he thought] advisable to attempt the reducing of it otherwise than by a very considerable force, which . . . ought not to be less than 20,000 horse and foot . . .'
Then too they must:

> consider that, towards the more speedy and effectual succour in relation to Ireland as well as with regard to France, there must be such a fleet as [might] in conjunction with the States, make it so entirely master of the sea that nothing [could] be sent from France, either to Ireland or anywhere else that may give disturbance to us or our allies.

Money must be granted for the purpose he named. It would be properly applied; and he, the King, would do nothing without Parliament's advice.

It was not surprising that the notion of intervention from France should at this time receive recognition in the royal mind. News, scarcely week-old, readily crossed the Channel and effective government intelligences were a feature of the age:

> Letters from France say that the late King of England had taken

his leave and was gone towards Brest in order to goe on board for Ireland (February 23rd). Letters from Paris say that the late King James, in his way to Brest was taken with a paralytick fitt (March 5th)

and this day, the 8th March, even as the distinguished throng dispersed, a report of much more than usual circumstantiality circulated in the city.

Letters from Morlaix in France say that King James sailed from Brest the 25th of last month, with 16 men-of-war and 7 tenders, for Ireland; but was beat back again the 27th, the men on board are English, Scotch and Irish, few French . . .[26]

Shrewsbury, on leaving the gathering, wrote by command to Lundy telling him that the King's 'greatest concern hath been for Ireland and particularly for the province of Ulster which he looks upon as most capable to defend itself.' He assured Lundy that two regiments waited at the sea-side ready to embark and that they would be followed by a 'considerable body'. On Lundy's 'fidelity and resolution' the King relied. Of Ireland's needs, Parliament, only that morning, had again been made aware. Lundy might confidently expect the King's favour.[27]

To return to the Irish Committee. At some time on Friday 8th the Commissioner of Customs, whose department had been requested to assist search for suitable vessels to transport soldiers to Ireland, tendered report. Whitehaven, it was said, had perhaps fifty colliers, unemployed because of interruption of trade with Ireland; Liverpool boasted sixty to seventy good ships—few at home—driving 'a universal foreign trade to the Plantations and elsewhere'; a score Chester and Mostyn craft were thought to be mostly of too low tonnage for employ. At this point Major General Kirke entered the picture. He was to be appointed to visit immediately the regiments intended for Ireland. The Victuallers of the Navy answered summons to tell of their procedure in hiring seven ships for 1,200 men at Chester. The cost, on the basis of 1 lb biscuit, 1 lb cheese and 1 gallon of beer *per diem* would total 341 L for a ten day voyage, to which figure must be added, for freight of the men and accoutrements, a further 240 L. The Victuallers were informed that the troops were at Liverpool and

that the two regiments might be supposed to consist of 1,500 not
1,200 men. Herbert would order the vessels round to the Mersey
and the Navy Board deal with the augmented requirements. The
Committee closed its proceedings by finally agreeing about the
list of colonels of regiments–thirteen in number–to be proposed
to the King.[28]

Herbert's orders of Friday the 8th were some seven in number.
They related to the transfer of officers and men, guns and stores
(three or four ships involved), more explicit guidance to the Navy
Board in the matter of sending troops from the River and Harwich
to Holland, a definite instruction to the Navy Board to continue
the customary provision for the sick and wounded and a particular
command to Captain Byng of the *Constant Warwick* in Spithead to
sail to Torbay, where, after waiting, if necessary, six days, he
should collect whatever merchant ships in the bay intended
voyage to Ostend or Rotterdam.[29]

Herbert's interim authority ended. It is worth mention that
three times just before and during his temporary executive control
the First Commissioner was in touch with Pepys; on the 26th
February he obtained desired lists[30] on the 27th, miscellaneous
information on pilots' pay, 'protections' from pressing for the
crews of the packet boats, musters and the eviction of the military
occupants of certain Sheerness officers' dwellings. Some correspondence from abroad Pepys sent to Herbert on the 5th March–a
letter from Killigrew included[31] (see p. 80).

The Committee was concerned on Saturday 9th to ascertain
from Herbert an estimate of Ordnance Office stores for his fleet.
(Had the Office commented, evasively, on its ability to meet the
detailed demands Herbert had just placed upon it? Celerity of
supply by a department which provided guns and ammunition
for the army and navy was never (certainly not at a time of joint
mobilization) to be taken for granted; but the Irish Committee
was at least in a position to attempt to secure attention to its
wishes![32]) The Committee still more desired to learn how many of
the ships named in Haddock's disturbing list had reached the
Downs–in brief, the real degree of readiness at that time of the
fleet 'intended for Ireland'. It recapitulated, re-examined much
other business and learned for the first time since the 20th

February (and no doubt with relief) news, from Sir John Lowther in Cumberland, concerning Captain James Hamilton[33] (see p. 54 *ante*). Hamilton, considering the contents of a letter from Shrewsbury, dated 21st February (and received by him before or with the formal instructions deriving from the meeting of the Irish Committee upon the 20th February and issued out of the Secretary's office under date, the 22nd February), no longer understood that he must, as the formal instructions ordered, make post haste to Ireland, with a single frigate and a single Chester ship, which should sail by way of Whitehaven to obtain additional stores. At Chester, having placed aboard the *Pelican* (owner and master Mr Nicholas Ward) arms and nearly £600 collected from Anderton, Hamilton properly requested Captain Beverley, in the *Jersey* frigate, to convoy him, with the *Pelican*, to Whitehaven. Beverley told him that he, with his frigate, did not dare to meddle with that Cumberland coast and would ride in Ramsey Bay, Isle of Man, while the *Pelican* took Hamilton in. But the *Pelican* was slow to load and the arrangement broke down. Consequently, Hamilton, with no more than Gawain's enthusiasm, set out from Wirral on the '115 scurvy miles' to the place 'not within the post road' well knowing that, when he got to Whitehaven, the finding of a ship, and transport of the stores from Carlisle to the found ship thirty miles distant, would greatly delay his Londonderry mission.[34] Though Lowther could report that Hamilton had placed arms and ammunition aboard the *Deliverance* of Whitehaven[35] he could not forecast when Hamilton would make contact with Beverley— still less when any one of the three aidant ships would reach the Foyle.

It was at Herbert's lodgings, in Channell or Cannon Row, Westminster, and not at the Buckingham Street, Strand 'residence-office' of Pepys that, on Saturday the 9th March the Commissioners of Admiralty first met.[36] All members were present. The letters-patent of William and Mary, dated the 8th March, were opened and read.[37] The draughtsmen had taken for model the commission to Sir Henry Capel, K.B., 14th May 1679. In broad terms the document gave to the Commissioners or any three of them:

full Power and authority to doe, Execute, exercise and perform all & every act, matter and thing, which to the office of Lord High Admirall of England appertaineth and belongeth, as well in and touching those things which Concerne our Navy and Shipping as those things which concern the Rights and Jurisdictions of or appeartaining to the Office or Place of High Admiral of England.

When however, generalization moved to particularization[38] it was made plain that the function of the Commission would be solely executive and non-initiatory, the Admiralty the servant of the Crown and Privy Council–as it had been long before the days of James, Duke of York and King. Decision was taken that:

Mr Phineas Bowles be . . . Secret[y] for the Affaires of Admiralty.[39]

The day's business? Captain Mees to replace Beverley of the *Jersey*, Ackerman of the *Dreadnought* to answer, at the Board, a complaint of Ashby of the *Defiance*. Sir John Berry, commanding the fleet at Sheerness, to apply to the Commission for any orders; the same instruction to Sir Richard Beach Commissioner at Portsmouth. Captain Fitzpatrick of the *Assurance* to proceed from Sheerness to Harwich, take on thirty-one Dutch officers from the *Phoenix*, and sail thence to Goree. He should guard any packets waiting to go out from, or return to, Harwich. (It appears from the actual terms of the order to Fitzpatrick (10th) that he had to act as protector to some seventeen ships taking soldiers to Holland.)[40] The captain of the *Jersey* or *Swallow* to convoy from Liverpool to Londonderry 1,200 men in ships provided by the Navy Office, then return to station. The *Guernsey* to be reconverted at Woolwich from a fireship to fifth rate. Captain William Sanderson to be captain and master of the *Henrietta* 'yacht'. Francis Lambert gunner of the *Isabella* 'yacht' to be gunner of the *Henrietta*. Resolved . . . 'The a Lr. be written to Mr Pepys to deliver unto Mr Bowles our Secret 7 all Bookes, Papers and things belonging to the affaires of Admiralty'.[41] The Navy Board to attend upon Monday at five at Channell Row. That Captain Cornwall of the *Swallow* at West Chester assist Captain Mees of the *Jersey* in taking possession of the said ship 'if there be occasion for it'. The unwillingness, previously noted (see p. 63), of Captain Beverley, commander of the *Jersey*, to take Captain Hamilton to the Whitehaven coast, suggests that there might be reason for a captaincy change!

'Inconsequence' characterizes the minuting of the decisions of this the first meeting of the newly constituted Commission. Doubtless it indicates the manner in which business was taken and cleared, a procedure which set the pattern for the sessions that henceforth followed almost daily sometimes more than once the same day.

Either before or after this meeting another–but not of the Board –was held in the same place. The Dutch emissaries who had arrived in December last for the negotiation of Anglo-Dutch alliance (see p. 34), crossed from Pall Mall to confer with three English Commissioners recently appointed by the King–the Earl of Nottingham, Admiral Herbert and Mr Russell. The representatives of the Provinces had reached decision to ask for bolder naval action than had been envisaged under the 1678 treaty. If England would provide five-eighths and the Provinces three-eighths of an allied fleet of eighty sail the combined effort, fifty English and thirty Dutch, would equal, so it was estimated, the French line strength. To the allied eighty, supporting craft should be added and, distinct from the eighty, a flotilla of ten frigates set aside for a specially indicated task. The Dutch emissaries, in no way hesitant, proposed not only the terms of strength but strategical allocations for the ships. For the Channel and Irish Sea fifty; for the Mediterranean thirty; for the North Sea narrows, Dover to Walcheren, the dozen frigates. The Dutch also asked for an expedition to America; but this extension of mutual activity the English declined. At this meeting the English claimed the right of commanding any allied fleet. It was accepted that ship preparations in the Provinces were already advanced. The Deputies suggested, as the date of rendezvous, the 30th/20th April, six weeks ahead; the English Commission asked for the 30th April/ 10th May seven weeks on, as the *whole* English fleet could not by any earlier date be at sea. The Dutch were not accommodating, even when reminded that England, with forty ships already at sea (here the English Commissioners must be allowed the exaggeration of intention rather than the accuracy of truth) had already fulfilled all obligation under the existing treaty. Might not the Dutch 'well be content to be at sea ten days before the last ten English ships arrived?' The Dutchmen remained unyielding and, in effect, gave the impression that putting to sea at even the suggested date depended on the expected prompt payment of the invasion expenses due to the Provinces from Parliament. Which fact between the 5th and the 10th March Nottingham told the King. [42]

Here it is convenient to observe that the United Provinces had by this time reciprocated Louis' declaration of War on the 16th/26th November. The declaration had issued from the Hague upon the 9th March/27th February. England still formally delayed diplomatic defiance, proclaiming only, since mid-February, 'an embargo . . . that vessels will not goe into France untill they give security accordingly'. Proclamation and enforcement did not necessarily go hand in hand. On the 21st February the full Privy Council was listening to the complaint of the Commissioners supervising the Wool Trade that certain merchants were loading wool into privateers and shipping it to France. [43]

Sunday the 10th March saw no business transacted, either by the Irish Committee or Commission of Admiralty, and Monday 11th only by the latter. On the morning of Tuesday the 12th March, the Admiralty was again in session. Its meeting was adjourned till the evening, possibly to allow the attendance of the Admiral at the afternoon consultation of the Committee of Irish Affairs when the instructions of Colonels John Cunningham and Solomon Richards, whose embarkation from Liverpool with their regiments was regarded as imminent, came under discussion. Their ordered destination was, of course, Londonderry, failing that, Carrick-fergus or Strangford; but, should the worst come to the worst, the regiments must return to Liverpool. For Colonel Lundy supplementary orders were being drafted, prescribing the reception he should accord and the use to which, in unsurrendering resistance, he should put these succours. [44]

The *post-meridiem* meeting of the Admiralty was duly held at the usual place, Herbert's Channel Row lodgings. First the business of detailing *Assurance* to convoy to Holland seventeen named transports, eleven from Gravesend and six from Harwich, was disposed of; next a report delivered express from Vice-Admiral Berry at Sheerness received consideration. Berry, answering demands which were the consequence of the Board's deliberations of the 11th ('fowle or cleane', every possible vessel, the *Cambridge* and *Pendennis* included, to be directed to Spithead), claimed that he had used 'his best endeavour', submitted a required ship list and requested leave 'to go on Shore for the recovery of his health'. For answer he was firmly told to sail for Spithead with the: '*Plymouth, Advice, Portland, Greenwich, St Albans, Foresight, Elizabeth, Yorke, Deptford, Woolwich, Bonadventure, St David, Warspight, Diamond*', picking up such of 'his Majts ships as he should meet with in his way thither, and to continue there till his Majty bid another to relieve him.' After that he might expect leave. The Vice-Admiral was encouragingly informed that the Commissioners of the Navy would be going down to Portsmouth to pay off the 'turned-over men' (ratings arbitrarily transferred from one ship to another); 'and, in a little time after, other money [would] be Ordered to pay off ye whole fleet now in Seapay for two months'. Two vessels, the *Dartmouth* and the *Guardland*, Berry was ordered to detach to convoy to Scotland the 2,000 troops already waiting at Gravesend.

In the course of the three meetings of the two days, the 11th and 12th March, the Commissioners of Admiralty continued to make routine appointments. More than a dozen captains were commissioned or transferred. Captain [Grenville?] Collins asked for and received promise of employ; Captain Legge of the *Dartmouth*, he was Lord Dartmouth's brother, was superseded and ordered to meet the Board. Captain James Smith obtained leave, through disablement, to lay down command. At a lower level the recommendations of commanding officers secured for a carpenter and a purser transfers; and for another purser a minuted promise of the next vacancy; a master-carpenter gained his objective of senior shore employ. One or two ship movement orders unconnected with the gathering of the fleet went out and (was it in a spirit of helpfulness?) the Board expressed itself willing to meet 'Captain' Mackay [Major-General Mackay] who would be in command of the soldiers bound for Scotland.

The extent to which in the same short space of the two days, the Principal Officers and Commissioners of the Navy had found themselves hustled by the Commissioners of Admiralty should interest the student of naval administration. Two considerable reports had been demanded – the figures on which to base the promise of pay to the 'turned-over' men and the whole fleet and a thorough conspectus of the victualling situation. (Of the former requirement an earlier order by Herbert had given warning.) Upon the unlucky representatives of the Board who, at the morning meeting of the 12th failed to honour an undertaking made at attendance upon the Commissioners 'last night', a promise to produce a list of the ships ready to effect the transport of the 2,000 troops from Gravesend to Scotland, reprimand had descended. Let them 'not fayle to send [to] the same Admll Herbert at the Councill Chamber [that afternoon] at 3 of the Clock!' It is to be hoped that when, that evening, the Commissioners, on behalf of their Admiral First Commissioner, indented of the Navy Board for: 'Sixty printed bookes of the General Sailing and Fighting Instructions'[45] copies were not reported in 'short supply'! The Deal postmaster, like the Navy Board, was made aware of the Commission's existence – returns of all ships entering the Downs must be forwarded *daily* to Channel Row!

Three meetings in one day can have left the Admiral little time to reflect upon the contents of a paper received, at earliest, the previous afternoon or evening. It came from the office of the newly appointed Principal Secretary of State Daniel Finch, Earl of Nottingham. Dated the 11th March; it was addressed, with customary preamble: 'To Our Right Trusty and Well-beloved Councellor Arthur Herbert Esq. Admirall and Comander of our Ships in ye Narrow Seas.'[46] and required him 'immediately upon receipt' to 'repair on board ye ship' – and take under command the ships 'named in ye margent', their commanders required to obey the orders they should 'from time to time receive'. But the name of the flagship was not inserted and the admiral was not 'edified by the margent' – which was blank. He was expected immediately to sail to the 'chops of the Channel', and, when off Scilly, to send a warship to 'Kinsale, Cork or some other port of Ireland' to learn whether 'the late King James' had arrived in that kingdom, and, if so, notion of his strength. While waiting for news he must cruise between Ouessant [Ushant] and Scilly off the coast of Ireland or elsewhere, to prevent the enemy sending troops and arms to Ireland or Scotland. Should King James be landed, the Admiral would be expected to dispatch some of his strength to cruise between Ireland and Scotland, and, with the rest of the fleet, endeavour to take or destroy the ships which brought over the said late king. Any French ships of war met with in the Irish sea or within twenty leagues of the coast of Ireland, or any vessels of any nation whatever ('not sent by us') bringing arms, ammunition or soldiers to Ireland or Scotland should be regarded as enemy. The Protestants in Ireland would require to be assisted. Without unduly hazarding his ships Herbert should look in upon Brest and report any activity. He was expected to give all the assistance and protection he could to ships belonging to the States General, 'so as' he did not prejudice the other services.

Addenda to these orders noted the necessity to recommission all commanders, since their commissions would, normally, be held of King James, and all commissioned and warrant officers were to be made to take the 'oaths of fidelity and test against Popery'.

With the main paper the Admiral received a sealed order, not to be opened unless he intercepted James on the sea. In that case he would be expected to treat the said King with respect, transport him to some port belonging to the States General and dispose of him into the hands of such persons as the said States might appoint. This delivery was not to be a cause of jeopardy to major dispositions.

The admiral in London – what ships at rendezvous at Spithead? In Bowles's office, clerks, using incoming information, built the table which makes possible an answer. 'A List of the Shipps in Seapay, together with their Comanders, Men, Guns, at where they now are, and in W[hat] Readiness for the Sea.' Bearing date the 13th, that list was sent to the King.[47] It forecast [the letters M (Mediterranean), C (Channel), I (Irish), R (Reserve), here used to indicate to which of the 12th January allocations the ship belonged, are not on the list] as follows: At Spithead four thirds, *Defiance* (C), *Dreadnought* (R), *Edgar* (R), and *Mary* (R) to which might be added *Tyger* (C), at Portsmouth, 'suddenly ready' (five in all). In the Downs no thirds; but *Advice* (I), *Foresight* (M),

*Portland* (M), *Greenwich* (C), *Mordaunt* (I), *Antelope* (C), *Ruby* (C), all fourth rates and *Saudadoes* (I), a sixth (eight in all) working through. Somewhere on their way out of Sheerness four thirds, *Elizabeth* (M), *Plymouth* (M), *Warspight* (M), *Yorke* (M), with *Deptford* (M), *St David* (M), *Diamond* (M), *Woolwich* (M), *Bonad-venture* (I), all fourths (nine in all), likewise ordered from the River. Twenty-one middle rates – of which only five were represented as on station – Berry to bring along the remainder and *Saudadoes*. Dartmouth had 'returned' forty-three thirds and fourths. Where (omitting the three 'counted out' at the 12th January allocation) were the nineteen others? Might not the Admiral expect addition beyond the incoming strength? Partly the list answers[48]. Four fourths were at sea. *Portsmouth* (R), cruising off Jersey, might be considered as already with him; but the *Swallow* (I) and *Jersey* (I), off Chester-water, *Assurance* (M), convoying soldiers from Harwich to Holland, and *Constant Warwick* (R), collecting trade at Torbay for the Downs and Ostend, would clearly not be available. *Cambridge* (R) and *Pendennis* (R) 'ready in 8 or 10 daies', *Hampton Court* (R) and *Kent* (R), 'wanting only men and provičons', four fourths, and *Tyger Prize* (R), a third, 'busy manning', were reinforcement of which Herbert could scarcely be sanguine. He perforce wrote off the two thirds *Henrietta* (R), *Resolution* (R), both 'in great need of repair' together with the four fourths *Crowne* (R), *Newcastle* (R), *St Albans* (M) and *Phoenix* (C), which were listed as in the shipwrights' hands – as well as three fourths not named in the report – *Centurion* (R), *Bristol* (R), *Dover* (I) of the condition and whereabouts of which he would undoubtedly be aware. Nine ships of the line quite out of action! Of the lesser ships allocated in January, only the *Saudadoes* (I), already mentioned, could do service; the sixth *Larke* (I) lay damaged at Rotterdam; the *Firedrake* (R) and *Quaker Ketch* (R), sixth rates, respectively needed 'a few days' and 'a month'. Of ships not assigned in the January plan, *Dartmouth* and *Guardland*, fifths, were appointed escort for Mackay's troops to Scotland, the fifth *Swan* was victualling, the *Salamander*, a sixth, asked yet 'a few days'. It might be remotely useful to Herbert to learn that in the Thames were four yachts, at Portsmouth, Guernsey and Chester, each, one; the information supplied by the list concerning fireships would approach the disheartening! Three fireships were said to be in dock, four regarded as too small for the Channel, and, while one 'wanted men and victuals', three others would not be ready for a week, two for three weeks, one for a month. Fireships were an essential component of a fleet.

It remains to add a brief statement on naval finance for the period of the 14th February to the 12th March.

That the 26th February had been reached before the Commons began to consider matters of supply, that the 11th March had arrived before the House voted to consider authorizing the revenue collection customary in the last two reigns, are matters of constitutional interest without demonstrable bearing upon naval preparations. The naval debt at the end of December stood at about £200,000.[49] It continued to rise between the 13th February and the date here reached – the 12th March; but the accounts of the Navy Office indicate a receipt in that period of just over £50,000 shared as the subjoined table shows:

| | £ | |
|---|---|---|
| For the current service of the Navy | 12,200 | |
| For payment of wages of ships and yards | 6,991 | £50,191[50] |
| For Victuallers | 31,000 | |

The evidence is that almost £112,000 was made available to the Navy from the 1st January to the 12th March.[51] In that case the naval debt can scarcely have grown much faster in the January-March interim than the credits passed from the Treasury to Lord Falkland, the Treasurer of the Navy. It is not the interim increase in the total debt which claims attention but the smallness of the allowance to the wages of the ships and yards.

In the foregoing pages at the accepted risk of a charge of some prolixity, a factual journal to illustrate the course and routine of naval business in the critical month from the 14th February to the 12th March 1688/9 has been attempted. A less detailed presentation would have suppressed data on which judgments which follow depend.

## II

In spite of William's pessimistic remarks to the Lords and Commons on the 8th instant (see p. 60), the situation of the Allies then and upon the 13th of the month was far from desperate. The news coming in from Sweden, from the Allies by the Rhine, from Spain and from distant Vienna encouraged a sober satisfaction. There could be no real doubt that the English Parliament would honour the outstanding cash debt to the liberator–the liability so insisted upon in the recent royal speech to both Houses assembled; that treaty troop-commitments to the Provinces would be met; that the horse and foot necessary for subjugation of Ireland would be forthcoming; and that an effective naval liaison between the two sea-powers would result from the negotiations set in train (now to all intents and purposes concluded) to produce an array of strength sufficient to excel the potentialities of the French marine.

Not that it is to be supposed that William was popular!

I heard my Lord Privy Seale say that, as the nation now stood, if the King [James] were a Protestant he could not be kept out four months; but my Lord Danby went further–for he said that, if he [James] would give the satisfactions in religion he might, it would be hard to resist him as he was.

The date of Reresby's oft quoted observation is the 13th March. But the Lord Privy Seal's remark was pointless–James was *not* a Protestant; and Danby's disgruntled comment–James being James, and the nation quite unprepared for toleration of catholicism or (as the Declaration of Rights had indicated) of a Catholic on the throne–had little practical worth.[52] The sober records of the daily proceedings of the Lords and Commons, the minutes of the Privy Council and its Committees, of the departments of State, are of more significance than court gossip, born of understandable reaction to William's undemonstrative, perhaps at times boorish, Dutch aloofness. The city and the ports traded; the writ of the law ran to the county boroughs and the rural parts. Considered domestically (Jacobite intrigue and the dissidence in James's old regiments not overlooked) the course and happenings of two months of *de facto* and one of *de jure* rule contributed, as with inevitability, to William's establishment upon the English throne. The invader could afford to send back in numbers his trusted, Dutch troops. And while he considered it wise to put into Carlisle and Berwick units to watch the Border and to ship to Leith, under Major-General Mackay, reliable Scottish regiments

brought with him to Torbay, he had ever expectation that a
Convention, due to meet in Edinburgh upon the 14th March,
would, under the guidance of Duke Hamilton, proceed to offer
him a second throne.[53] . . . Abroad, in England, in Scotland,
events sorted well enough with predestination and the pursuit of
the grand design.

But the turn of events in Ireland, the bare thought of the compelled diversion of 20,000 horse and foot to fight Richard Hamilton or Earl Tyrconnel, troops it were more desirable to hurl,
under Schomberg or himself, against Louis in his French confines,
irked William, who, as has been observed, on the 8th March,
could do no more than smother his fear that the situation might,
through French intervention, worsen before 'such a fleet as
[might] in conjunction with the States make it entirely master of
the sea' could mobilize to prevent the eventuality.

No historian urges that, at this time, William's handling of Irish
affairs contributed lustre to his reputation. The King had seen
(18th February) in Ireland 'dangers grown too great to be
obviated by any slow methods' and properly held in view the
need to send assistance to Londonderry. Sentiment and the
necessity to retain, against the worst, a foothold in the island
dictated that aid should be shipped. Yet, by the end of the fourth
week from the King's accession, no food, ammunition or arms,
no special commission to Colonel Lundy or contingent money for
his use had been delivered. *Swallow* rode at ease off Neston or
tossed in Liverpool Bay; the loaded *Pelican* of Chester earned for
Mr Nicholas Ward its master its daily rate of hire and failed to
follow Beverley in the *Jersey* to sight of the Point of Ayre. . . . Still—
no irreparable harm had accrued; the city of Londonderry was
not straitly shut up, the tidal Foyle ran navigable to and from its
walls; and the main body of oncoming enemy troops were not
much nearer than Loughbrickland some sixty miles away. Time
yet served; foothold in Ulster held.

It is in respect of the more gross neglect to guard against French
intervention in Ireland, whether or no headed by James in person
—but, so undertaken, invasion parallel to William's own appearance
at Torbay—that a charge against the King must lie. Admittedly,
the chances of the sea, wind, tide and fog were, in 1688, such that

the passage of an *isolated* ship or *limited* venture might well have eluded the most stringent vigilance and placed James in the other kingdom. Against that contingency only the initial prevention of James's expected escape into France could have completely guarded; and it is somewhat strange that historians have not debated whether a Machiavellian surveillance of the fugitive's second flight and the diversion of the fugitive's smack to Holland would not have been a mark of statecraft. Perhaps, as the King read Nottingham's draft of the sealed order which Herbert was to receive with the Instructions handed to him on the 11th March, and wrote his William R at the top left-hand corner, he questioned his own lack of prescience and wisdom in December.[54] Be that as it may, the escape of James to France allowed, it should have been William's constant preoccupation to forestall the landing by France of material aid, which, in any quantity, could only be forwarded in men-of-war or by men-of-war convoyed merchantmen, in either case (given an English squadron on appropriate station) likely, or at least possible, objects of detection when moving upon the high seas.

In a pamphlet,[55] written when Irish affairs had been three years under debate, purporting a dialogue between a Deputy and the Lord Lieutenant of his county, occurs the sentence:

I could never find any other reason, why *Forty Sail* of Stout Men of War, well equipped, delivered up by my Lord *Dartmouth*, and *Forty more*, which came with our K. from *Holland*, were kept in Port useless, when a Part of them might, *without resistance*, have possessed themselves of the Harbors of *Cork* and *Kingsale* in *Ireland*, being then neither *fortifyed* nor *garrisoned*, and that alone had prevented all the Designs of *K. James* and the *French K.* upon that Kingdom, and saved all that *vast Expense of Blood and Treasure*, which it hath since cost to reduce it, besides the Spoil and Destruction by War, which hath laid a great Part of that Country *wast* and *desolate*.

I dread the thoughts of the Account that must be given of three or fourscore thousand Mens Blood, needlesly spilt in that Kingdom.

If part of the Fleet had been thus imployed, the rest had been sufficient to have crushed all the first preparations of the *French* for a Naval War . . . It had been an easie work in the early Spring of 1689 (if the Advices of those faithful to our K had taken place) . . .

To turn to p. 30 of this study and count the 12th January allotment of Dartmouth's vessels to projected squadronal services and retention in sea-pay, is to recognize the reasonableness of the pamphleteer's figure 'Forty Sail of Stout Men of War'. His reference to the 'Forty more which came with our K from Holland' is an equally fair estimate. Herbert's fleet had consisted of forty-nine ships of war—some large, some small—exclusive of fireships. One recalls Dartmouth's declaration (see p. 25) of his personal intention to prevent 'any French forces landing or making any descent upon these Kingdomes', (the number of the noun is plural) and his expectation that the fleets would be merged 'no distaists . . . given to what either may be liable'. But no such union, no stay of Herbert's Dutch fleet on our coast is in this pamphleteer's mind. The Deputy Lieutenant does not ask for fusion and a single admiral. He would certainly have agreed that the 'Forty Sail of Stout Men of War' comprising the mobilization and reserve which, at the Prince–Herbert–Pepys meeting of the 12th January had been so optimistically agreed, would have provided an English Admiral with effectives sufficient to claim command of the Channel; the rest of the total November amassed naval strength he pictured as kept on a war footing (he does not suggest where) for other 'Work in the early Spring'. As the Deputy Lieutenant implies, the Channel command could have been exercised, had William been willing and prepared to provide the battalions, in a descent on Kinsale, Cork or Waterford. Kinsale fort was in Protestant hands till the first days of February, Bandon, a few miles up the river behind Kinsale, a month longer; Dungannon fort, guarding Waterford, resisted Tyrconnel through much of February. The less ambitious exercise of command dictated at least the spread of a net of scouts and the appropriate application of force for the destruction of an intercepted or disembarking expedition. No attempt was made until the penultimate morning of the period under review, 13th February–12th March, to send a Channel squadron to sea. Except for a fourth rate off Jersey–the *Portsmouth*–was any scout abroad?

The pamphleteer's 'Forty Sail of Stout Men of War', reasonable estimate for a layman, needs, in one respect, qualification; for it took no account of the condition in which Dartmouth's vessels were, in fact, 'returned', thirds, fourths, fireships, from the Winter seas. Of his forty-three capital ships (thirty-five original plus eight reinforcement), thirteen at least had sustained appreciable hurt.[56] Indeed eleven were, on the 12th March, still refitting –including the nine which, placed in the 12th January allocation, were for Herbert, on the 12th March, quite out of call. But all this duly pointed out to the pamphleteer, he would, no doubt, have countered with the observation that, presumably, Dartmouth's campaign ended with thirty thirds and fourths intact–a sizeable force–and asked whether the Navy did not possess another forty thirds and fourths. What the pamphleteer could not know–an argument to clinch his case–was that in November, additionally to the reinforcements–the eight–already posted to Dartmouth, Pepys had offered to order out three more fourths, two more thirds and 'any of the thirds save two' which the Admiral might desire with his flag.[57]

The provision out of thirty thirds and fourths, of twenty, or even ten good rates to patrol from the Scillies to Kinsale or Cape Clear was as feasible as desirable. Dartmouth's thirteen damaged vessels could reasonably have been sent to the royal yards of Chatham, Deptford, Sheerness and Woolwich, leaving to the royal yard of Portsmouth the minor repairs needed by a maintained, patrolling squadron, which, already manned and stored– Dartmouth had not fired a single angry shot!–could have been victualled from sea and port as occasion best answered. Why then was a Channel squadron or patrol not provided?

One hypothesis alone explains the omission. For William the Mediterranean appeared twice as important as the Channel, as important as the strategic needs, in terms of ships, of the Channel and Irish waters combined. Intent on his grand design to humble Louis, he, at this critical juncture of his affairs, surveyed France from the Hague rather than from London, gazed across Louis' confines to the Bay and Middellandsche Zee and proposed to send the largest of his squadrons to the Streights–by no means solely to provide safe convoy for the 'trade', reaching as far east as

Smyrna and Scanderoon – but, by show of force, to distract Louis' policy, strengthen the friendship of Spain, Genoa and Venice, impress the Turk and the rulers of African Tripoli and Algiers. At once, with twelve thirds and fourths under Berry and before the return of Killigrew with latest reports from the Streights and the inward-bound trade? Almost certainly not. It will be borne in mind that, before December 1688 had ended, Dutch emissaries had arrived in London (see p. 34) to discuss closer Anglo-Dutch relations and, in particular, negotiate a naval Convention; it will also be recalled that, not long after the 12th January allocation to squadrons and reserve, William specially asked for the presence of the Secretary of the Admiralty of Amsterdam at the Council table (see p. 35). Till completion (at a date which William forecast for the near future) and implementation of the Convention, he, so it seems, was prepared to wait events—satisfied with having effected token squadronal and reserve arrangements, which he would later expand and employ in a European rather than traditional English manner. Sound naval strategy dictated that Dartmouth's intact ships, or the greater number of them, should have been retained in Spithead as a Channel-Irish squadron. William, with his Mediterranean obsession, had sacrificed the needs of the belligerent present for a peace-time ideal, for a desirable tomorrow a present today. On the morning on which Gabaret put out from Brest, the 11th March, the English King instructed his Admiral – in London – with five ships at rendezvous in Spithead, no reinforcement nearer than the Downs and the Mediterranean squadron, reluctantly ordered at the last moment to the Admiral's assistance, still off Sheerness, to prevent that which, to all intents and purposes, was already accomplished. William had forgotten his father-in-law. He omitted, though with English naval forces available, to close the Irish back door. Had no one advertised him of his peril?

An expression occurring in the pamphlet *An Impartial Enquiry . . .* already laid under quotation in this chapter (see p. 74), comes back to mind: 'If the Advices of those faithful to our K. had taken place.' But we have no knowledge of the text of any such English-tendered considerations. Dartmouth, who had clearly appreciated the possibility of French descents 'on these

Kingdomes' and at one time thought that his own and the 'invading' fleet 'no distaists given' might be combined in common defence, advanced, on the 29th December, in a letter to Pepys (for the Prince's attention) the need for a considerable force to be maintained at sea. Lacking the private papers of Herbert, it is not possible to exhibit him as an adviser. At the conference of the English representatives, Nottingham, Herbert and Russell with the Dutch emissaries, upon 9th/19th March, it was the Dutch who proposed, in order to induce Nottingham to discussion, fleet dispositions.

> *tot voortsettingh der gemeene intressen so wel in de Midlandse Zee als in de Boght [Bocht van Frankrijk] en 't Canael*[58]

That approach, so much in keeping with the 12th January design, with its highest quota intended under Berry for the Mediterranean, suggests that the Dutchmen voiced an expression of what, from the first, had been their Stadholder's own idea. It is difficult to imagine Herbert placing the Mediterranean convoy needs at the head of the 1689 naval programme. Not Herbert nor William's Keeper of the Privy Seal, who wrote: 'Martha, Martha thou art busy about many things, but one thing is necessary . . . Look to your Moat,'[59] nor indeed any of their contemporaries— least of all Dartmouth—could be credited with willingness to leave the Channel indefinitely exposed for the sake of increased protection of the Streights' trade or a demonstration against Louis' 'flotte du Levant'. 'William [was] a masterful man, preferring subordinates to advisers . . . he was his own prime minister; . . . no Englishman had any influence in foreign affairs or much in anything except what was departmental.'[60]

William had welcomed Herbert to Holland and, while over-ruling, at sailing, his professionally sound advice to blockade the Dartmouth fleet, advice which, 'nothing but his the Prince's authority and Schomberg's credit could have withstood',[61] adroitly used him as invasion admiral. But there is nothing to show that he ever particularly sought or respected Herbert's opinion in other than routine matters; and he had never entertained the idea of placing the prestige and patronage of a Lord High Admiral in Herbert's or anyone else's hands. Herbert's rôle, seen in his contact with the King and Pepys, and particularly in his temporary authority over the Navy Board, was solely executive. Confidence between King and Admiral probably never really existed. It must stand that: 'upon him [William] constitutional fictions apart . . . responsibility for that year's policy [and consequently for that critical month's policy] must ultimately rest.'[62] William, with a soldier's outlook and no clear notion of the use of force at sea, culpably failed to make, or have made, dispositions calculated to prevent the landing of James with French officers and supplies in Ireland. James's descent, made as has been described in the preceding chapter, gave the military initiative for at least two years, to the growing danger of the grand design, to the French king.

In turning the page upon the fateful month one is tempted to ask whether the resources of the royal dockyards had been really extended upon the task of repair. Had ordnance and ordinary stores been readily supplied? Had victualling proceeded smoothly? Could it be said that manning deficiencies hindered materially readiness for sea?

When, on the 14th January, the Navy Board received details of the allocations of the 12th, it immediately wrote Pepys, 'Wee shall take the best care Wee can for furnishing them [the ships of the Streights, Channel and Irish squadrons] with what *Stores of any Sort* shall be wanting for, fitting them for the Services on which they are designed'. Turning to 'the other list [the Reserve] of Shipps and Vessells' it suggested to which of the five yards the sixteen middle rates, lesser rates and fireships should be sent.[63]

The yards immediately found their tasks of repair heavy. Sir Richard Beach, Portsmouth Commissioner wrote to the Navy Board, 'Ye Ord^y [Ordinary] here is not strong enough to do halfe the Worke that is required',[64] and the Navy Board complained to Pepys that the ships' crews at Portsmouth and elsewhere were not giving to the 'ordinary' the expected aid.[65] The Commander-in-Chief of ships in Portsmouth harbour was ordered to provide it.[66] Sheerness dockyard staff endured a special annoyance – some of their housing accommodation had been appropriated for soldicry! 'Now there is so much Business at Sheerness . . .' protested the Board, what would Pepys do about it?[67] While it cannot be shown that the yards defaulted of daily routine or that captains were

denied stores, ordnance or ordinary, it is certain that repair and
storing and re-victualling were not carried out, from the 12th
January to the 12th March as work to be pursued against
time.[68]

The ships had been brought in by the crews with which they
had sailed and remained in commission in sea-pay with complements in many cases purposely reduced. Physically therefore,
manning presented no problem so long as the commanders could
persuade their volunteers not to seek discharge (or prevent them
from obtaining it) and check dock-side desertion by them or by
the pressed men who formed by far the greater part of the crews,
conscripts who could not hope to be clear of the service till their
respective ships paid off—nor indeed then if they, the pressed men,
had the misfortune to be 'turned-over' from one naval vessel to
another still at sea. Understandably enough, William was averse
from resort to the press to secure replacements for ratings who
managed to disappear ashore or to supply deficiencies with which
a ship may have originally sailed.[69] Admittedly it was difficult to
convince all ratings, 'turned-over' men especially, that new King
would pay old King's debts. The declaration of the 16th January
was intended to provide that assurance; but talkative unrest
no doubt persisted. Questions put by Herbert to the Navy
Board, on the 2nd and 6th March, 'What would it cost to pay
half the wages due to all ships three years or more in arrears?'
'What money would be required to secure the whole fleet two
months' pay?' indicate official concern with the problem to which
the promises of the Board of Admiralty, meeting on the 12th
March, to the 'turned-over' men and 'ye whole fleet' (see p. 67)
were a palliative answer.[70]

To sum up. There were indeed twelve middle rates[71] and a
number of fireships unrepaired as the date the 12th March was
reached, four middle rates either victualling or manning or both[72]
and one manning.[73] But, had they all been ready they would
merely have been passed to their respective allocations and the
fatal grouping would, till the 11th and the issue of Herbert's
instructions, have remained. Not the shortcomings of eight weeks
in the yards but William's policy placed James on the afternoon
of the 12th March undetected in Kinsale, Ireland.

## REFERENCES

1 *Journals of the House of Commons, 1688–1693* (*v.* 10). The royal assent to the bill for making the Convention a Parliament as and from 13th February was given upon 23rd February.

2 P.R.O. P.C.6/2, 'Irish Affairs 14 February 1688 to 25 September 1691 being the Register of the Irish Committee' [of the Privy Council] and *H.M.C. XII, App. Pt vi, H. of L.,* p. 179 (*v. ante* p. 36, note (53). The main Register of the Privy Council, P.R.O. P.C.2/1 'Council Register February 1688 to 1690' records the appointment of this Committee and mentions matters referred to it.

For biographies see *D.N.B.*, noting the sea service of Devonshire and Mordaunt. Note should be taken of the fact that the attitude of Paymaster Harbord towards sending assistance to Ireland was worse than lukewarm and completely mercenary. *v. H.M.C. XII, App. Pt vi, H. of L.,* pp. 143–4. 'What should we make such haste into Ireland, for, if we do, we shall get no estates there' . . . 'God's wounds! What do you tell me of Ireland? I would not go over the threshold for Ireland' and, after the constitution of this Irish Committee, Mr Harbord told Mr Hugh Hamilton, who had been sent to him by the Committee, 'he [Harbord] would not go to Whitehall if it would save the nation from sinking. This was at his home at Newport Street.'

3 P.R.O. P.C.6/2; *H.M.C. XII, App. Pt vi, H. of L.,* pp. 160–2.

4 P.R.O. P.C.6/2; *H.M.C. XII, App. Pt vi, H. of L.,* pp. 162–8.

5 'As for the state of the Navy at the time of his ceasing to act (which was on the 20th February) he takes leave humbly to observe etc.' Mr Pepys' Report to the Committee on Miscarriages in Ireland, P.R.O. P.C.6/2 9th Aug. or *H.M.C. XII, App. Pt vi, H. of L.,* p. 185. The Report includes a table which shows 'The State of every Ship & Vessel of his Majesty's (whether at home or abroad, of L. Dartmouth's Fleet, or under any other's command) being in Sea-pay upon 20 Feb. 1688/9.' The rate, name and location of each warship is entered. From P.R.O. Adm.8/1. Ship Disposition Lists, 2nd Feb., commanders, lieutenants, time in sea-pay could be supplied.

6 On the enclosure page of a set of papers, Rawl. A. 186, f.112, one reads: A Copy of ye Entries of all ye Acts of His Highness the Prince of Orange, prepared by Mr Pepys, relating to ye Admiralty & Navy from ye time of his Coming to Whitehall . . . to that of Mr Pepys's voluntary ceasing to act further therein.

The *Diary of John Evelyn* now printed in full . . . ed. de Beer, E. S., 6 v. Oxford, 1955, V, p. 538: 'he layed down his Office, and would serve no more . . .' The complete eulogy is, of course, well known.

7 Pepys' Adm'ty Letters, f.584, 18th Feb. Captain Grenville Collins, later Hydrographer to their Majesties and author of *Great Britain's Coasting Pilot,* 1693 which contains post-1689 editions of the Charts referred to.

8 *Ibid.* f.589, 22nd Feb.

9 *Ibid.* f.591, 22nd Feb. For note on pendants *v.* p. 107, note (36) infra. This particular pendant was broader than others at the halyard and red. It is illustrated in the Pepys' MSS referred to in the note at its p. 333.

10 *S.P.Dom.* . . . *1689–1690*, p. 6, P.R.O. Adm. 7/169 Salary £1,000 per annum.

For biographies see *D.N.B.*–Sir Michael Wharton not included–and Ehrman, J. *op. cit.* pp. 278–81 for some supplementary facts. Lee had served on the Commission of Admiralty 1679, Chicheley, rear admiral since 1673, had seen service in the Dutch Wars and in the Mediterranean. He could also call upon experience as a previous Commissioner of Admiralty and a member of the Navy Board and Ordnance Commission.

It should be noted that the personnel of the Navy Board and Victualling Board remained unchanged–i.e. as in October 1688. (Powley, *op. cit.* p. 164, citing, for Navy Board, Jackson, (Sir) G., *Naval Commissioners 12 Chas. II– George III*, ed. Duckett, (Sir) G., 1889. *v.* also for Victualling Board, Ehrman, *op. cit.* App. IX, using National Maritime Museum MS. Sergison A.135. Officers of the Navy. Ehrman's work is a massive, thorough and meticulously detailed study of naval administration in all its aspects 1688– 1697. A concise account of the administrations of the English, French and Dutch Navies is given by Powley, *op. cit.* Appendix.

*Navy Board*

| Treasurer | Anthony, Viscount Falkland | |
|---|---|---|
| Comptroller | Sir Richard Haddock | Principal |
| Surveyor | Sir John Tippets | Officers |
| Clerk of the Acts | James Sotherne, Esq. | |

| Comptroller of Victualling | Sir John Berry | |
|---|---|---|
| Ditto of Stores | Sir William Booth | |
| Deptford–in Charge at | Balthasar St Michell, Esq. | Commissioners |
| Chatham ditto | Sir Phineas Pett | |
| Portsmouth ditto | Sir Richard Beach | |

(Treasurer £3,000, the rest £500 each, the appointments by Patent.)

*Victualling Board*

Sir Richard Haddock
Sir John Parsons
Anthony Sturt, Alderman
Nicholas Fenn, Esq.

Haddock, Berry, Booth, Beach and St Michell (as Muster Master) had served at sea. Tippets and Pett were shipbuilding experts, Sotherne was promoted from the Navy Office, Falkland was a figurehead.

11 Chamberlayne, E., *Angliae Notitia or the Present State of England*, 1687 issue, p. 137.
12 But speculation is attractive! See *Appendix B.*
13 P.R.O. P.C.2. P.R.O. Adm'ty 1/5139, Secretary's In Letters. Burnet, *op. cit.* iv, p. 8.
14 P.R.O. P.C.6/2. *H.M.C. XII, App. Pt vi, H. of L.*, pp. 179–180 gives dates and attendances not only of the original members but of others who were present at various dates.
15 P.R.O. P.C.6/2. P.R.O. P.C.2.
16 *S.P.Dom.* 1689–1690, p. 11. P.R.O. Adm. 2/1743 for text.
17 P.R.O. P.C.6/2. *H.M.C. XII, App. Pt vi, H. of L.*, p. 166.
18 Haddock was also one of the four Commissioners of Victualling, *v.* note (10).
19 P.R.O. P.C.6/2. *H.M.C. XII, App. Pt vi, H. of L.*, p. 167.

20 For the list, note (19) supplemented by Pepys's table of vessels in sea-pay 20th Feb., 1688/9, in *H.M.C. XII, App. Pt vi, H. of L., p. 186.*

21 P.R.O. P.C.6/2. *H.M.C. XII, App. Pt vi, H. of L.,* pp. 167–8 and p. 180. Mr Arnoll 'lately come from North Ireland' met the Committee on the 5th. Mr Cairnes sent from Londonderry officially to the Honourable the Irish Company in London, was interviewed on the 7th; and he it was who took back the message. For life of Councillor David Cairnes see *D.N.B.*

22 For date of Nottingham's appointment *v. H.M.C. Finch II,* p. 208. (Notes made 8th May 1689). From 14th February to 5th March Shrewsbury was sole Secretary. He now relinquished to Nottingham control of what came to be denominated 'Northern Department', himself retaining that which would later be referred to by the title 'Southern'. For biography *v. D.N.B.* noting service as a Commissioner of Admiralty 1681–4.

23 For mention of the indisposition and for the complete list of Herbert's orders under date until the opening of the Patent of Commission of Admiralty 9th March, see P.R.O. Adm. 2/1743. See also *H.M.C. XII, App. Pt vi, H. of L.,* pp. 187 and 191. Luttrell, *op. cit.,* makes entry for the 5th inst. 'Admirall Herbert was suddenly taken very ill.'

24 Nothing unusual in this. Dartmouth's 1688 fleet, when fitting out, was first intended to victual for four months. Dartmouth, to hasten matters, proposed three; but, on 3rd October, Pepys wrote, 'he [the King] with the Lords are most forward in their agreeing with it, as seeming to wish the fleet out, though it were but with 2 monthes proviĉon rather than have it stay but two hours for two months more'. Powley, *op. cit.* p. 51.

25 *S.P.Dom. . . . 1689–1690,* p. 15. For biography of Henry Killigrew see *D.N.B.* At this date he was Commodore of a small squadron sent in 1686 to take out and bring back the trade and to suppress piracy. The cruise was uneventful except for a fight with a Sallee cruiser which shot away the fore and main topmasts of the *Dragon* and escaped. Killigrew was grievously wounded by the bursting of a gun. The cruise is described in B.M. Additional MSS 19306 by Killigrew's Clerk, G. Wood. Dr. A. C. Wood, in his valuable work, *A History of the Levant Company,* Oxford 1935, misses reference to this voyage.

26 *Journals . . . H. of C.,* 8th March. Luttrell, *op. cit.* under dates indicated. [Kennet, White (Bishop)] *A Complete History of England . . .* III, p. 552 (2 edn 1719); for news reports see Luttrell under dates indicated. James went aboard the *St Michel* at 5 p.m. Monday, 7th March/25th Feb. but did not make any show of sailing till Sunday 13th/3rd March and again on 15th/5th March. He cleared Brest on 21st/11th March.

27 *S.P.Dom . . . 1689–1690,* p. 16.

28 P.R.O. P.C.6/2. *H.M.C. XII, App. Pt vi, H. of L.,* pp. 168–9.

29 P.R.O. Adm. 2/1743. The soldiers to be shipped to Holland were 1st Regt Guards, 2nd Regt Guards, Schomberg's, Churchill's, Hodges's, Fusiliers, 10 battalions.

*H.M.C. XII, App. Pt vi, H. of L.,* p. 191; P.R.O. Adm. 1/4080 Secretary's In letters from Secretaries of State.

No time had been lost in attending to the complaint of the drapers of Exeter and Taunton who, a week previously, had complained to the Council of losses by French privateers; but the corn merchants of Burnham, Brancaster and

Wells, whose Holland-bound cargoes had, so it was alleged, often been plundered and the ships put on shore, waited longer for redress. P.R.O. P.C.2. 21st/28th February.

30 Pepys's Adm'ty Letters, XV, f.96.

31 *Ibid.* ff.596–8.

32 *H.M.C. XII, App. Pt vi, H. of L.*, p. 169. Letters to Herbert.

33 P.R.O. P.C.6/2. *H.M.C. XII, App. Pt vi, H. of L.*, pp. 169–70.

34 *S.P. Dom.* . . . *1689–1690*, p. 8. P.R.O. P.C.6/2, 26th March. *H.M.C. XII, App. Pt vi, H. of L.*, p. 173 same date.

35 As note (33).

36 All 'Admiralty Minutes' references are from P.R.O. Adm.3/1–(1689–) read in microfilm. See under dates. Since reappointment in 1684 as Secretary of the Admiralty, Pepys had conducted official business from part of the private house situated at the south-west corner of the river end of Buckingham Street, Strand, described by Dr Thomas Gale of the Royal Society as 'the Paradise which looks into the Thames near the Watergate in York Buildings'. In 1689, over the 'front of the Office towards the Thames' hung 'the anchor of the Lord High Admiral of England with the imperial crown and cipher' and 'the King's Arms at large' were ready for erection as a 'pediment'–both achievements the work of Matthias Fletcher 'Carver to the Navy at Deptford and Woolwich'. Herbert and Bowles cast acquisitive eye on the accommodation; but, in spite of attempts to oust the holder– efforts continued till the Spring of 1690–what had been Mr William Hewer's house from at least 1679 to 1684 and Pepys's from that date onwards remained Pepys's property till his death.

   Tanner, J. R., *Mr Pepys*, pp. 243–4, 265, citing 'Mr Philip Norman's MS' as authority. See also Bonner Smith 'Samuel Pepys and York Buildings' in *Mariners Mirror*, XXIV, No. 2, p. 232.

37 For text see *Patent Rolls* or, with negligible literal variations, P.R.O. Adm. 7/685 (Entry book of Patents, etc. 1673–1727). Ehrman *op. cit.* prints the *Patent Rolls* text in an Appendix.

38 See *Appendix C* for a Summary.

39 Bowles who, shortly before William's invasion had sought Pepys's good offices for appointment to the Victualling Commission (Rawl. A.186, f.173), secured the post of Admiral's Secretary and Muster Master in Dartmouth's fleet. He was sent by Dartmouth to London to the Prince, Dartmouth thereby offending Pepys. (Powley, *op. cit.* pp. 54, 153, 156/7.) He was acting as Herbert's Secretary as early as 1st March (*v.* p. 59 *ante*) and was, no doubt, pushed into this appointment by the Admiral. On 1st April he is found writing to Herbert 'This Post wᶜʰ by yoʳ interest and favour I am established in . . .' (P.R.O. Adm. 2/377 Secretary's Out Letters.) The contrast between Bowles's position and that of Pepys is sufficiently indicated by the fact that Bowles held appointment by minute of the Board he served, Pepys by patent under the great seal of the realm; Bowles's salary, fees apart, was £500 per annum. (P.R.O. Adm. 7/169 Estimates); Pepys's office was four times as lucrative. Bowles will not be found to initiate business.

40 For Fitzpatrick's order *v.* P.R.O. Adm.2/1473.

41 For the full text of this letter see Rawl. A.170, f.23, P.R.O. Adm.2/1473. He was asked for

'All Bookes, Acc^ts, Registers, Precedents or any other thing whatsoever, relateing to y^e Affaires of the Admiralty . . .'
The letter was signed 'Yo^r affect^te friends, A. Herbert, Carbery, Tho. Lee, M. Wharton, J^o Chichley, J. Lowther.'
It is well-known that the Commissioners had great difficulty in securing what they desired (Rawl. A.170, ff.73, 75, 77) but the transfer was more complete than has been commonly supposed and the Public Record Office has ultimately benefited. For the best treatment of this subject see Ehrman, J. in 'The Official Papers transferred by Pepys to the Admiralty by July 12th 1689' in *Mariners' Mirror* XXXIV, 4, pp. 255-70. Of the unique official MSS retained by Pepys and now in Bibliotheca Pepysiana, Magdalene College, Cambridge, three may be especially mentioned–'A Register of Ships of the Royal Navy . . . 2nd May 1660 . . . December 18th 1688', 'Sea Commission Officers . . .', covering the same period, and the fourteen volumes entitled 'S. P's Letters, Admiralty'. The two former, following an invaluable introduction, which is in effect a history of the administration of the Royal Navy for the period covered, are printed in full by Tanner, J. R., . . . *Naval Manuscripts in the Pepysian Library* . . . (Navy Records Society, XXVI, 1903). Tanner began the editing of the letters, which cover the period 1673 to Pepys's retirement, but only reached the year 1677 (Navy Records Society, XXVII, 1904 and XXXVI, 1909). Other of Pepys's official papers found their way into the Rawlinson MSS now in the Bodleian Library. Pepys's single published work *Memoirs relating to the State of the Royal Navy of England for Ten Years determined December 1688*, 1690, has only limited 'compendium' value.

42  *H.M.C. Finch II*, p. 208 and Clark, G. N. Ch. II. Warnsinck, J. C. M. *De Vloot van den Koning Stadhouder*, Amsterdam 1934, pp. 9-24. The English refusal to co-operate in America follows the principle of a clause in the Westminster Treaty 1677/8 (*v.* p. 34 *ante*–'le tout pourtant dans l'estendüe de l'Europe seulement').

43  For declaration 9th Mar./27th Feb. Du Mont, *op. cit.* pp. 213-220. Declaratie van Oorlogh mitsgaders Placeat van de Hoogh Mogende Heeren Staten Generael de Vereenighde Nederlanden . . . : Déclaration de Guerre et Placard de leurs Hautes Puissances des Provinces-Unies contenant une Defense à tous les Habitans de ces Païs, et concernant la Navigation et le Commerce des Puissances Neutres aux Ports de France, aussi bien que les Marchandises de Contrebande, les Assurances des Vaisseaux et les Denrées appartenantes aux Sujets du Roi de France . . . *Bibliotheca Lindesiana– Hand-list of Proclamations . . . 1509-1714*, v. I. Aberdeen 1893 (12th/2nd Mar.). Luttrell, 5th March. *London Gazette*, 7th-11th March issue.
For complaint P.R.O. P.C.2, 21st Feb. For embargo Luttrell, 13th Feb. *See Appendix D*.

44  P.R.O. P.C.6/2. *H.M.C. XII, App. Pt vi, H. of L.*, p. 170.

45  In Bib. Pepysiana, Miscellanea IX is found in MS 'Sailing Instructions . . . The Signals appointed by the Instructions for Fighting & Sailing with the Placings thereof'. Were these printed in book form?

46  *H.M.C. Finch II*, pp. 194-5. This instruction is summarized much too succinctly. *v.* original MS. (in Leicester Record Office) for full text. There is a copy of the sealed order in B.M. MSS Lansdowne. 849, fol. 79.

47 *S.P.Dom. . . . 1689–1690*, p. 22. This list is not printed in the Calendar. *v.* P.R.O. King William's Chest 5, No. 8.

48 Though this list does not mention them there were certain ships abroad in New England, Virginia, Jamaica, the Streights, *v.* Pepys' List for 20th Feb. (p. 55 *ante*, note (5)). *H.M.C. XII, App. Pt vi, H. of L.*, p. 186.

49 P.R.O. Adm. 49/173, f.11. There the debt, but with a figure for Victualling omitted, is given as £159,537.16.7. £200,000 is a likely estimate.

50 *Ibid.* f.3.

51 *Ibid.*

52 *Memoirs of Sir John Reresby . . .*, ed. Browning, A. Glasgow, p. 564. For the justification of the adjective 'disgruntled' applied to Danby see B.M. Additional MSS 28042, f.34.

53 *London Gazette*; Luttrell, *op. cit.* passim. Dalrymple, *op. cit.* I, p. 281–.

54 *v.* p. 69 *ante*.

55 B.M. *An impartial enquiry into the causes of the present fears and dangers of the Government . . .*, 1692. Bodleian Pamphlet, Godwin, 1789, No. 21.

56 A Special Commission of Admiralty appointed in March 1685/6 and charged with the complete rehabilitation of the Royal Navy had been wound up, only a few months previously, on 13th October 1688. In notable achievement it had built three fourth rates, rebuilt twenty ships, repaired sixty-nine and provided all that was necessary for repair of another eight; indeed it had gone beyond the prescribed norm to put in order another twenty-nine and built a hoy and a lighter. There is, apart from Pepys's assertions as to the thoroughness of the work performed, the finding of a Commission of Public Accounts, appointed under Act of Parliament, December 1690 to enquire into the work of the Commission of 1686–88. Reporting in November 1692 it declared:

> That the ships built, rebuilt and repaired by these Commissioners and the buildings and other works by them erected and made during the continuance of the said Commission were done with great exactness . . .

No less than thirty-eight of the forty-three Dartmouth thirds and fourths (2 new, 13 rebuilt, 23 repaired) had been taken from the 'Special Commission' ships. All but three of those still refitting on 12th March were of that category. The exceptional damage Dartmouth had suffered had not been wrought on hulls and rigging sent unready to sea!

Text of report in Bib. Pepysiana, No. 1440, p. 76, quoted by Tanner, *op. cit.* (i.e. *N.R.S. XXVI*, pp. 92–6) (*v.* p. 64 *ante*, note (41)).

*N.B.* The new third rate *Sedgemore*, lost on the way round from Portsmouth with Dartmouth's fleet (*v.* p. 29 *ante*) is not included as one of the forty-three. She did not, apparently, join Dartmouth before the 'surrender' of the fleet.

57 Powley, *op. cit.* p. 109.

58 'to the furtherance of the common interests as well in the Mediterranean as in the Bay of France and the Channel.' Warnsinck, *op. cit.* p. 14. Warnsinck is quoting.

Warnsinck goes so far (*op. cit.* p. 22) to suggest that William may have thought of keeping the French Mediterranean forces in that sea, since 'bewesten de Straat' they would be a menace even to Ireland. Surely the greater danger to Ireland was from Brest.

59 Savile, George, 1st Marquis of Halifax, *A Rough Draft of a New Model at Sea*. The date ascribed 'some time in 1694', is immaterial. Reprint in Foxcroft, *op. cit.* p. 445.

60 Clark, *The Later Stuarts* . . ., p. 179.

61 Burnet, *op. cit.* III, p. 787.

62 Foxcroft, *op. cit.*, I, p. 110.

63 P.R.O. Adm. 1/3557 Secretary's In-Letters [Navy Board].

64 *Ibid.* 7th Feb. Beach's trouble was with the *Mary*'s crew. The men were unwilling to work except on their own ship. He required 60 taking turns once in every 4 or 5 days. He could have stopped 'victuals and wages' but that would have made the men 'run' and cause 'clamour' in London!

65 *Ibid.* 9th Feb. 'We desire you will move his Highness that the Comanders of the Ships in every Port may have Orders to give such Assistance to the Workes that are to be done . . . the Ordinary being too Weake to answer the Same since the Guardships have been taken away.'

66 P.R.O. Adm. 2/1743 Order by Herbert 20th Feb.

67 P.R.O. Adm. 1/3557 23rd Feb.

68 The 2nd March order (*v.* p. 59 *ante*) to send to sea ships victualled for two months only points in that direction. The several changes in central direction (of which the table below is a reminder) militated against application of pressure.

| | |
|---|---|
| To 13th Feb. | Prince–Herbert–Pepys régime. |
| 14th–20th Feb. | King–Herbert–Pepys régime. Pepys retires. |
| 22nd Feb. | Names of Board of Admiralty announced. |
| 28th Feb. | Herbert given authority to direct Navy Board. |
| 2nd March | Privy Council Committee for Irish Affairs takes interest in naval matters. |
| 9th March | Board of Admiralty meets, Herbert's authority ends. |
| 11th March | Nottingham, Secretary of State, drafts operational order from the King to Herbert. |

69 When through some misunderstanding certain mariners were marked R [run] by the Purser of the *Newcastle* they appealed to Herbert and were reinstated. P.R.O. Adm. 1/3557 6th March.

70 The theory and practice of the Navy were clear–payment could only be claimed by a crew (and even then by custom rather than legal right) when a ship was laid up, or by survivors of a wreck. 'It is the ancient course of the Navy not to pay off the Seamen till they discharged their ships' Sir Thos Lee, in the Commons, 9th Dec. 1689 (Grey, A. *Debates of the House of Commons . . . 1667 to the year 1694 . . .* 10 v. 1769, v. IX, p. 475). Herbert, 2nd March, ordered the Navy Board to pay off the crews of the wrecked hospital ship *Heldrenburg* and the *Sedgemore*, Adm. 2/1743. 'Turned-over' men would regard the ships from which they had been moved as 'laid-up', even though technically that might not have been the case, the transfer having taken place between vessels both 'at sea'.

71 *St Albans* (M), *Phoenix* (C), *Dover* (I), *Henrietta* (R), *Resolution* (R), *Crowne* (R), *Newcastle* (R), *Centurion* (R), *Bristol* (R), *Montague, Rupert, Lion* unallotted.

72 *Cambridge* (R), *Pendennis* (R), *Hampton Court* (R), *Kent* (R). For (71) and (72) *v.* p. 69, note (47).

73 *Tyger Prize* (R).

# CHAPTER V

# Ireland – Londonderry besieged

## *13th March – 30th April*

### ARGUMENT

*Gabaret, 13th March, reports arrival at Kinsale–James reaches Dublin, 24th March and a Parliament is summoned; the choice before James, 'consolidation' or a Scottish adventure?–By 7th April the Irish cross the Bann and a general retirement of Protestants towards Derry follows–James moves northward reaching Omagh 14th April.*

*Derry during the month elapsed–Captain James Hamilton arrives, 21st March, and swears Lundy governor; the decision taken, 13th April, to defend the Foyle fords; and next day* Swallow *and transports, bringing Cunningham's and Richards' regiments, appear in the Lough–The consternation of James and his reassurance on learning (on 17th April) that the ships had disappeared–The explanation of the withdrawal of the ships in terms of the cowardice of Lundy and the pusillanimity of Cunningham. James joins Rosen on the 18th before Derry–Murray's cavalry reinforce the besieged–Baker is elected governor, Walker coadjutor; the populace prevent negotiation; the city is invested and James, rebuffed, returns to Dublin; Lundy flees–The first sortie; the fall of Culmore; a second encounter; Derry–its discipline and challenge.*

ARRIVED IN KINSALE, Gabaret ordered his son, in a fast frigate, to bear to Louis the news of disembarkation and himself proceeded to sound and chart the ample harbour.[1] At 9 o' clock on the morning of Friday, 15th/25th he had cause to consult d'Avaux over an order given by James concerning an English frigate anchored off Cork, *'qui ne veut point se laisser aprocher d'aucun autre bastiment'* and would sail for England next day. Louis had arranged that, on Gabaret's return to France, three French frigates were to be left at James's disposal. These, with one other, James wished to despatch against the disobliging vessel. Not unnaturally Gabaret demurred at posting a fourth which might not come back soon enough to accompany his intended return to Brest. d'Avaux backed Gabaret and, reporting to his King, observed that it could reflect no credit for four Frenchmen of thirty guns to attack an Englishman of twenty-eight![2] James's three, their officers duly commissioned, sailed but did not intercept the English vessel which, with Lord Inchiquin[3] on board, made for England.[4]

Gabaret, by the 17th/27th, had received 'old' letters from both

Seignelay and d'Estrées. The Minister of Marine informed Gabaret that English and Dutch ships might be expected to combine in the Channel to frustrate his return, that the King had ordered scouts to observe and, if necessary, report to Gabaret, who, in any case, should sail large on leaving Ireland. The later-penned advice of the Vice-Admiral of France[5] suggested that, as information pointed to a concentration of an English fleet at Plymouth, it might be wise to make Belle Isle rather than directly approach Brest. All stores by this time landed, Gabaret waited only for the first fair wind.[6]

James arrived in Cork on Friday the 15th March[7] and in due course received report from his Viceroy who could claim: 'that he had sent down Lieutenant General Hamilton with about 2500 men . . . to make head against the Rebels in Ulster, who were masters of all that Province except Charlmont & Caricfergus'. Elsewhere Castle Martir and Bandon in Munster having surrendered to Lieutenant General Macarty, all was quiet.[8] Five days later, James, having conferred on Tyrconnel a dukedom, took, with his entourage, the road to Dublin.[9] James reached the capital on the 24th;[10] something of a state of Kingship was instituted, a Council[11] named and matters such as the regulation of currency, the minatory recall of fugitives, the disbanding of surplus irregulars received attention. Parliament was summoned for a date five weeks ahead. Thus far – popular acclamation and a semblance of royal purpose; henceforth – sharply divided counsels and conflicting interests. Duke Tyrconnel and Ambassador d'Avaux, the one from a soldier's standpoint, the other for his master's gain, urged James to occupy himself with the consolidation of an Irish Kingdom, throwing, perhaps, two or three thousand men into Scotland to support the Highlanders, whose activity might be expected to alarm William and hamper or prevent his intervention in the island. All thought of speedy passage across the water to the English throne ought, they contended, to be set aside. Equally authenticated is the evidence of the quite opposite influence of the Earl of Melfort, who, as Secretary for Scotland, had, till the downfall of James, practically ruled the northern kingdom. Melfort, though far from sharing James's delusion that welcome awaited a royal appearance on the English shores, considered himself at least sure of a Scottish greeting. England by way of the Isles could prove a winning insinuation![12] Therefore, when Richard Hamilton came to Dublin to report success and temporary checkmate – the Protestant rout at Dromore, no stand made at Hillborough or Lisburn and a sixty mile pursuit past the swamps of Lough Neagh till the broken Protestant ranks found respite and refuge in Coleraine – James not unreadily, and not unreasonably, sent Pusignan and young Berwick to Hamilton's aid.[13] Five leagues of Channel separate Antrim from Kintyre, a lee shore to lure the Scotland-gazing Melfort and tempt the England-exiled James.

It was the westward passage of the Bann at Portglenone fourteen miles south of Coleraine, on the 7th April which, by opening the way through the mountains of Antrim to the outfalling Foyle, precipitated the evacuation of Coleraine and placed in jeopardy the horse and several thousand foot of Lord Kingston, retreating from Sligo towards Londonderry but temporarily at a stand by the mouth of the Erne. And all the fearful among the country folk (save the defiant Enniskilleners) came towards Derry as their last refuge.[14]

On the 8th April, by which date the news of the expected passage of the Bann could scarcely have reached Dublin, James, leaving Tyrconnel to organize a soldiery to which almost nothing of the supplies from France had been distributed – for the three frigates, the obvious transports, had apparently not yet worked round to Waterford[15] – headed northward with Rosen in his train. d'Avaux followed next day. The desolation through which, during a week of wretched weather, he pursued his route, his dispatches then or later unsparingly display.[16] The royal cavalcade reached Omagh on the night of the 14th.[17]

Between the 15th March and the 14th April, the month of James's sojourn in Cork, his progress to Dublin, his stay in the capital and advance via Armagh, Charlemont and Dungannon to Omagh, events of importance occurred in Londonderry. On the 20th March, at much the same time as James was setting out from Cork, Captain Beverley, in the *Jersey*, obeying the orders of the assiduous and worried Captain James Hamilton – William's original envoy to Londonderry who, it will be recalled, had assumed his mission as far back as early February (see p. 37 *ante*) – passed, with a single storeship, the Innishowen Head north at the Lough entry. Hamilton's dealing with the Chester Customs' Officer, the lading of Mr Ward's *Pelican*, his road excursion to Carlisle and Whitehaven, his orders to the *Jersey*'s Captain to await him with *Pelican* off the Isle of Man, have been recorded (see p. 63); it remains to add that Hamilton had cleared Whitehaven on the 8th March in the *Deliverance*, trader of that port, and picked up the frigate, without the *Pelican*, in Ramsey Bay.[18] On the 21st March Hamilton disembarked at Londonderry and, as enjoined, called aboard the *Jersey* the mayor, the civil and chief military officers that they might witness Lundy take the oath of fidelity and receive commission as governor of the city. The occasion was less public than some desired; but the consequent proclamation of King William and Queen Mary lacked nothing of popular 'solemnity and Joy'. It does not appear that the money and such stores as Hamilton had brought were put to the best use.[19] Much later – on the 10th April[20] – Mr David Cairnes, last heard of on the 8th March (see p. 59 *ante*) arrived to deliver to the governor Shrewsbury's letter of the 8th March, containing the assurance of two regiments shortly to arrive. He found Lundy less than lukewarm as to the defensibility of the place – indeed bestowing passes on such officers as desired to quit. A council of war, persuaded by Cairnes and Hamilton, drew up a resolution branding as coward any who held back in allegiance or effort. This Lundy signed with the rest. Yet the murmurs increased.

On the 13th a general council of war gathered; whereat it was decided that all available troops – the influx from Coleraine and Portglenone, the Londonderry strength, the forces from the Erne, summoned suddenly from Ballyshannon – should, if not already on station, 'appear on the fittest ground near Cladyford, Lifford and Long Causy . . . [And] Colonel Lundy was chosen to be commander-in-chief in the field.'[21] For it was now plain that the enemy, fast centring on Strabane, would cross the Foyle, attempt to force the fords of the confluent Finn, Mourne and Foyle at Clady, Lifford and at Long Causey, a score miles, or less, to the south of Londonderry, in order to come upon the city from the landward side. Easier to swim horse and men across the upper

Tyrone-Donegal fords than to attack, without naval forces, across the city's natural moat, the thousand-feet-broad, deep, tidal Foyle, in which, to give semblance of strength and sink such of the enemy as might venture in boats from the Antrim shore, rode the vessel that had brought Mr Cairnes on his mission.[22]

Through the 14th, the outposts, encouraged neither by the presence of Lundy nor assisted with reinforcements, held. Then the welcome news spread that ships had been sighted endeavouring to beat into the Lough.[23] They were *Swallow*, Captain Wolfran Cornwall, and her transports, possibly a dozen in number, which had sailed on the 10th after windbound delay in Chester Water.[24] Under Colonel John Cunningham's orders the ships brought Cunningham's own and Colonel Solomon Richards' regiment and stores to Lundy's aid.

The morning after his night arrival, on the 14th, at Omagh, James heard *'dans le même moment'* that three or four thousand 'rebels' were close at hand and that thirteen English vessels had been sighted in the Lough. In a state bordering on panic he sent Rosen to join Hamilton; but, though better news shortly came, of the passage of Pusignan and Hamilton across the Foyle below Strabane, James decided, with Melfort and d'Avaux, to retrace the twenty-three weary miles to Charlemont.[25] This he did on the 16th. Disquieting news greeted the dismounting. Vice-Admiral Herbert, so letters from Kinsale alleged, with sixteen warships, rode at anchor just out of range of the fort. James, regretting the likelihood *'que les François eussent tout l'honneur de la prise de Dery'*, recognized that Dublin demanded the royal presence; James would start next day. But the morning of the 17th brought an advice from the Duke of Berwick informing his father that Rosen, Hamilton, Maumont and de Lery had joined forces and that he, Berwick, *'ne croyait pas qu'il fut venu en ces quartiers là les treize vaisseaux Anglois comme on l'avoit dit et que les officiers generaux disoient que si le Roy d'Angleterre paroissoit devant Londonderry les rebelles ouvriroient les portes . . .'* James and Melfort lost no time in re-saddling and rode to join the main army advancing on Londonderry, whilst d'Avaux, despairing of any power to counter the subtle lure of the Isles and England, determined to return to Dublin.[26]

What then of the ships the presence of which in the Lough Berwick encouraged his royal father to doubt? At 10 o'clock on the morning of the 15th the convoy had passed through the mile wide entry to the Lough, Greencastle to starboard, Londonderry distant about twenty miles.[27] Cunningham immediately informed Lundy that he had brought two regiments to his aid. At two in the afternoon, *Swallow* then off Redcastle, also to starboard and almost halfway down the Lough where the Lough approaches its widest room, news reached the ship that Lundy's forces had gone out to fight the enemy at Clady. Cunningham thereupon respectfully submitted to the Commander-in-chief that, if the fords of the Finn could be held till the two disciplined regiments which he, Cunningham, had on board could join the 'raw men', advantageous battle might be given. No answer to either communication reached *Swallow*, which, with her charges, continued under way to the extremity of the Lough; then the tide stopped them. Anchors were dropped under the fort of Culmore, set on the western bank, where the Foyle river enters the Lough well under four miles from the Londonderry quays. Cunningham then sent Major Tiffin, Captain Lyndon and Cornwall, the commander of the frigate, to interview Lundy. On their way they received Lundy's reply to the two earlier messages, an allegation of cowardice at the fords, a declaration that his troops were 'on the run' before an advancing enemy. He would have Cunningham march his soldiers 'all night in good order lest they be surprized'. They should have what accommodation Londonderry could afford. Indeed, if the men were not landed, they had better be put on shore and march immediately. But when Lundy met Major Tiffin, Lundy represented the plight of Londonderry as hopeless, ate his written words and sent back the three emissaries with orders to Cunninhgam not to disembark the regiments till Cunningham and his fellow-colonel Richards, with some of their officers, could, on the morrow, come to the city for consultation. That next day, the 16th, to a carefully picked council of war, Lundy presented the picture of a city about to be beleagured by 25,000 foes but with public and private provisions sufficient only for three thousand troops for ten days; and, he no doubt added, five or six times that number of persons were within its walls or anxious to crowd to its

protection. Against the proposal that the regiments should return
to England; 'only Colonel Richards argued . . . because he looked
on the deserting that garrison not only as the quitting that city but
the whole kingdom'. And well he might! For, as the clerk to that
council of war, Mr John Muggeridge, revealed to another council
two days later, the outcome of deliberation was an order that
Colonel Cunningham should return with the two regiments and
all gentlemen and officers quit the garrison and accompany him!
So, while Lundy sent the sheriffs on fools' errands through the
city to find billets for the supposedly arriving troops, *Swallow* and
her transports dropped back from Culmore to Redcastle and the
considerable remnants from the Clady-Lifford débâcle forced,
rather than received, entry through gates closed against them by
Lundy's orders. And under the leadership of Captain Murray,
'There being no forage in the town the horse went all generally to
Culmore.' Small wonder that, throughout the next day, the 17th,
suspicion of the integrity of the Commander-in-chief and resentment at the desertion of several officers grew. With messengers
going and coming, it could scarcely be hidden that pourparlers
for surrender were afoot and 'some in the town' sent to Colonel
Cunningham to assume the governorship. He refused.

At night-fall the advance guards of the royal army, with James
not far off, reached St Johnstown, rather more than five miles
south of the city; and the morning of the 18th brought Rosen's
army and the expectant James 'to the strand above the windmill,
at the south-end of Derry hill, and there [they] stopped waiting
what answer or salutation the city would give'. Again a council
met – in the main ignorant of the terms of the order with which
Lundy and the council of the 16th had turned away aid and
encouraged the secession of officers. Though startled by Muggeridge's revelation, it was, none the less, inclined toward surrender. The event was countered. Upon a section of the wall, the
garrison considering that some of Rosen's troops were, in spite of
an agreement,[28] approaching too near the city, and encouraged
to defiance by the appearance of Captain Murray advancing from
Culmore with a considerable number of horse, opened cannon
fire, killing several of James's own escort. Lundy ordered Murray
to retire out of sight of the city and the council addressed them-

selves to forwarding an apology to James for endangering his life. But Murray, with his troops, entered by the Shipquay Gate – to become the arbiter of the hour, the hero of the 'overwhelming majority of the garrison and the people [who] were determined not to surrender'.[29] Before night, the crestfallen James with the army had fallen back toward St Johnstown. The ships were again at Greencastle – three days after their passage into the Lough.

On the morrow, the 19th, a new governor,[30] Major Baker, was elected, Murray, at his own desire, standing aside. Baker then nominated as his coadjutor the Reverend George Walker; and the command of eight regiments into which it was decided to organize the able-bodied was settled. An augmented council, in which Murray would not participate, turned yet again to discussion of composition with James. Twenty ambassadors were appointed to the task. They never left the city! 'The multitudes on the walls and at the gates . . . threatened, that if a man of them offered to go out on that errand, they would treat them as betrayers of the town, the Protestant religion and King William's interest.' That evening, as 'some of the aged people, women and children with some few others to the number of near a thousand' quitted Derry and a trumpet came in vain to the walls, *Swallow* and her convoy, clear of the Lough, were standing to sea. James could not endure to stay near a city which had four times refused his summons to capitulation. On the 20th, leaving the lieutenant-generals Maumont and Hamilton with the major-generals Pusignan and Berwick in command of some 10,000 men, but with little artillery to carry out the siege, he headed, with Rosen and de Lery, for Dublin, which he reached on the 25th April, three days after the arrival of d'Avaux from Charlemont.[31] The day of James's departure was that of Lundy's disguised flight via Culmore to the sea.

Next morning a single gun from across the river opened fire; and during the day, Murray with his horse made a sortie northward toward Pennyburn mill encountering and himself slaying Maumont. Two days later the fort of Culmore submitted to Hamilton, giving the Jacobites promise of the means of prevention of further access to or egress from the city by sea. Two more cannon began to play. Early on the 25th, Murray again sallied forth toward the mill; at that day's end Pusignan had been mortally, de Pointis dangerously, Berwick less seriously wounded. These two sorties encouraged what was a volunteer garrison to accept discipline and helped to confirm the new governors in their rule. And henceforth for 'good understanding' Episcopalians and Non-conformists alike shared for their separate services the solemn facilities of the cathedral church. The first steps towards a con-servation of supplies were now taken.[32]

The siege proper had begun. Set upon rising ground, cinctured by an oblong of ramparts, four-gated and bastioned of earth and stone – the stone wall failing for the more part of three yards of thickness–one shorter side, the north eastern, protected by the Foyle, the city, designed to 'accommodate at most a few thousand people' now held (but scarcely sheltered) at least twenty thousand men, women and children. Of that number, the volunteer light regiments (of 341 officers and 7,020 men) and auxiliary combatants totalled less than half. They possessed eight sakers and twelve demi-culverin. The flag upon the tower of the cathedral of St Columb at the landward southernmost corner of the city, bade defiance to some 10,000 besiegers, advanced now from St Johns-town to dispositions by the walls or flanking the Foyle on its way to the Lough and the sea.[33]

## REFERENCES

The story of the Jacobite War in Ireland has been frequently told. Reference has already been made (p. 35, note 52) to the general standard works of Bagwell, R. *Ireland under the Stuarts and during the Interregnum*, and Murray, R. H., *Revolutionary Ireland and its Settlement*, the latter giving a very full list of authorities. Much the fullest treatment of the siege of Londonderry is the official volume, Milligan, C. D., *History of the Siege of Londonderry*, Belfast 1951. Hempton, J. in *The Siege and History of Londonderry*, Londonderry, Dublin, London, 1861, makes available, *inter alia*, the (broadly) contem-porary verse, Aickin, J. *Londeriados*, (or a *Narrative of the Siege of Londonderry*). Dublin 1699; Walker, (Rev.) G. *A True Account of the Siege of Londonderry*. London 1689; Mackenzie, (Rev.) J., *A Narrative of the Siege of Londonderry* . . ., 1690; Ash, (Capt.) T., *Extracts from a Circumstantial Journal of the Siege of Londonderry*, 1792. Dwyer, P., *The Siege of Londonderry in 1689*, reprints Walker's *A True Account . . . A Vindication of the True Account . . .* other original material, together with valuable Notes, etc.

1  *Négociations . . . d'Avaux*, p. 24, d'Avaux–Louis, 23/13 Mars.
2  *Ibid.* p. 25.
3  William O'Brien, second earl (1638?–1692), sometime Governor of Tangier, supported William in Munster; Governor Jamaica, 1689. See *D.N.B.*

4 *Négociations d'Avaux* . . ., p. 30, d'Avaux–Louis.

5 Estrées, Jean (Duc de) (1624–1707) fought during the Fronde and in Flanders, became lieutenant-général by 1656, turned to the sea, was given the honour of Vice-Admiral du Ponant, and was employed on American and African missions. He commanded the fine French (white) squadron of the Anglo-French fleet which, in the Third Dutch War, 1672–4, fought de Ruyter at Solebay, Schoenveldt and the Texel. His detached tactics displeased his ally. His further and more successful command in the West Indies with Cayenne and Tobago wrested from the Dutch 1676–7, ended in catastrophe when his fleet ran upon the rocks of Aves. None the less, 'Vice-roi d'Amérique' and Vice-Admiral du Ponant, he retained favour and, 1681, was the first 'marin' to be made a 'maréchal de France'. He was active against Tripoli, Tunis and Algiers–Hoefer, Larousse.

6 *Négociations* . . . *d'Avaux*, p. 46, Gabaret – d'Avaux with enclosures.

7 *Ibid.* p. 28, d'Avaux–Louis.

8 Clarke, *op. cit.* ii, p. 327.

9 *Négociations d'Avaux*, p. 37, d'Avaux–Louis.

10 *Ibid.* p. 48, d'Avaux–Louis.

11 Murray, *op. cit.* p. 84.

12 *Négociations* . . . *d'Avaux*, pp. 49, 50, 51. 4th April/25th March d'Avaux–Louis. Also p. 87 same to same 23rd/13th April; p. 105, same to same 27th/17th April.

James wrote to the 'earl of Balcarrase' [Colin Lindsay, 3rd earl of Balcarres, had been to sea with James] in appeal to raise troops 'Being resolved to come ourself as soon as it is possible for us to do it with safety . . . we have thought of sending five thousand men, whereof 100 horse and 150 dragoons . . . a greater number of horse and dragoons will be inconvenient to ship over to you'. James asked at what place troops should be landed and stated he had sent letters to the chiefs of clans and the likely nobility; and blank commissions could be supplied. 29th March, Dublin. *H.M.C. The MSS of the Duke of Buccleuch and Queensberry, v. II, pt i*, p. 38.

Tyrconnel also addressed the Duke of Hamilton. He described the landing and extent of French aid, expressed the hope that the news would encourage Hamilton 'to stick by him [James] and yourselves' and added, 'I hope before the end of July to have the honour to embrace you in Scotland'. Dublin. 15th March. *Ibid.* p. 36. In much the same sense Tyrconnel wrote to the earl of Perth, Lord Chancellor of Scotland, *ibid.* p. 36. Tyrconnel was not averse from stirring up trouble in Scotland but the consolidation of Ireland and viceroy rule remained his real aim.

For the career of Melfort, John Drummond (1st earl and titular duke) (1649–1714) see *D.N.B.*

13 Clarke, *op. cit.* ii, p. 330. *Négociations* . . . *d'Avaux*, p. 73, d'Avaux–Louis. Mackenzie, *A Narrative of the Siege of Londonderry*–as edited by Hempton, J., pp. 180–5. Berwick–James Fitz James, 'Mémoires du Maréchal de Berwick'–in *Collection des Mémoires relatifs à l'histoire de France depuis l'avènement de Henri IV jusqu'à . . . 1763*' ed. Petitot, A. et Monmerqué, LXV, Paris 1828, p. 338.

14 Mackenzie, *op. cit.* (Hempton) pp. 196–198. 7th April Robert King, 2nd Lord Kingston (–1693). On learning of Lundy's duplicity he dispersed or

D

sent into Enniskillen his soldiers and crossed to Scotland and William (*v.* *D.N.B.*).

15  *Négociations* . . . *d'Avaux*, p. 74, d'Avaux–Louvois, 14th/4th April.

16  *Ibid.* p. 435, d'Avaux–Colbert de Croissy, 30th/20th August; p. 85, d'Avaux–Louis, 23rd/13th April; p. 96 same to same 25th/15th; p. 99, d'Avaux–Louvois, 25th/15th.

17  *Ibid.* p. 96, d'Avaux–Louis; p. 99, d'Avaux–Louvois.

18  *H.M.C. XII, App. Pt vi, H. of L.* Hamilton to Committee for Affairs of Ireland, 13th March p. 173, 26th March.

19  Mackenzie, *op. cit.* (Hempton) pp. 193–200. It may be remarked that this Captain Hamilton (1656–1734) succeeded to the Abercorn earldom–6th of the line. See *D.N.B.*

20  From this point to the end of the paragraph 'Lundy's aid'. Mackenzie, *op. cit.* (Hempton) pp. 199–202.

21  Mackenzie, *op. cit.* (Hempton) p. 201.

22  *Ibid.* p. 200.

23  *Ibid.* p. 202.

24  P.C. 6/2 23rd March. Cunningham alleges he is only waiting for a wind. A *London Gazette* 5th April report from Liverpool states that the ships had put out but had been forced to anchor off Highlake (Hoylake) between Chester and Liverpool; a 10th April message shows they had sailed.

25  *Négociations* . . . *d'Avaux*, p. 96, d'Avaux–Louis, 25th/15th April.

26  *Ibid.* pp. 102, 104, d'Avaux–Louis, 27th/17th April.

27  'At 10 o'clock' to 'were standing to sea' (pp. 93–5). Mackenzie *op. cit.* (Hempton) pp. 202–218. To follow topographical references to the Londonderry and Foyle area see Charts D, E and F.

28  Mackenzie does not mention the question of agreement, *v.* Milligan, *op. cit.* p. 122, for discussion of the fact of agreement and estimates varying between four and two and a half miles.

29  *Ibid.* p. 133.

30  The question of precedence of governors is discussed by Milligan, p. 158.

31  *Négociations* . . . *d'Avaux*, p. 106, d'Avaux–Louis 3 Mai/23 April; d'Avaux–Louis 6 Mai/26 April.

32  Mackenzie, *op. cit.* (Hempton) pp. 218–24 for the paragraph to this point, except for (a) the fall of Culmore, the loss of which the besieged did not learn till the end of the first week in May, Walker, *op. cit.* (Hempton) p. 117 (b) the wounding of de Pointis and Berwick. For (a) *A Full Relation of the Surrender of Kilmore* B.M. 807, f 36, 13; for (b) *Mémoires du Maréchal de Berwick*, p. 342.

33  For the last paragraph Walker *op. cit.* (Hempton) p. 101 and p. 112 except for estimate of total number at this time within the walls. 20,000 is Milligan's carefully arrived at conclusion *op. cit.* p. 311. For besieger's numbers *v.* Bennet, Joseph. *A True and Impartial Account of the Most Material Passages in Ireland since December 1688, with a Particular Relation of the Forces of Londonderry* . . . 1689, p. 23; *Mémoires du Maréchal de Berwick*, p. 341, shows at this time St Johnstown–trois bataillons et neuf escadrons; two miles from Derry beside St Johnstown–quatre bataillons; across the river 'vis-à-vis de Derry' . . . deux bataillons, quelque cavalerie, et quelque petites pièces de campagne. Apart from these 'quatre cents hommes de pied . . . sept cents chevaux' by

Culmore; Bodleian, Carte Papers, v. 181, f 343 b has A Liste of fforces at Derry, Dwyer (*op. cit.*) prints pp. 218–19.

A demi-culverin, 4 in. bore fired a 10 lb. shot; a saker, $3\frac{1}{2}$ in. bore a 6 lb. shot.

# CHAPTER VI

# England – Herbert Late to Sea

## *13th March – 30th April*

### ARGUMENT

*Admiral Herbert's three commissions; to command a fleet, hold courts-martial, assume the Vice-Admiralty of England.*

*A detailed examination of naval finance in its relation to national expenditure, customary naval dispositions and the provision of 'a fleet . . . in conjunction with the States' – The slow mobilization of the English units begun; Vice-Admiral Berry weighs from the Nore, 16th March, picks up ships in the Downs and, on the 26th, joins Herbert, waiting with three rates at Portsmouth – The vexed question of seamen's pay – The Admiral's orders and strategy; in essence to command a limited area of sea girdling southern and western Ireland and, if possible, to 'look in' on Brest – Delay in Portsmouth till 4th April – Cruising off Ireland 12th April; James's landing confirmed – Herbert's instructions strengthened – 23rd April the fleet blown into Milford Haven; but, 26th April, again moving toward station.*

*Major General Kirke ordered with reinforcements to Londonderry. A King's messenger sent thither to report.*

T HE READER may be reminded that Nottingham had, on the 11th March, drafted instructions for Herbert as 'Admirall & Com̃ander' of the 'Ships in the Narrow Seas' and it has been assumed that the instructions were straightway delivered (see p. 68). Not till the 14th was the Admiralty requested to prepare his commission.[1] It followed the customary lines:

willing and requiring [him] forthwith to take upon [him] ye Charge & Com̃and of their Ma$^{ts}$ said ffleete as Admirall & Chiefe Com̃and$^r$ and authorizeing & Empowering [him] to wear ye Union Flag at ye Maintopmast head . . . all Com̃and$^s$, Captains, Mast$^s$ and other Off$^{rs}$ and Companys of ye sd ffleete to obey [him] . . . & [he] likewise to observe and execute all such Ord$^{rs}$ & Instructions as [he should] from time to time receive from . . . the L$^d$ High Adm$^{ll}$ of England or Com̃iss$^{rs}$ for Executing ye Office of L$^d$ high Adm$^{ll}$ for ye time being . . . [He was authorized] in case of neglect, disabillity or other default or defect in any of ye S$^d$ Off$^{rs}$ or Seamen, to displace them and appoint and constitute others in their stead . . .

The commission was sealed and signed by all the Commissioners, countersigned by the Secretary and bore date 15th March.[2]

A supplement to the Commission ordered him 'to observe and follow such other Ord$^{rs}$ and Instructions as [he should receive] from ye King's Ma$^{ty}$ giving [the Commissioners] from time to time an Acct of [his] Proceedings.'[3]

With this commission concurrently was issued authority to hold courts-martial

Whereas by an Act made by the Parliament begun and held at Westminster the 8th of May in the 13th year of King Charles the second Entitled An Act for ye Establishing Articles & Ord$^s$ for ye Regulating & better governing their Mats Navy . . . Authority is given to ye Lord high Adm$^{ll}$ of England . . . to grant Commissions to Vice Adm$^{lls}$ or Comand$^{rs}$ in chiefe of any Squadron of Ships to call and assemble Courts Martiall consisting of Comand$^{rs}$ and Captaines of the said Ships, for the putting in Execucion the sd Articles & Ordrs & for the Tryall of such p$^{s}$ons as shall offend against the same. These are . . . to authorize & empower you . . . as often as their Ma$^{ts}$ Service shall require the same, to call & assemble Courts Martiall consisting of Comand$^{rs}$ & Captaines . . . to enquire into and examine concerning all Crimes and Offences which have or shalbe comitted by any Person or Persons serving in their Ma$^{ts}$ Royall Navy . . . in such way & mañer as has been usually practised therein & to give Sentence . . . either of paines of Death or such other paines or Penaltys as shalbe thot fitt . . . to be executed accordingly unlesse in the case of Death, w$^{ch}$ Sentence is not to be executed (except in the Case of mutiny) without further Ord$^{rs}$ therein from this Board or the Lord High Adm$^{ll}$ or Comm$^{rs}$ for Executing that Office . . . And in case of the absence of the Judge Advocate of their Ma$^{ts}$ ffleet or Deputy you are empowered from time to time . . . to appoint some fitting p$^{s}$on to execute the place of Judge Advocate . . . for ye more orderly proceeding of ye same.[4]

In a further document,[5] which was not completed before the 16th March the Commissioners, having recited their names and affirmed their competence under their letters-patent to declare their 'trust and Confidence in ye Valour, prudence,

Circumspection, Ability and fidelity of ye Rt honoᵇˡᵉ Arthur Herbert Esq.,' stated that they had 'Nominated, Constituted, Appointed, Deputed & made [him] . . . Vice Admirall of England,' to which 'Office & place' adhered the place

of Lieutenant of ye Admiralty of England, as also of ye Lieu-tenancys of ye Navys & Seas of their Maᵗˢ Kingdome of England together with all & singular such jurisdic̃ons, Authori-tyes, Powers, ffees, Proffitts, Wages, Emolluments, Rewards, Advantages, Comodities, prehemencies and priviledges what-soever . . . in as large & ample manner . . . [as to] Henry Duke of Grafton, Prince Rupert, Count Palatine of ye Rhine, Ed'wd Earle of Sandwᶜʰ or any other Vice Admirall or Lieut Admirall heretofore . . .

To 'have hold & enjoy' the aforementioned offices and dignities gave entitlement to

twenty shillings by ye day & Wages, Entertainment & Allowan-ces for Sixteene Men every of them at ye rate of Tenn shill.p. mensem accounting twenty eight dayes to a Month . . . at & by the hand of ye Trear of the Navy . . . ye foure feasts or Termes⁶ . . . of ye Yeare by equall portions . . . Provided allwayes that this Grant be within . . . Six Months next ensuing . . . viewed, perused ratified, allowed & granted [in whole or part] by . . . Their Maᵗⁱᵉˢ . . . to take its due & full effect after it shall be soe allowed

As the pay of an Admiral of the Fleet was at the rate of £4 per day (including £1 per day table money) and the office of Vice-Admiral of England brought to its possessor an annual £469,⁷ apart from the perquisites of the post, as, moreover, Herbert remained a member of the Commission of Admiralty at a salary of £1,000 per annum, he could, so long as fortune smiled, count upon a regular income of almost £3,000 a year.

The 'Admirall and Com̃ander', possessed of instructions and equipped with commissions, was still without a mobilized fleet. A member of the Commission of Admiralty, he had attended, upon the 13th, 14th, 15th (twice) March, the meetings of that Board—all the more easily because the Commissioners' sessions continued to be held at his 'Channell Row Lodgings'.⁸ He had then travelled down to Portsmouth arriving late on the 18th.⁹ At departure from town, Herbert would be aware that the Earl of

Nottingham had notified the Admiralty what ships the King, varying the conclusions reached upon the 12th January (see p. 30 *ante*) desired to have in service during the coming year, and he had no doubt a shrewd idea of the detail, in terms of ships and complements of men, in which the demands of the King, worked out for the Commissioners by the Navy Board, would reach the House of Commons.[10]

It has been said that the 'historic import of the Revolution of 1688 . . . lay in the passing of the mediaeval concept that the King should live on his own – that out of "his own" income he should run the country and should only come to Parliament for financial help on extraordinary occasions, such as war, etc.'.[11] The House had just voted, 15th March, £600,000 as the appropriate figure for a settlement of the 'extraordinary' claim of the States General for services rendered in equipping and forwarding the late expedition[12] and, on the 20th March, stood engaged to credit a sum of £1,200,000 to the King as his 'own'[13] – meaning thereby the cost in a peace-time year of 'the Civil services (including the Civil List as we now understand it and ambassadorial service, secret service and pensions) . . . the three fighting services, Navy, Army and Ordnance'.[14] At the same time it set up a Committee to consider the extent to which the fighting services in peace-time made claims on the £1,200,000. By the 21st the House had come into possession of an estimate, obtained by William's orders of the Secretary at War, William Blathwayt, and the Ordnance Office, to give the cost for a year of the 22,330 men, horse, dragoons and foot, with artillery, necessary, as the King had told the assembled Parliament on the 8th March (see p. 60 *ante*), for the 'reducing' of Ireland. Towards the asked-for £714,117.6.4, on the 22nd, the Commons voted just over £300,000, promising a further £300,000 in six months' time should the war 'so long continue'![15] The counterpart of the military estimate, the naval document above referred to, reached the House on the 26th. It represented an attempt to meet the King's supplementary request of the 8th for a 'fleet . . . in conjunction with the States'. The King's amended requirements can more easily be grasped if thrown into tabular form:

| Designed for | Rates | | | | | | Fire-ships | Total ships | Total Cost for a year of 13 months |
|---|---|---|---|---|---|---|---|---|---|
| | 1st | 2nd | 3rd | 4th | 5th & 6th | Total | | | |
| Narrow Seas | | | 4 | 16 | | | | | £892,060 |
| | | | | 20 | | | | | 17,155 men @ £4 per month† |
| Mediterranean | — | 1 | 13 | 16 | 50   15 | 65 | 8 | 73 | |
| | | | | 30 | | | | | |
| Service for Convoys and to attend the Plantations | | 1* | 19 | | 2 | 22 | 2 | 24 | £236,080 / 4,540 men @ £4 per month |
| | | | | hired | | | | | |
| *The *Mountague* | | | | | | | | | |
| †13 months to the year | | | | | | 87 | 10 | 97 | £1,128,140 |

*see note 16*

A copy of the Anglo-Dutch Treaty of 1677/8 had, on the 23rd, been requested by the House;[17] but, at this later date, with the new naval convention almost ready for signing, it is likely that the members were already aware that the ratio of 5:3 (English to Dutch) for main armament in the Mediterranean and Narrow Seas would replace the former 3:2 arrangements. A Committee of the House, considering, on the 5th April, all aspects of the question of naval supply, reported that it would be wise, in dealing with the King's demands, to calculate expenditure on the basis of £4.5.0 rather than upon that of £4 per man per lunar month, the extra 5/- an allowance for Ordnance and lifted the Admiralty figure £1,128,140 to £1,198,648.15.0. Then, deducting the calculated expense of a peace-time winter and summer guard—£366,080[18] it struck a figure of £832,568.15.0 which, with the cost of 'the ordinary'[19] put at £130,000, might be regarded as the approximate likely expenditure for the coming year, £962,568.15.0 in all. Three weeks passed before the Commons voted, on the 25th April, the round sum of £700,000 'towards the occasions and services of the Navy' and proposed, on the 27th April, that, of the King's 'own' of £1,200,000 (see p. 103 *ante*), £600,000 should be earmarked by the Crown for the Navy and Ordnance,[20] which apparently left but £600,000 for the rest of the King's customary responsibilities–namely, his peace-time liability to the Army and Garrisons, with, to re-quote Shaw, 'The Civil services–including the Civil List as we now understand it and ambassadorial service, secret service and pensions'. Impossible budgeting! It is by no means clear that the issues at vote before the House were understood or the consequences of the decisions foreseen. But it is obvious that, had the Navy, in this first year of the joint reign, been able to count on receiving £700,000 and £600,000 minus the amount to be diverted to the Ordnance[21] it might have approached the unwonted experience of paying its way, at best have met current liabilities and even thought of repayment of instalments of the February debt. A mirage not to deceive the lords of Admiralty–still less their honours the Principal Officers and Commissioners of the Navy! The Treasurer of the Navy would receive nothing like the sums suggested.[22]

In any case, what the Treasurer of the Navy would draw at the Exchequer would very seldom be in cash. The yields of customs and excise, taxation, rents, loans, and the produce of a whole miscellany of sources of revenue, were collected with much uncertainty and reached the Treasury with an irregularity which admitted of small liquid supply to the departments of state. Payments to the Treasurer of the Navy were commonly made in ticket credit or wooden tallies, which, as 1689 went on, would usually be 'unappropriated' on any particular part of Exchequer revenue for their redemption, bear no interest and be encashable only at Exchequer will, or more correctly, Exchequer ability to receive its own again. Clearly the trading difficulties of the Navy Board and of the Victuallers (which latter received their allotments on demand made upon the Treasury by the Treasurer of the Navy) were multiplied at every turn by having to pay in such unattractive long-term tender. The Navy Office (with the Victuallers) more than any other department of the state lay at the mercy of the merchants. The Office kept meticulous account of receipt and expense and learned to co-habit with indigency. In one considerable respect circumstances assisted the Navy Office. Once sailors were at sea they could be kept aboard their floating homes for at least the periods of the ship's commission; over half the current floating debt of the Navy was at this time borne by the wave-tossed crews.

It may be observed that only slowly did the Commons, quite unable for a while to exclude constitutional issues from financial debate, move towards the conception of a rounded outlook on estimating,[23] taxing, allocating, efficiently disbursing and, finally, auditing its fiscal affairs.[24] Nor for that matter did the collection of the national revenue suddenly become an efficient art.

To return to Admiral Herbert. The King's broad 'European' rather than Channel mobilization plan (involving dispositions which, it has been suggested (see p. 30), can never have had the admiral's whole-hearted approval) and speculation as to what added strength, in terms of Dutch ships placed under English command, the new already part-written naval treaty with the Provinces would provide, must, from the moment of his setting forth for Portsmouth, have assumed for the admiral secondary importance. At the well-advanced naval conference Lord Carbery could, he knew, take his place, join with Nottingham and Russell 'to perfect the treaty' and urge de Wildt and Dykvelt to entice the Dutch ships from their wharves.[25] Not general policy but particular duty occupied Herbert's thought—the task of collecting, unifying and using the first post-Revolution English fleet.

At most, since three vessels had been sent away to the Downs to intercept any enemy ships bound from Dunkirk to Scotland, five thirds and one fire-ship swung at their anchors in Spithead or tugged at Portsmouth moorings.[26] Vice-Admiral Sir John Berry, ordered through the Downs on the 14th with all ships not detailed to stay there or to return to the Nore for particular services,[27] had not had time to arrive with any of the expected thirteen (or possibly seventeen) middle rates and the sixth rate *Saudadoes*. And the Admiral certainly did not suppose that *Cambridge* and *Pendennis* ('ready in 8 or 10 daies') with the ancillary tenders, fire-ships, yachts and an hospital ship (a Gibraltar-bound storeship disburthened of her supplies and adapted for duty[28]) would yet be out of the River. Actually Berry weighed upon the 16th,[29] the day on which, presumably, Herbert had left London for Portsmouth. Seven of his ships—the thirds *Plymouth*, *Yorke*, *Cambridge* (unexpectedly declared ready for service), the fourths *Woolwich*, *Deptford*, *St David* and *Bonadventure*, with *Assurance* bound for Harwich, had gathered at the Buoy of the Nore, saluted with nine guns the Union at the foretop of the third rate, the *Elizabeth* and, in the course of the windy, snowy day, accompanied the flag down the Swin to anchorage beyond the Long Sand Head but short of the Galloper. In rowdy weather which sprung the foretopmast of *Elizabeth* 'a foot above ye capp'[30] and split the main topsail and spritsail of the *Cambridge*,[31] the somewhat scattered squadron, at nightfall of the 17th, anchored in sight of the North Foreland light.[32] On the 18th it struggled through the Little Downs. The eight ships, with the fourth, the *Diamond* (which had probably preceded them from the Nore) and those which were already awaiting Berry's arrival, *Foresight*, *Portland*, *Greenwich*, *Dover*, *Mordaunt*, *Advice*, *Antelope* and *Ruby* – all fourths – swung windbound before Deal Castle till the 22nd, when the flagship 'hauled home her foreTopsaile Sheets & fired a gunn for all ye rest of ye ffleet to gett Under saile . . .' If the lieutenant of the *Elizabeth* correctly informs us, there were '19 Saile of ffrigotts & 2 Yatchs & ye *Kingfisher* Ketch all bound for *Portsmouth*', two more than those named above. One may have been the *St Albans*; possibly the sixth rate *Saudadoes* was counted; the two 'Yatchs' were presumably the *Fubbs* and *Henrietta*.[33] The squadron was blown back to the Downs; but the Vice-Admiral, clearing again on the 24th and taking with him several merchant-men, sailed, anchored, weighed as ebb tides served and winds allowed, past Dungeness light[34] and the high land of Fairlee, till he sighted Dunnose at dawn on the 26th, and, before the twilight, brought in 'all' his charge under the Gilkicker.[35] He found Herbert in the third-rate, the *Defiance*, the thirds *Dreadnought* and *Edgar* with him. The Commander-in-chief next morning transferred his flag, the Union, to the main of *Elizabeth* – 'all our Ships [records the captain of the *Woolwich*] shifted pendants & saluted ye Admirall'[36] with nineteen guns.[37] Berry 'went away' with his captain John Nevill; and Captain David Mitchell took command of the flagship.[38] The wind was east, the weather fair; but the reinforced Commander-in-chief was in no case to sail westward.

Berry, it will be recalled (see p. 67), while at Sheerness, had been told that arrangements were being made at Portsmouth to 'pay off the turned over men and, in a little time after, . . . ye whole fleet now in sea-pay for two months', and he, with Sir Richard Beach, the resident Commissioner at Portsmouth, had been appointed to supervise, with the tellers, the pay-off. Portsmouth had been selected because, in the Spithead, Herbert's whole fleet was to mobilize. Herbert, immediately on reaching Portsmouth, had pressed both Nottingham and the Admiralty for the 'two months' money for all crews. It would be of 'infinite service'![39] The administration was making a real attempt to meet at least the claims of the turned-over crews. A sum of £42,000 stands booked by the Treasurer of the Navy as received on the 16th March out of the Exchequer to naval use, of which £37,000 was earmarked for payment of the ships and yards. Additionally £5,000 was to be issued to Admiral Herbert 'for contingencies of the Navy'.[40] If the estimate made by the Navy Board to the Admiralty upon the 11th March[41] were accepted, the £37,000 was likely to be taken up in settling only with the transferred sailors. A further £30,000 would be necessary for meeting the two months' pay.[42] To Portsmouth the Navy Board had sent £17,000 but only two tellers.[43] When Herbert, who would suppose three tellers to be necessary,[44] commented to the Admiralty, he was informed that two would suffice, that 3,000 pay tickets had been forwarded, that 1,100 more were being sent by coach and that a further 3,000 would be provided.[45] Herbert, at much the same time as the money arrived on the 21st for Berry and Beach to disburse at Portsmouth, had learned of Berry's wind-bound condition off Deal. He therefore suggested to the Admiralty that he himself should sail with the money to his Vice-Admiral and that such payments as might be possible should be made in the Downs. The delay which must follow Berry's appearance at Portsmouth would then be reduced. By the time the Admiralty reply reached Herbert, Berry's ships were on the horizon. Upon Berry's arrival, on the 26th, the Admiral reported it would take two days to deal with the turned-over ratings.[46]

What, in these last days of March, actually took place at Portsmouth, or elsewhere, to settle the claims of the men moved from one ship to another or how far the non-transferred crews received at that time ticket advances is not clear. The bulk of the ships listed to be with Herbert on the 26th March had been in sea-pay since the preceding autumn. There had certainly been the usual opportunities for crews of ships refitting to 'run'; and impressment, the common device for replenishing manning, had, for policy's sake, so far been avoided. Inducement was held out to deserters to return–their 'Rs' in the ships' books would be removed.[47] It is perhaps not surprising that, in a revolution juncture, when rumour flourished, sailors questioned the worth of promises intended to reassure them.

On one of the fourths, working round behind, rather than with Berry, trouble occurred. In a *Journal begun on board their Majesties ship Greenwich*, the 17th March 1688/9 by Captain Christopher Billopp... riding at anchor in the Downs, these entries may be uncovered.[48]

Mar 29 Off Fairlee About 6 this evening the Desarters began to mutiny, so that I was forct in a Sick condition to goe amongst them to appease the mutiny. four of the Leaders put into Irons by name John Thacker, Rich. Paine, Geo Gabriell and Richd Richards.

30 About 7 o'clock this morning sent my Lieutenant to acquaint Adml Herbert with the mutiny whereupon he comanded the 4 that were in Irons to be sent in board his ship *Elizabeth* which was done. From this day to the 5th of Aprill was taken very ill

When Herbert reported the mutiny to the Admiralty he remarked that the 'preservation of government' could not be maintained but by 'martial discipline' and, as one of the commissions which he held entitled him to do (see p. 101), asked for a Judge-Advocate and Marshall to be 'speedily sent him'.[49] To the proposal the Commissioners, having secured, so their Secretary reported, approbation at a conference with 'the Parliament', gave their assent.[50] Strong reasons existed to prompt the King and Admiralty to desire to make pay advances to the men in any vessel sent to sea.

On the morning of Thursday the 28th March, Herbert held a council of war 'for all commanders'[51] and, presumably, unfolded to the assembled Captains the nature of his instructions for the campaign.

The Instructions which Herbert received upon the 11th

March (see p. 68) were, in effect, to assume a command of the sea area separating England from Ireland as well as of a band of waters sixty miles broad girdling the southern and western coasts of Ireland–a command to be extended, should James be found to have landed, to the waters between Scotland and Ireland. The station from which he would exercise that command would be the Chops of the Channel or somewhat further to westward– exercise of a negative and preventative nature rather than of a positive, aggressive kind. Indeed, shots would not be fired unless the French squadron were caught in attempting or concluding a major act of intervention, or individual ships, French or not French, accepted the challenge to land suspects, soldiers or ammunition upon the Irish or Scottish shores. Behind the shield of such a command the 'Protestants in Ireland', that is to say those of Londonderry, could be 'assisted'. To them supplies and troops could be forwarded from England. And it might be possible, weather permitting, for a fast frigate to 'look in upon Brest' and observe any activity in progress in that part.

At this council Herbert no doubt informed the captains that the gale would probably bring in the *Mary* from a mission to westward[52] and explain how, in obedience to orders, he was arranging to put into English ships arms and ammunition on board Dutch vessels at Exmouth. It is not likely the Admiral divulged that the orders had come to him from the Committee for Irish Affairs and that, though he had told Nottingham he would not let the Service suffer for a nicety, he had asked for further orders to be sent only 'in the proper way', proceeding from the Admiralty or bearing the signature of the King.[53] For yet a week the wind veered north and south of west; ships put up and took down their topmasts and yards, and, in the waiting intervals, found work to do aboard or took in wood, water or provisions.[54] Herbert, who received a reminder to send some lesser ships to cruise between Scotland and England, fretted and wished, so he told Nottingham on the 30th, that he had 'a regiment or two on board'. 'I fancy [he said] we mought make very good use of them, I proposed it long before I came out of town but had no answer. If they were sent to Chester, we could easily get them to the fleet.'[55]

Thursday, the 4th April, broke with cloud and rain; but the wind had changed to hang around north-east–'a fine gale'. At 8 o'clock *Elizabeth* unmoored, at '2 in the afternoon . . . wayed' and, under sail, 'answered' the 'Salutes' of the Portsmouth fort guns.[56] By 8 o'clock that evening, Dunnose bearing five leagues W.N.W., Herbert's company of six thirds, ten fourths, two sixths, two ketches, a yacht and a smack were seeking the Channel sea.[57]

Several of the rates already mentioned, which might have been expected to sail with Herbert, remained behind. 'We left 2 third Rates and one fourth rate at Spithead that were not ready to sail'. Thus the log of Herbert's flag captain[58]–presumably referring to the thirds *Cambridge*[59] and *Edgar*; the fourth is not easy to identify. *Edgar* sailed next day.[60] *Foresight* had been allocated to convoy Irish soldiers from the Wight to Hamburg.[61] *Dover* and *Mordaunt* stayed in Portsmouth.[62] *Bonadventure* left harbour at the same time as the fleet, 'ran between the Island & the Maine' and reached 'Dolish [Dawlish] Bay' on the 6th, where, arrived to take charge of a convoy from Exmouth to Londonderry (see p. 110), she watched the fleet pass westward.[63]

By the 9th Herbert was buffeted off the Isles of Scilly.[64] Thereabouts he encountered a Jamaica merchant ship in distress, sent the *Ruby* to inspect and, deciding that 'it would be a little hard to leave her soe . . . for she had neyther masts nor rudder to help herself', detached *Advice* to tow her into Plymouth. A fine example of the camaraderie of the sea! Without delay, he hoped to 'double Scilly' and gain more certainty of French naval movements than various reports had so far given him. Men-of-war, an unspecified number, had, he believed, sailed out of Brest and seven had left Rochefort. To 'meet with them all together' was not his wish; for he had, so he reported to Nottingham, 'but twelve and one fireship'.[65]

On Friday, the 12th April, the Admiral made the coast of Ireland between Cork and Kinsale. A boat sent into Cork harbour brought him 'eyght Irishmen' who gave him news of James's arrival 'abowt a month since' in a French squadron 'two and twenty under English colours', of James's departure for Dublin and the return of the ships to France. In the afternoon, a French sloop came out of Kinsale (for Cork?), eluded the *Henrietta Yacht* and ran in again. On Saturday the 13th, Herbert found roading 'between the harbour's mouth and the old Head' and, to spy the harbour, sent in the *Elizabeth*'s boat, at which the castle fired. 'Three English' came that night to the admiral who was told that the French sloop was *avant-courier* of a fleet of forty sail, on which were embarked 'a considerable number' of French soldiers, every day expected. Herbert said he would 'wayte there arrivall, thought [he] could hartily wish [he] were strengthened by the conjunction of at least those ships destined for these seas'. All this Herbert reported to Nottingham in a long dispatch on Sunday 14th; but the main and inevitable theme, as he lay in sight of so fine a haven, was a return to that request for 'two regiments', expressed before he had weighed from Spithead and originally advanced 'long before [he] came out of town'.

I am [he protested] mightily confirmed that two regiments in the fleet would have been of infinitt servisse, for with theyr help and a number of arms I am very confident wee mought not only have made owr selves masters of this place but put all this cuntry into sutch a posture as would at least have given a great diversion. I cannot yet thinck it to late if his Majesty thincks it fitt and indeed I cannot but believe it of mighty importance to put the ennemy owt of possesion of a place of security to all ships that at any tyme may be ordered to bring them succours, withowt which I doe not thinck the late King can make such stay in Ireland or the Irish hold owt against any reasonable force of the King's This is my opinion which I humbly as I ever have done submitt to his Majesty . . . All the best of theyre forces are drawne towards the north and this part of the cuntry left to the guard of new raysed men that as I am informed dayly desert . . . me thincks the King of France would hardly venter any number of men withowt a secure place by which he may relieve or withdraw them, and if the French are wonce in possession of this place and have time to fortify it to the land as well as it is to the sea, it will not be reduced withowt much blood, tyme and money, I doe not know whether I reason right but thinck it my duty to desire you will please to lay it before his Majesty, to whome as in duty bound I submitt as becomes a faithfull subject.[66]

A southerly gale swept Herbert from sight of Kinsale as far east as Dungarven, moderated and allowed him, by the 17th, to lie again before Cork. There were fruitless chases of French sloops. Then, even as he reported, the wind veered to S.E. and promised to set easterly. That would bring out the French and, so the Admiral hoped, waft him 'the rest of our frigats'.

> 'tis possible [he told Nottingham] we may stand in need of them . . . for, though the battell is not allways to the strong, yet the ods seem to be on that syde, and I am sure we have hitherto found the race to the swift and it is therefore that I the more earnestly desire cleane [and therefore fast sailing] ships

It would be useful, he further remarked, to be informed how he should behave himself 'towards the Irish papists'. There might be 'frequent oportunities of doing them mischief'[67] Herbert wrote to the Admiralty the same day putting his strength twelve men of war, one fireship, two yachts and four smacks, stressing the need for clean ships, 'those he had failing it'; he wishes the *Warspight* changed for the *Montague*; he asked for a hulk to lie at Plymouth and he informed their Lordships he had ordered a survey of Milford Haven, to which the Admiralty had decided victuals for the use of Herbert's fleet should be sent.[68]

Some at least of Herbert's reinforcements were moving Channel-wards. *Pendennis* reached Spithead on the 6th April. *Cambridge*, which had arrived there with Berry's squadron on the 26th March, but (see p. 111) had been unable to follow Herbert's exit on the 4th April, nosed to sea on the 9th. She had obviously left Blackstakes too soon, 'fowle' and ill-stored, for her lieutenant's log now records that the crew 'healed & scraped ship', took in cables, returned 'old cables of best bower', received many tuns of beer, hogsheads of pork, puncheons of beef and pork, a quantity of ballast and several hoy loads of wood. Off St Helens that afternoon the third rate was saluted by the sixth rate *Greyhound*, bringing along two ketches and the hospital ship. The salutation was returned with nine guns. *Greyhound* and her charges went on; the larger vessel anchored on the night of the 10th off Dunnose, used the next morning to take in more provisions from a victualling hoy advantageously arrived from London. The loss of the 'best bower buoy' was annoying, the firing of '21 Guns to Solemnize the Coronation of the King & Queen' on the 11th gave no doubt great satisfaction. When, on the 16th April, *Cambridge* entered Plymouth Sound she found *Greyhound* and the ketches. On the 19th the *Advice* (with the Jamaica derelict) and the *Dreadnought*, which had sprung a leak too large for the carpenter sent for from the *Yorke* to patch at sea, came in from the fleet. *Antelope*, leaking too, in her powder room, *St David* sans bowsprit, foremast and topmasts, *Portland* seeking shelter, all, parted from their admiral, joined them. *Dreadnought* and *St David* would, of necessity, go on to Spithead; but *Pendennis*, from Spithead on the 19th, the fifth rate *Dartmouth*, in also on that day, the *Cambridge*, together with a more ship-shape *Portland*, a more sea-worthy *Antelope* and the *Advice* were able, on the 24th, to watch the citadel and Penlee fade to northward as they plied against the westerly winds to the fleet. *Cambridge* had not failed to improve the occasion of the wind-bound delay at Plymouth to take in twelve more tuns of beer and send her empty casks and staves ashore! [69]

Report that James had landed in Ireland reached London within a week of the event [70] and the presses prepared to print details. [71] (Herbert could have heard of the rumour before, on 17th March, he left town for the fleet) (see p. 102.) The King and Nottingham read with some apprehension the latest letters received from Dublin; for since the 12th of April, they had known that James 'designed to go into the North'. [72] Would an attempt be made to send a regiment into Scotland? Would James himself essay to cross to the Northern Kingdom? By the terms of the Instructions of the 11th March the Admiral had been required, should James be landed, to dispatch ships to the waters dividing Scotland from Ireland; on the 30th March he had been reminded of the order – 'to be obeyed whether James were landed or not'. [73] That reminder he acknowledged on the 1st April. [74] A letter of the 12th, now on its way to the *Elizabeth*, bade Herbert arrange upon arrival of the ships in the North Channel, to give 'notice to Duke Hamilton'. [75] Yet further Instructions were to issue on the 19th. Two 'little frigates' were to be sent to join '*Swallow* and *Jersey*' to cruise between Ireland and Scotland to prevent the transport of men and all materials of war. Their Captains should make it their concern to 'take or destroy any French ships they might meet and . . . take away or destroy all boats and little vessels in the ports or on the coasts of Ireland which might be used for . . . transport.' For himself and the rest of the fleet the Admiral might 'cruise as he [should] judge most proper to prevent the French coming out of Brest.'

These instructions gave to the negatively drawn orders of the 11th March (see pp. 68, 69) a positive emphasis which fell little short of a demand for a strategic blockade of Brest. They were the consequence, as a covering letter made plain, of a roused official attitude; the Privy Council had placed 'an embargo' on 'all ships' and granted permission to apply the press; the Commons had addressed his Majesty with a promise to support open war. Nottingham ventured the hope that the full tale of the Admiral's listed vessels was now with him—apart from some few which still wanted men. They certainly were not! And Herbert can scarcely have been encouraged to learn that though 'the King has pressed the Dutch Ministers to send such of their ships as [were] ready to join . . . they [were] not as forward as [the English fleet].' The letter concluded with a request by Nottingham that the Admiral would facilitate the efforts of a certain Captain John Spurrell to run his small vessel safely into Kinsale from which place he could observe and 'give intelligence' of happenings in Ireland. The package—orders and letter—was 'sent by express to Minehead' and thence to the fleet.[76]

Exactly when the letter of the 12th which conveyed official recognition of James's presence in Ireland and the letter and orders of 19th were delivered aboard *Elizabeth* cannot be decided. A letter of the 20th,[77] answering Herbert's of the 14th, acceded to the reiterated request that two regiments be put aboard the fleet, the arrangements for placing them there to be made with Mr Robert Henley, merchant of Bristol. The rest of the communication revealed William thinking in his original terms of provision of a Mediterranean as well as a Narrow Seas fleet; for Herbert was asked to state which of the two he would prefer to command, it being intended that Mr Russell should be offered the other flag. Not that, added Nottingham, the King had any thought of calling Herbert 'for some time' from his present station, his presence there 'being so necessary for his [the King's] Service'.

It is curious that Nottingham did not tell the Admiral that he was about to transmit, or had already that day sent, to the Admiralty at the King's behest, the strictest instructions that any ships of the quota of sixty-five rates and eight fireships allocated for service in the Narrow Seas and in the Mediterranean (see p. 104 *ante*), which might be at or near condition to go to sea, should sail suddenly to join the Admiral, proceeding singly, if necessary, to avoid delay. The ships should steer for Plymouth and, if they there failed to obtain news of the fleet, seek the approaches to Kinsale. The Admiralty immediately gave urgent orders to the commanders of the two thirds—the *Rupert*, fitting at Portsmouth, and the *Warspight* in the Downs, to the two fourths—the *Tiger Prize*, fitting at Deptford, and the *Hampshire*, ready at that place, as well as to four fireships—the *Charles* and the *Cygnet*, both ready at Deptford, the *Owner's Love* and *Thomas and Elizabeth* already on their way.[78]

Blown off the Irish coast, Herbert, on the afternoon of the 23rd took refuge in Milford Haven.[79] A court-martial occupied the forenoon of the following day: 'about 9 of ye Clock in ye morning [*Elizabeth*] hoisted a Union Flagg in ye Mizon Shroudes for a Councill of Warr for all ye Comd[rs] to come on board to try ye Master of ye *Plymouth*'. The charge and the verdict are not recorded by the Lieutenant of the flagship, but it was common gossip that, with the captain, two others were charged with endeavour to take the ship over to King James. All were condemned to death.[80]

The continued bad weather and consequent disablement of ships had obliged the Commander-in-chief to seek the commodious Milford anchorage in order to put the fleet in a condition to keep the sea.

I now mean [he declared] to sail (with thirteen ships) before Brest judging that the properest station to prevent the French, since it is not certayne where they meane to attempt, though I doe really believe Kingsale in Ireland is the place designed . . . Weak as we are [Herbert resumed] I do not doubt givin them trouble if the weather will suffer . . . not but that I could

hartily wish wee were stronger to make the worck sure . . .
The *Dreadnought*, *Antelope* and *St David* are bore away for
England disabled and the *Portland* is missing, soe that I suppose
she is gone too: the *Pendennis*, *Cambridge*, *Advice* not yet come;
The only fireship I had disabled, so that wee have but thirteen
ships of warr to trust to and those but weakely man'd for we
have many sick.

Herbert did not know (see p. 114) that *Antelope*, *Portland* and *Advice*
were on their way to rejoin him and that *Pendennis*, *Cambridge* and
*Dartmouth* were with them.

On the Admiral's table lay, it is reasonable to suppose, his
drafted, signed Sailing Instructions, which happily have been
preserved, to a fleet of eight thirds, twelve fourths, two sixths,
two fireships, one ketch and four yachts, a tender and an hospital
ship![81] With but 'thirteen ships of warr'[82] in place of a score or
more rates, he yet purposed obedience to the more positive
spirit of the orders of the 19th instant, strategic blockade of the
port of Brest–to attempt an operation long recognized as an
orthodox opening in the establishment of command, a gambit
which was not successfully to be applied against Brest for another
three-quarters of a century. Did the King mean to send ships to
make good storm damage and give additional strength? In that
case it would be well for him to appoint more flag officers 'for
beside that a line may stretch to far for one man to govern, I am
not imortal [declared Herbert] and if I should fall it would
occasion great confusion, not only during the tyme of battle but
after it too'.

Lesser matters were referred to in the dispatch. Ships which
had followed the Admiral in had informed him that 'the man he
had sent ashore to Kinsale'–probably Nottingham's spy Spurrell–
was captive in the castle and that light batteries were being
mounted at the harbour entry. Herbert stated that he had seen a
list of men-of-war designed for the Narrow Seas, the Mediterranean and for convoy duty and, if it were not 'too presuming to say
so' he thought it would require 'considerable alteration'. The
invitation of the 20th to choose for the forthcoming command the
Narrow Seas or Mediterranean flag drew no comment. There was
a note of satisfaction in the remark that, because the officers of

Customs at Milford had not been able to 'stop' the merchant ships in that port 'according to the orders', he had practised an 'effectuall way' and pressed their men. Herbert had hope of sailing on the morrow.

That day, also, in a brief later letter,[83] he asked for 'plain and positive order' how to behave toward the French generally. His first Instructions of the 11th March limited hostility to a stretch twenty leagues from Ireland's coast-line; those of the 19th April which required him to cruise where he might 'best prevent the French ships coming out of Brest', gave him no direction 'to attack them there or anywhere else'. Herbert assured Nottingham that he meant to lose no opportunity 'for falling upon them'; but he would like, he said, an explicit order for 'better justification'. He ended with the querulous remark, 'whatsoever his misfortunes might be at court he would never be lacking in his duty'.

As soon as the Admiralty had become aware of Herbert's presence at Milford, copies of the Commission's minutes and therefore news in respect of the eight ships ordered to join him were forwarded.[84]

At their sitting on the 24th April, the Irish Committee received advice from Liverpool that Colonels Cunningham and Richards were returned from Londonderry![85] The next day, the 25th, the Committee took steps to prevent the two ships with '5,000 arms and ammunition' lying in Torbay on the 13th instant from proceeding to Londonderry now believed to have fallen into enemy hands. If a messenger sent from London could not find the ships in Torbay or intercept them at Plymouth or Falmouth and they had rounded Land's End, it was expected that Herbert would have sufficient oversight of their movements to be able to direct them into Chester to unlade. He was not to be precluded from taking the arms for his own use. Nottingham notified Herbert immediately.[86] In point of fact *Bonadventure* (see p. 111) had accepted them at Topsham bar upon the 10th, sailed immediately and by the 16th rounded the Lizard. Off the Smalls, eight leagues or more west of Milford, on the night of the 17th she lost her charges but collected at morning light. Bound for Londonderry, at eight in the evening of the 20th, she hove to off North Rock and spoke with *Swallow* returning to Chester Water with Cunningham's abortive 'relief ships'. Cunningham is alleged to have sent another vessel – Colonel Richards aboard – to inquire whether the presence of *Bonadventure* indicated the proximity of part of the English fleet. Cunningham represented that, should such be the case, he would hope to obtain a fortnight's provision, which would enable him to return to Londonderry.[87] *Bonadventure* ran into Lough 'Reane' on the 21st and remained at anchor till the 24th on which day her crew enjoyed the extra benefit of a hogshead of beer leaking 'by defect of cask'. She put into Lough Foyle on the 25th (with what convoy, if any, is not evident) and apparently did nothing to affect the Londonderry situation. Weighing on the 3rd of the next month *Bonadventure* reached Chester on the 9th.[88]

It so happened that Herbert's dispatch and postscript communication of the 24th found their way not to London but to Hampton Court and William 'had the curiosity to open them'. Thereupon he, on the 28th, commanded Shrewsbury to forward them to Nottingham who should tell Herbert that 'the warr being now declared with France . . . he [might] fight the French fleet wherever he [met] them'.[89] This Nottingham did on the last day of the month enclosing an actual order from the King who 'approved' of the going before Brest.[90] He did not mention that already a proclamation had issued on the 25th forbidding the import of goods made or produced in France, a prohibition which the Admiralty would, on the 27th, translate into necessary orders against enemy shipping.[91] And he left it to the Admiralty to include in their next communication copies of two further proclamations – one of the 29th recalling seamen from service with foreign princes; another of the same date ordering all pressed men on pain of punishment by the Privy Council to seek their ships.[92] The Secretary hoped that the Admiral really would receive 'a very considerable addition' to his ships and reported the assurance of the Dutch ministers that twenty-four of the States' ships were ready to sail. The Admiralty, he said, would send Herbert two flag-officers – Captain [William] Davies and Lord John Berkeley.[93] Sir John Berry was too sick to serve and Captain Killigrew still in the Streights. It would be left open to Herbert to 'regulate' the details of the composition of the two squadrons intended for the Narrow Seas and the Streights.

It was Nottingham's duty to inform Herbert that the King had just signed an order for sending four regiments under Major General Kirke to Londonderry. The strange facts of Lundy's treachery, his refusal to admit Cunningham's and Richards' regiments into the city and its determination under a new governor to continue its resistance had become known—hence 'this alteration' and a hope, in the Secretary's opinion not very strong, that 'that very important place' might be saved. The note on which the communication ended was well calculated to remove the Admiral's fears, real or imaginary, of court intrigue: 'I would not have you apprehend any misfortunes at Court where no man is better than yourselfe, the King being entirely satisfied both of your fidelity and conduct and therefore 'twill be but little complement to you to assure of my service'. Nottingham was destined to become well skilled in the art of mollifying admirals! It is improbable that Nottingham's communication of the 25th reached the Admiral before he sailed; that of the 30th could not.

Not on the 25th was Herbert able, as he had hoped, to catch a favourable wind; but at two in the morning of Friday the 26th. The flagship

> fired 2 Guns and put 3 Lights in [her] main Topmast Shrouds being a Signall for all ye Fleet to Unmore . . . by 4 [she] had ye small bower to ye Bowes . . . by 5 hove Short upon [her] best . . . by 9 loosed [her] ForetopSaile and ffired a Gun it being a Signall for all ye Fleet to waigh . . .

Shortly they came to anchor in 'Thick Fogg', waiting till next morning to clear the Haven. The happenings of the next three days are best recounted in the Admiral's own words:[94]

> I intended directly for Brest, if the wind had been such as would not have suffered the French to come out; but its coming up easterly made mee steer away for Kingsale; judging that the likeliest place to meet them as alsoe to meet with the ships wanting to make up my squadron. On the 28th of Aprill, somewhat short of Cork, I mett the *Pendennis, Camebridge, Antelope, Salamander*, three small tenders and the hospital ship. On the 29th off of Kingsale we mett the *Portland* and towards evening one of our scouts made signalls that he discovered a fleet keeping theyr winde, which made us keep ours all that

night before Kingsale to prevent theyr getting in there. In the morning Tuesday April 30th, not seeing them, and being informed by our scouts, as likewise by the *Advice* and *Dartmouth* that joined us that day, that the French fleet, consisting of forty-four sayle, were gone into Baltemore, made me beare away for that place, but found no sign of them there. In the evening our scouts got sight of them againe to the westward of Cape Clear. Wee steered after them and found that they were gott into the Bantry; we lay off the place that night . . .
A fresh gale blew from the north-east–the eight thirds, ten fourths, and less than half a dozen smaller vessels kept company and waited for the morn.

The decision to send additional succours to Londonderry, mentioned by Nottingham in his letter of the last day of April to Herbert, had not waited on the abortive return of Cunningham with his and Richards' regiments to Liverpool on the 23rd of the month.[95] As far back as the 18th March,[96] more than three weeks before Cunningham had sailed, Lord Churchill had told the Irish Committee that the King intended two more battalions, 1500 men, which proved to be of Sir John Hanmer's and Major General Kirke's regiments, for Ireland; and the Commissioners of the Admiralty, waiting on the Committee, had been ordered to make the requisite arrangements. For that embarkation Mr Russell and Mr Harbord were to act as liaison with the Commissioners.[97] On the 28th April Marshal Schomberg ordered Major General Kirke[98] to hasten to Liverpool, take command of his own and Hanmer's forces as well as of Cunningham's and, if desired, Richards' soldiers and proceed to Londonderry. The four contingents were part of the 22,290 men for which Parliament had voted supply for six months (see p. 103) and which were all to be embarked from ports between Chester and Carlisle as soon after the 1st May as possible. The fourths *Swallow*, *Jersey* and *Bonadventure*, were regarded as available for convoy to the transport ships which Brigadier Charles Trelawney would engage (to the hired ships the 'embargo' was not to apply) in the port of Liverpool. Their captains were instructed that orders from Kirke should supersede any previously received from Admiral Herbert.[99]

Kirke's full instructions, dated the 29th April, were drawn by Nottingham.[100] There could be no doubt that the plight of the besieged city was appreciated by William and his advisers. So Mr Stevens, 'a messenger from King William with orders to go to Londonderry and make his report of that place', sailed in a twenty-ton Liverpool ship on the last afternoon of the month of April.[101]

## REFERENCES

1  P.R.O. Adm. 3/1 under date.
2  P.R.O. Adm. 2/3, p. 18. The Union was of course identical with the present jack minus the red saltire of St Patrick.
3  *Ibid.* p. 19.
4  *Ibid.* p. 20, 15th March. For the Act, 13 Chas II, v. *The Statutes of the Realm* . . . *printed by command* . . . *MDCCCXIX*, v. V.
5  *Ibid.* p. 1. But see entries P.R.O. Adm. 3/1, 24th May. Commission 'as Vice-Admiral of England where unto he is appointed' to be drawn; *Ibid.* 1st June, Commission to be issued as 'Lieutenant or Admirall and Captaine Gen[ll] of the Narrow Seas' (Incidentally, Narrow Seas as defined by Pepys= 'R of Thames to ye Island & Islands of Scilly and ye Coasts thereof', Rawl. A. 451) and P.R.O. Patent Roll A° 1[mo] Gul et Mai. 14th Sep. for ratification of grant of Vice-Admiralty by the Commission.
6  Christmas, Annunciation of the B.V. Mary, Nativity of St John Baptist, Michaelmas.
7  B.M. MS Harleian 6003 gives a convenient table of flag officers for the whole of King William's War; names, exact rank, dates of commissions, and rates of pay are shewn. Herbert's Vice-admiralty is entered as worth £469.5.9. per annum. The question of naval pay generally is dealt with in Tanner, *op. cit.* (*v.* p. 64 note (41)). *N.R.S. vol. XXVI (Introduction)* pp. 140–151.
8  P.R.O. Adm. 3/1.
9  *Ibid.* 20th inst.
10  *S.P. Dom.* . . . *1689–90* 16th March, p. 27. Admiralty to Nottingham, *H.M.C. Finch II*, p. 196, to King and thence to Mr Richard Hampden (Chancellor) for the House. For biography of the son of the famous father see *D.N.B.* He is notable as one who refused emoluments from William. *Journals* . . . *H. of C.*, 23rd, 25th, 26th March.
11  Shaw, *op. cit. v. IX, Pt 1*, p. x.
12  *Journals* . . . *H. of C.*, 14th, 15th March. The account is fully set out and amounts to F.7,301,322.1.8. which, as may be seen by the note to a summary of the debt in Rapin de Thoyras, M., *The History of England*, trans. Tindal, N. (with Additional Notes), 4th edn corrected 1757, v. 13, p. 142 might reasonably be equated at a rate of exchange of 1 guilder=1s.10½d. to about £686,500. Provision for payment of the £600,000 was long delayed. A bill for 'appropriating monies' was presented in the Commons on 10th August, read, referred to Grand Committee, certain objections considered, and read

again the same day; on the 12th it was taken a third time and, *nemine contradicente*, carried to the Lords. The Lords received it on the 12th and on the 13th, considered the objections of counsel representing 'divers servants of King Charles II' that they 'had Securities appropriated to them out of several Duties which are passed away from them by this Bill'. None the less a second unamended reading followed and, on the 14th, the Lords, after deliberating in Committee and resolving on an address to the Crown to meet the claims of the 'divers servants', returned to session. To the motion 'Whether this Bill shall pass for a Law' their lordships voted affirmatively. *Journals of the House of Lords beginning . . . 1685 [to 1690 Dec.].*

On 30th Oct. the royal sign manual was granted for a payment to Engelinburg, Witsen, Odyck, Citters, Dykvelt of any portion of £100,000 which Sir Hen. Amhurst *et al* had agreed to lend into the Exchequer of 600,000 l. due to the United Provinces. Shaw, *op. cit. v. IX, Pt 1,* p. 291.

13 *Journals . . . H. of C.,* 20th March.
14 Shaw, *op. cit. v. IX, Pt 1,* p. xliv.
15 *Journals . . . H. of C.,* under date. For the Londoner William Blathwayt (1649?–1717) a great civil servant left till Victorian times his mark on his office and, like Pepys, missed peerage, see *D.N.B.*
16 *Ibid.* under date. (Victuals @ 20, wages @ 30, ordnance @ 8, wear and tear @ 27 shillings.)
17 *Ibid.* under date.
18 The Summer and Winter Guard–provision for,

| Stations | 3 | 4 | 5 | 6 | F.s. | Y. | K. | Number Ships | Men |
|---|---|---|---|---|---|---|---|---|---|
| | | | Rate | | | | | | |
| Streights | 1 | 10 | — | 1 | 2 | — | — | 14 | 2495 |
| Channel | 2 | 10 | — | — | 2 | 5 | 2 | 21 | 2815 |
| Ireland | — | — | 1 | — | — | 1 | — | 2 | 130 |
| Newfoundland | — | 2 | — | — | — | — | — | 2 | 400 |
| Canaries | | | Supplied from Channel | | | | | | |
| Jamaica | — | 1 | 1 | — | — | — | — | 2 | 305 |
| Barbados | — | 1 | — | — | — | — | — | 1 | 200 |
| Leeward Is. | — | — | 1 | — | — | — | — | 1 | 105 |
| New England | — | — | 1 | — | — | — | — | 1 | 105 |
| Virginia | — | — | 1 | 1 | — | — | — | 2 | 180 |
| Iceland | — | 1 | 1 | — | — | — | — | 2 | 305 |
| | 3 | 25 | 6 | 2 | 4 | 6 | 2 | 48 | 7040 |

F.s.=Fireships  Y=Yachts  K=Ketches.
Charge, including Ordnance, £4 per man per month=£28,160 and for 13 months of 28 days=£366,080.
*Journals . . . H. of C.,* under date. Also Shaw, *op. cit. v. IX, Pt 1,* pp. xliv–v.
19 A useful summary of what constituted the *Ordinary* of the Navy is to be found in Shaw *op. cit. v. 1742–5* p. xxvi under the heading 'The Navy Estimates'. Shaw is there dealing with the year 1742. One may run together the items thus:

The salaries of my lords Commissioners of Admiralty and of the Principal Officers and the Commissioners of the Navy; the payment of all Clerks, disbursements to superannuated officers, pensions to flag and other sea officers [to widows of Navy Commissioners and relatives of sea officers]; wages at the yards, Chatham, Deptford, Woolwich, Portsmouth, Sheerness, Plymouth and at outports; wages to ships lying up; harbour victuals and 'moarings', graving and repairs to ships; repairs to the yards; half pay to flag officers; [Greenwich Hospital].

The items enclosed in square brackets should not be included for 1689.

20 *Journals . . . H. of C.*, under date, and Shaw, *op. cit.* p. cxxvii.

21 Shaw, *op. cit. v. IX, Pt 1*, p. xlv, gives the peace-time charge of the Ordnance Office as £22,600, of the Guards and Garrisons (Army) as £200,000. With the peace-time charge for the Navy (a) Ordinary £130,000 (b) summer and winter guard £366,080, the total for the fighting services (in peace)= £718,680!

22 February debt (*v.* p. 105) £200,000.

The difficulty of marshalling and considering the inter-related figures placed before the House for the King's 'own', peace-time and war-time (Navy, Army, Ordnance) defence expenditure is considerable. How complicated the matter may be gathered from the lengthy attention given to it in *The MSS of the House of Lords, 1693–1695, New Series, vol. 1 No. 751* (pp.12–29)

There was delivered at the Bar on 20th Nov. [1693] by the Secretary of the Accounts Committee, . . . 'A State of the yearly supplies of money intended for the Navy for the years 1689 to 1692, including what was deficient, as also the debt owing to the Navy on 5th November 1688.'

What baffled in 1693 must still remain unelucidated. Shaw, *op. cit. v. IX, Pt 1*, p. xliv–discusses the question; so also Ehrman, *op. cit.* p. 333–.

23 *Journals . . . H. of C.*, 8th and 9th Oct. 1690 for what Shaw *op. cit. v. IX, Pt 1*, p. cxxxvii calls 'the first genuine estimate in the modern sense' submitted to William's Parliament.

24 *Ibid.* 6th and 8th Nov. 1689, appointment of a Committee 'to inspect the expenses of the War the last year'; 14th April 1690, for further progress *v.* also Shaw, *op. cit. v. IX, Pt 1*, p. cli, but note that 'the actual payments to the Forces in these years 1688–9, were not produced to the House of Commons until 1707, a matter of 18 years after the event', p. cxxxiii.

25 'The Deputies from Holland being not returned from Hampton, the Treaty could not be signed today, as I hope it may tomorrow. I pray your Majesty to press the dispatch of their ships.' *H.M.C. Finch II*, p. 200. Nottingham to King, 16th April. *Ibid.* p. 208. Note by Nottingham.

26 *Ibid.* p. 196. Herbert to Nottingham, 19th March.

27 P.R.O. Adm. 3/1.

28 *Ibid.* 19th March.

29 Various Ships' Logs. A number of logs of ships taking part in this 1689 'Irish expedition' or in operations in the Irish Sea are available.

(A) P.R.O. Adm. 51 (Captains') 52 (Masters'). Logs and journals by lieutenants are to be found among them.

| | 51 | 52 | | 51 | 52 | | 51 | 52 |
|---|---|---|---|---|---|---|---|---|
| Defiance | — | 20 | Elizabeth | 4180 | — | York | — | 123 |
| Plymouth | — | 88 | Pendennis | — | 87 | Foresight | 364 | — |
| Ruby | 4322 | — | Portland | — | 89 | Bonadventure | — | 9 |
| Diamond | 244 | — | Deptford | 4160 | — | Henrietta (yacht) | 3863 | — |
| Advice | 13 | 5 | Woolwich | 4398 | — | Jersey | 4228 | — |
| Mary | 582 | 65 | Greenwich | 414 | 40 | | | |
| Edgar | — | 30 | Cambridge | 4135 | — | | | |

(B) Rawl. C 968–*York* (Captain's), C 969 *Cambridge* (Master's), C 198 *Swallow*.

All have been read. It should be noted that, contrary to expectation it will not invariably be found that logs of this period follow the accepted practice of record from noon to noon. See P.R.O. Adm. Sec. In Letters 1086 'A' 1554 for post 22nd Oct. 1805 usage. Reference is made only where it seems desirable to give authority for a particular remark.

The official Ship-Disposition Lists P.R.O. Adm. 8/2, prepared at frequent intervals for the use of the Admiralty, purport to show the positions of ships in, and sometimes out of, sea service and are of great value if read with caution. Ships' logs, provided they are not carelessly written or 'hooded', are, of course, the final authority for disposition.

30 Log *Elizabeth* (Lieutenant Crawley).

31 Logs *Cambridge* (Captain Clements and Master Gates Naylor).

32 Log *Cambridge* (Master's).

33 Log *Elizabeth* (Lieutenant's) P.R.O. Adm. 3/1, 20th March. The *St Albans* was with Herbert on 6th April–Log *Elizabeth* (Captain's).

34 Logs *Cambridge* (Master's) and *Bonadventure*.

35 Fairlee, east of Hastings; Dunnose, below Chine Head and just north of Ventnor; Gilkicker, a cape at the western entrance to Portsmouth Harbour directly opposite Southsea Castle.

36 Log *Woolwich*. The pendant proper, the distinguishing mark of an English warship, was a streamer that floated rather than flew, from a tiny spar slung close to the mast head. Less than a yard broad at the spar, it was twenty to thirty yards long and, properly, in 1687, a tricolour in horizontal stripe or plain red, white or blue, save for a St George's Cross at the spar and tapered to a fimbriated end. Vice-Admiral Berry's ships probably came in wearing, apart from jacks at the bowsprits and ensigns (red flags with a St George's cross in canton) at their poops, pendants tricolour or red at their foretops; but, falling under command of an Admiral (the Vice-Admiral departing) ran up their pendants at the main. (For an earlier instance of ships that 'shifted their pendants to the main-topmast-head', at a transfer of command–in that case to a 'Commodore'–v. Powley *op. cit.* p. 158. The occasion is referred to p. 31 *ante*). The best known sources for information concerning the English usage of flags in the first three quarters of the 17th century are Boteler, N. *Boteler's Dialogues*, ed. Perrin, W. G. 1929 (*v.* Index 'Flags'); Monson (Sir) W, *The Naval Tracts of Sir William Monson in six books*, ed. Oppenheim, M. v. IV 1913, v. pp. 1–119; Teonge, H., *The Diary of Henry Teonge, Chaplain on board H.M's ships* . . . *1675–1679*, ed. Manwaring, G. E. 1929 (v. Index Flags, Pendants). Pictorial evidence becomes available for the latter half of the century. The Van de Veldes,

father and son, were at work—part of the time for Charles II. But the more one studies (say at the National Maritime Museum, Greenwich) their drawings, or the canvases of their school, the less is one enabled to make firm statements about 'mast' as distinct from 'bowsprit and ensign' staff flags. The final evidence on English pendants and flags is to be found in Admiralty orders and ship logs. These at this time indicate movement away from display toward the codified utility which Pepys was much concerned to obtain, v. Bib. Pepysiana, Miscellanea IX. 'A Collection of Papers and Notes upon the Subject of the Sovereignty of the British Seas and the Right of the Flagg and all Matters relating to Salutes and Colours' (MS) pp. 333, et seq. On flags generally v. Perrin, W. C. op. cit. viz. British Flags—Their early history and their development at sea . . ., Cambridge, 1922.

That the pendant was the distinctive mark of the warship—not only here but abroad—is corroborated by Teonge. He describes the launch of a Maltese brigantine. The religious ceremony being concluded, 'they hoisted a pendant, to signify she was a man-of-war' (op. cit. p. 128). This work, among its many references to pendants, makes incidentally, one sad record—'Summersett Evins going up the mizzen chains to clear the pendant fell down and was drowned' (p. 194).

37  Log Cambridge (Captain's).
38  Logs Elizabeth (Lieutenant's and Captain Mitchell's).
39  H.M.C. Finch II, p. 196.
40  P.R.O. Adm. 49/173 f.3. cf. Shaw, op. cit. 12th March for £20,000 and 16th for £17,000 and contingency £5,000—all Disposition Book entries. The Auditor of Receipt had, in respect of the £17,000, been warned that the money was 'intended for mariners' wages . . . the Exchequer officers not to go away till the money is paid as his Majesty's service requires the despatch of same this morning'. These demands were met out of customs or excise money which had just been paid in. The fact that the Treasurer of the Navy, Lord Falkland, had, on 12th March, been granted an 'Imprest' for £200,000 was of little practical significance. The grant of an imprest, the opening of a 'credit fund', as Shaw op. cit. 1731–4, p. iii calls it, could not, at this date, produce the cash; and hence one cannot, for 1689 and the immediately following years, assert, as does Shaw for the later period, 'by standing entirely by the imprest it is possible to form a tolerably correct idea of the sums actually paid to the [particular] establishment'. The final authority for Naval receipt must be the data of the Navy Office itself—conveniently accessible in Adm. 49/173. An itemized statement of expenditure of Contingency Money by Torrington (entered as paid by Mr Abraham Anselme) from 24th March 1689 to 24th Jan. 1690 is given in B.M. Additional MSS 28084 f.265. The total amounts to £3,659.14.8.
41  P.R.O. Adm. 3/1.
42  Ibid. same date.
43  Ibid. 15th March.
44  For discussion on the usual method of payment see Report on Admiralty Pay Books; Bodleian MSS, Firth, p. 107. It is strange that museum specimens of sailors' pay tickets are not common. I have not seen one.
45  P.R.O. Adm. 3/1, 20th March.
46  H.M.C. Finch II, p. 196.

47 P.R.O. Adm. 3/1, 14th March. R='run'.

48 National Maritime Museum MSS. Adm. L/G/188. There is also a fair copy of the Captain's log P.R.O. Adm. 51/414 with similar entries.

49 P.R.O. Adm. 3/1, Ap. 1. There is a record 23rd May of appointment of a Dr Philip Foster to 'attend all Courts Marshall' P.R.O. Adm. 2/3. The Commissioners gave instructions to their Secretary to send to Herbert, who remained one of their number, 'from time to time' copies of the Board's Minutes.

50 P.R.O. Adm. 2/377, 6th April.

51 Logs of *Elizabeth* and others.

52 As note (51). She arrived on 28th March.

53 *H.M.C. Finch II*, p. 196.

54 Logs–various.

55 *H.M.C. Finch II*, p. 197.

56 Log *Elizabeth* (Lieutenant's). The *London Gazette* reported in its next (8th–11th April) issue and continued to publish fleet movements on notifications received from the Downs, Portsmouth, Plymouth, Kinsale, etc. and from on board the fleet.

57 Log *Elizabeth* (Captain's).

58 As note (57).

59 Logs *Cambridge*.

60 Log *Edgar*.

61 P.R.O. Adm. 8/2.

62 As note (61).

63 Log *Bonadventure*.

64 Logs *Elizabeth* (Lieutenant's) and *Bonadventure*.

65 *H.M.C. Finch II*, p. 198. Log *Elizabeth* (Captain's) refers to the disabled ship by name—*Terra Nova* (Mr Daniell, Commander).

66 *H.M.C. Finch II*, p. 198.

67 *Ibid.*, p. 200, 17th April.

68 P.R.O. Adm. 3/1, 22nd April; *H.M.C. XII, App. Pt vi, H. of L.* p. 188, 18th April.

69 Logs of *Cambridge* (Master and Captain), *Elizabeth* (Lieutenant and Captain), Herbert to Nottingham on 24th *v. infra.* 'staves'–presumably 'staved casks' casks broken into.

70 Luttrell *op. cit.* 17th March. The French counterpart of the *London Gazette*, *Gazette, Recüeil des Nouvelles* . . . [pendant l'année mil six cent quatre-vingt-neuf, à Paris, . . . avec privilege] notes, in its issue Du 2 Avril (23rd March O.S.), as reported in a letter from London dated (begun?) 24 Mars (14th March O.S.) the arrival of James at Cork from Kinsale! James reached Kinsale late on 12th/22nd March, Cork late on 15th/25th March. A problem in journalism!

71 *A Full and True Account of the Landing and Reception of King James at Kinsale* . . . *in a letter from Bristol, 1st April 1689*–licensed 4th April–(B.M. 807 f.36/7 or 816/50 m.23.)

72 *H.M.C. Finch II*, p. 198, Nottingham to Herbert, 12th April.

73 *Ibid.* p. 197–Additional Instructions.

74 *Ibid.* p. 197, Herbert to Nottingham.

75 *Ibid.* p. 198, Nottingham to Herbert. William and Mary had been proclaimed

King and Queen of Scotland on 11th April and William Douglas, 3rd duke of Hamilton (1635–1694) was designated 'President of the Convention of Estates'. See *D.N.B.* for Hamilton's career.

76 *Ibid.* p. 201, Nottingham to Herbert and Additional Instructions. Date of embargo 15th April. P.R.O. Adm. 3/1. *v.* also P.R.O. P.C.6/2. For Commons' address *v. Journals* . . . 19th April. The Admiralty made immediate demand through the Navy Office upon the Rulers of the Waterman's company to provide 50 men for each of 10 named vessels, the thirds *Lyon* at Portsmouth and *Henrietta* at Chatham, the fourths *Happy Return, Oxford, Phoenix* and *Tiger Prize* at Woolwich, *Centurion* at Chatham, *Kingfisher* at Deptford and *Mary Galley* and *James Galley* at that place. *v.* P.R.O. Adm. 3/1, 20th April. The application of an embargo led straightway to requests by ships' masters for 'protections' against impressment for their crews. Such were issued by the Commissioners at discretion, *v.* P.R.O. Adm. 3/1 and Adm. 2/3.

77 *Ibid.* p. 201, Nottingham to Herbert.

78 *H.M.C. XII, App. Pt vi, H. of L.*, p. 188, 20th April. *S.P.Dom.* . . . *1689–1690* under same date. The *Warspight* in the Downs and the *Henrietta* at Chatham were insufficiently manned. The Captain of the *Warspight* (Bootham) had been told to take Englishmen or foreigners out of the returning Virginia fleet—the embargo would cover that. The Admiralty ordered the Navy Board to find turned-over men and to send, in the *Katherine* yacht, one of their Board and the necessary clerks and tellers to the ships in question to effect pay. P.R.O. Adm. 3/1, 23rd April. P.R.O. Adm. 2/377.

79 *H.M.C. Finch II*, p. 202, 24th April.

80 Log *Elizabeth* (Lieutenant's) and Luttrell *op. cit.* 5th May.

81 B.M. MSS. Additional 3650, p. 73. These signals are not noticed by Sir Julian S. Corbett in *Fighting Instructions 1530–1816* or referred to in *Signals and Instructions 1776–1794*, which are respectively vols. 29 and 35 of the *N.R.S.* publications. See Appendix E.

82 As note (79).

83 *H.M.C. Finch II*, p. 203.

84 P.R.O. Adm. 3/1.

85 *H.M.C. XII, App. Pt vi, H. of L.*, p. 177. *H.M.C. New Series v. VIII, The MSS. of the Marquess of Ormonde*, p. 21 'The two regiments that went a fortnight ago are come back last night' Charles Thompson to Henry Gascoigne, Chester, 22nd April.

86 *Ibid.*, P.R.O. P.C. 6/2 under date; *H.M.C. Finch II*, p. 203.

87 For the contact of *Bonadventure* and *Swallow, v.* Mackenzie on the evidence of Sir Arthur Rawdon and Captain Hugh Magill who were in Richards' vessel.

88 *H.M.C. Finch II*, p. 203, 25th April; *S.P.Dom.* . . . *1689–90*, p. 77, 25th April (4 entries); Log *Bonadventure*. Reane=Ryan—the Lough between the northern end of the Mull of Kintyre and the mainland. 'And if you go into Lough Reyn you may bear in at all times' *The English Pilot* II, Pt 1, Seller, J. 1672, p. unnumbered, between 20 and 24.

89 *H.M.C. Finch II*, p. 204, Shrewsbury to Nottingham, 28th April.

90 *Ibid.* 30th April.

91 For this and similar proclamations, P.R.O. Privy Council Registers P.C.2, P.R.O. Patent Rolls 1–14 William III. *London Gazette* or, for summary,

*Bibliotheca Lindesiana Catalogue of Tudor and Stuart Proclamations*, vol. i.
England and Wales, Oxford 1910. For order to Herbert and from him to his
captains to seize French ships, P.R.O. Adm. 2/3, p. 96.

92 *Bibliotheca Lindesiana Handlist of Proclamations . . . 1509–1714*, v. 1– Aberdeen
1893.

93 P.R.O. Adm. 2/3, 1st May, for appointments; Vice-Admiral to wear the
Union at the fore. Davis was assigned to the *Resolution*, Berkeley asked for
the *Hampton Court*. They made requests to the Board for their captains–
Butler and John Munden respectively, *Ibid.* 23rd, 24th April. William Davies,
a lieutenant in 1664 and captain next year, gained his experience against
the Dutch and commanded a score of ships before becoming Dartmouth's
flag captain in *Resolution* 1688. For Berkeley, John (third baron Berkeley of
Stratton) (1663–1697), who had served as Dartmouth's rear admiral in
1688, see *D.N.B.* The *D.N.B.* (to which biography reference has already
been made) following Charnock, does not make mention of the operation
now brought to a close.

94 *H.M.C. Finch II*, p. 204, Herbert to Nottingham.

95 *H.M.C. XII, App. Pt ii, H. of L.*, 24th April.

96 *Ibid.* p. 172.

97 *Ibid.* pp. 172 and 174.

98 For the career of Kirke, Percy (1646–1691) to date see *D.N.B.*, noting that
he had learned his soldiery in France under the duke of Monmouth, 1673
and with Turenne, Luxembourg and de Creci later. He reached the rank as
lieutenant colonel in 1680, before proceeding to Tangier to become colonel
of the old Tangier regiment, with its famous badge the Paschal Lamb. The
brigadier of Sedgemoor (1685) notoriety is now a major-general.

99 P.R.O. P.C.6/2.

100 *Ibid.*

101 Richards' *Diary of the Fleet*, under date in *Two Diaries of Derry . . .* with
Introduction and Notes by Thomas Witherow . . . Londonderry . . . 1888.

E

# CHAPTER VII

# Bantry Bay

## Late April to mid-May

### ARGUMENT

*5th May/25th April a second French expedition to Ireland sails from Brest; Chateaurenault its commander; his relations with Gabaret, second in command; Forant rear admiral—Course laid for Cape Clear rather than (as prescribed) Kinsale or Galway; on 30th April landfall made in Bantry Bay and disembarkation at Balgoben planned—Mayday morning, Herbert enters the Bay—Mutual preparations for battle; the strength of the French fleet; and of the English—The conflict joined across the top of the Bay from east to west and out southward to the sea till Chateaurenault breaks off the engagement—The French admiral's report—Herbert's reflections upon failure; his intention to detach ships toward the Irish Sea and, if not reinforced, to return to Portsmouth; the damage and losses Herbert sustained; emergency repairs as the fleet lies to and Captain Aylmer is buried—Rooke is detached to Scottish-Irish waters. On 6th May, Herbert is off the Lizard, on the 7th enters Plymouth Sound reaching Spithead on the 12th where he learns of the King's approbation—15th May the King, aboard the Elizabeth, knights two captains, rewards the ratings and Herbert (a peerage in prospect) leaves for London. Chateaurenault returns to France to learn that his victory has been received with restrained approval; Chateaurenault's criticism of Gabaret, who sharply retorts; Forant's observations; Louis' measured satisfaction.*

*A plain naval verdict on Bantry—the tactics employed by the admirals used by Hoste, in L'Art des Armées Navales, for illustration—Dublin and the battle. Should Chateaurenault have headed eastward and northward to Dublin and Londonderry?—Losses before Londonderry cause d'Avaux alarm.*

*Other happenings in the first half of May—Killigrew, 5th May brings in the trade from the Streights—The unsatisfactory conduct of certain captains contrasted with the exploit of the Nonsuch.*

*General command of the Narrow Seas and especially of the Irish Sea—The King's messenger Stevens returns from Londonderry; Captain Jacob Richards' mission to the city awaits in Liverpool opportunity to sail—Kirke in Liverpool is reprimanded for delay in embarking with regiments to the relief.*

*King William's Declaration of War upon Louis, 7th May; the Anglo-Dutch Naval Convention, backdated to 29th April, signed 11th/21st May; unjust criticism of Nottingham.*

---

FOR SOME FIVE WEEKS before 5th May/25th April the second expedition to be sent by Louis to Ireland lay ready in the harbour of Brest.[1] On the morning of Friday, 6th May/26th April, the wind at north-east, the weather dull, the expedition weighed, twenty-four warships of between sixty-two and forty-four guns, several vessels about twenty, half a score fireships and two merchantmen, under the command of the comte de Chateaurenault.[2]

François-Louis de Rousselet, comte de Chateaurenault, born in 1637, the son of François de Rousselet—the Frondist—governor of Belle Isle, created marquis by Louis XIII, was the youngest of four brothers in a family of nine. Like so many other marine officers achieving in this era high command, Chateaurenault first chose a military career. He was present at the siege of Dunkirk, passed in 1661 as enseigne to the service of the sea and conducted himself with bravery in African and Mediterranean campaigns—serving with the duc de Beaufort, taking part in the capture of Djidjelli, reaching the rank of captain, and, in 1672, destroying the forts at Salee. Promoted chef-d'escadre in 1673, he, for many months, fell short of the proper expectations of the great Minister of Marine, Colbert; yet, before the end of the war with Holland he had met and fought creditably with young de Ruyter, Tobyas and Evertsen and recovered his reputation with Colbert. Between 1679 and 1688 Chateaurenault's services were not continuous. He found time to marry. Early in 1688 the death of du Quesne opened the door for further promotion. Therefore, it was as *'lieutenant général des armées navales'* that he left the company of d'Estrées and Tourville in the Mediterranean and reported at Brest for this particular expedition. The personal bravery, breadth of gathered experience and attained rank, of the short, stockily built Breton noble suggested fitness for an undertaking which presented strategic challenge and demanded tactical skill.

The appointment of Jean de Gabaret as Chateaurenault's second in command, the leader of the van, might not have been made had Colbert père, and not Seignelay his son, controlled at this time the Ministry of Marine. At least the memory of Chateaurenault's démêlé with Gabaret fifteen years earlier (an incident in that period of official dissatisfaction with Chateaurenault to which reference has just been made) would have revived in the Ministerial mind and prompted caution. Ordered to unite his squadron with that of Gabaret the maimed and renowned chef-d'escadre, Chateaurenault, the junior chef-d'escadre, had obeyed and presented himself to his senior officer with the expectation that the service visit would be reciprocated to one of the same rank and—a count! The visit was not repaid and the count took his grievance to Versailles. He can scarcely have been prepared for the reprimand which Colbert administered. In a letter, comparable to the like compositions of the English Pepys, the French Pepys informed the rising officer of official surprise that one who had previously shown all due concern for the etiquette of the royal service should fail in essential duty *'l obéissance à* [*ses*] *supérieurs'*. Arguments such as the complainant had advanced were *'chicane'* savouring too much of *'l'esprit qui régnait d'autrefois dans la Marine'*. As to the unpaid call, Chateaurenault must understand

> *que cela ne s'est jamais pratiqué entre le supérieur et l'inférieur et que Sa Majesté aurait trouvé fort mauvais que le dit Gabaret eût été vous visiter dans votre bord*

Let him cultivate subordination, reflecting that, by seniority, he owes it to five or six officers only whereas there are some two or three hundred junior to himself who might be influenced, should they ever come under his command, by his bad example! One cannot know whether gossip of Chateaurenault's indiscretion at Versailles ever reached Gabaret's ears or whether the reprimanded Chateaurenault continued unreasonably to harbour resentment against Gabaret. Certainly Gabaret, approaching his seventieth year, can hardly, in any case, have relished the assignation to serve under one who, no greater in merit but more fortunate in birth, had outstripped him in promotion. He had but recently safely conducted that sacred personage, James Stuart, to Ireland. Why, he may well have questioned, should not this second command have been allotted to his care?

Job Forant, born at la Tremblade in 1630, of Protestant family, to whom was entrusted Chateaurenault's rear, was much nearer in age to his commander. Forant had fought the Spaniards in the River Plate, the Turks from Portugal to Candia. A full captain by 1665, he was employed by Louis in Holland upon ship-construction duties; none the less he took his full combative share in the war with Holland, under d'Estrées encountering de Ruyter at Walcheren. He had reached the rank of chef-d'escadre in 1686 and was credited with sang-froid and navigational skill.[3]

By nightfall (of 6th May/26th April)[4] the fleet scarce clear of the Iroise, the wind hardened, blowing from the north and carrying fog. To keep formation, Chateaurenault sent '*les frégates*' – two vessels of twenty guns – through the fog to tell each ship the course he, the admiral, held; and, when the fog cleared next afternoon, 7th May/27th April, he found his charge more or less in company. Standing north-westward till noon on 8th May/28th April, by which time an English ship bound for France had been intercepted but allowed to continue her voyage, and a Portuguese, which had run into the fleet, permitted to sail on to London, the admiral hove to and 'some consultation was held aboard the admiral'. Chateaurenault, moved, as he says, by the fear of further dispersal of the fleet in fog, had, it seems, already decided not to abide by what one must assume were his original orders – certainly intention – to head for Kinsale or Galloway (Galway) but to set '*une route certaine au cap de Clare*', which promontory at the southern extremity of Cape Clear Island, is, of course, twenty or more leagues west of Kinsale Old Head.[5] At dawn on 9th May/29th April, the admiral, having been observed by three English warships, which he had vainly chased to windward, was sufficiently near land to be able to identify the coast as that west of Kinsale.[6] He stood in and dispatched a shallop to the shore. It brought back an Irish colonel, who assured the French commander that the English had been a fortnight on that coast and that he, the informant, had counted '*du même lieu le même matin*' twenty-three English sail. With the wind east-north-east and, therefore, blowing '*directement contraire pour aller à Kinsale*' and with what he believed to be vessels of the English vanguard at hand, Chateaurenault could not think of beating backward and eastward to Kinsale harbour; still less, he reflected (as if in self-justification) entertain the notion of attempting, pursued, the fifty leagues to Atlantic Galway. He realized (with no degree of composure!) that he might be called upon to essay disembarkation in view of his enemy – '*rien n'est si dangereux!*' – that he could expect no friendly port protection from landward whilst the operation was in progress and that his only course was to go with all speed down the wind, past Baltimore, hang south (presumably) of Clear, the Mizen Head and the Sheep's Head [Dunmanus Point] and turn into the commodious if unwelcoming bay of Bantry. He reached it at 11 o'clock on the morning of Tuesday the 10th May, the Irish 30th April. His anchorage was close inshore to the Sheep's Head some four leagues south of the town of Bantry.

Through five hours, 'the English, Scotch and Irish to the number of about 1500, with all the money, arms and ammunition brought from France, and four days' provision for each man',[7] were put aboard the frigates *L'Empressée* and *La Pressante* and six fireships to be taken up the bay to Balgoben,[8] on the Bantry Creek, the place selected for disembarkation. Not all had been transferred when Chateaurenault's two guard vessels, under command of the Chevalier de Coetlogon, signalled that the English, numbering twenty-seven vessels, were beating up from sea. The remnant of troops was, during the cold and probably part moonlit night,[9] ousted to the nearest rocks; and, at peep of day ['*au point du jour*'] another '*fregatte*', *L'Argent* took care of two of the fireships, which had not previously been able to stand clear of the fleet to head for Balgoben, and of the two heavily laden merchantmen, which were finding special difficulty in moving up the bay. Chateaurenault addressed himself to battle; but, knowing he had the wind of the oncoming English, '*pour plus grande sûreté*' of the disembarkation vessels, determined not to fight, unless compelled to do so, till 11 o'clock and the turn of the insetting flood. In a bay in which there is 'scarcely any tidal stream' and less on the eastern than western or Bere Island side,[10] the assistance which his transports received from six hours of the spring flood cannot have been considerable. At 11 o'clock '*la marée finissait*' and longer delay was impossible; the English vanguard had caught up with the French fleet and was, according to the French admiral, pressing to engage. Chateaurenault, quickly forming line, ordered his own van to fight, knowing full well that only success in battle could insure the continued safety of his charge.

Herbert was anxious for battle, and he was well advised of the strength of his enemy; for, on the preceding morning, he had called aboard, 'Mr Andrew Hopkins master of the *Adventure* of Byddiford homewards bound from Maryland with tobacco', who had, the day before, seven leagues west of the Cape of Ireland

[Clear] sailed through Chateaurenault's fleet. Hopkins had, probably correctly, counted twenty-five capital, eight fireships and four tenders formed in line ahead.[11] Now at four o'clock this fine May day morning,[12] the presence of the French in the Bay had been confirmed by the *Fubbs* yacht which, scouting ahead, had 'lett fly her Maintopsaile sheets';[13] and, as the English ships, hugging the shore, worked round the Sheep's Head peninsula, the anchored French fleet with transports moving beyond 'along the reef' (as the English admiral puts it), had come into view.[14] By five o'clock the Union flag at the mizen peak of the *Elizabeth* had flapped, to signal to ships, already cleared for action, to form line;[15] but, against the 'fine fresh gale'[16] veering from E.N.E. to E.[17] 'blowing directly out of ye Bay',[18] yet not greatly ruffling the water,[19] Herbert's ships, which gained little from the flood,[20] had only been able to make headway by persistent tacking.[21] More than one English log[22] records how, on first sight of the incoming English, the French admiral, his anchors already 'a-peak',[23] weighed and plied further up the Bay, keeping the while close to the peninsula shore[24]–in the near wake of his 'fregatte' *L'Argent*, the two fireships and the two merchantmen hustled off since first light. How far, in shielding his transports, Chateaurenault had sailed along the Bay's rock coast from his night anchorage, a league within the Bay and four from Bantry,[25] before the threatening proximity of the English compelled him to face attack, it is impossible to say; but it is certain that the sea area of initial encounter cannot have been very far south-west of Bantry, where the Bay is appreciably less than its maximum seven and a half miles wide. It was therefore a restricted sea area within which, from a protective formation, Chateaurenault swung his ships into what Herbert calls, in his despatch to Nottingham, 'a very orderly line composed of twenty-eight men of war and five fireships',[26] but which Chateaurenault declares consisted of 'twenty four warships and four fireships'.

As was proper, Gabaret's 'avant-garde' took station in the van, followed by the 'corps-de-bataille' of Chateaurenault. Forant's 'arrière-garde' completed the line (see overleaf).

Whether any of the 'fregattes', *L'Empressée, La Pressante, L'Argent, La Tempête*, which sailed with the fleet[28] were in attendance on

## Gabaret's 'avant-garde'

|  |  | Canons | Equipages |
|---|---|---|---|
| Le François | Panétié | 46 | |
| Le Vermandois | De Machault | 58 | |
| Le Duc | De Saint Marc Colbert | 48 | |
| Le Fendant | De Real | 52 | 350 |
| Le Saint Michel | Gabaret | 54 | |
| Le Fort | Le Chevalier de Rosmadec | 52 | 350 |
| Le Léger | Le Chevalier de Fourbin | 44 | |
| Le Précieux | De Salampart | 56 | 330 |

## Chateaurenault's 'corps-de-bataille'

| | | | |
|---|---|---|---|
| Le Capable | Le Chevalier de Bellefontaine | 56 | |
| L'Arrogant | La Harteloire | 54 | |
| Le Diamant | Le Chevalier de Coetlogon | 56 | |
| L'Ardent | Le Comte de Chateaurenault (Champmeslin–Capitaine de pavillon) | 62 | 350 |
| Le Furieux | Desnots [Desnol] | 60 | |
| Le Faucon | Le Chevalier d'Hervaut [Dervaut] | 44 | |
| Le Modéré | De Saint-Hermine | 50 | |
| L'Entreprennant | De Beaujeu [Beaulieu] | 56 | |

## Forant's 'arrière-garde'

| | | | |
|---|---|---|---|
| Le Neptune | De Palières [de Lahire] | 46* | |
| L'Arc-en-ciel | De Perinet [de Permet] | 44 | |
| L'Excellent | La Vigerie [de la Noyene] | 60 | |
| Le Courageux | Forant | 62 | 350 |
| Le Sage | De Vaudricourt | 52* | |
| L'Emporté | De Roussel | 42* | |
| L'Oiseau | Du Quesne Guitton | 40* | |
| L'Apollon | De Montortié [de Montfortier] | 56 | |

27

the battle-line is not clear. Herbert's estimate of twenty-eight suggests that it was so.[29] Some of the half-score 'brûlots'–Herbert counted five–would hover behind the moving French line in readiness to swoop on the wind upon disabled rates.

It is not possible to set out with certainty the English line. The following purports to be

a perticular List . . . when they engaged the enemy[30]

| Rate | Ships' Names | Men | Guns | Comanders | Division |
|------|-------------|-----|------|-----------|----------|
| 3 | *Defyance* | 400 | 64 | Cap. Ashby, John | |
| 4 | *Portsmouth* | 220 | 46 | St Loe, George | |
| 3 | *Plymouth* | 340 | 60 | Carther, Richard | |
| 4 | *Ruby* | 230 | 48 | Froud, Frederick | |
| 4 | *Diamond* | 230 | 48 | Wallters, Benjamin | |
| 4 | *Advice* | 230 | 48 | Grenville, John | |
| 3 | *Mary* | 365 | 64 | Col. Aylmer, Matthew | |
| 4 | *St Albans* | 280 | 50 | Cap. Layton, John | |
| 3 | *Edgar* | 445 | 70 | Shovell, Cloudsley | Admirall Herbert |
| 3 | *Elizabeth* | 460 | 70 | Mitchelle, David | |
| 3 | *Pendennis* | 460 | 70 | Churchill, George | |
| 4 | *Portland* | 230 | 48 | Geo. Aylmer | |
| 4 | *Deptford* | 280 | 54 | Rooke, George | |
| 4 | *Woolwhich* | 280 | 54 | Sanders, [on] Ralph | |
| 5 | *Dartmouth* | 150 | 36 | Lay, Thomas | |
| 4 | *Greenwhich* | 280 | 54 | Billop, Christopher | |
| 3 | *Cambridge* | 400 | 70 | Clements, John | |
| 4 | *Antelope* | 230 | 48 | Wickham, Henry | |
| 3 | *York* | 340 | 60 | Delavall, Ralph | |
| | Fireships | | | | |
| 5 | *Firedrake* | 65 | 12 Gu. 6 Pat. | Cap. Leake, John | |
| 5 | *Saudadoes* | 75 | 10 Gu. | Wivell, Francis | |
| – | *Sallemander* | 35 | 2 m. | Gother, James [Votier, John] | |

That the nineteen ships first named were all present may be accepted. An official list confirms it; in the *Mary* '18 Saile and the *Dartmouth*' was logged; and a report 'from on board' the *Elizabeth* on the 2nd May to the *London Gazette*[31] testifies similarly. With the nineteen were the three vessels named in the table; the *Fubbs* yacht was at hand (see p. 135) and, one would suppose, the *Henrietta* yacht (see p. 111). Chateaurenault wrote to Seignelay of twenty-two ships of war and six yachts – an exaggeration; but, in conveying that five of the English vessels were bigger than his largest and none smaller than his weakest, he, as a comparison of the tables will reveal, was not far from the truth. What really signifies is the fact that twenty-four French ships of the line,

mounting at least 1200 guns, confronted nineteen, mounting not
more than 1062. The leading ships at 11 o'clock were *Defiance*,
*Portsmouth*, *Woolwich*, *Plymouth*, *Advice* and the order of the rest is
uncertain.[32]

The French line 'edged down' on the starboard tack[33] and
Herbert, who seems to have indulged at least a partial hope that
he could turn the French line and win the weather gage,[34]
perforce conformed to his enemy's plan for the battle. As the
heads of the lines converged, the captain of the *Greenwich* observed
of the French, '3 had pendants–at the maintopmast, foretopmast
& Mizen topmast heads each ship with a white Flagg at Mizen
Peak & he with a Pendant at Maintopmast head put abroad a red
Flag at foretopmast head & fired 3 gunns'.[35] Herbert likewise
spread, at the foretopmast head, his 'bloody' flag.[36] When the
*Defiance* and Panétier's *le François* were within musket shot of each
other 'small & great shot' were loosed off by the French.[37] Captain
Ashby answered with a whole broadside and, while *Defiance* and
*Le François* engaged, *Portsmouth*, *Woolwich*, *Plymouth*, *Advice* went into
action, presumably against the next following units of Gabaret's
van.[38]

Chateaurenault's account of the battle from this stage onwards
is lucid and credible. It amounts to saying that all Gabaret's vanguard and the corps-de-bataille as far as Chateaurenault's own
ship, *L'Ardent*, were in line by the time the *Elizabeth*, Herbert's
flagship, drew abeam; that firing thereupon became general to
the sternmost ship of the French line; that the starboard tack was
held by both himself and Herbert, till the latter found it expedient
to take note of the nearness of the land–obviously the western
shore of the constricted water–and change course. This, Chateaurenault states, Herbert did 'with the wind', so that *L'Ardent* was
not able for awhile easily to keep the *Elizabeth* abeam. Nevertheless, it must have been encouraging to see that the English flagship
had lost its main topsail. Each admiral, Chateaurenault affirms,
after the alteration of course, sought contact with his opponent's
line and, as far as it was found, ship fought against ship. This–for
four hours, during two of which the French admiral claims to have
been involved with the centre of the English line. Gabaret and
Forant, he briefly remarks, '*combattaient chacun dans leur division*'.

At the end of six hours of conflict, being seven leagues from the scene of the beginning of the encounter—in other words some nine or ten leagues from Bantry and Balgoben, with Dursey Island to starboard, the Mizen Head to port and the open sea before him— Chateaurenault decided to return to hasten whatever might remain unaccomplished of the work of disembarkation. Upon an enemy, drawing out of reach, what more, he asked himself, could be accomplished? The wind, he noted, was blowing harder; he had six feet of water in hold and had been forced to stop five leaks caused by hits below the water-line. Chateaurenault does not this time make reference to the tide; but, in *'revirement'* and till he could re-enter the Bay, the young flood may have given him a limited assistance.

Nothing in the official report of the English admiral counters the Frenchman's narrative so far followed. During the first phase of the battle, Herbert, working from leeward, was not able to bring his line to continuous close range. Of the second phase he writes:

I 'stretcht' of to sea, as well to gett owr ships into line as by that way to have gott the wind of them but found them soe cautious in bearing doune that wee never could gett an oportunity to doe it, so continued battering upon a stretch till about five a clock in the afternoone that the French admirall tackt from us, but indeed had soe disabled us in owr masts and rigging that I was not, nor half owr ships, in any condition to follow them or make any further attempt upon them.[39]

The log of the *Advice* (Master's) confirms that the engagement was first upon the starboard and then the larboard tack; the master of the *Cambridge* supplies the time of the turn 'abt noone' and indicates that it was late, '½ past 4', before the two rears were in, or broke off, action. All important is the continuation: 'they having the wind of us would not bare downe in reach of our Guns: but we recd ye damage . . . by there randome shot'. That indeed was the rub! And the master(?) of the *Mary* was of like opinion: 'for the most part they kept Soe farr to windward that our Shott would not Reach them when we found theirs went over Uss and throe us'. Chateaurenault first, between five and six, took in the 'bloody' flag. Herbert delayed the gesture.[40] By sunset, the

English fleet was, for the more part, well to the S.W. of the Mizen.⁴¹

Chateaurenault's report reveals, in the sequence of its narrative, that he returned to Balgoben in critical mood. He had time to reflect a lack of co-operation by the '*seconde et troisième divisions*'. Why had they not during that four hours when he considered himself '*le maître de la tête des Anglais*' likewise crowded sail? He had been constrained to outsail Gabaret to the extent of putting himself at the head of the battle line. Not to have done so would (he was persuaded) have been to allow Herbert to manoeuvre to windward, set the French fleet '*entre deux feux*' and sail on to destroy '*le débarquement*'. Two of the three leading ships of the corps-de-bataille, *Le Diamant* and *L'Arrogant*, had kept close to their admiral; so also three of the four in the flagship's wake, *Le Furieux*, *Le Faucon*, small and poor sailer, and *Le Modéré*. But not his foremost or rearmost vessels, *Le Capable* and *L'Entreprennant*. They had lagged behind. Gabaret and Forant, he would tell Seignelay, could, better than he, account for their divisions – they were really too far away from the corps-de-bataille for him to be able to pass judgment. But two days elapsed between the battle and the completion of the dispatch and time availed for Chateaurenault to move to the settled view that, on the whole, he had done well. It pleased him that it was to Herbert, '*le plus capable et le plus brave de leurs généraux*', this experience had befallen; but he was piqued at the lack of congratulations from the English Jacobite gentlemen he had safely set ashore and protected! '*Je n'ai pas reçu le moindre compliment de leur part sur ce fait*'. He had completed an imposing list of 'mentions' and recommendations, transacted business with d'Avaux and was arranging to send his report by the hand of [his nephew] the Chevalier de Chateaurenault in *L'Emporté*. For him he requested, after eleven years' service, promotion '*à présent*' to captaincy. That would be an honour to a loyal house – and he felt that he might look forward to the time when the young man would succeed him! Chateaurenault said that he left it to his *commissaire* – paymaster – to report detailed damage to ships and loss of life and limb. Panétier's vessel he mentioned and that of Coetlogon, in which the poop had been shattered by a ball, a magazine exploded and a violent fire started. Both officers were highly commended. It is known that the paymaster's casualty list showed forty killed and ninety-three wounded.[42] On the 13th/3rd May, Chateaurenault was off Cape Clear with all the vessels except *La Tempête* and *La Pressante* which he had sent back to Bantry.

The after battle reflections of the English admiral likewise demand attention. At the core of his dispatch to Lord Nottingham Herbert allowed himself exaggeration. 'I must confesse that as long as I have gone to sea, I never saw soe much modesty in any men's behaviour as the French shewed upon this occasion; for considering the advantage of the place, the wind, their fire-ships . . .' The implication that, had *he* possessed such advantages, he would have pressed home the fight more closely may be allowed –not so the bald assertion that the French were 'at least dubble [the English] force as to the quality and number of ships'. Yet the apologia was commendably brief; and, from the parting gibe, 'surely a temper unaccountable' he passed to the sailor-like recognition. ''Tis trew they have gaind theyr poinct, for wee have not been able to hinder them from landing whatever they brought, though I can trewly say it has not been my fault'. The damaged ships, said the admiral, had been put into 'pretty good repayre' in the three days since the battle and he was making his way to the rendezvous 'ten leagues west from Silly', where, if he could meet with 'any number of [the] frigets . . . or . . . any number of the Dutch that [would] follow [his] orders', he would try fortune against the homeward bound Chateaurenault. The *Deptford* (Captain Rooke) with *Antelope, Portland, Dartmouth* and *Henrietta* yacht would be detached to strengthen 'those ships already cruysing between Scotland & Ireland, lest the French should take a fancy to make a detachment that way'. Should no reinforcements appear out of the eastward, Herbert intended to make for Portsmouth where new orders would, he hoped, em-power him to select and man an adequate fleet. Enclosed, his lordship might find an account of the damage and losses which his ships had suffered.

Finally, items of old correspondence received attention. The two regiments which the King now promised Herbert obviously could not at this juncture be employed. To the renewed invitation to select command of one of the two main summer fleets he answered as before (see p. 115). He ventured to suggest the desirability, whilst the fleet refitted, of waiting upon the King in town.

The inventory of ship-damage and the casualty lists are not with the covering dispatch; but its nature can be gathered from extant log entries. *Elizabeth* lost her maintopsail (as Chateaurenault had noted) and at that juncture towards the limit of the starboard tack was so damaged in her tacks and sheets that she had to wear to regain the line. *Ruby*'s foretopsail was shot away, her foreyard and her maintopsail yard were broken, her rigging much torn; she was 'crank' and took in 'much water'. The 'boltsprit and Maintopmast' of *Cambridge* suffered; she had been hit twice 'between wind and water' and nursed several shot in her side. *Mary* had to 'fish' her mast, nail on shot boards, bend several sails. *Deptford* hit 'under water' . . . 'proved very leaky'; *Woolwich* was 'much disabled in sails & rigging with guns dismounted or split'; *Diamond* was hurt. The midshipman of the *Defiance* puts the matter thus: 'The [French] ships all [at] a distance having very Damnified our Masts and Riggins [we] was Forctt to Beare away and Knott our Riggine and secur our Masts'. An officer of the *Portland* is explicit:

[Our] Maintopsaile shott away or Maintopmast wounded our spare topmast quite shot asunder and 1 ffire bome and one studing Saile Bome shot to pieces, all our sailes very shattered. Re[ceived] shot . . . underwater [Our] Long boat Shot in pieces

The above are indicative and by no means exhaustive entries. And ship after ship recorded its dead, its 'dismembered' and its wounded. One–the *Portland*–had lost its commander. In all–a captain, a lieutenant and 94 seamen killed and as many as 250 wounded.[43]

The emergency repairs to which Herbert refers were put in hand as 'all the fleet lay by' from nightfall of the 1st 'till noon' of the 2nd or later. The captain of the *Cambridge* informs that 'Capt. George Aylmer . . . was *this morning* thrown overboard'; the master of the *Portland*, fifteen leagues S.S.E. of Dursey, records: '*by 5 afternoon* we buried Capt. George Almer in ye sea the Admirall and all ye Cap[tts] at his ffunerall ea[ch] shipp ffireinge their [guns] and boats their Small shott.' And, he added, 'Captt Shelea [John Shelley] Comd<sup>r</sup> of ye *Dartmo[uth]* came on bord with the Admirall['s] comition to Com<sup>d</sup> the *Portland*'.[44] With the fleet under sail the unfinished work went on. The *Mary* (Captain Mark Aylmer) sped ahead bearing Herbert's report to Nottingham.[45] Fair weather obtained. Captain Rooke with the *Deptford* and his four charges fell away for St George's Channel on the 4th and, at 'breake of day' on the 5th, observed Chateaurenault's fleet so 'very intent on getting home' that it ignored the English squadron entirely. On the 6th, Herbert passed the Lizard; on the 7th anchored in Plymouth Sound. The *Portsmouth* took on two prizes to Spithead–two others which the *Ruby* had fetched out of Cork harbour had been brought in from Milford to Falmouth. The *Half Moon* came in–so that they were 'in company 14 saile'. Herbert was greeted with salutes; he, with '42 gunns', returned the compliment. In the forenoon of the 8th 'with 26 saile' he weighed–not without incident. For the *Elizabeth* ran on a rock 'in ye middle of ye Sound Right of ye West End of ye Cason & continued 2 hours'. The fleet was skirting the Wight on the 10th; on the 12th made the Spithead.[46] A letter from Nottingham dated 8th May awaited Herbert.

> The King tells me to let you know that he is very well satisfied of your conduct in the engagement, and tho' the French have gained their point in landing the succours they brought, yet you have sufficiently shewn your zeal and fidelity . . . in attending to prevent them upon so vast disadvantages . . . that I am from him to assure you of his great esteem of you.

The King, Nottingham said, intended to be in Portsmouth on the following Monday.[47] It was on the 8th that the Admiralty read a letter from Herbert delivered by the hand of Captain Mark Aylmer–a statement of the condition of the damaged fleet–to the repair and strengthening of which the Navy Office was forthwith required to give extraordinary attention. Dr Pierce, Chirurgeon General, was ordered, with surgeons to Portsmouth.[48] On the 13th 'fine delightful weather' during which the sick and wounded were sent ashore. Another twenty-four hours of 'dilicate fair weather' and the second council of war in two days! For the King's coming 'Great p<sup>r</sup>par<sup>a</sup>tion was made'. Wednesday the 15th came!

This day fair weather. This morning about 11 of ye Clock his Maj^tie was Entertained most magnificently coming on board at ye time w^th Guns fireing from all Ships & all Forts on Shore who after Respect was payed him from all ye Cap^ts in ye Fleet was pleased to bestow ye Hono^e of Knighthood upon 2 of them Viz Capt Clowdsley Shovell Com^dr of ye *Edgar* & Capt John Ashley [Ashby] Comd^r of ye *Defyance* & alsoe ten Shills a man to Every one yt Engaged.[49]

From the *London Gazette* of 16th–20th May, whose readers had on the 9th been given, 'From on board . . . *Elizabeth*', an inspired and coloured account of the action its result and casualties, one gathers that the sum provided for disbursement was £2600 (actually it was £2,583) and that Herbert received indication that a patent of earldom would be granted him.[50] He struck his flag on the 16th[51] and, having given his flag-captain Mitchell leave, left for London.[52] Ships were moving to the new rendezvous. The flag of Vice-Admiral Davies, the Union, flew at the foretop of the *Montague*.[53]

Chateaurenault, off Cape Clear on the 13th/3rd, stayed but briefly on the Irish coast. In the course of his homeward passage he captured seven Dutch merchantmen, returning richly laden with the spices of Curacoa, and entered his port on the 18th/8th, just a week after the battle.[54] Dreux de Chateaurenault had delivered his uncle's packages and given his eyewitness account of the sailing and battle. His news was received with such restrained approval that Chateaurenault, two days after return, 20th/10th May felt bound in writing to counter criticism.[55]

It was certain, Chateaurenault maintained, that the battle against Herbert would have been more decisive if Gabaret and Forant had done their duty. After the first firing, the said Gabaret had neglected a signal to bear down *again* on the enemy; he had 'gone about' and, after that–well, one couldn't say he had fought at all! That was why, Chateaurenault reiterated (see p. 140), he had been obliged to assume the lead and grapple with the head of the enemy line which bade fair to place itself between him and Bantry. Five times did he especially crowd sail to fall on Herbert . . . Even those most favourable to Gabaret might be heard to comment that it was because he, Chateaurenault, was not one of Gabaret's friends, that Gabaret would do nothing to increase the glory of the action! Unsupported as he thus was–again he reiterates–the adverse wind strengthening, the sea rising (to the extent that the lowest gun ports could not be opened) prudence dictated he return to attend to the last stages of that *débarquement* which was his *principale affaire*, to collect his brûlots, before the Dutch joined with the English–a contingency he feared–and to look for the English the next day–which he did.

Gabaret sharply rebutted blame. He did not know why Chateaurenault had not borne down on the English centre while he, Gabaret, had so successfully attacked the van and forced disabled English ships to leeward of their own line, any more than he understood why at five o'clock action should have been discontinued. Chefs-d'escadres are not masters of their movements; the commander in chief decides, his 'avant' and 'arrière' guards follow. But, of course (observed Gabaret), the necessary knowledge for competency in issuing orders from the bridge of a flagship can only be acquired '*par une longue pratique à commander des divisions avant de commander en chef!*' Gabaret hoped that the expression of his views would not be taken ill, although he, who had for fifteen years commanded divisions, could now only speak 'comme un particulier dans l'armée'–just an ordinary figure in the navy!

Less splenetic and more informative, Forant advanced that Chateaurenault indeed had the initial advantage but, after the first half hour, left the centre of the line, assumed the lead that should have been reserved to Gabaret and threw all into confusion –'*confusion par sa faute*'–so that captains then ranged themselves indiscriminately to fight. He complained that no signal was ever given to him to bear down, though, after long waiting, he did damagingly attack the enemy rear. Had Chateaurenault signalled at the outset to the whole line to bear orderly down, probably no English ship would have escaped . . . And nobody can understand why, so early in the evening, return to Bantry began. The enemy beaten, Chateaurenault could have returned at leisure for his few brûlots.

Officially, the French inquest on the battle might have been expected to end with a letter of the 24th/14th of May from Louis to 'Monsieur le Comte de Chateaurenault' . . .

J'ai appris avec beaucoup de satisfaction le détail du combat que

vous avez rendu contre les vaisseaux anglais commandés par
Herbert, et je suis bien aise de vous assurer qu'on ne peut être
plus content que je suis de la conduite que vous avez tenue en
cette occasion espérant cependant que, dans la suite de cette
guerre, ou trouvera moyen de remporter sur mes ennemis des
avantages plus décisifs en les coulant à fond et en leur prenant
des vaisseaux.

But Seignelay could not, 8 Juin/29th May resist a postscript![56]

A plain naval verdict on Bantry is necessary.

Twenty-four warships with frigates and other craft had not been
sent out from Brest for the purpose of engaging in set battle an
English (or Anglo-Dutch) fleet but to convey, rather than convoy,
money, munitions of war and men to Ireland.[57] Chateaurenault
had but half completed the purpose of his expedition when, in the
May-day dawnlight, his enemy appeared by the Sheep's Head.
For six hours he withdrew before the threat – respite invaluable to
the slow process of disembarkation, retiral that placed him at the
narrow head of the Bay in a position which Herbert, against the
wind, found it impossible to turn. Maintaining the windward
gage, the Frenchman accepted the combat when he could no
longer avoid it, a battle which he could not afford to lose but which
he was not compelled to win. The initial, the starboard tack
phase, followed (van to van, centre to centre, though hardly rear
to rear) the orthodox plan. But whether, outranged by Chateaurenault's gunnery, much directed against the masts, yards, sails
and rigging of the English vessels, Herbert, after the turn from the
Bay's western shore, denied the weather gage, *could* successfully
have continued from leeward ('under the wind' as the French
would say), on the larboard tack, close ship-to-ship, line encounter, is open to question. He certainly did not attempt to do
so. He 'lasked' away across the wind to southward, in hope to
draw on his adversary to the open sea, where, perhaps, the
weather-gage might, in the closing hours of the evening, have been
obtained and the disembarkation, leagues away, left uncovered.
Chateaurenault refused the lure and, properly, returned to assure
the completion of his disembarkation, his *'principale affaire'*. Yet,
had Herbert, at that late stage, gained sea-room and the gage, it

would have profited him nothing. On his own showing, he was not 'in any condition to follow them or make any further attempt upon them'. A night and a morning he lay licking his wounds before he was ready to sail for his rendezvous off Scilly. And, though the English admiral knew it not, the absence of amity between the French admiral and his chefs-d'escadres, as also of agreement among them concerning the functions of the squadrons of the line and the right use of signals, had almost certainly saved him from a worse defeat.

In his celebrated treatise, le père Paul Hoste[58] makes reference to Bantry Bay. From theorizing of the battle line and the advantage of fighting 'with the wind' he turns to consider whether a commander, equal in strength to his enemy, would ever prefer to do battle from an 'under the wind' station. There be some, the writer declares, who hold that the benefits of the leeward outweigh the advantages of the windward gage–a choice mistaken! Yet the benefits are real. In strong wind, the sea running high, in any case in which the weaker must face the stronger, they are undeniable. To particularize–the use of the lowest tier of guns will be assured; a damaged ship can quit the line, go 'down the wind' to repair; the commander may usually exercise the option of breaking off the combat. It is true that a strong force may pursue at will a broken enemy to leeward; but, if night be coming on, or wind or sea rising or a would-be pursuer be burdened by responsibility for other duties such as protection of convoy or a disembarkation, the pursuit will not occur. Referring to Herbert's force as though it were an Anglo-Dutch fleet, Hoste declares, '*Les Alliez profitèrent de ces avantages dans le Combat de Bantri l'an 1689*', for then the '*escadre à peu près égale*' used the leeward gage in a manner of which he, Hoste, theoretically approved. Equally, Chateaurenault, achieving and prudently assuring his '*débarquement*' but robbed of battle victory, deserved in Hoste's opinion the full measure of the '*applaudisement*' he received of Louis upon his return home.

At the news from Bantry the French and the Irish in Dublin lost all sense of proportion:

It was not thought enough to cry up the advantage of the French at Bantry over a single squadron only of the English fleet into a complete and glorious victory, though never a ship taken or sunk or the pursuit followed. Every day supplied us with fresh fables of the entire defeat of both English and Dutch fleets, and with hyperbolical and monstrous relations of the greatness of the French both as to the number and bigness of ships: whilst both the former, which for so many years had been the terror of the seas . . . were vilified to such a degree as if they had been but a few Algiers pirates or Newfoundland fishermen. The incredible number of arms reputed to be brought from France would have furnished Xerxes' army and they, added to what were before in the kingdom, made not up 50,000 men. The millions of money spoken of would have impoverished Croesus and broken the bank of Venice, . . .[59]

My Lord Dover, under no restraint and, doubtless, some provocation, declared that no battle had even taken place at Bantry–the English had looked in to reconnoitre and, having seen what they wanted, sailed off with random shots![60] But if James was as disinclined as Lord Dover to rejoice in the defeat of an English fleet as such,[61] he could do no less than order the singing of a *Te Deum* and fireworks for the diversion of the Dublin crowd.[62] His reaction to the news was a desire to exploit an unexpectedly promising situation. Intent on retaining the French fleet on Irish shores he first asked d'Avaux to request Chateaurenault to safeguard the reshipment from Bantry to Waterford or Dublin of the heavy munitions, which, unlike marching men or boxes of money, could not be passed over the bad mountain roads. When it was pointed out to him that he already had three frigates at Waterford to which could be entrusted that task he put in a 'mémoire'–a document of considerable interest which clearly revealed his mind. Chateaurenault's fleet should be brought into the waters separating England and Scotland from Ireland; the use he, James, would propose for them would shorten the business–a chance *'qui peutestre ne reviendra pas'*. For Chateaurenault would clear the intervening sea of the two frigates and five or six other vessels then interrupting communications with Scotland and, by taking siege cannon to Londonderry, expedite its fall. Under its cover 10,000 troops could, without delay, be landed at Troon ten miles from Glasgow; the Highlanders would collect and, in two days,

Stirling (its castle a weak store-house of arms) would be reached; three days beyond lay Edinburgh. To the fleet the operation could present no possible danger. Its work accomplished, it would slip away through the North Channel, along, and wide of, the West coast of Ireland and so, unobserved, home. A new French fleet (James assumed that such was already under mobilization)–or, alternatively, Chateaurenault returning–would do well to steer for Anglesey to put ashore the several thousand French troops such a fleet would no doubt bring. If then it were found that the Prince of Orange had committed himself to a march toward Edinburgh, might not his line be cut by the landed French troops? In the event of the Prince holding back to defend London, those troops could link with James marching toward the capital city. Chateaurenault had cleared Irish waters before the 'memoire', dated the 6th May, was placed in the hands of d'Avaux; it is practically certain that not even verbal indications of James's desires reached him, and it is most unlikely that Chateaurenault would in any case have heeded James's wishes. Two fourth rates *Swallow* and *Jersey* off Liverpool, the *Bonadventure*, a fourth, in Lough Ryan (?), the three fourths, *Deptford*, *Antelope* and *Portland*, the fifth *Dartmouth* and the *Henrietta* yacht, detached, under Rooke's command, off Scilly, by Herbert, even if collected into a single squadron could have done little against the French twenty-four ships of the line with attendant '*fregattes*'. The English ships, individual or in squadron, brushed aside, the briefest spell of command in the Irish Sea and North Channel should have availed Chateaurenault to place siege artillery on the shores of the Lough. A longer stay might have yielded incalculable sequelae. With nothing to fear if a second Bantry battle were forced upon him by markedly inferior forces, with the way home by western Ireland open and unimpeded, Chateaurenault might well have extended that stay to the time required by the Admiralty to equip from the half dozen ships in Irish waters, from those of Herbert in Spithead (in no happy plight!) and any others that could be sent to sea, a fleet capable of challenging with likelihood of success a second Bantry encounter. Who shall say that James's plan was unsound and that the interim would not have sufficed to bring about the fall of the rebel city–possibly allow of James's passage with troops

to beckoning Troon?[63] James, on the 7th May, the day after the
singing of *Te Deum*, the firework display and the drafting of the
memoire, opened an inexperienced and rancorous Irish Parliament anxious to recast the whole body of Caroline Acts of Settlement and Explanation. News came in from Hamilton before
Derry. Though, in the course of the night of 5th/6th May, a
surprise attack had dislodged from the Windmill Hill (a garrison
outpost some 500 yards from the south-western Bishop's Gate) its
defenders, by a determined sortie the besieged had redressed the
loss. Brigadier Ramsey, endeavouring to stay his fliers, had fallen,
together with many other officers and at least 200 men. 'Four or
five colours' and spoil had passed to the rebels.[64] Two days later,
d'Avaux, writing to Louvois, trying to put right misunderstanding
about, *'eschange de troupes Irlandoises contre des Françoises'*, after complaining that Hamilton, in disobedience to *'l'ordre expres'* of
James, still allowed numbers of 'mouths' to leave the city, handed
on news of the local Londonderry rout. Sunk in pessimism, he
concluded, *'j'apprehende fort que le Roy d'Angleterre ne fosse perir toutes
ses troupes en detail devant cette place.'*[65] But James could still make
promises. He would dispatch more troops; a great mortar and
two pieces of battery should be sent by land and the same number
by sea![66] As James had just turned down a suggestion made by de
Pointis that the three French frigates at disposal (see p. 148)
should be ordered to bombard Londonderry (a project which
Melfort, reminding his master of the presence of English forces off
the Foyle, had been the first to ridicule), he, James, cannot have
rated the gun-running chances as high. Nor, for that matter, can
an alternative proposal to dispatch the frigates to burn the
shipping of 'Erpoul' have appeared more feasible. In any case the
frigates were still carting arms from Kinsale to Waterford.[67]

James was destined to remain long in Dublin, there to receive
continuous bad news and, Melfort beside him, to work at cross-
purposes with Tyrconnel with d'Avaux and with the unloved
Irish. James's prophecy: *'occasion qui peutestre ne reviendra pas'*,
his Fate would ineluctably fulfil!

Though the Bantry affair dominates the naval scene in this the
first half of May, there are other happenings to tell.

Captain Killigrew in the *Dragon*–with him Hozier in the *Sapphire*–ignorant of danger survived, brought into Plymouth the expected seasonal trade convoy from Cadiz (see p. 59 *ante*). He had anchored on the 5th and passed forward to the Downs, cargoes, largely of silver and worth 'upwards of 300,000 l'[68] only three days before Chateaurenault and his fleet of thirty re-entered the Iroise with French flags streaming over seven captured vessels of the Dutch Curacao Spice fleet.[69] Gratifyingly to the Government Killigrew could report: 'the Algerines continue the war still against France and keep the peace with us'.[70]

The conduct of certain captains at this time attracts attention. Herbert, on the 9th, was informed that the Admiralty was not satisfied with Botham of the *Warspight* delaying in the Downs when he should have been with the Bantry fleet;[71] on the 10th Elliot of the *Centurion* was dismissed command;[72] by the 11th, so report ran, Hozier, suspected of intent to hand over the *Sapphire* to James, had been placed by Killigrew under arrest.[73] There is nothing to indicate that the authorities viewed these cases of political dissidence with special alarm. For a different reason–that of 'extorting great summs of money' from Protestants lately brought over from Ireland–Wolfran Cornwall, of the *Swallow*, was said to have cause to fear trial.[74] No pusillanimity characterized the widespread, incidental encounters at sea which preceded or followed the official Declaration of War upon the 7th instant. For example *Gazette* readers were proudly told how the *Nonsuch*, a small fourth rate of thirty-six guns, fell in, off Guernsey, with two French men-of-war, one of thirty guns and 120 men, the other of sixteen guns and six patereroes and 120(?) men convoying twenty small merchantmen for Newfoundland, how, in the engagement, the captain Roomcoyle, the master and the cook were killed, the carpenter wounded. The *Nonsuch* bore no lieutenant; so the boatswain, Robert Sincocke assumed command, fought for three hours, captured both French men-of-war and brought them into Plymouth. The *Tyger*, which was to leeward of *Nonsuch*, fell among the merchantmen and was assumed to have accounted for them.[75] The talk of the town went further–William, it was said, hearing of the exploit had ordered a gratuity, gold chain and medal be given to Sincocke and the command of the *Nonsuch*![76] It would indeed be interesting to know whether Boatswain Sincocke, receiving the surrender of the senior of two wounded French captains attached to the name 'Jean Bart' (supposing it to have been given) the significance of gathering fame.

In the preceding September, Seignelay, at the instance of Louis, had asked Patoulet the Intendant at Dunkerque to select and equip two vessels which he and M. Louvois (the one) and M. de Croissy (the other) would send out, *au pair*, as privateers. The Intendant was required to suggest a Dunkerque commander; and Jean Bart was selected.

The capture in October of a Dutchman (en français *le Cheval-Marin*), confirmed Seignelay's confidence[77] – *la Railleuse* (Bart), was doubtless among '*les armateurs françois*' which called forth William's mid-December instructions to Herbert (see p. 25 *ante*) and his orders against '*Corsaires françois dans cette mer*' (the Channel) (see p. 29 *ante*) at the month end. Late in April two Spanish prizes, one laden with mahogany, another with gold-dust, silver and pepper, were taken into Havre by Bart and Forbin. Bart, to utilize his earlier-gained knowledge of Dutch commercial navigation, proposed to Seignelay a scheme more systematic than promiscuous privateering; but the Secrétaire-d'état stated that the four vessels which Bart required for his purpose were '*destinés pour servir dans le corps d'armée*' and, in the same letter showed his personal predilection for profitable privateering. Consequently Bart, in *la Railleuse*, and Forbin, in one of the adapted Spanish prizes now named *Les Jeux* prepared for sea – their orders, the moment war should be declared, '*courir sur les Anglais*'.[78] Seignelay proposed, Louis disposed! Bart, Forbin subordinate, was ordered to convoy fourteen merchantmen from Havre to La Rochelle. He left the former port on 20th/10th May. Off the Casquetts on the 22nd/12th an English forty-eight and a forty-two, say the French, were sighted. Intent to board, Bart steered to port, Forbin (at Bart's command) to starboard of the larger English vessel; three of the merchantmen better armed than the rest were to hold off the lesser Englishmen and aid the convoy to escape. Forbin did succeed on a wind in reaching his enemy's decks. Bart was less fortunate and his lieutenant deserted in the action. The lesser Englishmen came back from chasing the merchantmen and the carnage of two hours or more ended as the *London Gazette* told.[79] But of Jean Bart–more anon!

By the 4th May, the Irish soldiers previously interned in the Isle of Wight had been embarked for service with the Emperor;[80] the second troop of English guards had been put aboard for Holland,[81] and the Earl of Marlborough escorted to take charge of the English forces in the Low Countries.[82] The Hague packets sailed as was necessary; collier and fishing protection obtained.[83]

Thus, though in the Channel and North Sea French privateers roamed and made captures, neither the English–nor the Dutch– use of those waters was seriously disputed and, by default of Chateaurenault and the presence of Rooke's squadron, command extended firmly over St George's Channel and the Irish Sea where it was especially needed.

Major General Kirke, obeying Marshal Schomberg's orders (see p. 121, accompanied by Brigadier Trelawney, reached Liverpool by the 5th May, gave to Colonels Stewart and St George command of John Cunningham's and Solomon Richards' regiments (see p. 121) and held 'several councils-of-war about embarking the four regiments'. Three days later, Stevens, the King's messenger to Londonderry (see p. 122), returning, landed at Liverpool, informed Kirke that Londonderry was still in Protestant hands, gave some account of the action at Pennyburn on the 21st April and hurried to Whitehall. For the last fortnight, a certain Captain Jacob Richards and four French officers, appointed in London to carry out a special Londonderry mission, had been waiting for Kirke to complete arrangements for them to sail. Richards now–on the 10th–received the detailed instructions which Kirke had been empowered to draft; and, on the 12th, with the four Frenchmen, a lieutenant, ensign and fifty gunners and miners, embarked in the merchant ketch *Edward and James* (master Mr Meers) of Liverpool. Next morning 'among sands great and many' of the Mersey-Dee outfalls, the frigate *Greyhound* (Captain Gwillam) and the *Kingfisher* ketch, from Highlake, 'where also lay the *Swallow* and *Bonadventure* and several other ships under convoy', picked up Mr Meers' ketch. Richards transferred to the *Greyhound*. His instructions were to sail within cannon

shot of Culmore, prospect for batteries or boom, acquire information and report; he might proceed to Londonderry only if the
venture were likely to leave intact the ship.[84] In London the
arrival of Mr Stevens provoked, no doubt, the sharp reminder
which this same day, the 13th May, went out from the office of the
Secretary of State for the South, of the King's 'no little concern'
that Kirke 'was still this side of the water'. Fully ready or not, let
him 'immediately sail for Londonderry'.[85]

Lastly, diplomatic matters. Almost six full months had elapsed
since Louis had declared war on the rulers of the United Provinces,
five since William expelled Barillon, ambassador to the court of
St James, two since the States General, in return, had issued their
declaration against Louis. In spite of continuous French privateering and the support given to Louis by James, William, no less King
than Stadholder, had not (much else upon his hands) considered
it convenient to address diplomatic challenge to his royal rival. On
the other hand, the King of France simply did not recognize the
Stadholder's regal existence and, as treaties and declarations of
war were only negotiated or made between princes, he was under
no obligation of etiquette to threaten a pretension. The declaration
of war, formalizing the hostility that Bantry had made unmistakable, was dated the 7th May. Its naval significance was general;
but the reference to seized colonies, interrupted trade, the pre-
eminence of navigation, the 'right of the flag' and, to some extent
the mention of Ireland, point to the recognition of the necessary
rôle of the Navy in the expanding war.[86]

Four days after the publication of the Declaration, 11th/21st
May, the Anglo-Dutch Naval Convention, debated since early
January (see p. 34) was at last signed; but 'at the request of the
English commissioners' was ante-dated to 29th April.[87] As Sir
George Clark has observed:

In the naval history of Europe this treaty is important because,
except for the details of the number of ships, it lays down the
lines on which the co-operation of the English and the Dutch
was to continue throughout the two great wars of William III
and Anne.[88]

It consisted of fifteen clauses which completed the basic agreements concerning fleet ratios, theatres of operation and command tentatively attained two months previously. These, already outlined in this work (see p. 65), need not be repeated; but, for the appreciation of the degree of understanding reached over such matters as councils of war and discipline, the allocation of prizes, the mutual acceptance of convoy duties and the protection of West Indian possessions the summary provided in Appendix H must be consulted.

At the date on which signatures were mutually appended to the documents no single Dutch ship had reached rendezvous. Some folk were complaining that, had Nottingham accepted on the 9th March, at the first meeting of the joint Commissioners, the date originally proposed by the Dutch for the union–*viz.* the 20th April, rather than the 30th April, Herbert's fleet at Bantry would have been larger and more effective. Nottingham, in an aide-mémoire of self-justification, reveals no qualms. The reasons for refusing the 20th had been well-known to the Dutch–the sheer inability of the English to get the whole of the fifty large ships, the projected new treaty quota, out of dock by that date. With forty of those fifty ships at sea, and the English obligations to the States under the old Treaty of 1677/8 or that of 1685 fully kept, it had surely been reasonable to expect the Dutch not to hang back with *every* ship of their thirty till all the English fifty were with the flag? When Nottingham reflected on all he had done by 'frequent consorting w$^t$ ye admty wh was not properly [his] business', he could well 'presume to say [it] did follow y$^t$ Adm$^{ll}$ Herbert was at Sea some days perhaps weeks sooner than otherwise he would have been'.[89] With that the historian must agree.

### REFERENCES

1 A *Journall of my Travels since the Revolution* . . . edited by Murray, R. H. as *The Journal of John Stevens* containing a brief *account of the War in Ireland 1689–1691* Oxford 1912 pp. 41–5; a list of the fleet given by Stevens differs little from that which actually sailed; pp. 39–41 provide a careful account of the appearance and organization of the port of Brest. John Stevens, scholar and soldier, who, at the time of the Revolution was collector of Excise in Wales, crossed from England to Paris, volunteered for the cause of James and sailed with this expedition. For life, amending that of the *D.N.B.*, see preface to the above-named work.

2 Archives de la Marine, B⁴ 12 f.69. Relation du combat contre le Vice-Amiral Herbert–written in Chateaurenault's own hand to Seignelay–transcribed by Sue, *op. cit.*, IV pp. 317–325. Troude O. *Batailles Navales de la France*, Paris 1867, VI, pp. 190–4 made use of Sue and de la Roncière, *op. cit.* pp. 47–51, of both Sue and Calmon-Maison for whom see Note (3).

3 Calmon-Maison, J. J. R., *Le Maréchal de Chateau-Renault (1637–1716)* Paris 1903; *La Grande Encyclopédie* . . . Paris, Larousse and Hoefer for biographical detail. For the reprimand to Chateaurenault, Archives de la Marine, B² 28, f.345, as referred to and quoted by Calmon-Maison pp. 47–9.

4 From this point to the conclusion of the first paragraph on p. 134 ('safety of his charge') the authority is Chateaurenault's dispatch referred to, note (2), p. 131 with additional data introduced from Stevens' *Journall*.

5 Stevens *op. cit.* p. 43, speaks of 'very thick fog'; he is the authority for the meeting of the ships and the holding of the consultation. Fog (which today means a visibility of under ½ mile) is infrequent over the open sea especially west of Ireland; but at any hour of observation *may* be encountered as often as 35 to 40 days in the year off Scilly–*Irish Coast Pilot, 1954*, p. 30, and *West Coast of England Pilot, 1948*, p. 34, Hydrographic Department, Admiralty. The identification by Sue in a note, *op. cit.* p. 317, of Galloway (Galway) with the Galloway of the Scottish Mull is an unexpected lapse! d'Avaux will be found (in a letter to Louvois 14 Aoust) employing the spelling 'Galloway' for Galway 'Car Galloway n'a point de port, ce n'est qu'une rade, et la grande mer y est si violente quand il soufle un vent d'ouest que les vaisseaux en hyver en pouroient bien in commodez' *Négociations* . . . *d'Avaux*, p. 388. One may comment that Chateaurenault would not have found Galway Bay an ideal Springtime anchorage!

6 Stevens, *ibid.*, says they approached within half a league of Castlehaven, roughly two thirds of the way between Kinsale and Cape Clear and that Chateaurenault captured a small Ostender.

7 Stevens, p. 44, speaks of the 'extraordinary bay . . . between four and five leagues in length . . . The largest ships may anchor anywhere, close under the shore there being for the most part within a hundred yards of it fourteen or fifteen fathom water'. He most carefully remarks the place of anchorage. Chateaurenault's own estimate 'huit lieues' from the intended place of disembarkation was a miscalculation.

The estimates of numbers landed vary. *A Jacobite Narrative* . . ., p. 71 'gentlemen and officers Irish, English, French and with about three thousand Irish soldiers who had been in England the winter before against the invasion of Orange'. There can be no justification for the latter part of this statement. Such as came over were interned in the Isle of Wight. Troude, *op. cit.* p. 190 says 6,000! After all, Stevens, a meticulous narrator, was at the landing.

A Chart of the battle is provided.

8 Balgoben. This place is not marked (though perhaps indication might have been expected) on any Petty map. *v. Hibernia Deliniatio quoad hactenus licuit Perfectissima Studio Guilielmi Petty* . . . *1690*; but it is to be found on two other maps of the period *L'Irlanda o'vero Hibernia* . . . del Molto R. P. Agostino Lubin . . . Geografo Ordinario de S. M. Christianissima . . . Giacomo Rossi, Roma 1689, the map can be seen in *Atlante Veneto* . . . studio del

Padre Maestro Coronelli . . . Venetia 1690– and in *Le Neptune François Carte Générale des Costes Occidentales d'Angleterre.* In the former map Balgoben is placed at the head of Glengariff Bay at the outfall of the river Glengariff, in the latter, as Balgobban, at the head of the outfall of the Bantry River. Stevens's narrative, p. 44, points conclusively to the Bantry Creek. d'Avaux often refers to Bantry as the scene of disembarkation.

9 For the cold and the suffering of the men, Stevens, *op. cit.* p. 44. Various English ship logs note the weather (*v.* note (12) *infra*). The moon was four days past the full. Pond, *An Almanack for the Year of our Lord God 1689,* Cambridge 1689.

10 *Irish Coast Pilot, 1954* (Hydrographic Dept. Admiralty) p. 223.

11 *An Exact Relation of the most Remarkable Transactions that happened lately in Ireland With an Account of a great Sea Fight between the English and French Fleets,* in B.M.807, f.36, 12.

12 Logs of *Elizabeth* (Captain's and Lieutenant's), *Cambridge* (Master's and Captain's), *Defiance, Mary* (Master's) for the time and Logs of *Elizabeth* (Lieutenant's), *Advice* (Master's), *Ruby* for weather.

13 Log of *Advice* (Master's).

14 Logs of *Advice* (Master's), *Defiance;* H.M.C. Finch II, p. 206.

15 Logs of *Elizabeth* (Captain's), *Greenwich* (Lieutenant's), *Mary* (master's), *Deptford, Ruby, Diamond* (at 5 o'clock) for signal. For examples of clearing, log of *Defiance*–as early as the 29th; and log of *Elizabeth* (Lieutenant's) 'gott down Chests & hammocks & by 12 at night [Ap. 30] gott a Clear Ship'.

16 Log of *Advice* (Master's).

17 *Ibid.*

18 Log of *Ruby.*

19 Log of *Elizabeth* (Lieutenant's) 'smooth water'.

20 *v.* note (10) *ante.*

21 Log of *Ruby* 'we made divers boards before we could get up w$^{th}$ them'.

22 *Cambridge* (Master's), *Defiance, Advice* (Master's), *Elizabeth* (Lieutenant's).

23 Stevens *op. cit.* p. 44. An anchor is a-peak when the cable holding it is vertical to the ship's side–the anchor ready for lifting from the sea-bed.

24 Log of *Cambridge* (Master's).

25 Stevens *op. cit.* p. 43.

26 *H.M.C. Finch II,* p. 206.

27 All 24 warships, or, rather, their commanders, are named by Chateau-renault as taking part in the battle. The list above is as it appears in a version of Archives de la Marine B$^4$ 12 f.60 printed by Calmon-Maison *op. cit.* Where the commander's name as given by the admiral in his report materially differs from that in Calmon-Maison's transcription, it is placed in square brackets. The figures for 'canons et équipages' are supplied from the data for the same ships in the battle of Bévéziers (Beachy Head)– Archives de la Marine B$^4$ 12 f.404 reproduced in Calmon-Maison, *op. cit.* p. 321. Further figures are inserted, for 'canons' only, from tables given for ships engaged in the battle of La Hougue shown in Ordre de Bataille de Combat de l'année 1692, le 25 de juillet–Bibliothèque Nationale, Estampes 1c, 6. reproduced in de la Roncière, *op. cit.* p. 69. It may be conceded that a given ship at different times might not carry precisely the same number of

guns–but variation was not wide. The 'canon' entries which are asterisked are inserted from Troude, *op. cit.* p. 192. I have not traced his source. Troude's entries for other ships are sometimes more, sometimes less than those selected. Total guns shown in above table = 1258. Troude = 1244.

28 All mentioned in Chateaurenault's report.

29 The Master of the *Cambridge* counted 28. Aboard *Advice* and *Ruby* 27 were noted. *v.* Logs.

30 The 'perticular list' is that contained in *Memoirs relating to the Lord Torrington*, ed. Laughton (Sir) J. K. Camden Society, 1889, p. 37. The author is unknown. For critical comment on his use of Burchett, J. *Memoirs of Transactions at Sea during the War with France 1688–1697*, 1703, *v.* Powley, *op. cit.* Appendix. In the short account of the battle of Bantry Bay, which includes the 'perticular list', verbatim quotation of Burchett (by unacknowledged incorporation) extends to about one-third of the narrative; but Burchett does not provide the 'perticular list' or any other–though he must have had access to all usual official material. In the list 6 Pat. = 6 patereroes (small guns). (For derivation and variants of this interesting word see *N.E.D.*) 2 m = 2 minions–also small guns.

The 'official list' referred to in this work (p. 138) is part of a document in the possession of the earl of Dartmouth, Patshull House, Wolverhampton, entitled: 'Mr Pepys' report to the Honorable the Committee appointed to prepare an address about Ireland . . . and the reason of Admirall Herbert having but 19 ships in the fight at Bantry.' A table shows ships (*with* guns and complements but not commanders) in commission at various dates, 1st Nov. 1688, 16th Dec. 1688, 20th Feb. 1688/9 and present at Bantry. The first three sets of entries are obviously extracted from Pepys's own papers. That for 20th Feb. is, slightly rearranged, identical with the last submitted for that date to the Committee on Miscarriages of Ireland (9th Aug. 1689, *H.M.C. XII, App. Pt vi, H. of L.*, p. 186), obviously the 'Committee' referred to in the Patshull document. The document is in one hand. It is not printed at p. 252 in *H.M.C. XI, v. Dartmouth.* This Patshull list gives for the nineteen 3rds and fourths 12 guns less than in the *Memoirs . . .* table. It shows *Saudadoes* present–but not *Firedrake* or *Sallemander.* According to Pepys's 'Register' in Tanner *op. cit.* (*v.* p. 64, note (41), p. 298; *Fire Drake* and *Salamander* had been fitted as Bombers in 1688 and 1687 respectively.

The Christian names of the Captains are not included in either list; they are added to the 'perticular list' from P.R.O. Adm. 8/2, Ship List 7th May, which includes the vessels returning from Bantry. The names of the lieutenants of those ships are also given. To complete the information missing from both the 'perticular' and Patshull lists, add, from the 7th May table,

Yacht Fubbs        35 — John Johnson
Yacht Henrietta    30 — William Sanderson

The 7th May table makes Votier captain of the *Sallemander.*

31 Log of *Mary* (Master's). *London Gazette*, 6th–9th May. Referred to by *Luttrell, op. cit.* 6th May.

32 Log of *Advice* (Master's).

33 Log of *Mary* (Master's), supplemented by logs of *Advice* (Master's), *Deptford.*

34 *H.M.C. Finch II*, p. 206.
35 Logs of *Greenwich* (Captain's and Lieutenant's–the latter specifying 'upon his crosstrees at maintopmast head') and *Mary* (Master's).
36 Log of *Greenwich* (Lieutenant's).
37 *H.M.C. Finch II*, p. 206 and Chateaurenault's dispatch Archives de la Marine B⁴ 12 f.69.
38 Logs of *Greenwich* (Captain's), *Defiance* and *Advice* (Master's) and Chateaurenault's reference to Panétier leading the line. According to Chateaurenault two of the leading English ships, on their way into the line, were roughly handled by two of Forant's rear-guard, which were themselves struggling into position.
39 *H.M.C. Finch II*, p. 206.
40 Logs of *Elizabeth* and *Mary* (Master's) for Chateaurenault's flag (by 6 o'clock) and *Elizabeth* (Captain's) and *Diamond* for Herbert's. (*Elizabeth* ¼ hr after Chateaurenault, *Diamond* 7).
41 See positions as plotted for 8 p.m. from entries in the logs of *Elizabeth* (Captain's), *Cambridge* (Captain's), *Diamond*, *Edgar*, *Advice* (Master's).
42 Archives de la Marine B⁴ 12 f.60. tabulated by Calmon-Maison *op. cit.* p. 319.
43 From 'The after-battle reflections of the English admiral . . .' (p. 141) *v.* Herbert's dispatch, Finch II, p. 206. The authority for damage is, of course, the logs. *Elizabeth* (Captain's), *Cambridge* (Master's), *Mary* (Master's) the rest as indicated in Ch. VI, p. 106 note (29). For casualties, *London Gazette* 'From on board H.M.S. *Elizabeth*, 2 May 1689' in issue of 6th–9th May. For comment on the casualties, *v.* Keevil, J. J. *Medicine and the Navy 1200–1900*, 3 v. London and Edinburgh, 1957–. v. II, p. 171.
44 For times of 'lying by', logs of *Cambridge*; for funeral the logs indicated. The log of *Elizabeth* 2nd May (Lieutenant's) records that the flagship 'Knowled ye Capt Helmer'. His widow received a pension of £100 under the sign manual of the King, 11th June. P.R.O. Adm. 3/1 19th June.
    John Shelley's career provides an interesting example of ship changes which an officer of this era, lucky enough to keep in more or less continuous employ, might experience. Commissioned in 1664 as lieutenant in the *Assurance* (4th), Shelley captained, in turn, four fireships, served as first lieutenant aboard the *London* (1st), became second captain of the *Monmouth* (3rd), then captain, successively, of the *Portland* (4th) and the *Diamond* (4th), after which he had two more appointments to fireships followed by command of the *Dartmouth* (5th) in this expedition, before being once more piped aboard the *Portland*! (*v.* Pepys's 'Sea Commission Officers . . .', Tanner, *op. cit. N.R.S. xxvi.*)
    The replacement of Aylmer by Shelley resulted in the transfer of Leake from the *Fire Drake* to the *Dartmouth*. If we are to credit Sir Stephen Martin Leake, *The Life of Sir John Leake* (edited by Callender (Sir) G., N.R.S. v. LII, it was *Fire Drake* which, 'by means of a cushee piece' (p. 23) wrought the havoc in Coetlogon's *le Diamant* (*v.* p. 140) but I do not know on what demonstrable authority the assertion stands, believable only on the supposition that the *Fire Drake* was ever near enough, and lucky enough, to be able to lob into the stern of the Frenchman a projectile from one of its two mortars–a bomb, the fuse of which was lighted before insertion in the

barrel for firing. Chateaurenault's dispatch referring to the matter, does not rule out the possibility

> Il arriva une aventure terrible au chevalier de Coetlogon par le feu qui fut mis, à ce qu'on peut juger, par un boulet aux gargousses de poudre qui étaient dans la chambre de conseil, qui enleva la dunette . . .

45 For detaching the *Mary*, logs *Elizabeth* (Lieutenant's) and *Mary*.

46 Rooke, off Kinsale, reported to Nottingham on the 5th, *H.M.C. Finch II*, p. 207. Rooke's Instructions, dated the 4th, had ordered him to sail to the Copelin (Copeland) Islands, find and take under his command the *Bonadventure, Swallow, Jersey, Greyhound* and *Kingfisher Ketch*. On the way, arrived there or sailing on an otherwise chosen station between Scotland and Ireland, he was required to take or destroy any ships encountered belonging to the French King, or his subjects, and to deal likewise with the ships of 'any nation whatsoever' known to be concerned in the transport of men, arms or ammunition without the King's authority to the Irish or Scottish shores. Rooke should, moreover, seek out and destroy 'all boats and little vessels' sheltering in Irish harbours and capable of the work of transport. He was required on his arrival in the North Channel to report to Duke Hamilton and, thereafter, to send dispatches to Lord Nottingham and Herbert. The Admiral hoped that Rooke would find time, in some suitable harbour, to clean and tallow his ships!

Rooke, off Kinsale, reported to Nottingham on the 5th, *H.M.C. Finch II*, p. 207, and, in due course, 11th May, to Duke Hamilton, sending the Duke with a covering letter 'a Truè Copy' of Herbert's Instructions. The true copy and letter are in the Lennoxlove MSS. For letter see *H.M.C. Hamilton*, VI, vi, p. 184. Log of Elizabeth (Lieutenant's) except for the reference to the *Ruby's* prizes for which see *London Gazette* 9th–13th May. The passage of the fleet from Bantry could be followed in many logs. The Master of the *Cambridge*, for instance, notes the mishap to the flagship—how it happened and when she got off. *London Gazette*, 13th–16th May.

47 *H.M.C. Finch II*, p. 208. The *Mary* bearing Herbert's report to the King had reached Portsmouth by the 7th. Logs *Mary*.

48 P.R.O. Adm. 3/1 under date.

49 Log of *Elizabeth* (Lieutenant's). For further career of Shovell, (Sir) Clowdisley (1650–1707) destined to a distinguished career and a watery grave, see *D.N.B.*; for Ashby, (Sir) John (d. 1693) also see *D.N.B.*

50 *London Gazette*, 6th–9th May, 2nd May: 16th–20th May, Portsmouth, 16th May. For amount of bounty P.R.O. Adm. 49/173 f.9. For other English accounts see Newsletters, e.g. in *H.M.C. XII*, App. vii, *Le Fleming MSS*, pp. 240–1—One states that the King also ordered £10 to each seaman's widow and £3 to each fatherless child. Another reported that Herbert had redeemed his repulse by taking eight of the French fleet and killing their admiral. *v.* also p.135, note (11)–that account anything but veracious! Evelyn's was condemnatory alike of admiral and government 'A fight by Admiral Herbert with the French, imprudently setting on them in a Creeke as they were landing men &c in Ireland by which we came off with Great slaughter, & little honour so strangely negligent & remisse in preparing a timely & sufficient fleete' *Diary* (ed. de Beer) IV, p. 639. The *Gazette* [de France] follows 'Par privilège du Roy' its issue du 21 Mai with a factual

and fair 'Relation du Combat . . .' dated 27 Mai, based on Chateaurenault's report to Seignelay.
51 Logs of *Elizabeth*.
52 Log of *Cambridge* (Master's).
53 Log of *Elizabeth* (Lieutenant's) 2nd June entry. On that day 2nd June Davies transferred to *Resolution*. P.R.O. Adm. 3/1 1st May for commissioning Captain Davies as vice and Lord Berkeley as rear *v.* p. 119, note (93).
54 *v.* Gazette referred to in note (50) which supplies some details of Chateaurenault's return to Brest missing from the report to Seignelay. Also *London Gazette*, 20th–23rd May, Paris, 28th/18th May and for the fact that six Dutch sail, which parted company with the unfortunate seven on the 46th parallel reached the Texel 24th/14th, *ibid.* 23rd–27th May, Amsterdam 27th/17th May.
55 'Extrait de lettres de MM. de Chateaurenault, Gabaret et Forant, sur ce qu'on leur a écrit que les nouvelles d'Angleterre portaient qu'ils pouvaient remporter sur Herbert un avantage plus considérable 20 mai 1689' as given by Sue, *op. cit.* p. 323.
56 Archives de la Marine, B² 68, f.111, quoted by Calmon-Maison, *op. cit.* p. 123. For Seignelay's later comment *v.* p. 206 note (34).
57 The order 'l'argent, les munitions de guerre, et tous les passagers' is that of d'Avaux. *Négociations . . . d'Avaux*, p. 143, d'Avaux-Louis, 14th/4th May.
58 *L'Art des Armées Navales ou Traité des Evolutions Navales*, Lyon 1697, p. 54.
    Hoste–le père Paul, 1652–1700, of the Society of Jesus, was chaplain to the maréchaux d'Estrées and Tourville in turn. His work, published in Amiens 1697 is of great theoretic and practical value–*La Grande Encyclopédie*.
    It is worth remarking that, among the many illustrations in Hoste's work is a large plate of a French warship, the parts of its hull, masts and rigging named.
59 Stevens, *op. cit.* p. 67.
60 *Négociations . . . d'Avaux*, p. 190, d'Avaux–Louis, 5th June/26th May.
61 *Ibid.* and Dalrymple *op. cit.* p. 332–for the remark attributed on being told of an English defeat 'C'est bien la première fois donc'.
62 *Négociations . . . d'Avaux*, p. 147, d'Avaux–Louis 14th/4th May.
63 For the whole paragraph from 'His reaction . . .' *Négociations . . . d'Avaux*, p. 142, d'Avaux–Louis 14th/4th May; p. 144, 16th/6th; p. 148, 17th/7th; p. 150, 18th/8th; Memoire from James dated 16th/6th–p. 150 p. 155 d'Avaux–Louvois, 14th/4th May; p. 157, 16th/6th and p. 158, 18th/8th p. 160, d'Avaux–Seignelay, 14th/4th May; p. 161, 16th/6th; p. 163, 17th/7th; p. 188, d'Avaux–Louis, 5th June/26th May. The same facts are several times referred to. In an exceeding long letter, Louvois–d'Avaux, le 13 Juin, *Négociations . . . d'Avaux*, p. 284, occurs the sentences: 'Comment est-il possible aussy, que le Roy d'Angleterre puisse penser que la flotte du Roy puisse passer au nord d'Irlande? De pareilles propositions mortifient au dernier point, car elles ostent toute esperance que les affaires du Roy d'Angleterre puissent se restablir . . .'
64 Mackenzie, *op. cit.* (Hempton), p. 225.
65 *Négociations . . . d'Avaux*, pp. 159, 60, 18th/8th May.
66 T.C.D. MSS Siege Letters Box E 2–19, No. 543, 10th May, referred to by Milligan *op. cit.* p. 191.

F

67 *Négociations* . . . *d'Avaux*, p. 135, d'Avaux–Seignelay, 7th May/27th April.
d'Avaux complained to Seignelay that de Pointis hid from him his
actions and dared to put his schemes direct to James in Council! A scathing
reprimand from Seignelay in store. It would tell de Pointis that, apart from
his ordinary duties, he had played 'un bien mauvais parti!' Could he not
see that, on return to France, he would risk being regarded as 'un homme
qui par son incompatibilité seroit absolument inutile au service de Sa
Majesté?' Complete subordination to Rosen, faithful communication with
d'Avaux were demanded. Bombard Londonderry from the sea? Unreason-
able idea. Burn the English coast towns? 'Imagination vive!' . . . But that
much said, the letter (it would be dated 2 Juin) would convey the news that
Louis had graciously granted de Pointis a gratification of 1500 livres in
respect of a wound (by that time received) and it would end more gently
than it began–reprimand toned to solicitation.
Clément, P. *op. cit.* pp. 343, 6.

68 *London Gazette*, 6th–9th May. Luttrell, *op. cit.* 6th May.

69 *v.* note (54), p. 144.

70 Luttrell, *op. cit.* 6th May.

71 P.R.O. Adm. 3/1 under date. On 29th April Sir Henry Bathurst had
attended the Board of Admiralty presenting a Privy Council Order that the
*Benjamin*, Leonard Brown, Master, 80 seamen and soldiers aboard, be given
a protection from impressment to proceed to the East Indies. The Board
had decided to seek the King's 'further directions'. Meanwhile, Botham,
who had been ordered to impress any Englishmen he found in 'foreign'
ships, held up the *Benjamin* and sent an express to the Admiralty asking
whether he should let the ship pass. He was told to do so. *Ibid.* 30th April,
4th May. To stop the *Benjamin* and examine her papers was not blame-
worthy.
The incident is here mentioned because it enables attention to be drawn
to B.M. MS Additional 18989.
Journall of our Intended Voyage by Gods Assistance in the Good Shipp
Benjamin Leonard Browne Comand^r: From England towards East
India. In ye Servise of ye Honerable India Company.
The journal consists of 117 double folio pages neatly written and illustrated
with beautifully executed colour sketches of ports visited. It covers the
period April 1689–31st Oct. 1693, and the voyage to Malacca and back.
The MS. would be well worth editing and annotating.
The fact that Ovington, J., who sailed as chaplain in the *Benjamin*,
published, in 1696, *A Voyage to Suratt in the Year 1689*, a highly instructive
but discursive quarto (the preface of which presents, nonpareil, a fulsome
epistle dedicatory to the Earl of Dorset and Middlesex followed by verses
not the worst that Nahum Tate could write) does not render the suggestion
superfluous.

72 *Ibid.* This dismissal is not surprising. The extent to which Capt. Edmund
Elyott was in the confidence of James can be gathered from the fact that, on
21st December 1688, he was made the emissary of the King, at Rochester,
to Lord Dartmouth at Spithead. Powley, *op. cit.* p. 155.

73 Luttrell, *op. cit.* 13th May.

74 *Ibid.* 10th May. If so, the storm blew over.

75 *London Gazette*, 13th May (Plymouth) and Luttrell, *op. cit.*, both 13th May.
76 Luttrell, *op. cit.* 16th May.
77 Bib. roy. MSS Colbert Seignelay–Patoulet, quoted by Sue *op. cit.*, iv, p. 136.

Born in Dunkerque, in 1650, of Corsair stock, Bart went to sea at twelve, before sixteen served as mate to a brutal captain, contrived to volunteer aboard de Ruyter's *Zeven Provincien* to share in the Anglo-Dutch Four Days Fight of 1666 and witness, off Chatham, the blockade of London in the year following. When Louis declared war on the Provinces in 1672, Bart surreptitiously returned to Dunkerque and his corsair career began, at first in close association with Keyser. In 1676 in *La Palme* (24) Bart took a Dutch frigate (32) and received from Louis a chain of gold. Colbert, entertaining the idea of forming 'une escadre de course' under Bart's command, stimulated inquiries at Dunkerque which were not to bear fruit till 1690; but Bart's pre-eminence in the home port was beyond question and his marauding in 1678 and '79 as spectacular as ever. For the next few years his course is more obscure; in 1679 he was made lieutenant in the French Navy, served in the Mediterranean and was severely wounded; in 1686 he was promoted capitaine de frégate, *v.* note (79) for authorities.

For the capture of *le Cheval-Marin*, *v.* Sue, *op. cit.* p. 137. This was the encounter (so the legend runs) in which Bart's son, François-Cornille, aged twelve, showed uncontrollable fear. The father, at the tiller, ordered he face the prow and be bound to the mizzen mast, dying men at his feet.

78 Seignelay–Patoulet, Intendant de Dunkerkque 9 Mai 1689, quoted by Sue, *op. cit.* v. p. 141.

Forbin, Claude de, born 1656, at Gardanne (Bouches-de-Rhône) of aristocratic family. Violent and brave, he had so far served in the Mediterranean, America, before Algiers and in Siam. He was destined to continue a colourful career, under Tourville at Bévéziers, 1690, soon after operating with Bart, in 1696 serving with d'Estrées before Barcelona, and, in 1706, unsuccessfully attempting to land the Old Pretender in Scotland. He died 1737. He left *Mémoires* (*v.* Authorities). (*La Grande Encyclopédie*).

79 Sue, *op. cit.* v. p. 142.

Sue in his *Histoire de la Marine Française* is much concerned with the picturesque figure of Jean Bart and dedicates his XVII-century volumes to him. The article on Bart in *La Grande Encyclopédie* is compendious. Fauconier, P. *Description Historique de Dunkerkque*, Bruges, 1735 is of interest; Vanderest, –. *Histoire de Jean Bart*, . . . 1844, and Malo, H., *Les Corsaires: Les Corsaires dunquerquois et Jean Bart*, 2 v. Paris, 1914, (très documenté) are the chief biographies. Norman, C. B. *The Corsairs of France*, 1857 contains a notice of Jean Bart.

80 *London Gazette*, 7th May.
81 Luttrell, *op. cit.* 5th May.
82 *Ibid.* and *London Gazette*, 23rd–27th May (Rotterdam 27th/17th May).
83 P.R.O. Adm. 3/1, *passim*, for whole paragraph.
84 From 'Major General Kirke' (p. 153) to this point Richards' *Diary of the Fleet*. Captain Jacob Richards (*v.* Dalton, C. *English Army Lists and Commission Registers 1661–1714*, 6 v. 1904 III, p. 41) was the son of Colonel Solomon Richards. He had served as an Imperialist engineer at the siege of Buda 1686. See also *D.N.B.* Richards' passage to Ireland is recorded

in detail in the *Diary of the Fleet* and, as typical of the wind, weather and tidal hazard of the then crossing, is worth notice.

On the 15th–breeze 'round the compass'–Anglesea lay S.W. 6 leagues; on the 16th a N.W. wind and the Isle of Man 'bearing N. but three'; Ramsey Road, in 'indifferent weather' next day; again a N.W. wind and two leagues off Ardglass Point at close of the 18th. Then the weather turned 'foul' and, though they captured, while held up, three small ships, they were right back in Ramsey Road by the 22nd. They logged two leagues from Carrickfergus, wind N.W., at noon on the 24th and saw the Mull of Galloway at night. But they were in Castle Road, Douglas on the 25th! Weighing on the 27th with wind S.W., the three ships anchored off the Copeland Islands on the 28th. In 'Custenden [Cushendun] Bay' on the morning of the 29th 'betwixt the two heads'; two great ships and a yacht, which they were prepared to fight, looming up in the afternoon. Rooke–to their great satisfaction! N.W. winds and 'very cross tides' held the three in 'the road of the Island of Rathlin' all through the 30th. On the 31st–the Foyle Lough entry.

85  *S.P.Dom* . . . *1689–90*, p. 101.

86  The résumé which is given as *Appendix G* is from a broadsheet deposited by Earl Crawford in the Library of the University of Cambridge. The summary in *S.P.Dom.* . . . . *1689–90*, p. 93, is somewhat inadequate.

87  Clark, G. N. (Sir) *The Dutch Alliance and the War against French Trade*, Manchester, 1923, p. 40 for ante-dating. Clark remarks, 'it may have been intended to record the fact that the treaty was drafted before the English declaration of war which had now been made'. Publication of declaration was upon the 7th; but none the less, William on 28th April spoke of war as declared (*v.* p. 119). The 29th was, of course, just before the clash at Bantry and the day before the day on which the English had originally demanded that rendezvous of the fleets take place. For text of treaty *v.* Du Mont, *op. cit.* p. 222. A summary is provided as *Appendix H*. For *MS* Text State Papers Foreign Treaties No. 325–the ratification by the States General, 2nd July 1689. This treaty is noticed, with partial quotation in Davenport, E. G. and Paullin, C. O. *European Treaties bearing on the History of the United States and its Dependencies*, 4 v, Washington, 1917–(v. II, 1650–1697, p. 332).

88  Clark, *op. cit.* p. 40.

89  *H.M.C. Finch* MSS 8th March (The notes are summarized *H.M.C. Finch II*, p. 208).

# CHAPTER·VIII

# Allied Grand Fleet – Tourville
# (Toulon to Brest) eludes Torrington
## Mid-May to the end of August

---

### ARGUMENT

*Herbert arrives in London 17th May–on the 21st is thanked by the Commons and moves provision be made for the wounded; on 1st June takes his seat as a peer; his election to the mastership of Trinity House.*

*Events of the week 24th to 31st May. William's persistence in his original and continuous policy of assigning his major naval strength to the Mediterranean, though no decisive victory brought home from Bantry and no Irish settlement in sight! The Mediterranean idée fixe suddenly dislodged (but not shattered) in favour of the mobilization of a single three squadronal Anglo-Dutch fleet; for the government has become aware of the French design to unite the Toulon with the Brest fleet–Nottingham drafts Torrington's instructions; Russell to be Vice-Admiral and Admiral of the Blue–Certain judicial appointments and disciplinary matters.*

*Torrington's orders as first drafted require him (1) to sail 'the length of Scilly' in order to discover whether the French be on the Irish coast: (2) not finding them there, he should go before Brest to hinder the junction of the Toulon and Brest fleets; (3) should that union be found accomplished, let him weigh the possibility of destroying the French in harbour; (4) suppose that impracticable, he must at least blockade Brest and render safe the English and Irish shores–The traditional and novel in these orders, which, however, do not reach the admiral unmodified; for specific mention of the threat from Toulon is omitted and emphasis placed upon the necessity to blockade Brest to guarantee the immunity of the three kingdoms–7th June, Torrington rehoists his flag in the Elizabeth; on the 14th the first Anglo-Dutch fleet, 20 English 9 Dutch, stands to sea; on the last of the month lies before Brest; and by 8th July numbers 70 sail.*

*Tourville, 9th June/30th May weighs from Toulon, passes Gibraltar a month later, stretches to the Azores to secure sea-room and insure evasion; is happily 'spotted' by Jean Doublet's Sans Peur; by 23rd/13th July rides thirty leagues south of Brest and, a week later, enters the Iroise undetected.*

*Torrington, whose fleet had been blown some fifty miles north-westward of Ushant, returns to close blockade; Torrington, 23rd to 25th July, probes (not for the first time) the outer harbour of Brest; then, certified by Nottingham that Tourville had passed Gibraltar and was believed to be making for Belle Isle or Ireland (which latter would constitute a threat to Kirke lately arrived in Lough Foyle) decides to sail for Scilly and the Soundings.*

*The imposing battle line presented by the Anglo-Dutch fleet–28th July, Scilly is in sight; victualling; a court martial; 30th July, the news of Tourville's entry into Brest reaches the Allied fleet–A month's cruise off southern Ireland; the loss of the Portsmouth; 31st August, anchors cast in Torbay.*

*Tourville's August cruise off Belle Isle; his return to Brest; Doublet's amusing reconnaissance; Louis' naval policy (in effect to maintain a 'fleet in being') revealed.*

*The success and limitations of Torrington's command. The consequences of failure to intercept the Toulon squadron regrettable; but the establishment and support of Rooke's secondary command in the Irish Sea the all-important achievement—d'Amblimont's July exploit off the Texel, the single challenge to Anglo-Dutch military control of the Narrow Seas—No such dominance evidenced in respect of denial of the sea to French trade or protection of English and Dutch shipping against French privateers. The Admiralty and letters of marque—The French Ministry of Marine and the corsairs—escape of Bart and Forbin from Plymouth.*

*The Allies' Treaty of 12th/22nd August to interdict all traffic, including neutral, with France; its unique place in International Law—The refusal of the English to release Dutch captures, temporarily carried into English ports, for adjudication in the courts of the captors.*

*A third Anglo-Dutch Treaty 24th August/3rd September of 'Amity and Alliance'.*

*Prize Court appointments—A Commission for Sick and Wounded Seamen, relief of Widows and Orphans and for Prisoners of War—The Commons Committee, set up in response to Herbert's (Torrington's) notice of 21st May concerning naval casualties; takes evidence from the Governors of the Chatham Chest and Trinity House and others; reports and recommendations.*

---

HERBERT ARRIVED in London on Friday the 17th May the day after striking his flag (see p. 144) and at once resumed attendance at the Board of Admiralty,[1] which, by the 22nd, had, as the Minutes reveal, found, in York Buildings and not far from Pepys's fine house (see p. 63), a home more suitable than Herbert's Channel Row lodgings. On the 21st he made an appearance in and before the House of Commons in which he represented Plymouth.[2] 'Admiral Herbert', declared the Speaker,

This House hath taken Notice of the great Service you have performed, in the Engaging the *French* Fleet: They do look upon it, as one of the bravest Actions done in this last Age: and expect it will raise Reputation of the *English* Valour to its ancient Glory. I do therefore, by the Command of this House, return you their hearty Thanks for this service; and desire you, that you will communicate the like Thanks, in their Name, to the Officers & Seamen that served under your Command; & to let them know, That this House will have a particular Regard of their Merits, & take care, as much as in them lies, to give them all due Encouragement.

Herbert, who privately looked back on the action as an English tactical failure (see p. 141), comported himself (as well he might) as one 'in some Confusion at [so] great and unexpected

Honour' indeed, without 'Words to express [his] Sense of it' and (with irony not officially cognizable!) declared himself determined to 'deserve it by future action'. He promised to convey to those under his command the gratitude the Speaker had expressed. Then with a bluntness that did him credit, continued: 'And, since the House have so favourable Opinion of their Actions,' he would beg 'leave to make an humble Motion . . . a Thing becoming the Greatness of this Nation . . . [to] assign some Place and Revenue, for the Support of such as are maimed in the Service and Defence of their Country'. There was, he said, 'no sufficient Provision made, at present, in this Kingdom; and indeed, it [was] too great a Charge for the Crown'. He therefore humbly moved it be ordered: 'That an Act may pass, That they may have a Support and Subsistence, after they have, by Wounds, been made incapable of further Service.'

The proposal of the distinguished member who had himself lost an eye in service led to the establishment of a committee of twenty-six, of which he was one, which met next afternoon[3] and was, shortly afterwards, augmented by the calling in of the sea-port members.[4] The Committee produced its report in less than two months from inception.[5]

From the Commons to the Lords! The record of the entry of Arthur Herbert, Baron of Torbay and Earl of Torrington in the County of Devon, to the Upper House, on Saturday, 1st June, is preserved:[6]

This Day Arthur Earl of Torrington was introduced, between the Earl of Pembrooke and the Earl of Oxon; the Gentleman Usher of the Black Rod and Garter King of Arms going before, carrying his Patent and Writ of Summons; and the next to them the Lord Great Chamberlain, and the Earl Marshal of England. His lordship delivered his Patent and Writ to the Speaker, on the Knee; who delivered the same to the Clerk of the Parliaments; who brought them to the Table, and read them.

The Patent bears Date the 29 of May Anno 1º *Guil.* et *Mariae*; and the Writ of Summons is dated the 30th of May, Anno 1º *Guilielmi Regis* et *Mariae Reginae*.[7] And then he was brought & placed at the lower End of the Earls Bench.

Arthur, Earl of Torrington took the Oaths and made and

subscribed the Declaration, appointed by the Acts.

Herbert was not the first 'Earl of Torrington'. Did he choose the title because it had once formed part of the more honorific appellation of George Monck, first Duke of Albemarle, under whom he had served?

At the College of Arms the heralds were busy supporting an armiger Herbert shield:[8]

> On the dexter side A Mariner proper in a Wastcoat Azure the Breeches Argent striped Crimson hose and Shoes Sable neck-cloth Silver and Cap Gules holding in his dexter hand a Falchion of the first, hilt and Pommel Or standing upon an Anchor proper the shank Gold And on the sinister side a like Mariner habited as aforesaid holding in his sinister hand a Terrestial globe Argent the frame Or standing upon a piece of Ordinance proper.

Balancing the superimposed earl's coronet, a scroll wound beneath the shield. It bore '*Sine his nihil*'. Chosen by an admiral who had so recently countered the adulation of the Commons with plea for a 'Place and Revenue' for mariners 'maimed', Torrington's augmentation declared, far from hollowly, the tribute of a seamen's admiral.[9]

Earlier in the week in which Torrington entered the House of Lords the Mastership of Trinity House for the ensuing year fell to his lot by, presumably, unopposed election.[10]

The week, the 24th to the 31st May, was a period of more than ordinary significance in the conduct of the naval side of King William's War. It will be recalled that, in estimates submitted to Parliament, 26th March (see p. 104 *ante*) the King's determination to apportion a larger number of English naval units to the Mediterranean than to the Channel was made plain and that the policy stands fully revealed in the opening clauses of the Anglo-Dutch Naval Treaty of the 29th April (see Appendix I, Ch. VII), eighty English and Dutch warships, provided in a five to three ratio, to constitute, in the same ratio, the Mediterranean and Channel fleets. On Friday the 24th May,[11] Torrington at the Admiralty Board, it was resolved, 'That a ltre be writt to the Navy Board letting them know that his Ma^ts Commands have lately been

Signified by ye Earle of Torrington' to the effect that the allocation of English ships for the Mediterranean and Channel fleets should stand at:

| | | |
|---|---|---|
| 1—2nd rate<br>13—3rd rates<br>16—4th rates<br>6—fireships } | Mediterranean | { Victualled at<br>Portsmouth<br>and Plymouth<br>for 6 months |
| 10—3rd rates<br>7—4th rates<br>4—fireships } | Channel | { Ditto<br>for 3 months |

For the Mediterranean no alteration; for the Channel three rates less, though with some compensation of gun power. William's determination persisted–inflexible, even though no victory had been brought home from Bantry and no Irish settlement was yet in sight! Tuesday the 28th and Wednesday the 29th saw Torrington again at the Board. On Friday, the 30th,[12] he entered late. Immediately, as 'next business', Captain Russell was appointed 'Admiral of ye Blew' and direction given to the Navy Board: 'Blew Colours to be made with all despatch for ye Fleete as many as will be required for that Squadron and likewise Unjon Flaggs and Flaggs for Signalling, if there be not Suffishont in Store.' Obviously a single three squadronal grand fleet, large as those of Dutch War days, is envisaged. Vice-Admiral Davies's ships at Portsmouth as 'Red', the gathering Dutch vessels as 'White', Russell's the 'Blue'.

What, in the course of a week, had occurred to produce such sudden reversal of policy? Nottingham, at this week's end, is revealed possessed by the disturbing conviction that a squadron of French *flotte du Levant* was under orders to leave Toulon and make junction with *flotte du Ponant* right opposite our shores in the commodious harbour of Brest.[13] The King-Stadholder's *idée fixe* was dislodged–not shattered–the King-Stadholder forced to agree with himself to invoke the escape clause in Paragraph IV of the Treaty and admit that, for the summer of 1689 at least, security would demand that the allied strength be deployed at home. To Nottingham's knowledge and William's unwilling deliberations Torrington must perforce have been privy and, of them, Russell, anyway, informed.

Nottingham, before the 1st June, was busy preparing Instructions for Torrington, who would, on William's nomination, take command of the allied fleet, and on the 1st June the Board of Admiralty, Torrington attending, minuted 'A commission Signed for the Rt Honable Edward Russell to be Vice-Admirall of the Fleet now fitting to sea [he to wear] Ye Blew Flagg at ye Maine Topmasthead.' Russell's star was in the ascendant. He had recently, on the 4th April, succeeded Lord Falkland as Treasurer of the Navy.[14]

Three necessary judicial appointments were dealt with by the Admiralty Commissioners at the end of May. Dr [Matthew] Tindall to be Deputy Judge Advocate, Dr William Oldys to be Advocate General and Dr [Sir Charles] Hedges, Judge of the High Court. The Marshal of Admiralty, Mr [William] Joynes, held under arrest two captains – Wilford of the *Eagle* (it was aboard the *Eagle*, then guardship in the Thames, with Wilford captain, that James, in the course of his second flight, had for a time sought refuge) and Hozier of the *Sapphire* (see p. 151 *ante*), the former to be handed over to Torrington at Portsmouth, the latter to Russell.[15] And Roach, captain of the *Charles Galley*, together with his lieutenant and master, recently reported to the Admiralty by Vice-Admiral Davies as 'guilty of an Unusuall peice of cruelty' against three boys whom they had interrogated on captured prizes, also waited with apprehension the likely return of Torrington to Portsmouth. These officers had, the Vice-Admiral said, placed 'burning Matches between their Fingers to extract a Confession touching the Place whereunto those Prizes belong'.[16] Less to fear, but with need to be ready with his case, Captain Aylmer of the *Mary* was due to appear at the Board to account for what petitioning London merchants alleged was irregularity in making prize (on his way back from Bantry?) of the *Mary Ann* laden with brandy.[17]

The original draft of Nottingham's 1st June Instructions addressed to, 'Our Right Trusty and Right Wellbeloved Cousin and Counsellor Arthur Earl of Torrington, Admiral of our Ships in the Narrow Seas'[18] ran thus:

So soon as you shall have received these: ... take under your Com̃and such of Our Ships, as also of the Ships belonging to the States General of the United Provinces as are now at Portsmouth ... and immediately sail to the length of Scilly and inform yourself as best you can whether the French fleet be upon ye Coast of Ireland or come out of Brest ... [if it be] still in Brest, you are forthwith to sail with your whole Fleet (as also such other ships as shall come to you) before that Port and endeavour to hinder the joining of the French ships from Thoulon with those in Brest: or if they be already arrived there to prevent their coming out to sea, by burning & destroying them in that harbour: if it may be attempted: or by lying before that Port as you shall judge most proper to prevent the French from landing in England or Ireland & you are to take all opportunity of taking or destroying them.

These Instructions, in preliminary draft, are remarkable of their kind and well worth scrutiny. Nottingham pictures the admiral sailing in confidence of possessing command of the Channel waters, reminds him that the Brest fleet may have stretched over to Ireland–if so, he will fight it–or be still in harbour–in which case he must hold it of first importance to keep the Toulon ships, believed to be navigating Brest-ward, from working in. There is, of course, the contingency that the two French fleets have already joined; in that event the admiral should 'if it may be attempted' put beyond peradventure his assumed command by 'burning and destroying' the combined armament, *flotte du Ponant* and the arrived *flotte du Levant*, in the great arsenal anchorage or (and it is at this point that the draft develops the line of thought discernible in Nottingham's earlier transmitted orders to a lesser fleet) (see p. 109 *ante*) maintain that command by 'lying before that Port' in order to make it impossible for the French to get to the shores of England or Ireland. Here, for the first time in English operational orders, the alternatives of assurance of command by battle decision through destruction of a fleet within the enemy's own harbour or maintenance of the command by strategic blockade are specifically balanced.

In 1217, John, at Damme, had burnt the collected transports of an intended invasion. By the attack he made upon the French ships at the port of Sluys, Edward III had settled that the Hundred

Years' War should not be fought on English soil. Drake had
singed the King of Spain's beard by attacking the convoying fleet
in the harbour of Cadiz; but for a turn of the wind which swept
Lord Howard of Effingham from the coast of Spain, possibly the
Armada would never have quitted the port of Corunna; and, when
it did sail, no small part had been 'smoked out' of Calais roads in
which it had sought refuge. These all were operations aiming at
assurance of command by forcing battle decision even within the
enemy's own ports and shelters.[19] In the three Dutch Wars the
series of battles (the bitterest the Royal Navy had hitherto or
since has been called upon to wage) engagements for the more
part beginning coastally and developing out to sea, provided, on
the English part no such new example of devastating oppor-
tunism; it was left to De Ruyter to send in Van Ghent and Brakel
to demonstrate, in the Thames and Medway, fort, store and warship destruction, on a scale which insured the Dutch six weeks'
rule of the North Sea. Nottingham's request to Torrington to go
in and conquer 'if it may be attempted' would be guidance
acceptable, traditional and orthodox. But the alternative, strategic
blockade on a Channel-Atlantic coast, was quite another matter,
for which but one partial and one comparable precedent could be
found—the former Lord Henry Seymour's co-operation with
Justinus of Nassau off the ports of the Spanish Netherlands in 1588,
the latter the intermittent hovering of Blake off the Spanish port
of Cadiz throughout the autumn and winter of 1656.

When the draft had thus far been completed a sentence was
added which apparently indicated recognition that the French
might be found united out of harbour and already taking to sea
or that they might break from a blockade and prove too strong to
be attacked. In either eventuality it would be for Torrington 'to
obstruct their course and watch all advantages against them', in
any case preventing a hostile landing.

Finally the draft gave guidance as to the disposal of ships
captured while trading into France or Ireland. If such vessels
proved to be Dutch or English they must be dealt with in manner
'pursuant to the Treaty', or, exigency compelling, destroyed and
the crews made prisoners. All other intercepted craft must be
brought into English harbours.

But it was not a fair copy of these draft Instructions which, on
or about the 1st June, reached the Commander-in-Chief's hand! A
vertical line was struck through the passage beginning 'before that
Port . . . destroying them' and then rewritten to read: 'you) and
cruise in such station as shall be judged by a Council of War most
proper to prevent their Coming to Sea or if that cannot be
prevented Yet at least to hinder them from landing in England,
Scotland or Ireland.' Torrington was therefore simply required,
the French being discovered in Brest, to blockade that base! The
Toulon squadron was not specifically mentioned. What considerations lay behind the alteration are not obvious; nor can it be
decided whether the change was made by Nottingham without,
or as a consequence of, consultation with a second or third party–
the King or Torrington himself. With the drafting of operational
Instructions neither Privy Council nor Admiralty was concerned.
The interposition of a council of war at a particular stage of a
voyage is not perhaps particularly significant; for councils were
held on all sorts of occasions. It remained for Torrington–Vice-
Admiral of England, First Commissioner of the Board of Admiralty,
Commander-in-Chief for the present expedition–to hasten toward Scilly and thence before Brest.

The Commander-in-Chief returned to his old flagship, the
*Elizabeth*, during the afternoon of Friday the 7th June–the Union
at the maintop, jack at bowsprit, ensign at the poop. Whether
foremast and mizzen were left 'naked', as would be the case if the
Pepysian 'establishment' were followed, may be doubted.[20] His
squadronal Vice-Admiral, Davies, had, several days earlier, transferred his Union flag from the *Montague* to the *Resolution* and only
that morning, the Rear-Admiral, Lord Berkeley, had run up his
flag, also the Union at the mizzen of the *Hampton Court*.[21]

In the three weeks during which the Commander-in-Chief was
in London, reconditioning and strengthening of the fleet at
Portsmouth had proceeded with unwonted smoothness, thanks no
doubt to the effectiveness with which, even before the battered
Bantry vessels had come in, the Admiralty had roused the Navy
Board to appreciate the need for emergency action, requesting it
to dispatch one of its number to Portsmouth, to co-operate with
the resident Commissioner there that 'no manner of time be lost'

and ordering ships in the River and Downs 'though not fully manned' and three rates at Plymouth to sail immediately to Spithead.[22] By the time Torrington resumed command a score of English ships were fit to sail and the Dutch Vice-Admiral Philips van Almonde had already half-a-dozen large ships at anchorage.[23] He wore his flag, that of Vice-Admiral of Amsterdam, to the concern of Torrington, at the foretop.[24]

None the less, writing to Nottingham on the 10th June,[25] Torrington congratulated himself that the French were not reported out; for, wind-bound, he could not have got at them. Three more Dutch ships came in on the 12th – one, 'Rear-Admiral' Brackell's too leaky to proceed. On the 13th a wind change,[26] and, early on the 14th,[27] the first Anglo-Dutch fleet, about twenty English and nine Dutch,[28] was standing off St Helens.[29] By this time the English seamen would recognize that their ships constituted a Red squadron; for, at the fore of Davies's *Resolution* and the mizzen of Berkeley's *Hampton Court*, red ensigns had replaced the Union flags.[30] The Dutch no doubt spread States flags. Although Russell had been appointed Admiral of the Blue (and Vice-Admiral of the Fleet), and his Vice- and Rear-Admirals commissioned, namely, Henry Killigrew, blue flag at the fore, and John Ashby, the like at the mizzen,[31] the Blue squadron had not yet been organized.

Torrington held course past the familiar sea-marks – Dunnose, Portland, the Berry, Start and Deadman toward the Lizard and Scilly. Off Falmouth a fireship exploded; near the Lizard Sir Francis Wheeler's half dozen frigates, which had been cruising since the beginning of June in the Soundings, came to the Admiral's flag, so that the fleet mustered, by the 23rd June, rather more than forty ships of war (thirty-two English and at least eleven Dutch) and a dozen fireships, victualled, the admiral remarks to 'the 23rd of August'.[32] A signalling code was now existent or in course of compilation.[33] It is surprising that at no time had Chateaurenault, supposed to be at sea with ten vessels, been sighted.[34]

While, on the 27th, the Admiral lay, as his Instructions required, ten leagues west of Scilly, Captain Byng, of the *Dover*, who had been detached from Wheeler's squadron to look in on Brest, returned to report no discovery made.[35] As there was nothing to suggest that the French were out Ireland-ward Torrington called the enjoined council of war and notified Nottingham that it was 'by all concluded that Brest [was] the properest station–or at least Ushant'.[36] The north-west wind blew away the close thick weather; and, on the 29th the lieutenant of the *Yorke*, leader of the Red Squadron, logged 'at 4 this afternoon we saw Ushant at topmast head . . . E.S.E. distant 9 leagues.' The wind dropped;[37] forty-three sail and twelve fireships[38] rode 'a great rowling sea'.[39] On the last day of the month, a Sunday, toward sunset, from the *Yorke*, Ushant bore S.E.$\frac{1}{2}$.S. 6 leagues;[40] the flagship was even nearer the French shore.[41] The first attempted English blockade of Brest had begun.

While the fleet cruised in the offing, Byng was given three more ships and ordered to reconnoitre. He entered Broad Sound, drew French gunfire but returned scarcely wiser than before.[42] The fleet had twice been reinforced[43] by ships, English and Dutch, before the afternoon of the 8th July, by which time the north-west wind had also brought in Russell, Admiral of the Blue, in the powerful second-rate, the *Duke*, the *Hampshire* with him. Noting the arrival of the English ships, Torrington's flag-captain added, 'Admr[ll] Evertson, Vize Adm[ll] Vanderburg, Admr[ll] Colemburg Reer Admr[ll] Evertson & 5 Saile of Dutch men of warr more joyned us'.[44] The 'whole Fleet of English & Hollanders' now totalled '70 saile', standing to in sight of Ushant,[45] three squadrons, the Dutch the English 'Red' and 'Blue'–but the Blue without its full quota of ships; for its Vice-Admiral, Killigrew, in the *Kent* with five fourths, two fifths, a yacht and two fireships, held back for special service, the 'Discovery of and meeting w[th] Some French Men of Warr said to be coming out from Dunkirk & bound towards Brest' had only just received orders to come off the French-Flemish coast and, with the *Kent* only, join Torrington. The rest of the detachment was dispersed.[46]

It was, in all probability, in the early part of May that Anne Hilarion de Constantin de Tourville,[47] Lieutenant-général des armées navales, travelled from Paris to Toulon, accompanied by Chef-d'escadre Villette,[48] charged with a mission (of which he said nothing to his companion) to prepare twenty ships of the line and subsidiary vessels[49] for a cruise–ostensibly in Mediterranean waters?

To Richelieu is attributed the statement: '*Il semble que la nature ait voul·i lui* [*la France*] *offrir l'empire de la mer par l'avantageuse situation de ses deux côtes pourvues d'excellents ports aux deux mers Océane et Mediterranée.*'[50] But the arsenals and harbours of Toulon and Brest are, through the interposition of the Iberian peninsula, separated on the shortest routes by 1,700 miles of sea. The first blockade of Brest was in progress, the first attempt to solve what a recent French writer has called '*L'éternelle difficulté de faire concourir à une même action les forces navales du Ponant et celles de la Mediterranée*'[51], began.[52] Down to Brest in good time had gone the Minister of Marine, Seignelay. Having arranged the supersession of the Maréschal d'Estrées he issued his orders from *le Souverain*[53] and looked forward to the direction if not actual command of a powerful combined fleet (p. 186 *infra*).

By 9th June/30th May, Tourville in the 90-ton *Conquérant* put astern with his fleet Iles d'Hyères[54] and, if, before leaving Paris, he had not been taken into confidence, sealed orders, now broken open,[55] told him his distant assignation–rendezvous with the Brest fleet. Against westerly winds, he took a full month to pass the Strait of Gibraltar[56] and, encountering in the Atlantic strong north-westerlies, crossed to the Azores intent on winning sea-room sufficient to secure him, on rising to the latitude of Finisterre, relative immunity from discovery wide of the coast of Spain. So concerned was Tourville with evasion that he elected not to seek contact with vessels which he could expect would be out in the Bay to ascertain his progress and supply him with such information as might be to hand of the whereabouts and strength of the Anglo-Dutch fleet.[57] One such look-out, Jean Doublet, commandant of a 'barque longue' the *Sans Peur*, of eight guns, cruising from Belle Isle with Sieur de Levy of *La Lutine* had put back to Brest for victuals and new orders at a date in July when the absence of news of Tourville's whereabouts had begun seriously to alarm the Court and Seignelay and the presence of Torrington's blockading fleet, with, no doubt, estimates of its numbers, had become the talk of Brest. Without delay Doublet and another were ordered back to sea, no courses prescribed, to look for the Toulon squadron;[58] and, left to his own judgment, Doublet laid his course eighty leagues west of Brest and south to as many west of Finisterre. Far out at sea he was ignored by an English frigate and, half an hour afterwards, his look-out sighted the Toulon sails! Aboard the flagship *le Conquérant*, Doublet, the commandant, was interviewed and, retailed, no doubt, what he knew of the situation at and off Brest. Then with all speed, he turned for home. Again, an hour before sunset, the English frigate! Night–Tourville unobserved of the frigate and *Sans Peur* (name for the nonce belied) threshing through the Atlantic under a press of canvas that scared Doublet's crew! Three days later–Bertheaume and Brest and the tidings delivered to the Minister, roused sleepy-eyed to hear it. Doublet well deserved the order for a hundred pistoles on the treasury at Brest.

On the 23rd/13th July, approaching two months at sea, with victuals largely spent, Tourville lay well south of the latitude of Brest some thirty leagues from the land. He had gathered by that time, from a captured Dane, news of the general disposition of the enemy off Ushant. To challenge with a score sea-strained ships of the line a force which could justly be assumed to be considerable, perhaps three times his number, believed to be barring entry to the Iroise, was not a reasonable naval risk, especially since there could be no assurance that ships would opportunely emerge from Brest to aid the entrants. Consequently, it is not surprising that, at a council-of-war held before the 23rd/13th, the voices of Lieutenant-général d'Amfréville and Chef-d'escadre de Nesmond,[59] were raised in advice either to return to Provence or to retreat to Lisbon–counsel which Villette alleges he alone countered. Should not messages be sent to Maréschal d'Estrées, believed to be commanding in Brest, to throw on him the burden of advising Tourville's retreat? Or, alternatively, should not d'Estrées indicate how the Toulon ships could enter the Iroise? It is not clear that any steps to communicate with d'Estrées were taken. The French Admiral, loth to disappoint his King, clung with fear to his purpose, his determination indicated by Villette, the working of his mind more explicitly demonstrated by le père Paul Hoste of his immediate entourage. Tourville, declares Hoste:

*voit que le vent de Sud-Oüest règne fort dans ce parage et il étoit résolu de l'attendre, sachant bien que d'un vent du Sud Oüest force les Alliez ne*

*pourroient pas tenir sur Oüessan et qu'ils seroient obligez de donner dans
la Manche en même temps que nous donnerions dans l'Iroise.*

Still cruising at great distance from the shore, the admiral watched,
a whole anxious week, his vane-pendants. Then, on the morning of
Monday the 29th/19th July, the longed-for change of wind
occurred. Two frigates with crowded sail were ordered abroad–
M. de Chalard toward Pennemarc, M. de la Mothe d'Héran in
the direction of Belle Isle.[60] The squadron's off-shore distance
rapidly shortened. At noon, twelve estimated leagues from land,
a thick mist was drifting. Tourville became apprehensive of the
rocks of a lee-shore he had not recently coasted and, for awhile,
held his vessels off shore.[61] His latitude can fairly be fixed. He lay
rather more than his estimated twelve leagues, indeed eighteen,
west of the little isle of Groix, which is some three leagues south-
west from the place where the Blavet (L'Orient to the north and
Pt Louis to the south) falls into the sea. He was just far enough out
to enable him, when the last stage of his voyage should begin, to
weather Pennemarc and avoid the promontories of Douarnenez
facing the Raz de Fontenaz and the threatening Saintes, for, here
or hereabouts, Tourville was again found by Doublet, who,
having cashed his order for a hundred pistoles on the treasury at
Brest, had with another captain been bid reconnoitre between
Pennemarc and Glennan.[62] One report[63] declares that the evening
brought assurance from Tourville's scouting frigates that Ushant
had been sighted and no enemy seen on the skyline; another that
de la Mothe d'Héran had been engaged and du Chalard had not
returned before Tourville, '*ne découvrant point les vaisseaux ennemis
qui devoient estre en garde, et jugeant par là que le mauvais temps du jour
précédent auroit tiré leur armée de sa post, entreprit de tenter le hazard de
passer brusquement*'.[64] The fact is that the hazard *was* accepted–
with complete impunity; for the Anglo-Dutch fleet was, as will
appear, far from the scene of the triumph.[65] At break of day,
Tuesday the 30th/20th July, Tourville approached the Iroise.
Doublet–had he signalled Tourville a clear passage?–reached
Rade de Bertheaume at the northern entry from the Iroise seven
hours before the Toulon ships cast anchor.[66] Three days later
Louis in Paris learned the good news and the next *Gazette*
announced it.[67]

It was certainly a 'fleet of great strength', itemized in the dispatch, dated the 13th July, of Russell, Admiral of the Blue, direct to the Earl of Nottingham (a communication written under physical difficulty 'my shipp roles so much I can hardly sitt'), which, in the critical week, 13th/23rd–20th/30th July, rode before Brest – a fleet of nearly three score ships of the line, ten lesser and a score of fireships.[68] Yet it missed Tourville's sore-tried squadron!

The truth is that, during those days, the Anglo-Dutch force steered courses which, for the more part, held it nearer latitude 49° than 48°, while Tourville appears to have stayed well below the 48° line. In fair but close weather, with little wind (what there was veering from East to North and then to West) on the 15th, 16th, 17th and 18th, the Allies cruised in sight of Ushant, the island bearing S.E. and at times distant not more than four or five leagues; but, on the 19th/29th (joined now by the Vice-Admiral of the Blue, Sir Henry Killigrew), the whole fleet backed north-westward in thunder, lightning and heavy rain before Tourville's timely gale which piled up 'a great swell out of ye westward'. So that, by the 20th/30th, for the body of Torrington's three squadrons, Ushant must have lain fifty or more miles to the south-eastward. On that removed station Torrington was rejoined by the twelve rates and two fireships with which, on the 10th, he had ordered Wheeler not only 'to observe the French fleet but likewise the fortifications [of Brest] and know in what manner they [the Allies] could best attack the French in their own port'. Sir Francis had sighted round St Matthew's point, presumably in the Bay of Bertheaume '40 odd ships and a flag', provoked twenty to come at him; but, 'it being night and little wind', no action had ensued. The wind, round again in the north-west, had blown so strongly that Admiral Evertsen's 'driedekker' *Walcheren* had lost mizzen and bowsprit; it moderated and the van of the fleet, standing in at dawn on the 21st, when Evertsen transferred to the *Hollandia*, brought Ushant once more in sight; and, shortly, 'all ye Fleet', again at four leagues, 'lay by'.[69]

Nottingham, half-way through the critical week – on the 18th July – was in possession of a list of the French fleet in Brest and of the ships expected from Toulon. He could tell Torrington that Tourville was designated to command, that Seignelay proposed to lord it in the assembled armament. Naturally, the Secretary 'could wish [his lordship] could give some account of them'. A letter, received in Plymouth by Sir John Berry and confided by him for delivery to the captain of the *Firedrake*, should have been, and probably was, in the hands of the Admiral before midnight of the 21st. Two days at least too late![70] But not presumably too late to act as a spur to a further probe at Brest. The *Yorke* on the afternoon of the 22nd received orders to 'goe in against Brest w[th] 6 saile of Frigotts & we ye Chiefe ye *St David*, *Jersey*, *Centureon*, *Hampshire*, *Portsmouth* and a Hollander'. On a south west breeze the following morning, the 23rd, the detachment had worked in far enough to make the West point of Ushant bear N.W.b.N. when, '9 Saile of the French Fleet came out from under ye Rocks and showd themselves'. Nothing happened! *Yorke* and her companions lay off till a new day, the 24th, found them with a northwest wind and an insetting flood nine miles south of Ushant and about the same distance from Cape Mathieu. Frenchmen, the Captain of the *Yorke* once more records, appeared, 'then went in againe. They would [continues the captain] faine have dril'd us in further that ye Flood might have hove us in'. Apparently the ruse was avoided by sailing alternately north and south athwart the tide. The whole operation was given up on the 25th.[71] By that date, a supplementary letter, written by Nottingham on the 22nd, informed Torrington that Tourville was seen to pass Gibraltar on 2nd/12th July and that His Majesty believed the Toulon squadron to be at Belle Isle or gone to Ireland–which latter circumstance would be 'of very pernicious consequence' what with 'Major Gen. Kirke . . . in the Lough of Derry and the Count de Solmes . . . embarking for Ireland with 12,000 men'. The Secretary could only suggest that the Admiral should send scouts toward Belle Isle. The letter assured him that supplementary provisions for the fleet, which was supposed to be victualled to the 23rd of August (see p. 174), were in store at Plymouth and it told him that he should send for those provisions while remaining on station.[72] A 'Council of Warr' had already on the 22nd decided the fleet should 'saile for Sillia and keep 10 Leagues west from it [to] meet the Victuallers whome the Admr[ll] had Comanded to meet him there'.[73] So (another council first held) Torrington, interpreting the Secretary's injunction broadly, on the 27th, line of battle formed, 'ye Dutch leading ye Van w$^{th}$ their Starboard tack on board', the Red next and the Blue in their wake, laid course toward the Soundings[74] from which a watch, though distant, could be kept on Brest and attempt thence to penetrate St George's Channel in force prevented.

It is possible to present with fair certainty the imposing line

## THE VAN

| | | | | | |
|---|---|---|---|---|---|
| M | Eendracht | 70 | 360 | Kap. Snellen | |
| M | Honselaarsdijk | 50 | 200 | " Convent | |
| A | Haarlem | 64 | | " Manaert | |
| A | Gelderland | 72 | 400 | V-A. van Almonde | |
| N | Noord–Holland | 70 | 300 | S.b N. Jan van Brakel | |
| N | Wapen van Hoorn | 52 | 200 | Kap. Muijs | |
| A | Gaasterland | 52 | 210 | " Taelman | 7 |
| A | Kroonvogel (fregat) | 19 | 50 | Comm. Regort | 1 |
| A | Vesuvius (brander) | 6 | 22 | " du Pon | 1 |
| A | Holland | 70 | 360 | Kap. van Toll | |
| | | | | Lt A. Cornelis Evertsen | |
| A | Elswoud | 50 | 210 | Kap. van der Nieuburg | |
| N | Westfriesland | 90 | 450 | V-A. Callenburg | |
| A | Amsterdam | 64 | 325 | Kap. Graf van Nassau | |
| A | Schattershoef | 46 | 210 | " van der Goes | |
| Z | Cortgene | 50 | 200 | " de Boer | 6 |
| N | —— (fregat) | 14 | 42 | Comm. Grooes | 1 |
| Z | Berg Etna (brander) | 6 | 22 | " Antonissen | |
| N | Maagd van Enkhuizen (brander) | 6 | 22 | " Muijsevanger | 2 |
| N | Huis te Vlaardingen | 46 | 170 | Kap. Pael | |
| A | Provincie Utrecht | 56 | 315 | " Dekkar | |
| Z | Zierikzee | 62 | 325 | S.b N. Gelyn Evertsen | |
| Z | Gekroonde Burg | 62 | 350 | V-A. van der Putten | |
| M | Ridderschap | 60 | 300 | Kap. der Liefde | |
| A | Vrede | 52 | 210 | " van Lieren | |
| M | Vrijhreid | 72 | 400 | " Rees | 7 |
| M | Phoenix (fregat) | 26 | 110 | Comm. Cornelis van Brakel | 1 |
| A | Zes Gebroeders (brander) | 6 Stukken | 22 Koffen | " de Jongh | 1 |
| | | 1293 | 5785 | | |

Admiraliteit

M=Maas, A=Amsterdam, N=Noorderkwartier, Z=Zeeland.

To these must be added *Europa* (48) Kap. Hidde de Vries, *Brak* (36) Tierck de Vries, *Windhond* (34) Kap.–Jantema–Friesland ships,

*Calansoog* (64–325) Kap. van Zijll and *Veere* (60–300) Kap.–
Mosselman, the former an Amsterdam, the latter a Zeeland vessel
–all, no doubt, with appropriate places in the line. Evertsen's
flagship *Walcheren*, a Zeeland ship of seventy with a crew of 400,
which commonly took station between the *Westfriesland* and the
*Amsterdam*, had been sent into Portsmouth as a result of her mishap
on the 19th/29th. The *Damiate* (36) Kap. van der Gijsen, of the
Amsterdam admiralty, had gone into Plymouth with '*King Fisher*
with all the Prizes'. With van der Gijsen was operating a vessel
unnamed captained by van der Zaan.[75]

## THE RED[76]

| | | | | | | | |
|---|---|---|---|---|---|---|---|
| 3 | *Yorke* | 60 | 340 | Cha.[Ralph]Delavall | | | |
| 4 | *St David* | 54 | 280 | Jno Grayden | | | |
| 3(f) | *Resolution* | 70 | 420 | [Henry Boteler] | | | |
| 3 | *Henrietta* | 62 | 355 | Jno. Nevell | | | Vice Adm[ll] |
| 4 | *Jersey* | 49 | 230 | { Jno. Beverly / [Geo. Mees] } | | 5 | Capt. Davisses |
| | Fireships | | | | | | |
| | *Rich^d & Jn^o* | [10] | 40 | [Edw^d Poulson] | | | |
| | *Jn^o of Dublin* | [6] | 35 | [Tho. Warren] | | 2 | |
| 4 | *Woolwich* | 54 | 280 | [Jas] Gooter | | | |
| 4 | *Advice* | 49 | 230 | [John] Greenvell | | | |
| 3 | *Edgar* | 69 | 445 | S^r Clow. Shovell | | | |
| 3(f) | *Elizabeth* | 70 | 460 | [David Mitchell] | | | |
| 3 | *Pendennis* | 70 | 460 | Geo. Churchill | | | Adm[ll] |
| 4 | *St Alban* | 50 | 280 | Jno. Layton | | 6 | Redd Ld. Torrington |
| | Fireships | | | | | | |
| | *Owners Love* | [10] | 40 | [Tho. Heath] | | | |
| | *Fire Drake* | | | | | | |
| | *S^t Paule* | [10] | 45 | [John Crofts] | | 3 | |
| | *Fubbs Ya^t* | [12] | 40 | [John Johnson] | | 1 | |
| 4 | *Happy Returne* | 54 | 280 | [Wm Bokenham] | | | |
| 4 | *Diamond* | 40 | 230 | Ben Walters | | | |
| 3 | *Mountague* | 60 | 355 | Tho. Leighton | | | |
| 3(f) | *Hampton Court* | 70 | 460 | Jno. Munden | | | Reer Adm[ll] |
| 3 | *Defyance* | 64 | 390 | Tho. Allen | | | Ld. Berkly |
| 4 | *Hampshire* | 46 | 220 | [Rbt] Robinson | | 6 | |
| | Fireships | | | | | | |
| | *Sophia* | [6] | 22 | [Wm Harmer] | | | |
| | *Halfe Moone* | [8] | 25 | [Jno. Bounty] | | 2 | |
| | | 1053 | 5962 | | | | |

The *Kingfisher* (46–220) [John Avery] was on duty to Plymouth.

## THE BLUE[77]

| | | | | | | |
|---|---|---|---|---|---|---|
| 4 | *Tyger Prize* | 46 | 230 | [Jas. Barber] | | |
| 3 | *Lion* | 60 | 340 | Chas. Shellton | | |
| 3(f) | *Berwick* | 70 | 460 | [          ] | | Reer Adm[ll] |
| 3 | *Cambridge* | 70 | 420 | Jno Clemans | | Sr Jno |
| 4 | Reserve | 50 | | [Rd Keigwin] | 5 | Ashby |
| | | [48] | 230 | | | |
| | Fireships | | | | | |
| | *Charles* | [6] | 20 | [Tho Dilkes] | | |
| | *Thomas & Elizabeth* | [6] | 40 | [Tho Marshall] | 2 | |

| | | | | | | |
|---|---|---|---|---|---|---|
| 4 | *Dover* | 48 | 230 | [George Byng] | | |
| 4 | Portsmouth | 46 | 220 | Geo. St Loe | | |
| 3 | *Rupert* | 66 | 400 | Sir Fran. Wheeler | | |
| 2(f) | *Duke* | 92 | 660 | Jno. [Edwd] Stanley | | Adm[ll] |
| 3 | *Suffolke* | 70 | 460 | Math. Aylmer | | Russell |
| 4 | *Centurion* | 48 | 230 | [Bazill Beaumont] | 6 | Blew |
| | Fireships | | | | | |
| | *Cadiz Merchant* | [12] | 45 | [David Greenhill] | | |
| | *Cygnett* | [8] | 25 | [John Shelley] | 2 | |

| | | | | | | |
|---|---|---|---|---|---|---|
| 4 | *Greenwich* | 54 | 280 | [Xtopher] Billop | | |
| 3 | *Warspight* | 70 | 420 | Wm Botham | | |
| (f) | *Kent* | 70 | 460 | [Edward Good] | | |
| 3 | *Plymouth* | 60 | 340 | [Rd] Carter | | Vice |
| 4 | *Oxford* | 54 | 280 | [Seth Thurston] | | Admiral |
| 4 | *Mordaunt* | 46 | 230 | [John Tyrrell] | 6 | Killigrew |
| | Fireships | | | | | |
| | *Charles & Henry* | [6] | 25 | [Wm Stone] | | |
| | *Salamander* | [10] | 35 | [John Voticr] | 2 | |
| 6 | *Fire Drake* | [35] | 50 | | 1 | |

1116  6130

On Sunday, the 28th July, Scilly lay visible from the topmast head of the leader of the Red and, coming in on the horizon, were, '20 Saile of Shipps . . . Victuallers . . . from Plymouth under ye Convoy of the *Kings Fisher*'[78], and the Dutch *Damiate*.[79] With them, it would appear, were seven or eight merchantmen bound for Bilbao. The process of swinging in bags of bread, casks of flour, cheese, puncheons of beef, iron or wooden-bound tuns of beer, butts of water and other supplies, and the lowering of empties for quick return to London immediately began.[80] Hove to, Torrington now found time, on Tuesday the 30th, to hold, in his flagship *Elizabeth* 'upon the high & open seas', a long-deferred court-martial. Six admirals and thirty-seven captains, 'all being officers or captains of their Ma^{ties} ships and ffrigates and now in their Ma^{ties} immediate service and actual pay', sat to judge Captain Robert Wilford of the *Eagle* in a 'criminal matter', the concealing of treacherous designs and words spoken on the 16th May last by Sir William Booth, Comptroller of the Storekeepers' Accounts till 25th March, 'pretended captain of the *Pendennis*', to carry that ship over to James. Wilford said nothing 'to enervate or weaken the deposition'–indeed would not assist the court. He was fined £500, payable into the Chatham Chest, and committed to the Marshalsea, 'without baile or main-prize', a year and a day from the 30th July last and–until he should pay. Sir William, whose place on the Navy Board had been taken by Captain Henry Priestman, had wisely cleared the country before the warrant of arrest for treasonable practices could be served upon him.[81]

It was no doubt shortly after being piped back aboard the *Kent* that Killigrew's flag-captain made the revealing journal entry: 'This day we heare yt ye Tollon squadron is joynd those at Brest wch doe Admire we continualy cruising about'.[82] London had received the report, perhaps as early as the 25th and anyway by the 27th, Tourville's strength on arrival at Brest being put at: '22 capital ships, 6 frigats and 8 fireships'.[83] It may well be that the fourth rate *Swiftsure*, which joined Torrington from England on the 30th, brought to the fleet the tantalizing news.[84]

The news in no way damped the top-dog assurance of Torrington's Vice-Admiral Russell to my Lord Nottingham.

We are a very Considerable strength and In my opinion able to fight the whole power of france should they come out, but In my Humble opinion they will not venter out while we are thus powerful; my Reson is should they meet with a mortification it would be Impossible for them this warre to Repaire it, but when our fleet comes In they may atempt something on us or Ireland.

Russell's reference to the incoming of the fleet, he elaborates, 'it will not be possible for the King to keep these great third-rates out in these seas longer than the latter end of August', even if there were sufficiency of the victuals which they were 'in great want of' would not surprise Nottingham; a suggestion that newly fitted thirds might temporarily be added to the Channel strength so that 'my Lord Torrington [could] send in some of the fourth rates to be cleaned and all the fourth rates in the River got ready against [the fleet] come in' would be well taken; so also the hint that some of the 'captains already afloat' with their men could be turned over to those fourth rates to face the autumnal gales and winter hazards. But the central section of this last day of July communication: 'The casks of provisions [are] full of gaules, which the seamen fancy is put on porpus to poyson them and attribut all their sicknes to that and often refuse eating the beafe and porke. Many ships in the fleet are extremely sickly . . .' no doubt raised apprehension which Russell's self-satisfaction, 'though God by praysed itt [the sickness] has not reached my schipp yett', would not cancel out.[85]

Revictualling and 'accommodation' as between one ship and another continued, the fleet hovering in the vicinity of the Isles, till, on the 8th, reiteration, by council-of-war, of the decision of the 28th July to cruise eight leagues south of the Old Head of Kinsale was given effect. Another fourth rate, the *Bredah*, had added (on the 6th) her reinforcement.[86] For the next few days the Old Head showed, off and on, upon the skyline.[87] There was talk, on Evertsen's ship, the Dutchman lying close up to the shore, of a raid on the castle.[88] Far from unseasonable the weather–yet an English ship had to report a bowsprit carried away and Schout-bÿ–nacht Brackel's ship *'sijn groote mast had verlooren'*.

The 13th brought a shock! In the words of the *Elizabeth's* captain, 'A Dutch privateer came into the Fleet this Morning & gave an Acc$^{tt}$ that he had seene ye French Fleet at sea ye 7 Instant SW$^t$ 30 Dutch myles from Ushant Steering to ye South Ward'.[89] A Dutch log speaks of a Swedish vessel bringing the information and putting the French strength at '90 zeijlen soo kleijn als groot'.[90] Of course–the inevitable council! 'When it was resolved to Steere to ye Eastward and bring Dungannon N° 16 Leagues of, Y$^t$ noe ffrench might hinder the Transporting of our Army.' It would have been the height of foolishness to go to look for the French and expose Rooke–So there or thereabouts for a day or two till the 17th, Torrington cruised, the *Monmouth* and

*Eagle*, thirds, in the meantime coming along from England; then
another council-of-war and back towards the Old Head. Report
that the fourth rate *Portsmouth*, Captain George St Loe, had been
'taken by a ffrench man-of-war named *Marqueese*', was scarcely
offset by ocular evidence of the capture of a small Irish vessel by
the *Diamond*. At yet another council-of-war, held off Cape Clear
on the 20th, it was decided to end all stay in the Irish waters and
once more steer for 'Sillia'. And, continues the informative log,
'in regard that our provisions & water was short & that the
Season of the yeare allmost spent it was likewise resolved that,
after the 26 Instant Torbay should be the place of Randivouze'.[91]
Meanwhile the Admiralty was doing its best to get and give
Torrington information of the strength and whereabouts of the
enemy. And, presumably in anticipation of Torrington's autumn
needs, to keep Torbay clear for his fleet. From its cruising ground
of the 20th well out towards the Mizzen Head, the fleet began its
uneventful run eastward. Fastnet and Baltemore for bearings at
sunset, 'Gallahead' on the 21st–but the 27th before a course set
for Scilly. The 28th, 'much wind and a great Sea but at night . . .
almost calme', the *Yorke* capturing a small vessel 'from Brest
bound for Ireland'. Scilly, 'the bodie of it', was sighted on the
morning of the 29th; Land's End fell astern before the evening;
on a following wind the fleet was short of Plymouth in the morning
watch of the 30th, of the Start at noon and up with the Berry in
the first dog. Anchors were cast at '6 a clock in Torbay ye berry
head S.W. the Fleet rid all over the bay'. The last of August
dawned with rainy haze over the first Anglo-Dutch fleet brought
intentionally into harbour.[92] Two letters from Lord Torrington to
Lord Nottingham, written respectively on the 24th and 29th,
were now delivered to the Secretary[93] and the Admiralty also
received from Torrington a communication forwarded by Mr
Addis at Plymouth.[94] They set forth the commander-in-chief's
reasons for his presence in the Bay.

In less than ten days after his arrival at Brest, Tourville was
prepared to take to sea[95] a fleet drawn from the combined armament of Brest and Toulon which now numbered some seventy
vessels of war and a hundred fireships.[96] Not the Vice-Admiral of

France, d'Estrées, ruled in Brest! But Seignelay, forbidden by Louis to order Tourville into the Channel to engage the Anglo-Dutch fleet unless descent were made '*en Normandie, Picardie et Boulonnois*' was compelled to o'ermaster his professed desire to observe a naval battle and content himself with the lesser excitement of the safer summer cruise. For the admiral the cruise presented an unprecedented opportunity for the large scale manoeuvres of which he was professionally fond and for which he was justly famed.[97] Ordering Doublet to precede him on a given course '*pour faire découverte*', the French admiral cleared the Iroise (by 8 Août/29th July) and stood south-west to a ground sixty leagues off Belle Isle. The weather was delightful; and Doublet observed that there was no great desire to encounter the enemy fleet! On the eleventh day out, Doublet was ordered by Tourville to take '*le grand major nommé Mr de Remondy*' in the '*canot blanc*' from ship to ship of the fleet to enquire of aught lacking aboard and the health of the sailors. For the sick '*flûtes hospitalières*' were available. Using Doublet's barque, Remondy made his inspection in three and a half days, exceeding sea-sick in the course of duty. Tourville stayed at sea till 20th/10th August and encountered nothing. Seignelay, who had accompanied the French admiral, developed a chest illness, dispatched a courier to Louis, waited a reply, which, received, ordered him to court and commanded Tourville, lying now by Belle Isle, to take in the fleet.[98]

It must not be supposed that the immunity which from 30th/20th July to 20th/10th August Tourville enjoyed had been accepted by him without question. Orders had been issued on the 17th/7th to le Sieur Dumené to look in on Plymouth, like instruction of the same date given to M. Desfrans of *le Trident*; also upon the 17th/7th le sieur de Lévy in *La Gratienne* had been sent to cruise off the Scillies.[99] But no certain knowledge was to hand by the 23rd/13th when Doublet made, through the flag-captain of Tourville's *le Conquérant*, Mr de Venize,[100] a startling offer ('*enterprise d'étourdi*'!) to Seignelay. It was accepted. With ample commission (signed Louis, dated Versailles, countersigned Colbert) and a promise that, if he, Doublet, were caught, Seignelay would do his best to get him exchanged, Doublet headed for Mount's Bay. Chased by a guard vessel, he dodged among the rocks by the

Lizard, then coasted towards Portland and, Ostend flag displayed, anchored off Exmouth. Out came a boat. Its officer boarded Doublet's barque, most of the crew of which were concealed from sight. French brandy? The English officer could certainly arrange for profitable disposal of the contraband! And an hour and a half later a brightly painted eight-oared boat brought a fine gentleman in a scarlet cloak, prepared, so it seemed, for an illegal deal. The gentleman scaled on board. Eight men in a boat soon saw an anchor weighed and counted themselves lucky to be left in their own Bay; the gentleman found himself a French prisoner! Nearing the Brittany coast Doublet was attacked by two Flushing frigates; but he ran for the hazards of Roscof, made the port, landed, fed well, took post horses for Brest, and arrived there on the evening of the 29th/19th. At 4 a.m. next morning, aboard *le Conquérant*, Tourville received '*très gracieusement*' Doublet and his English captive. Seignelay, roused from sleep, entered in dressing gown. Asked whether he had been robbed, 'scarlet cloak' took out a fine watch, exhibited a purse of guineas, extended a diamonded finger. His name? Thomas 'Fisjons' (Fitzjohns?) 'collector or receiver of the royal customs at Exmouth'. What did Seignelay desire of him? Full details of the Allied fleet. That, Fitzjohns said, he would be a traitor to give–but, if only his captor had investigated the contents of the '*portfeuille*', he could have discovered the information sought. Search followed. There, on one of '*deux pancartes*' a complete picture of the English and Dutch squadrons, commanders, guns, complements, all–even the signals of the fleet! Seignelay felicitated Tourville! Who could desire more? But another '*pancarte*' fell out–the equal picture of the French '*armée*' and its signals! . . . Seignelay asked Fitzjohns how he would like to return to England. Via Calais or Zeeland? By sea with Doublet was the choice. Four English sailors were taken from a French prison, an extra boat put aboard Doublet's barque; and, in due course, off Torbay–not too far from Fitzjohn's home!–the boat was lowered, occupied by the four lucky sailors and the Collector of the Customs for Exmouth! Whether Seignelay and Tourville, questioning Fitzjohns on 30th/20th August, could learn or deduce anything of value of the station of the Anglo-Dutch fleet–then off Mizzen Head–may be doubted. Presumably

Torrington was not in Torbay when Doublet returned his captive to safety. To Tourville, about to return to Brest, the urgency of information would lessen. It is uncertain when exactly that return occurred. *'C'est de bonne part que, si ma flotte ne sort point, et s'il n'y a point d'avantages sur elle, que les ennemis ne peuvent rien entreprendre de la campagne.'*[101]

A clear statement, on the French part, of the doctrine of the 'fleet in being'. At no time that summer had Louis intended to challenge Anglo-Dutch might.

There is little direct evidence that Torrington had watched for Tourville. It is true that Russell had gossiped to Nottingham (in the letter of the 13th July) accepting the hearsay evidence of a captured Frenchman to the effect that 'Turvil' was not to sail, 'till he had made peace with Algere and bin before Barcelona'. Indeed, convinced no French fleet would put to sea that summer, Russell had advised that the King should use his ships to cover an expedition to Ireland and effect seizure of a south coast Irish port for naval use in the coming winter. On the other hand, there is nothing to show that Torrington had not exercised circumspection. The sentence in the log of Killigrew's flag-captain comes back to mind: 'This day we heare yt ye Tollon squadron is joynd those at Brest wch doe Admire we continually cruising about.' But the entry does not assert, or necessarily imply, cruising designed to intercept forces from the Mediterranean. Whether the English frigate which Doublet's *Sans Peur* encountered just before he picked up, far west of Brest, Tourville's squadron, was a scout sent out, on a like but less friendly search by Torrington, one cannot tell. The form in which Torrington received his Instructions placed upon him no requirement to look-out for the French reinforcement; but it is hard to accept that he can have been entirely blind to the contingency that Tourville *might* be working up from southward and, to the extent to which that bare possibility—distinct from a probability—entered his thought, he would be desirous of preventing the junction of French forces by effecting the Frenchman's destruction. Out of Torrington's own mouth we have no clue to his thoughts, none to his reaction when *Swiftsure* brought him the news that Tourville had made Brest.[102]

The destruction by Torrington of Tourville's much inferior fleet *en route* for Brest, or a like outcome from a general mêlée off Douarnenez–Brest ships emerging to assist Tourville's passage of the Iroise–would not suddenly have solved William's Irish problem; but the news of a French naval defeat would unquestionably have added to the stature of William among his continental confederates and immeasurably strengthened his hand to deal with the neutral sea-powers Sweden and Denmark. What is certain is that defeat of Tourville would have rendered impossible the occurrence the following year of the encounter off Beachy Head, contested on the French side by the combined effectives of Brest and those score and more now brought thither by Tourville.[103] From the result of that engagement flowed great consequences of encouragement to the French Marine and to Louis, which were not to be negatived till decisive defeat struck at Barfleur–la Hougue.[104] It were, however, 'to consider too curiously of the matter' to entertain the further notion that, Tourville intercepted in 1689, the mid-May battle of 1692 would not have been fought.

Had the cruise of the Grand Fleet, as far as completed, ended then in comparative failure? Far from it. It was behind the shield of a major command of the Narrow Seas, of the Channel and Channel approaches, by this three squadronal first Anglo-Dutch fleet, a command established by blockade followed by more distant watch on Brest, that Rooke's small squadron had maintained with ease its lesser command of St George's Channel, the Irish Sea and the North Channel, upon which command depended all operations designed to press and effect the relief of Londonderry, encourage Enniskillen with tangible aid, protect Scotland, and place and establish the first contingents of Schomberg's force upon the eastern Irish shore. Rooke's maintenance of limited command, during the months mid-May to the end of August, is the subject of a following chapter. Other functions of Torrington's command require notice.

Neither the Allies nor the French had indulged in coastal raiding. Military stores were conveyed along the Channel shores to westward and into the St George's Channel with impunity. The exploit of the Chevalier Claude l'Amblimont, chef-d'escadre, against a squadron of Dutch warships conveying troops and stores to the West Indies was very much the exception.

Eighteen leagues W.N.W. of the Texel, at three of the morning of the 27th/17th July d'Amblimont had sighted five Dutch ships. They proved to be two Amsterdammers each mounting twenty-four guns–at least a dozen less than they were designed to carry–a Flushinger, armed with eighteen and six perriers, a flute of Amsterdam with six cannon and a galiot of that Admiralty with four. There were soldiers aboard. As the French squadron bore down on a wind, *la Sorcière* (Harpin) a twenty-six, *le Profond* (d'Amblimont), a flute of forty, *la Trompeuse* (de la Motte) a frigate of twelve, *La Serpente* (de Selingue) of twenty-six, so close in line that they were in each other's wash, the Dutch brailed their main sails and, with 'arrogance', took in their mizzens as they displayed their Dutch flags. At range d'Amblimont ran up French colours and 'la flamme de combat'. A fight to the death began. Selingue captured the leading Dutchman (she carried 100,000 livres worth of cargo 'argent de Holland' in hold); the Dutch commander's vessel, lying second in his line (her destination Guinea and her treasure comparable) was destroyed; the third, that is the Flushinger, bound for Surinam but of less value, was sunk; the flute, richly laden for Surinam, became a prize. Apparently the galiot escaped. In the mêlée d'Amblimont's *Profond*, after battering the Dutch commander, took fire, luckily brought under control. Selingue saw the doomed Dutchman 'sauter en l'air et en même temps couler à fond'; he watched would-be survivors of the holocaust take to boat, *'leurs mains jointes au ciel . . . demandant quartier et la charité'*, which he gave–wondering, since he had heavily reduced his own numbers by putting on the captured vessel a prize crew, whether it were wise to take aboard *la Serpente* so many survivors. Against a south-west wind d'Amblimont made for Dunkirk, adding a 'dogre qui venait de la pêche' to make his prizes three. His losses were negligible–a famous if small victory.[105]

But while, in its military aspect, Torrington's command approximated to control complete, no such dominance applied in respect of denial of the sea to French trade or protection afforded to English and Dutch shipping. The extent to which the belligerents

were disturbing each other's commerce on the high seas by capture
of each other's merchantmen is not readily ascertainable. The
sea-borne trade of France did not compare with that of England
and the United Provinces. Even if one does not go as far as Raynal
to affirm,

> '*Les rades du nord ne recevaient pas un navire français et celles du sud
> n'en voyaient que rarement. L'état avait abandonné jusqu'à son cabotage
> à des étrangers*',[106]

one can accept that the French had much shipping–all passing
into the Channel or moving in the North Sea–upon which to
prey. Each of the nations used the warship to chase and catch
merchant prize; each had long recognized the supplementary
warship, the privateer, sailing (whilst a war was in progress) on a
special commission, a letter of marque, which lifted the status of
the master of the vessel above that of pirate. While the warship
proper, moving as part of a squadron or fleet, or coming and
going on specific mission, might, by chance, intercept an enemy's
merchantman or suspected neutral, the privateer like the modern
submarine could range unfettered to kill. And though every non-
commissioned vessel had the right (which still obtains) to resist
arrest and though few were the trader craft of that era which did
not carry some sort of armament, only the larger could hope to
brush off the privateer attacker.[107] The Admiralty provided
regular warship convoy for trade to the Mediterranean, to and
from the Canaries, the West Indies, New England, the Newfoundland Banks and Hudson Bay; protection for the ships bringing
essential naval stores from the lands adjoining the Baltic and from
Holland, for Tyne colliers; it watched the North Sea fisheries,
listened to the needs of shippers of Norfolk grain, Welsh coal or
West Country wool. The Dutch were also concerned to provide
convoy on ocean routes–to the West Indies, the Mediterranean and
the Indies of the East. In any case there was constant passage of
warships to and from the Nore, off Vlissengen, through the
Downs and up and down the Channel. But do what the Allies
might they could not, short of destruction of all the usable ports
of France from Dunkirk to St Malo, eliminate the privateers, who,
on that coast, with the encouragement and under the supervision
of the Ministry of Marine, established, to the menace of all that

I. Samuel Pepys, by Sir Godfrey Kneller.

II. (Right) Arthur Herbert, Earl of Torrington, by R. White after J. Riley.

III. Anne Hilarion de Constantin, Comte de Tourville.

Daniel.
Earl of Winchilsea
& Nottingham;
1727,

IV. Daniel Finch, 2nd Earl of Nottingham (artist unknown).

V. Percy Kirke, Lieutenant General (artist unknown).

VI. A north-east view of the City of Londonderry *c.* 1680, by T. Phillips.

VII. Edward Russell, Earl of Orford, by Sir Godfrey Kneller.

IX. (*Facing*) Flagship masts in Het Y Voor, Amsterdam, by W. Van de Velde (the younger).

VIII. (*Below*) The flagship *Resolution*, by W. Van de Velde (the younger).

X. Contemporary model – the *St Michael*. Built at Portsmouth, 1669, by Sir John Tippetts. Length 125 ft, beam 40 ft 8½ in., hold 17 ft 5 in., draught 19 ft. 8 in., burden 1101 tons.

XI. A Dutch flagship coming to anchor, by P. Canot after W. Van de Velde (the younger).

## A Prospect of CARRECK-FERGUS.
*Being the Place where King William landed in Ireland.*

A. The King in the Mary Yacht Capt. Collins
B. Prince George in the Henrietta Yacht Capt. Sanderson
C. The King going a Shoare in Sr. Clo: Chowells Barg
D. Sr. C. Shovell Rear. Adm.ll of the Blew in the Monk with his Squadron
Æ. Bonfiers on the Shoare.

XII. King William landing in Ireland, *Great Britain's Coasting Pilot* (Map 32).

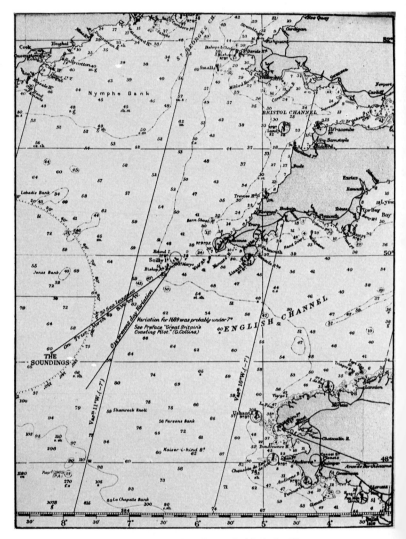

A. *Channel Approaches*. Part of *Admiralty Chart 2*.
By courtesy of H.M. Stationery Office and the Hydrographer
of the Navy.

B. *Battle of Bantry Bay.*

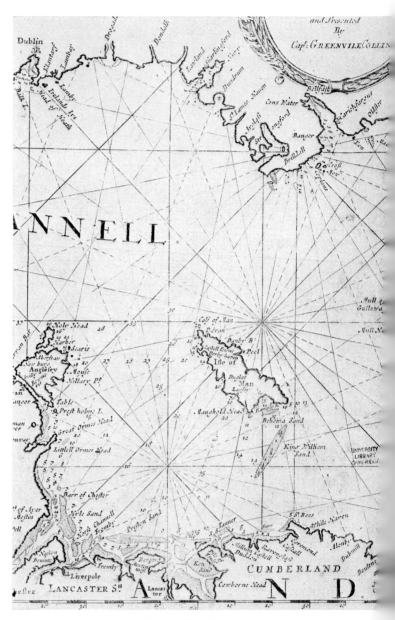

C. *Irish Sea*, Greenville Collins, from *Great Britain's Coasting Pilot*, 1693.

D. *Ireland North Coast* from *Le Neptune François*, 1693.

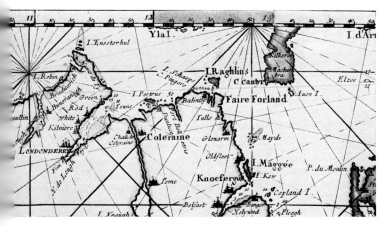

E. Northern Ireland, sketch map with selected place-names.

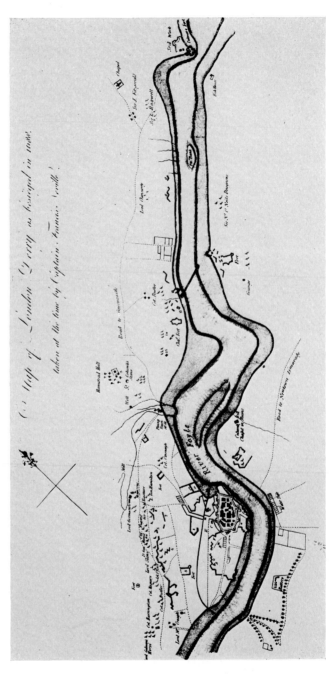

F. *A map of Londonderry as besieged in 1688*, Francis Neville.
Original in Trinity College, Dublin.

# KEY TO CHART F

## DESCRIPTION OF THE TOWN, ETC.

a Double bastion,
b Royal bastion,
c Platform,
d Hangman's bastion,
e Gunners' ditto,
f Coward's ditto,
g Water ditto,
h Newgate ditto,
i Ferry ditto,
k Church ditto,
l Church-yard ditto,
m Diamond,
n Queen-street,
o Silver-street,
p Gracious-street,
q School-lane,
r Butchers'-street,
s House of Correction,
t Pump-street,
u Bishop's House,
x Ravilin,
y Old Church-yard,
z Wapping,
A An old work made in the last wars,
B Foundation of cathedral, or long tower,
C Small redoubt,
D Cow market,
E Columb-kil's three wells, from which the besieged got water,
F A work made by the besieged, lest they should be forced out of the trenches at the windmill.

## DESCRIPTION OF THE ENEMY'S CAMP

1 An old Danish fort,
2 A fort,
3 A trench,
4 A platform of three mortars,
5 & 6 Two batteries,
7 A battery of two guns,
8 A trench, with small shot,
9 A line of approach,
10 A guard-house,
11 Ditch of the orchard,
12 Small ditch,
13 Last line of approach,
14 A ditch made across the strand,
15 & 16 Places where they kept advanced guards,

No. 17, 18, & 19, Three batteries to defend the boom.

It was between No. 17 & 18 that Captain Brownrigg's ship, after breaking the boom, ran on shore; but the tide coming in, and firing her chace guns, she got off safe. Here, also, Captain Brownrigg lost his life by a small shot in the head.

The boom was a float of timber, with iron sockets at the end of each piece, and so buckled together; it was about 200 yards long, and five or six feet broad, lashed about with small cables, and spiked through.

a, a. Ditches lined with small shot.

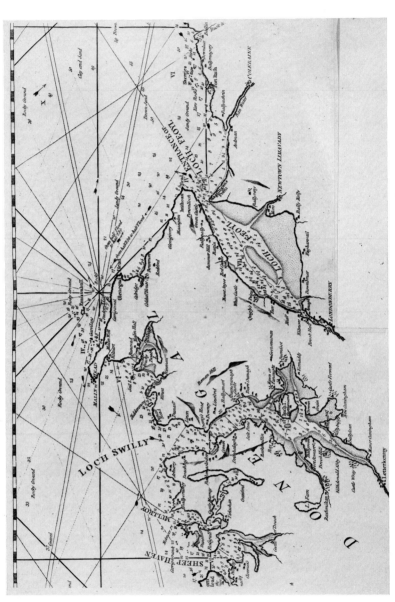

G. *Sheep Haven to Skerries*, from J. Huddart in *The Coasting Pilot*

passed into and out of the Channel or moved in the North Sea, a veritable trade.

The English government early decided to emulate the French, follow the example of the Dutch–particularly the Zeelanders–and encourage privateers to sea;[108] but there was appreciable administrative delay in giving effect to the plan. The tenor of a Commission for granting letters of marque, 'according to the Course of Admiralty and Laws of Nations', received Nottingham's signature on the 27th April.[109] This, as not properly directed nor under the great seal, the Admiralty did not consider adequate; and the Privy Council ordered Sir Charles Hedges, Sir Thomas Pinfold and Dr Oldys to prepare a satisfactory draft. The lengthy document and the articles and instructions to merchants and others who should receive letters of marque were drawn up.[110] On the 12th July, a letter with impression of the great seal of Admiralty was accorded Joseph Reade commander of the *Diligent of Lymerick* to sail belligerently 'against the ffrench King and his Subjects or Inhabitants within any his Dominions'. The Declaration, made before Hedges the day before, showed the *Diligent* to be of 100 tons with a crew of fifty. Her lieutenant, master, gunner, boatswain and cook are named. She was victualled for three months; her armament consisted of eight iron guns and fourteen patereroes, for which she carried six barrels of powder and 500 wt of shot. Small arms for fifty men were stored and *Diligent* possessed two suits of sails.[111] Before the close of August, application for six other letters had been made to the Board of Admiralty[112] and passed on, approved, to the Judge of the High Court or his surrogate for completion of legal formalities and granting.[113]

The special nexus between the privateers of Dunkirk, Dieppe and St Malo and the French Ministry of Marine should always be borne in mind. Colbert had seen the advantages of encouraging, disciplining, controlling men whose habitat, traditions and early-learned maritime skill, whose passions and greed drove them to choice of the corsair trade. Seignelay and Louis were, in 1689, fostering Colbert's schemes–indeed, in practice, integrating these restless seamen into a ruthless volunteer reserve. A successful corsair might attain naval rank, though without genuine acceptance by the noblesse officer corps,[114] be appointed to specific

G

naval duties to convoy or scouting or even squadronal command.
For the common mariner, danger and wounds but also reward.
The English privateers formed no such confraternity.

The capture of Bart and Forbin by Sincocke of the *Nonsuch* and
their incarceration in Plymouth has already been recounted (see
pp. 151–53 *ante*)–but not the sequel, known, one would like to
suppose, to every French school-boy. Stress of weather drove into
Plymouth a Dutch merchantman commanded by none other than
Gaspard Bart, the corsair's cousin, who learned of the identity of
the recently taken officers and received permission to visit his
relative. In the course of three visits, plans for escape were laid–
not in Gaspard's ship but in a boat stolen from a drunken fisher-
man by two English attendants who had been free at times to
come and go in the port and were willing for silver to enter a plot.
At length the bars of a tower window were filed and Bart, Forbin,
a French chirurgeon and the two 'mousses' at midnight of the
2nd/12th June dropped on improvised ropes to the quayside,
found their sail-less boat, eluded the guardship, and dared a
stormy Channel. But the sea calmed; and the escaped reached
little Harqui, on the Normandy coast six leagues from St Malo,
two days after leaving Plymouth. Bart was no doubt gratified to
learn that Seignelay had taken steps to obtain the release of
himself and Forbin *'mais surtot du Sieur Bart'* by prisoner inter-
change–two Customs' Officers or the Captain of a Dutch man-
of-war for Bart. Louis promoted both Bart and Forbin to the rank
of capitaine-de-vaisseau and Bart back in Dunkirk waited to learn
the wishes of Seignelay.[115] There is even a postscript to the sequel.
That summer, at sixteen and a half, René Duguay Trouin was
turning his back on the church and the University of Caen to
begin a corsair career which would place his name side by side
with that of Bart and Forbin. Before the war ended he had
captured the captor and *Nonsuch* had become *Non-Pareil*!

For an English or Dutch ship, naval or privateer, to capture a
French-owned merchantman and pass it, with all its cargo spiked
down (whatever that cargo might be) to the adjudication of a
prize court, was a routine procedure. Its counterpart was as
simple for the French enemy. But what of trade direct or through
intermediaries between English or Dutch merchant of the one

part and French factor of the other? And what of contraband (however that term might be defined) carried in neutral bottoms, direct or through intermediaries to the enemy?

A treaty concluded between William and the 'Seigneurs Estats Generaux' on 12th/22nd August[116] at Whitehall left no doubt of the manner in which William decreed and the Dutch consented that those questions should be answered. Its title proclaimed that it existed for 'Union' and 'Concert' of arms but, *'principalement pour interdire toute sorte de Commerce ou Traffic'* with France; it advanced through a brief preamble to the announcement that Allied fleets would blockade *'bloquer'*, all the ports, harbours and roads of the Most Christian King—in other words watch to achieve as far as possible the prohibitions set out in three following paragraphs. The first forbade English or Dutch subjects, using their own vessels or those of another state, to commerce with the French in any manner whatsoever; to bring French goods into the harbours of the Allies or carry such into any other state; to take any goods, whatever their place of origin, into French ports. Offence would be paid for by confiscation of ship and cargoes. The second[117] announced that, since several rulers and states of Christendom had already forbidden all commerce with France, the English King and the Seigneurs had decided that the subjects of states not at war with France must behave in the same way or suffer attachment of their vessels and condemnation as prize *'par les Juges competens'*. The third provided that these arrangements should be notified to all the European powers, some of which might have potentially offending ships in voyage. Such vessels would be ordered to return to their ports of origin, or, if intercepted leaving French harbours, sent back to unload. But for the time being only! Notification delivered, offending vessels would risk arrest as good prize. The English and Dutch expected the states allied with them to concur in this treaty. There was to be no delay in operating the Treaty; but a separate article,[118] absent from some copies, indicated that the contracting parties anticipated it might not work completely smoothly.

The smuggling of brandy and wines, silk or other goods from France, the 'owling'[119] of Romney Marsh wool would not be likely to cease because a treaty had been made in London to reinforce proclamations posted at the ports at intervals since the spring;[120] and if, as was the case, it had been necessary for the Privy Council, 22nd July, 'given to understand that considerable quantitys of Salt Petre [were] about to be exported', to threaten the 'Utmost Rigor and Severity', at any contravention of a proclamation engrossed the 20th July, it is obvious that not all English merchants were likely to behave impeccably.[121] Their Dutch rivals were certainly not expected to behave more patriotically.[122] And it was certainly not to be taken for granted that the two chief neutrals, Sweden and Denmark, though the latter was already in treaty with William (15th/5th August) (on a business basis) for the supply of troops, would acquiesce in the dictation inherent in the Anglo-Dutch agreement–that Lutheranism would develop emotion enough to outweigh mercantile interests and national pride, and align, as William professed to hope, these two countries not actually on Louis's doorstep against him.[123] Three days after the Treaty had been signed, the Privy Council took cognizance of Danish and Swedish vessels detained in English ports and ordered the taking out of all goods of the Allies or the enemy before sending the ships on homeward voyage.[124]

From the example of the Hanse towns, particularly Hamburg, limbs of the Empire, which, since 4th March/22nd February had been at war with Louis, or that of the Spanish Netherlands, part of the same Empire, Denmark and Sweden received no encouragement to co-operation on a single trade blockade; no example from Spain, made hostile to Louis since the 15th/5th April but with her north-west ports nests of entrepôt traffic. Neutral Portugal like Spain was especially well placed for that sort of commerce. Inside the Streights, in spite of William's paper allocations of ships to squadrons, nothing English or Dutch yet acted in sufficient strength to hinder French trade. The fact that the Treaty closed with a special article by which the signatories mutually assured each other of aid in suppressing any resistance which the application of the Treaty might entail pointed to no expectation of smooth working of the drastic prohibitions.

Summer of 1689 was advancing when the Treaty, supposed to come into force at once, was signed. Technically it was ratified on the 24th August/3rd September[125] but, seemingly, the procrastination of Zeeland could hamper the most expeditious schemes.[126] To the operation of the Treaty in the concluding months of the year, September-December, reference will later be made. It can at once be said that the English government found it politic to grant from time to time licences for imports. For example the German, David Loggan, needed a special paper for the work that had already begun to make him famous[127] and certain named merchants reasonably desired consent to bring in a large quantity of French silk which was on order.[128]

The Treaty occupies a unique place in the context of International Law. As Westlake observes:

> The blockade of 1689 is of great historical importance. It was the first appearance of England on the scene as a blockading power . . . It is probable that to the alliance of England with the Dutch on this occasion we owe her adoption of the placard of 1630 as the basis of her prize law on the subject 'the received law of nations' to which reference is continually made in the reports of the English Admiralty and United States Supreme Courts.[129]

The 'placard' referred to was a Dutch trade blockade pronouncement against the Flemings–an earlier attempt to dictate what this Treaty on a far larger scale now set out to achieve.

The Treaty just considered was directed at the capture of enemy ships or the arrest of offending neutrals–or friends! Yet one phrase of four words at the close of the second paragraph *'par les Juges competens'* had the intended effect of modifying clause XII of the Concert of the Fleets Treaty or Naval Convention of the 29th April which provided always for adjudication of prize in the court of the captor. It happened that, during the spring and summer of this year, a number of Dutch privateers ran their captures, for convenience, into English harbours only to find unwillingness on the part of English port authorities to allow later removal of the ships into Dutch harbours and jurisdictions. Once only did the Dutch succeed in getting a prize released 'as the Treatys direct'.[130] And when the King received from the Dutch representatives at Whitehall a long diplomatic memorial on the subject,[131] dated the 24th June, the Privy Council answered with an unequivocal legal opinion–for the purpose obtained. Met together on the 4th July,

the Lords Chief Justices of the King's Bench and the Common
Pleas, the Judge of the High Court of Admiralty, the Attorney
General, the Solicitor General and Advocate General agreed:
>   that it is not Consistent with the Lawes of England to make it
>   an Article of Treaty with another Kingdome or state that in
>   Case Prizes be taken by the Privateers of the One Kingdome or
>   State, and brought into the Ports of the other, They shall in all
>   Cases be judged by the respective Admiralty of that Kingdome
>   or State to which the said Privateer belong and shall be
>   permitted to go thether from out of those Ports to that purpose.

The ostensible ground of the judgement was the consideration that
a ship brought in by a foreign privateer might be a vessel in
respect of which one of His Majesty's subjects considered he had a
claim. Such subject had indefeasible right to sue for a warrant in
the High Court of Admiralty in order to test his claim and 'no
Article in any Treaty [could] exclude [subjects] from Such their
Right, or disable [his] Ma^{tys} Court to proceed therein'.[132] With
that, officially at least, the Dutch had to be content. The reason
for the vague phrase '*par les Juges competens*' becomes plain!

Bound together by two treaties–that for 'Of Concert of the
Fleets of England and Holland' (29th April/9th May) and that
'To forbid Commerce with France' (12th/22nd August) (to give
them contemporary short titles), the Allies proceeded to a third,
of 'Amity and Alliance'.[133] It first listed all existent mutual
treaties, beginning with that of Breda, 21st/11th July 1667, tied
the parties not to make peace whilst either was at war with the
arch-enemy and moved to the assertion that, as soon as possible,
the arrangements of the Concert for the Fleets Treaty would be
supplemented by new 'articles and stipulations' on the numbers
and use of troops and naval vessels–the decisions to be reached
governed by paramount need to use resources to the best advantage against the common enemy.[134] The war over, the Treaty of
Westminster 3rd March 1677/8 (see p. 34) would again come
into force. This treaty bore date 24th August/3rd September.

The survey, mid-May to the end of August, would be incom-
plete without mention of a number of individual and commission

appointments designed to assist the Lords Commissioners of Admiralty and the Principal Officers and Commissioners of the Navy in their work, and if note were not taken of the report to the House of Commons of the Committee appointed to consider Torrington's plea for the casualties of sea-warfare (see p. 167 *ante*).

On the 11th June one Earle was appointed to the office of Register of all goods, ships, wares and merchandise that shall be seized in any port, at a yearly allowance of £106.13.4 with an additional payment of £93.6.8.[135] A full Prizes Commission was set up on the 19th June. It consisted of Sir Thomas Littleton, Sir Edward Ascough, Sir Roger Langley, Benjamin Overton, John Parkhurst, John Carpenter and Charles Dereing paid severally £500 per annum, their secretary John Dyve remunerated at the same rate.[136] James Herbert, on the 29th August was made Receiver General of all Prize Money.[137] The relation of these patentees to the High Court of Admiralty, the manner in which they interpreted and exercised their duties, in the light of previously established practice and the provisions of the existent Anglo-Dutch treaties is a matter which must be outside present discussion.

Three full folios of the Minutes of the Privy Council for the 11th July are required for the setting out of the 'Instructions to the Comm^rs for Sick & Wounded Seamen and Marines & others Imployed in his Maj^tys Service at Sea and for Releif of Widowes & Orphans of Such as shall be Slain in his Maj^tys Service and for ordinary Prisoners of War'.[138]

Firth[139] has directed attention to the fact that the Long Parliament took thought for the casualties of the Civil War; and the manner in which the Commonwealth and Protectorate essayed to deal with the sick and wounded, the dependents of the slain and with prisoners of war receives notice in the pages of Oppenheim.[140] The Commonwealth's appointment, in 1653, the First Dutch War at its height, of 'Commissioners of Sick and Wounded at Little Britain', four in number with fifteen subordinates, provided a pattern for the Commission of 1664, set up when the Second Dutch War became imminent. Again four chief members—each drawing an annual salary of £300—of whom the diarist Evelyn was the most active. Re-appointed in 1671/2,[141] when a Third Dutch War developed, the Commission was modified next year and lasted till 1674 when its functions were assumed by the Navy Board. In 1678 and 1681/2 Orders in Council dealt with and kept alive these functions; and, in the last year of James's reign, the establishment of 1672/3 was (but without Commissioners), 'renewed and rendered universal as to time place and service wherein any person shall be slain in his Majesty's pay as against his enemies at the seas'. The truth seems to be that the responsibilities of the Navy Board from the 28th March 1674 onwards had, on warrant from the Lords Commissioners of Admiralty, devolved on James Pearse 'chirurgeon general of his Majesty's Navy' (see p. 34 *ante*). Pearse, to whom Tanner accords the tribute 'a man of method after Pepys's own heart' seems to have done his work well.[142] But he was on his way out[143]—a loss no doubt to Admiralty and Navy Board administration. Had he been retained, a new major war on hand, it would still have been desirable and necessary to re-institute a full Commission. Thomas Addison, Edward Leigh, Anthony Shepherd and John Starkey each paid the £300 per annum, were the named members.[144] And if their ordered duties and permissible disbursement scales, as set out in the Privy Council Register, are compared with those which were devised to govern the conduct of the 1671/2 Commission, to be found in 'Naval Precedents'[145] and summarized therefrom by Tanner,[146] the extent of innovation will be seen to be limited. Appropriate reception centres for the wounded changed according to the 'frontages' of war; Portsmouth, Plymouth, Bristol, Whitehaven, were indicated for the businesses now in hand. The directives that the Commissioners be ready to go down to ports near to the scene of an engagement, that mayors of all towns are to be assistant at need were indicative of serious intent.

By chance the Committee of the House of Commons, set up in response to Torrington's appeal of the 21st May (see p. 167 *ante*) on behalf of the seamen wounded in their Majesties' service or the wives and children of the slain, reported at this time—indeed on the 15th July.[147] The Committee had taken evidence concerning the working of the Chatham Chest, the benevolence of Trinity House, and from other quarters. The Chatham Chest it was told, by 'Sir

Richard Haddock and others', was an institution of Elizabethan origin, controlled by nine governors[148] yearly chosen by former governors and supervised by two Commissioners of the Navy, chosen by the other governors. It derived its revenue from (i) a deduction of 6d. per month made from the pay of 'every common seaman' in the Navy, of 4d. per month additionally subtracted from a seaman's pay if the ship in which he served was rated to bear, but did not actually carry, a chaplain, and of 2d. a month if the vessel should have carried a surgeon and did not (ii) lands purchased worth £400 per annum (iii) forfeits, fines, mulcts on officers for misdemeanours. Against the Chest a wounded seaman might prefer claim—in effect for a yearly pension payable in advance.[149] The scale of relief stood: Loss of a leg or arm, 20 nobles (£6.13.4); of two, 20 marks (£13.6.8); of an eye £5; other hurts according to 'view of surgeon'.[150] In May 1688, 650 such pensions existed totalling £5,694.7.7 but the income for that year, apart from profit upon lands, reached only £1,300![151] 'The rest was supplied (as it hath formerly been accustomed) by the King,' in theory by Lord Treasurer to the Treasurer of the Navy on presentation of deficiency figures: 'At the last Pay in May 1688 there was Two Years Pay in Arrears and in May 1689, there was Three years Pay due'.[152]

The Chest gave nothing to the widows and children of the slain; but customarily a widow might expect eleven months pay out of the King's bounty. A child unmarried at the father's death might receive a third of that sum; if the sum amounted to £20 or more it was put 'into the Chamber of London[153] for the Use of Such child', if less, 'the Churchwardens of the Parish where the Father dwelt' were to administer. A widowed mother of fifty years and indigent could receive a widow's benefit if the slain man had no wife. Though, 'all wounded Men during their Cure lie at the King's charge', no public hospitals, so the Committee was told, were appropriated by the King for the purpose. St Thomas's in Southwark and St Bartholomew in London were commonly used.

The Corporation of Trinity House of Deptford Strond informed the enquiring members of its Henry VIII origin, of charter duties of buoyage, beaconage and lighting and indicated income derived from (i) dues for, 'Buoys, Beacons, Lights, Load, Manage and Primage' and, lately, ballasting;[154] (ii) from lands yielding £250 per annum for the poor. The total revenue reached £3,591 in the year ending Lady Day last. The upkeep of buoys, etc. cost £700 per annum; there were fifty-seven almshouses to maintain (at £11 to £20 each house per month) and 1,350 monthly pensions (2/6–5/–) were regularly paid. On almshouses and pensions for the year just ended £2,717 had been spent. To that needed to be added an item 'other accidental poor'–£150 per annum. Every month the Warden read the accounts to the Court; every year an audit! The Corporation always kept in hand £1,000 for 'emergent occasions'. How many pensioners? The extent of the income decided that–never less than 1,200. Trinity House did not make grants to beneficiaries whom the Chest had gratified; the widows and orphans of merchantmen were for Trinity House admissible applicants.

The Parliamentary Committee appears to have pressed for details on income from the Corporation's four lights. 'Silly', demanding ½d. a ton of outward or inward bound English ships and double of strangers, yielded the Brethren a profit of £350 a year. For 'Lostoft light in Suffolke and Caster Light by Yarmouth' they could give no separate light figures; ships in that area paid 5/4 per hundred tons per voyage, buoyage and beaconage; Winterton Light[155] was expected to collect 12d. per voyage from all English ships and 'by Strangers the Double', which insured a profit of £80. These replies obtained, and the Committee, reminded by the Brethren that, by an Elizabethan Act of Parliament and a Privy Council Order of James I, the Master and Wardens, 'ought solely to have the Erecting & Disposing of all such Sea Marks and Signs', professed it saw no reason why *all* lighthouse gain should not accrue, 'to the good of them that paid it', and proceeded to a rough inventory of lights not owned by the Corporation–Spurne, Tinmouth, Dungenesse, three on the N. and S. Forelands, two at Harwich, three at Wintertonness and two at Orfordness. But, 'the Persons interested [in these] being unwilling to make any Discovery', the Committee ordered 'to be reported specially' its estimate that 'communibus Annis' the patentees for these beacons made a profit of £4,000 per annum.[156]

The Committee turned down the proposal made in the time of Charles II and James II to adapt the King's House at Greenwich as an hospital but was attracted by the idea that a tax 'on Paper to be sealed for certain Uses' might bring in £18,000 per annum. It recommended (1) An imposition on sealed papers used for mercantile purposes as, 'a proper Fund towards the Relief of wounded Seamen and of the Widows and Children of such as should be slain in fight.' (2) That: 'Fourpence in each Pound be raised out of the Wages of all Seamen serving in Merchant Ships.' (3) that the Justices of the Peace be required next Quarter Sessions to make a return of 'what Monies during the Seven Years last past have been annually raised for the "Relief of maimed Soldiers & Seamen in pursuance of the Act of 43 Eliz", what pensions are at present being paid and what balances should be available for "present Supply"';[157] (4) That his Majesty be advised to be pleased to make no further grants of lights till the next Parliament meet. These recommendations the House received and carried a motion that the same Committee consider further whether St Katherine's Hospital and its revenue should not be applied to the benefit of wounded seamen. There is no indication that the Committee looked ahead toward method of distribution of the new monies to be raised. Possibly it considered it sufficient for the day to await the legislation that would be necessary for the implementation of its plans.

## REFERENCES

1 He attended 17th, 18th, 20th, 21st, 22nd, 24th, 28th, 29th, 30th May and 1st, 3rd June. P.R.O. Adm. 3/1 under dates.
2 *Journals . . . H. of C. . . .* under date. Herbert who had previously sat for Dover, 1685, was returned for Plymouth, 17th Jan. 1688/9. *Members of Parliament Pt 1, Parliaments of England, 1213–1702* (1878).
3 *Journals . . . H. of C.,* under date.
4 *Ibid.* 28th May.
5 *Ibid.* 15th July.
6 *Journals . . . H. of C.,* under date.
7 P.R.O. *Patent Roll Aᵒ 1ᵐᵒ Gul. et Mar.* [C66/3326]. The patent opens in the customary manner stating the honour (barony of Torbay, earldom of Torrington—no viscounty mentioned) and, for reasons of bestowal, presents Arthur Herbert as a sometime Master of the Wardrobe, a naval commander of fame, opponent of repeal of the Test Act, contemner of Popery, who

crossed over to Holland and brought safely thence the imposing liberating fleet. The honours stand in descent to the heirs male of Herbert's body with remainder to Charles Herbert, esquire and his heirs male. The patent, in tortuous Latin, spreads, badly engrossed, over the equivalent of more than two membranes.

8 Per pale azure and gules three lions rampant argent.

9 College of Arms, 13th June 1689. Lengthy entry and painted exemplification.

10 Chaplin (Capt.) W. R., *The Corporation of Trinity House of Deptford Strond from the year 1660 . . . 1952*. The election took place on Trinity Monday, 27th May. His deputy was Capt. Henry Mudd.

11 P.R.O. Adm. 3/1 under date.

12 *Ibid.* Under dates.

13 The evidence is the reference to the Toulon ships made by Nottingham in the draft of Instructions for Torrington, 1st June, quoted in the text following. While *H.M.C. Finch II*, p. 212, provides an indication of the final form the Instructions took, no mention is made of this draft, for which *v.* P.R.O., Finch MSS, 1st June.

14 P.R.O., Adm. 3/1, under date. It is not however referred to in *Orders and Instructions . . .* P.R.O., Adm. 2/3. For previous reference to Russell *v.* p. 26 *ante*. For Treasurership, *v.* p. 56 *ante*, note (10), Jackson *op. cit.* The Patent Roll, cited Note (7) this chapter, has the engrossement.

15 *Ibid.* Tindall, 28th May; Oldys and Hedges (the latter at £400 per annum 'to run durante se bene gesserit') 31st May. Joynes and Wilford, 21st, 22nd May; (Clarke *op. cit.* p. 276, for James's refuge aboard the *Eagle*), Joynes and Tozier 21st May, 3rd June. For biographies of the three Oxonians, Tindall, Oldys and (Sir Charles) Hedges, *v. D.N.B.* For their duties, *v.* (under their names) *Orders and Instructions . . .* P.R.O., Adm. 2/3. One of Hedges' first duties was to prepare letters patent for Joynes (*v.* Hedges, *ibid.*). Russell received warrant for the necessary court martial, P.R.O., Adm. 3/1, 3rd June.

16 *Ibid.* 27th May.

17 *Ibid.* 28th May.

18 *H.M.C. Finch II*, p. 212, gives a very inadequate summary. Here original Finch papers are used.

19 Descents such as the raid by Essex on Cadiz in 1596, Blake's unsurpassed exploit against the treasure ships at Santa Cruz de Teneriffe, 1657, the plundering descent upon Dutch East India ships at Terschelling in 1666 were exercises of command not operations to establish it.

20 P.R.O. Adm. 51/4180. Log of *Elizabeth* (Lieutenant). Bib. Pepsyiana Miscellanea IX [*v.* p. 107 *ante*, note (36) of this work].

21 Log of *Elizabeth* (Lieutenant) and P.R.O. Adm. 51/4135. Log of *Cambridge* (Captain's).

22 P.R.O. Adm. 3/1, 8th May.

23 Warnsinck, *op. cit.* p. 27, refers to a letter from Van Almonde to the States General, Spithead, 7th June (28th May O.S.) which indicated that he had arrived there with 5 large vessels as well as a frigate and a brander and found there 1 large Rotterdam warship and a frigate, which had recently escorted merchantmen from Holland to the Thames. The log of *Elizabeth* (Lieutenant's) noted the arrival of the Dutch Vice-Admiral 28th May.

24  *v.* p. 34 note (42) for Dutch flags.

This matter of Vice-Admiral van Almonde's flag is far from easy to follow! It can (should the reader be interested) be studied in P.R.O. Finch MSS, 10th June, the original of *H.M.C. Finch II*, p. 214. *H.M.C. Finch II*, pp. 215 and 219.

What is Torrington's final position? He had been present at the Board which had minuted, 1st June, a Commission for Russell to be 'Vice Admirall of the Fleet now fitting for sea'.

Almonde, Philips van, born 1644 at Brielle, entered sea-service young, captained the *Dordrecht* in the Four Days Fight of 1666, commanded the fleet at Goree, 1672, rejoined Tromp and, in 1674, cruised off Spain and France. He took back the Dutch ships after de Ruyter's death in Sicily, assisted Tromp in defending Denmark against the Swedes. With Evertsen, Van Almonde ranked as a Lieutenant Admiral under 'Lieutenant Admiral General' Herbert in William's descent on England. Consequently Torrington and Van Almonde were not complete strangers. Van Almonde, in 1688/9, brought the Princess Mary from Holland to the Thames. He will be found, subsequent to this campaign, adding to his reputation at La Hougue 1692, and especially, with Rooke, in 1702, at Vigo Bay. Totally deaf he was forced to retire from service and died in 1711 at Haamyck near Leyden. *La Grande Encyclopédie.*

25  *H.M.C., Finch II*, p. 214.

26  *Ibid.* p. 215, Torrington to Nottingham and a signed fleet list enclosed.

27  *Ibid.* Torrington to Nottingham. An enclosed ship list there referred to is not printed. Included in P.R.O. Finch MSS, 13th June, it shows 20 named English ships ready to sail, 4 to be out of Portsmouth in a week and 6 waiting with Sir Francis Wheeler off Plymouth.

28  As note (26).

29  As log referred to in note (20) together with P.R.O. Adm. 51/4180. Log *Elizabeth* (Captain's).

30  P.R.O. Adm. 3/1, 11th and 13th June. Commissions to Davies and Berkeley as Admirals of the Red and 'to weare Red Flaggs at the Masthead as they formerly (when there were three Flaggs) did Union fflaggs'.

31  P.R.O. Adm. 2/3, 8th June. For biography of Killigrew *v. D.N.B.* For Ashby Ch. VII *ante* and *D.N.B.*

32  Logs *Elizabeth* and Log of *Yorke* (Lieutenant's). Rawl. C.968. *H.M.C. Finch II*, p. 219, Torrington to Nottingham. But the two papers, dated 20th June, giving names of ships and guns, English and Dutch are not in the *H.M.C.* volume. *v.* P.R.O. Finch MSS. None the less, admirals, like farmers, are allowed to grumble. When, on 23rd June, Torrington announced himself on station he reported this fireship loss with the comment that, if the rest of the dozen were as 'ill-fitted', he had 'as good be without them' and, having harked back to leaving the Dutch Rear Admiral Brackell behind in Portsmouth, he complained that he had had to send in to Plymouth another Dutch ship 'disabled without any the least bad weather'. He noticed the rest of the Dutch ships might 'hold out better . . . most [were] olde crasy ships', *H.M.C. Finch II*, p. 220. See also *Memoirs . . . Torrington*, p. 39.

33  See Appendix F. B.M. MSS Add. 3650. Like the Bantry signals not in Corbett, *op. cit. v.* p. 117, note (81) *ante*.

34  Seignelay, 8 Juin/29th May had indicated to Chateaurenault the intention
of Louis that cruising in the Channel continue till the end of the month.
At the same time, he, Seignelay, had rebuked Chateaurenault for wanting
to transfer the whole crew of *L'Ardent* to his ship *le Souverain*; and taken
occasion to comment upon the battle of Bantry Bay.

Mon intention n'est pas de blâmer votre action, mais je ne puis m'empêcher de vous dire qu'il a paru à tout le monde qu'elle auroit pu être
poussée plus loin . . .

Clément, P. *op. cit.* p. 347.

35  *Memoirs . . . Torrington*, p. 39.

36  *H.M.C. Finch II*, p. 220. The fleet was now definitely reported as 'forty-
three sail of men of war and twelve fireships'.

37  Log of *Yorke*.

38  As note (36).

39  As note (37).

40  As note (37).

41  Log of *Elizabeth* (Captain's).

42  *Memoirs . . . Torrington*, p. 39.

43  Log of *Elizabeth* (Captain's) for 27th June and 3rd July.

44  Log of *Elizabeth* (Captain's). For Dutch squadron list *v.* p. 181 *ante*. The
Dutch squadron came under the command of Lieutenant Admiral Cornelis
Evertsen (the younger). He was born at Flushing in 1642 and went to sea
at the age of ten. While commanding, at the age of twenty-three, a 22-gun
vessel, he was captured by the English but immediately released by Charles
II. Evertsen was second in command to Herbert in William's invasion fleet
1688. He was to serve similarly under Callenburg in the Dutch squadron
participating in the fight 'off Beachy Head 1690'. He became Admiral of
Zeeland and died at Middleburg 1706.

45  Log of *Yorke*, 9th July.

46  P.R.O. Adm. 3/1, 5th July. The ships which at the end of June (P.R.O.
Adm. 8/2 28th June) were with Killigrew were (3rd) *Kent*, (4ths) *Assurance,
Berkeley Castle, Coronation, Princess Anne, Success*, (5ths) *Supply, Peare*, (fireships)
*Eagle, Elizabeth and Sarah*, (Yacht) *Kitchin*.

47  Tourville, Anne Hilarion de Costantin, comte de, was born in Paris in 1642.
At the age of nineteen, the young 'Chevalier de Malte' served against the
Barbary pirates. Commissioned capitaine in 1666 he fought, in 1669, under
Beaufort against the Turks, under d'Estrées against Sallee and, under him
again, in the uneasy Anglo-French alliance of 1672 (Solebay) and 1673
against the Dutch. Tourville's career from 1675 to 1688 lay almost entirely
in the Mediterranean. He followed Vivonne and Duquesne against Sicily
and the latter against de Ruyter–in respect of which service Colbert, in the
King's name, felicitated him. After the battle of d'Agosta, 1676, Tourville
was placed at the head of a squadron which destructively attacked a
Spanish-Dutch fleet at Palermo. He was promoted Chef-d'escadre at the
close of 1677. His first squadronal command ended in shipwreck in the Bay
of Biscay. Hereabouts began his active assistance of Colbert's reforms and
ship construction; instruction of junior officers, naval manoeuvres henceforth much engaged him. None the less he incurred rebuke for tardy response
to new mobilization, 1682, against Algiers. Active against Spain, present,

under Duquesne, at the bombardment of Genoa 1684, he reached, in 1685, at the age of 43, the rank lieutenant-général des armées navales. In the Mediterranean his various services continued–among them a colourful fight, 1688, with the Spanish admiral Papachim to enforce the French claim to salute of the flag. The war declared by France against Holland, 1688, brought him with a small detachment, temporarily into the Channel where he took prizes. Then occurred the exploit which is here described.

Tourville's success off Bévéziers (Beachy Head) 1690, his 'campagne du large' of 1691, his defeat off La Hougue 1692, his capture of the Smyrna convoy 1693, are the best known happenings of the subsequent years. The honour of Maréchal de France was accorded Tourville in 1693. He died in 1701 and was buried in Paris.

Delabre, J., *Tourville et la Marine de son temps*, Paris 1889, main work on the career of Tourville; *La Grande Encyclopédie*.

48 Villette, Philip le Valois (Marquis de), *Mémoires*, ed. Monmerqué, M. Paris, 1844, p. 92. Villette, or Villette-Mursay after the name of his château, born 1632, had served twenty years in the army when Seignelay persuaded him to resort to the sea. He gained repute against the Dutch in the Mediterranean and with d'Estrées in American waters. He reached the rank of Chef-d'escadre in 1686. Long time a protégé of Mme de Maintenon, he, by 1687, embraced Catholicism and found promotion easier. Lieutenant-général des armées navales, before the close of 1689, the way lay open for responsibility as vice-admiral of the van at Bévéziers 1690 and, as vice-admiral of the centre at La Hougue, 1692. He continued his naval career and died in 1707.

49 Sevin de Quincy, *Histoire Militaire du Règne de Louis le Grand* 7 t. La Haye, 1726, t. II, p. 228, itemises the 20–3 of second, 9 of third and 8 of fourth rank, 4 frigates, 8 fireships, 2 flutes and 2 tartanes. Aitzema, L. van, *Tweede Vervolg van Saken van Staat en Oorlog* . . . 28 Boek, Amsterdam 1698, p. 144, names the ships with captains and men. The list agrees with Sevin de Quincy except that it tables 2 (not 4) frigates and 4 (not 2) flutes.

50 Tramond, J., *Manuel d'Histoire Maritime de la France*, Paris, 1916, p. 19.

51 *op. cit.* p. 254.

52 The following account to 'the Toulon ships cast anchor' (p. 183) is based on Villette *op. cit.* pp. 92–4; Hoste *op. cit.* pp. 101–2; *Journal du Corsaire Jean Doublet de Honfleur* . . . ed. Bréard, C., Paris, 1883, pp. 138–41; La Fayette, *op. cit.* pp. 263–8. Delabre, J., *op. cit.* pp. 159–62 is not, for the expedition, of much contributive value.

53 *Journal* . . . *Doublet* p. 139, note 1. Authority *Arch. de la Marine*; but Doublet says he was aboard *Soleil Royal*.

54 There is little doubt of the date, de Quincy, *op. cit.* p. 228. Bréard in *Journal* . . . *Doublet* (p. 139) de la Roncière, *op. cit.* p. 61, and others state thus; but I do not know their authority.

55 de la Fayette, *op. cit.* p. 263.

56 *H.M.C. Finch II*, p. 228. Nottingham to Torrington: 'the French fleet came out of the Straits on the 2/12th instant' [July].

57 A Dutch privateer captured orders of Seignelay to 'Sieur de Gaudemar' 7th July/27th June to sail twelve leagues west of Belle Isle to meet 'Chevallier de Tourville'. Hauling up to leeward of the fleet Gaudemar will observe the

admiral put out a red flag at the mizzen to which he will reply 'du mesme pavillon' at the main; Gaudemar to windward will put out his red and the admiral will reply with the same colour. The packet which Gaudemar was ordered to deliver to Tourville (l'escadre dud S<sup>r</sup> De Tourville est de vingt vx de ligne huit bruslots, une fregatte, deux flustes et deux tartanes) indicated that at the date in question, the King intended the Brest fleet to sail to Belle Isle to meet the Toulon ships. Had Tourville received this packet he would have been forbidden to seek Brest. *H.M.C. Finch II*, p. 221, supplemented by reference to Finch MSS.

Villette p. 91. *Journal* . . . *Doublet*, p. 139, note 2, cites 'Ordres au Sieur. de Beaugey aller croiser à l'hauter d'Ouessant'−14 Juillet and to 'Sieurs de la Guiche et de Septimes d'aller reconnaître la flotte ennemie'−14 Juillet (Arch. de la Marine).

58 *Journal* . . . *Doublet*, p. 139, note 2, cites 'Memoire Instructif au Sr de Levy, commandant *la Lutine*, pour aller à la recontre de M. de Tourville'−15 Juillet (Arch. de la Marine). For armament of the 'barque longue' *v. ibid.* p. 134.

59 Villette, *op. cit.* pp. 19 and 92−footnotes.

d'Amfréville, capitaine 1666, chef-d'escadre de Languedoc 1677, lieutenant-général 1688, (Etat abrégé de la Marine du Roy (1690) Archives de la Marine). de Nesmond, capitaine 1667, chef-d'escadre 1688, both, like Villette, destined to carry flags at Beachy and La Hougue.

60 Villette, *op. cit.* p. 93. The directions in which the frigates were sent suggests that Tourville lay well south of Lat. 48°. Du Chalard, capitaine, 1676, note 1, *infra*. La Mothe d'Airan, capitaine de galiote, 1684, *ibid.* note 2.

61 Hoste, *op. cit.* p. 102: 'fit mettre côte-en-travers à toute l'Escadre . . . cela faisoit trouver étrange à quelques-uns, qu'on perdît, à la cape, un temps si prétieux.' [la cape=mainsail.] 'Estre à la cape−c'est ne porter que la grande voile, bordée et amurée tout arrière. L'on se tient à la cape . . . [ou] pour attendre quelque chose'−Jal. *op. cit.*

62 *Journal* . . . *Doublet*, p. 138, note 3 'les Sieurs de Beaumont et Doublet ayant eu ordre de naviguer entre Pennemarc et Glenan pour découvrir si les ennemis s'estoient avancez jusqu'à ce parage, il [M. de Beaugey] les chechera et les ordonnera de revenir incessamment à Brest'−30 Juillet. (Arch. de la Marine, Ordres du Roi, Ponant) [Glennan island is between Pennemarc and Groys].

63 Hoste, *op. cit.* p. 102.

64 Villette, *op. cit.*, p. 94.

65 It is not necessary on reading Hoste's statement, p. 102, 'les ennemis qui étoient huit ou dix lieuës au vent, eurent le déplaisir de nous voir entrer à Brest' to suppose that he wishes to imply physical observation. Villette suggests the enemy learned 'lendemain' from 'des pecheurs', p. 94.

66 Possibly in the same bay−At least Tourville's flagship was there some days later. For Bertheaume and preceding place names, Jaillot, *op. cit.*(Carte particulière des Costes de Bretagne) and modern Charts.

67 *Gazette de France* 6 Août, p. 388 'Le 2 de ce mois le Roy reçeut avis que l'escadre commandée par le Chevalier de Tourville . . . estoit arrivée à la rade du Brest le 30 du mois dernier sans toucher à Belle Isle'.

68 *H.M.C. Finch II*, p. 226. The list there referred to, but not printed, may be seen in P.R.O. Finch MSS, signed Torrington.
69 For 'The truth is . . . lay by'. Logs of *Yorke, Elizabeth* (Captain's), *Cambridge* (Captain's), Adm. 51/4135 (see next page), *Reserve* (Captain's) Adm. 51/ 3953, *Duke* (Captain's) Adm. 51/4174, *Kent* (Captain's) 51/4230. *Yorke* and *Kent* remark heavy rain, the latter making special mention of thunderstorms; the 'great swell' is noted by Russell *H.M.C. Finch II*, p. 226. The *Elizabeth's* log gives 49°-03′ as latitude at noon 20th and '52 myles' as the distance westward from Ushant, observes Wheeler's return and Evertsen's mishap. For the quotation 'to observe . . . port' v. *Memoirs* . . . *Torrington*, p. 40; for 'laying by' v. log of *Yorke*. Incidentally *Reserve* records for the 20th, the burial of 'A man this day Hen. Marsh' and has a like entry next day for 'Jos Wyatt' followed by more cheerful notice of the taking in of 'beere from the *Duke*'. For this summer campaign the logs (Captain's and/or Master's) of about half of all the ships engaged are available. The entries for the last fortnight in July in the log (Captain's) of the *Cambridge* (Adm. 41/4135), apart from value in support of the text opposite, provide an informative specimen of a well kept sailing record of the period.

*Journaal van den Kapitein Johan van Convent* (of the *Honslaerdijk*) Rijks Archief. Adm. No. 1897, edited in Warnsinck, *op. cit.* corroborates generally the record of the English logs. For example, 29th/19th July '. . . outrent de vroegh kost schoot de wint mett harde regen, hooge zee, noordelijck . . . De koelte nam hardt toe mett mott regen, tegen den avont verloor den admiraal Evertzen sijn boegspriett en focke mast, lietent bij hem den heelen nacht mett 't hooft om de west drijven', (p. 182). He tells us that Evertsen transferred to Toll's *Hollandia* 31st/28th July (p. 183).

Sevin de Quincy, *op. cit.*, p. 228, remarks that the wind which served to take Tourville into safety 'éloigna la flotte ennemie'.
70 *H.M.C. Finch II*, p. 227. Nottingham to Torrington and Berry to Nottingham.
71 Log of *Yorke*. dril'd (drilled)=enticed [v. N.E.D.].
72 *H.M.C. Finch II*, p. 228 for letter and p. 230 for the forwarding.
73 Log of *Elizabeth* (Captain's).
74 As note (73) and Log of *Yorke*.
75 B.M. MS Add. 3650, pp. 17 v. 18 following upon the table of signals 'on ye Expedicon of Brest in ye Month of June & July 1689' and a list supplied by Russell to Nottingham 31st July, referred to *H.M.C. Finch II*, p. 232 but not there printed–v. original Finch MSS. The sailor-Anglicized Dutch names occurring in the above are corrected from a ship list Warnsinck, *op. cit.* p. 28, from which also the respective Admiralties, complements, names of commanders can be gained and gun-power which is, with the names of a few of the commanders, given in the English lists checked.

The whole of the paragraph 'To these must be added . . . prizes' is, apart from the reference to the *Kingfisher* (Log of *Yorke* 19th July) and some armament and manning figures supplied from Warnsinck's table (p. 28) dependent on daily entries, Julij 23–Augustus 6 (Jy 13th–27th) in Convent's *Journaal* (v. note (69), p. 179 *ante*). Warnsinck's table (p. 28) makes unnecessary more than passing reference to the old authority Aitzema, L. van, *op. cit.*, 27 Boek p. 37. For van der Zaan's v. Convent Junij 25.

| Month | Day | Wind | Course | Miles | Latitude Corrected | Longitude Corrected | | | Remarkable Observations and Accidents |
|---|---|---|---|---|---|---|---|---|---|
| [July] | 16 | NNW | E 7° N | 9 | | | [Ushant] Do | SSE | 15 m. | Calme for ye most part with hazy weather at noon saw Ushant |
| | 17 | Calm | | | | | Do | S° | 4 leag. | At noon saw Ushant |
| | 18 | WSW | | | | | Do | S½E | 7 leag. | Little wind At noon took our departure from Ushant |
| | 19 | WSW | N 24° W | 57 | | | | | | It blew hard. Our maintopsaile splitt |
| | 20 | Nrly | W 32° S° | 44 | | | | | | The wind blowing very hard at noon we tryed under a Main Course |
| | 21 | NNW | E 41° S° | 24 | | | | | | Blowing hard we all tryd under a Main Course most part of this 24 hours |
| | 22 | NE | E 19° N | 25 | 48 40 | 0 0* | Ushant | EbN | 7 leagues | Little wind hazy weather |
| | 23 | NNW | W 28° S° | 26 | 48 28 | 0 27 | Ushant | EbN | 6 le. | Little wind at 8 last night saw Ushant |
| | 24 | NNW | W 29° S° | 27 | 48 30 | 0 27 | Do | E 29° N° | 9 le. | Little wind |
| | 25 | Wrly | | | | | Do | ENE | 6 le. | Little wind |
| | 26 | NNE | | | | | Do | SE | 4 l. | Little wind |
| | 27 | ENE | N 55° W | 71 | 49 21 | 1 29 | Do | S 55 E | 71 miles | Little wind fair weather |
| | 28 | NE | N 36° W | 28 | 49 44 | 1 55 | Do | S 49° E | 97 miles | Little wind |
| | 29 | Ely | E 18° S | 19 | | | | | | Little wind Recd more water from one of the Tenders |
| | 30 | SSE | N 12° E | 25 | | | Silly | E½N° | 5 leag. | Little wind Recd some beer on board |
| | 31 | NNW | W 11° N | 22 | 50° 7 | | Silly | EbN | 5 le. | At 4 yesterday afternoon Silly as St Marys. |

*The meridian of Lands End

76 This table is based on B.M. MSS Add. 3650 and Russell list referred to in the preceding note with matter square bracketed taken from P.R.O. Adm. 8/2 for 1st Aug. See also Pepys's *Register* (*N.R.S. v. XXVI*).

77 As Note (76). The 'Blue' has been 'rearranged' upon the arrival of the Vice Admiral–Killigrew.

78 Log of *Yorke*.

79 Convent's *Journaal*, Augustus 7.

80 As note (78).

81 P.R.O. Adm. 1/5253, Reports of Courts Martial 1680–July 1698, for trial, Jackson, *op. cit.* Navy Board. At the same time as Priestman was appointed, another change occurred. Sir Edward Gregory replaced Sir Phineas Pett as Commissioner at Chatham, Jackson, *op. cit.* For the Booth warrant, *S.P. Dom. 1689–90*, p. 119.

82 Log of *Kent* (Captain's).

83 Luttrell under date. The *London Gazette* reported in 29th July–1st Aug. issue.

84 Log of *Elizabeth* (Captain's).

85 *H.M.C. Finch II*, p. 232 and original Finch MSS.

86 Log of *Elizabeth* (Captain's).

87 Logs generally.

88 Convent 19th/9th Aug.

89 *Ibid.* Log of *Elizabeth*.

90 Convent, Augustus 23. It will emerge (v. p. 186) that coming out of Brest Tourville cruised from 8 Août/29th July to 20 Août/10th Aug. towards and on a ground 60 leagues S.W. of Belle Isle–then retired to Belle Isle.

91 'Of course the inevitable council . . . Randivouze'. Log of *Elizabeth* (Captain's). Sevin de Quincy, *op. cit.*, pp. 229–30, deals with the capture of the *Portsmouth*. So also the *Gazette de France*, p. 485. de Quincy says this action was the result of an order to the Chevalier du Méné in *le Marquis* (58 guns and 300 men) to reconnoitre the Anglo-Dutch fleet off the Scillies. *Portsmouth*–Captain George St Loe–bore 46 guns and 220 men (v. p. 183 *ante*). du Méné lost his life, St Loe was badly wounded and suffered imprisonment in Brest and Nantes. For his later career as a Naval Commissioner see *D.N.B.* His two books, *England's Safety* or *A Bridle to the French King* (1693) and *England's Interest Or a Discipline for Seamen* (1695) are of importance.

*Memoirs* . . . *Torrington*, p. 40, mentions another small capture by Byng of the *Dover*, p. 40.

92 As Note (91).

93 *H.M.C. Finch II*, pp. 235–6 (These letters are dealt with in Chapter X.)

94 P.R.O. Adm. 3/1, 31st Aug.

95 Doublet, *op. cit.* p. 146.

96 Delabre, *op. cit.* pp. 162–5, gives names, commanders, guns and complements of the 70. Aitzema, *op. cit.* p. 144 has two lists–those Tourville brought in and those already in Brest.

97 de la Fayette, *op. cit.* pp. 265–8, for removal of d'Estrées to duties 'le long des côtes' and the rôle assumed by Seignelay just before and after Tourville's arrival. 'Il étoit général en tout, hors qu'il ne donnoit pas le mot'. Villette, *op. cit.* p. 95 for remarks on the cruise and manoeuvres.

The King's prohibition was contained in a letter to Seignelay, dated simply, 'Août 1689'. Since the appended 'Reflexions depuis avoir écrit' show the letter to have been written before Louis received news of Tourville's arrival at Brest (v. p. 178, ante) the fuller dating of 1, or, at latest, 2 Août can be given. The letter was no doubt, as Louis ordered, shown without delay to Tourville. Œuvres de Louis XIV, ed. Grimond et Grouvelle, 6 t. Paris and Strasbourg, 1806, t. vi, pp. 15–19.

98 Doublet, op. cit. pp. 146–7: Doublet remarked, 'je reconus bien que l'on avoit pas envie de rencontrer nos ennemys'.

99 Ibid. op. cit. p. 141, note 3. Archives . . . Marine.

100 For the career of Venize, ibid. note 4. From 'it was accepted' to 'returned his captive to safety' pp. 141–5.

101 From Louis' 'Réflexions' in his letter to Seignelay (v. note(97) ante) which so explicitly explains the naval policy of France in the summer of 1689 that it has seemed desirable to print it in full as Appendix I.

d'Hamecourt (Jean-Charles Horque) while chief clerk of the archives of the French Ministry of Marine 1745–1785, set out a day to day record of French naval events 1610–1750. The valuable MS, still unpublished, is preserved. d'Hamecourt by presenting the bare annals under 'les lumières de l'histoire' (the phrase from his own Introduction) can and does go astray. Tourville certainly did not, as d'Hamecourt alleges, seek the Allied fleet; so it follows that the statement (quoted by Delabre, op. cit. pp. 164–5), 'telles manoeuvres et tels moyens qu'il [Tourville] pût employer pour les engager au combat, il ne lui fut possible d'y parvenir, par le soin extrême qu'ils prirent de l'éviter', is astray. And others have followed him.

For emphasis on the non-belligerency v. Villette, op. cit. p. 94, 'M. de Louvois, qui n'a jamais esté favorable à la Marine, prenoit soin de faire entendre au Roy que les forces ennemis estoient de beaucoup supérieures à celle de Sa Majesté, et qu'il auroit de l'imprudence de hazarder toutes ses forces maritimes dans un combat très inégal, et duquel, quand on le gagneoit, on ne pourroit tirer de grands avantages, dans une saison déjà avancée.'

102 If Torrington had anything to say it is likely he expressed it in the dispatch or dispatches which were committed for carriage to Captain St Loo of the Portsmouth and thrown overboard by him when his ship was captured (v. p. 186).

103 The argument is not affected by the fact that Chateaurenault, dispatched to bring round, in the Spring of 1690, five more warships and three brûlots from Toulon, succeeded in his task. For lists of the fleets under Tourville's command in August 1689 and in 1690 respectively, see Delabre, op. cit. pp. 162 and 167 and for Chateaurenault's squadron from Mediterranean Calmon-Maison, op. cit. Appendix.

104 For a contemporary witness v. Villette, op. cit., p. 96. 'Celle (la campagne) de 1690 fut la plus glorieuse de toutes pour la Marine de France, et, si la victoire que nous remportasmes dans la Manche n'a pas eu toutes les suites qu'elle devoit avoir, elle servit au moins à faire connoistre que nos forces, bien employées et bien ménagées, estoient au dessus de toutes celles qui s'estoient liguées contre le Roy.'

105 The authority is a 'Relation du combat de M. d'Amblimont' by de

Selingue joined to a letter by d'Amblimont 6 août 1689 in Archives . . .
Marine B⁴12 f.101, B²70 ff.49, 61, 68; C⁴, 252, f.253, reproduced by Sue,
*op. cit.* IV, p. 325. See also Sevin de Quincey *op. cit.* p. 230 who adds a
further combat story of the French frigate *Intrepide* attacking, a few days
after d'Amblimont's return to Dunkirk, an English vessel of 300 tons off
Scilly; she was captured but lost off Ushant to three intercepting English
frigates.

106 Raynal, G. T. F. (Abbé) *Histoire Philosophique et Politique des Etablissemens
et du Commerce des Europeens dans les Deux Indes,* 12 t. and Atlas, Paris 1820;
t. 10, p. 205.

107 Such cases did occur. For an example, Captain Robson's *Castle* with 12
guns, was challenged on her way home from Barbados by a French
man-of-war which fired a broadside at her. She defended herself for an
hour and escaped. *London Gazette,* 10th–13th June, 11th June and Luttrell,
12th June.

108 P.R.O. H.C.A. $\frac{26}{1}$ Letters of Marque and Reprisals from the beginning of
the War declared against France from 7th April 1689 to November 1692.

109 *Ibid.* f.7.

110 *Ibid.* ff.9–12.

111 *Ibid.* f.22.

112 P.R.O. Adm. 3/2 *passim.*

113 P.R.O. H.C.A. $\frac{26}{1}$

114 Bréard, editor of Doublet, *op. cit.* p. 18, remarks on, 'La solide barrière qui
séparait les officiers proprement dits des officiers mariniers . . .'

115 Forbin, Claude (Comte de) *Memoirs du Comte de Forbin . . .* 2 v. Amsterdam
1730, p. 183. Sue, *op. cit. v.* p. 143.
    See P.R.O. Adm. 3/1, 26th June for the complaint to the Admiralty of
Sincocke, captor of Bart and Forbin, now captain of the *Nonsuch,* at their
escape. And P.R.O. Adm. 3/1, 10th July, for the order for fitting out the
two prizes which Sincocke had taken. They are referred to as 'the Play
and the Jester'.

116 du Mont, *op. cit.* VII, p. 238.

117 Et comme 'plusieurs Rois Princes & Estats de la Chrétienté sont déjà en
Guerre contre le Roi T.C.' and have already forbidden 'tout Commerce
avec la France il est convenu entre Sadite M. de la Grande Bretagne & les
dits Seigneurs Estats Généraux' que si pendant cette Guerre, les Sujets
d'aucun autre Roi, Prince ou Estat entreprendront de trafiquer, ou de faire
aucun Commerce avec les Sujets du Roi T.C. ou si leurs Vaisseaux &
Bâtiments seront recontrés, faisant voile vers les Ports, Havres, ou Rades,
d'obéissance du dit Roi T.C. sous un soupçon apparent de vouloir trafiquer
avec les Sujets dudit Roi, comme cy-dessus, & si les Vaisseaux apparte-
nants, aux Sujets d'aucun autre Roi, Prince ou Estat, seront trouvés en
quelque Endroit que ce soit chargés de Marchandises ou Denrées pour la
France, ou pour les sujets du Roi Très Chrétien, ils seront pris & saisis
par les Capitaines de Vaisseaux de Gerre, Armateurs, ou autres Sujets
dudit Seigneur Roi de la Grande Bretagne & desdits Seigneurs Estats, &
seront réputés de bonne prise par les Juges Competens.

118 Il a été arrêté qu'en cas que l'une ou l'autre Partie vint à être incommodée
ou troublée à cause de l'Exécution du présent Traité ou d'aucun Article

d'icelui, Sa Majesté Britannique, & les Hauts & Puissants Seigneurs Estats promettent & s'obligent de se garantir l'une l'autre à cet égard.

119 See p. 40 *ante*, note (37), for capture of an 'owler' 4th Feb.

120 25th Ap. Against the import of goods made or produced in France (coupled with encouragement of French Protestant refugees to England). 7th May Declaration of War '. . . défendons expressément d'avoir ou d'entretenir ci-après aucune Correspondance ou Communication avec le Roi des François ou avec ses Sujets'.
18th May Against the import of any description of French goods.
6th June Against traffic with Ireland.
*Catalogue of Tudor and Stuart Proclamations*, Vol. I under date.

121 P.R.O. Patent Rolls 1–14 Wm III (66/3326); P.C. 2/73, under date.
Luttrell, 3rd Aug., has an interesting comment on the 'balance of trade' with France: 'It's said that on the calculation of our trade with France, it appears, on the ballance, that a million more has been remitted thither in one year for goods imported than those exported by our merchants'.

122 The opinion of Sir G. N. Clark: 'the Dutch were worse still', *op. cit.* p. 72.

123 du Mont, *op. cit.* p. 237, for Treaty. William's attitude to Denmark and Sweden is well illustrated by Nottingham's letter to Duncomb, Envoy to Sweden, 13th July 1689, H.M.C. Finch II, p. 226.

124 P.R.O. P.C. 73/2, 15th Aug.

125 By the passage of the further treaty 'd'Amitié & d'Alliance'–q.v. p. 311 *infra*.

126 Clark, *op. cit.* p. 106.

127 P.R.O. P.C. 73/2, 18th July.

128 *Ibid.* 15th Aug.

129 Westlake, J., *The Collected Papers . . . on Public International Law*, Cambridge, 1914, p. 330.

130 P.R.O. 2/73, 6th May.

131 P.R.O. State Papers, Foreign (Holland), 84/220, seven large quarto pages, French.

132 P.R.O. P.C. 2/73 entered under 1st July. See also Marsden, R. G. . . . *Law and Custom of the Sea* v II, p. 124 for other references and for comment.

133 du Mont, *op. cit.* VII, p. 236.

134 'Et comme . . . il est arrêté et accordé, qu'ils conviendront au plutôt d'autres Articles & stipulations, pour le dénombrement & l'emploi de leurs Troupes & Vaisseaux de Guerre de telle manière qu'il sera trouvé le plus à propos pour agir avec d'autant plus de succès contre l'Ennemi commun.'

135 P.R.O. Patent Rolls 1–14 Wm III (66/3326).

136 *Ibid.* For Littleton see *D.N.B.*

137 *Ibid.*

138 P.R.O. P.C. 2/73 under date.

139 Firth, (Sir) C. H., *Cromwell's Army . . .* 1902, pp. 253–277.

140 Oppenheim, M., *A History of the Administration of the Royal Navy and of Merchant Shipping in relation to the Royal Navy from 1509 to 1660 . . .*, 1896, pp. 320–4.

141 Bib. Pepysiana, No. 2867, *Naval Precedents*.

From p. 533 onwards is a body of information dealing with appointment and Instructions including those to Chirurgeon General Pearse and to a Provost Marshal for 'takeing Care of all Prisoners of War'.

142 Pearse reported to Pepys, Sept. 1687, Bib. Pepysiana, *Miscellanea*, XI, p. 106.

Tanner, *op. cit.* (i.e. N.R.S. XXVI, pp. 132–139) carefully traces developments from the Commonwealth period to 1687/8.

143 'Mr Pierce, surgeon generall of the fleet is dismist that employ' Luttrell, *op. cit.* 30th Sept. One could wish that a biography of Pierce existed. There are thirteen references to him in Pepys's *Diary* (fourteen to his life 'la belle Pierce') and frequent mentions in Keevil *op. cit.*

144 As note (138).

145 As note (141).

146 See note (142), p. 134, Tanner.

147 *Journals of the House of Commons*–under date.

148 'The Two Masters of Attendance, the first Shipwright of Chattam, Two Boatswains, Two Gunners, and Two Pursers of the Great Ships . . . ordinarily the Officers of the First and Second Rate Ships are taken in turn'. *Ibid.*

149 The exact wording is: 'That when any Pension is settled, there is a Year's Pension given as an Introduction *gratis*: Which is commonly called Smart Money'.

150 The statement does not entirely agree with that found in Bib. Pepysiana Miscellanea VI, p. 71, a reply to a demand to the Clerk of the Chest from Pepys for details of scales etc.; nor is it as full. See Tanner, *op. cit.* (i.e. *N.R.S. XXVI*, p. 139).

151 If one supposes (for argument) that, in the year ending May 1688, no officers' forfeits or fines swelled the fund, the £1,300 could be taken as equivalent to 52,000 monthly 'common seaman' payments of 6d. That would imply the cash crediting to the Chest of a year's contributions by less than 4,500 sailors!

152 It is certainly not clear that most pensioners got their pensions!

153 The 'Chamber of London' still exists–called by that name. The office of Chamberlain dates from 1276.

154 The dues on 'Buoys, Beacons, Lights' would, no doubt, be collected by the Customs' Officers at appropriate ports.

Ballasting–from a reach of sand and pebble in the River.

155 Winterton is under 10 miles north of Gt. Yarmouth.

156 It was also pointed out by the Brethren that an Act of the 1st year of James II aimed at encouraging the building of ships in England. It levied 5/- per ton on all ships bought abroad and 'employed in carrying goods from Port to Port'; and it put 'another Duty of Twelve Pence per Ton on such Foreign Ships as were not free'. The Chatham Chest and Trinity House were to divide the receipts and devote them to the 'Relief of wounded and decayed Seamen, their Widows & Children'. Nothing had been received by Trinity House from that part of the Act which was in operation.

157 'An Act for the necessarie Releife of Souldiers and Mariners', 43 Eliz. c 3 A.D. 1601, which provided for the raising of a weekly rate of not less

than 2d. and not more than 10d. from each parish by the churchwardens, the money payable by them to the high constables for transfer at quarter sessions to 'the Treasurers' appointed by the Quarter Sessions. The 'treasurers' were to hold office for one year. A wounded man would 'make his complaint to the Treasurers of [his] County', presenting a certificate from his late commanding officer. The treasurers could grant a pension, payable quarterly, of £10 per annum for an ordinary soldier or marine, for any under rank of lieutenant £15, for a lieutenant £20. Provision was made for relief of soldiers, etc. travelling to their 'proper' counties; strict accountancy was enjoined and treasurers could be fined for unreasonably withholding relief . . . See *Statutes of the Realm* . . . *IV, Pt ii*, 1819, pp. 966–8.

# CHAPTER IX
# In Ireland
## *Mid-May to the end of August*

---

## *ARGUMENT*
### I

*Londonderry more closely invested; the second battle of Windmill Hill, 4th June; the besiegers rely on bombardment and starvation – de Pointis constructs a boom across the Foyle – Rooke, cruising between Ireland and Scotland, awaits the arrival of Kirke and his regiments, while Captain Jacob Richards, in the* Greyhound, *approaches Culmore and observes the boom; what befell the* Greyhound; *the besieged disappointed, the besiegers encouraged.*

*Kirke in Liverpool 3rd May; sails from Hoylake 30th May; reaches Lough Foyle 12th June – Richards reports to Kirke, who sends Leake, in the* Dartmouth, *15th June, to observe and report upon the prospect of relief of Londonderry by river – A Council of War, 19th June, pronounces the scheme impracticable; the sea officers who concurred in the finding – Kirke investigates from the maintop of the* Dartmouth *off Culmore; his efforts to make contact with the city; the messenger Roche succeeds in reaching Londonderry; but McGimpsey, swimming with three letters from the rulers to Kirke, is captured – Derry in the last week of June; the death of Governor Baker; the effect of de Rosen's barbarity in driving the neighbouring inhabitants beneath the city walls – Captain Hobson, in* Bonadventure, *sent to reconnoitre and report on the Island of Inch; a Council of War, 2nd July, advises the occupation – Kirke hears indirectly concerning the state of the besieged and indulges in a reprisal for de Rosen's barbarity – Landing made on Inch, 9th July. Two of the three messengers sent out on 12th July from Inch to Londonderry return on the 13th; Governor Walker wonders that Kirke 'had not all that time relieved him' – Hamilton's seductive offer to the besieged, who recognize with misgiving that surrender may be unavoidable at the end of fourteen days; but, nevertheless, on 11th July, propose obviously unacceptable terms – Lieutenant Mitchell's letter from the ships received whilst the envoys parleyed – Captain Hobson, in* Bonadventure, *ordered, 29th June, to deliver powder and ball to Ballyshannon (for Enniskillen), returns to the Foyle, 12th July; he looks in on Inch, 14th July – Kirke, visiting Inch on 19th July receives a startling reply to his latest letter (of the 16th) to Londonderry; which causes him to sail in haste with three provision ships for the Foyle, determined to relieve Londonderry!*

*Rooke, in chase of du Quesne Mosnier's three frigates (the three which Louis had lent to James), is too late to intercept the landing of a Jacobite contingent in Lochaber – The story of the* Pelican *and* Janet *of the Scots Navy; and the adventures of David Cairnes – How an intercepted letter disturbed the darkening outlook of Jacobite Dublin.*

*Kirke's second thoughts on Inch and the reception by his officers there of his plan for withdrawal – Londonderry in the closing days of July and, particularly, upon Sunday, 28th July – The relief as recorded by Kirke and as experienced by the city. Macaulay's mistaken assertion that Kirke's action was prompted by peremptory order from Schomberg.*

*The end of Kirke's amphibious operations and his final reports to Duke Hamilton and the King on the relief of the city; the later recommendation by Captain Cornwall (of the*

Swallow) *of his Boatswain Shelley and crew, who cut the boom – Rooke awaits Schomberg's expedition, his remarks (and some observations by d'Avaux) upon the Londonderry operation.*

*Schomberg, appointed 16th July, and in Chester since 20th July, sails on 12th August, to be met by Rooke next noon and land in Bangor Bay, Carrickfergus Lough – Supplies continue to reach Schomberg – Carrickfergus invested and taken within six days on 27th August – Schomberg, on 2nd September, advances toward Newry – The King's views expressed to Schomberg on the need for a winter port in Southern Ireland.*

## II

*Survey of Rooke's use of command mid-May to the end of August – The paralysis during the month of August of James's exiguous naval resources.*

*Historians hitherto unfair to Kirke.*

*Parliament and ' Miscarriages relating to Ireland and Londonderry'.*

## I

THE BLOODY REPULSE of the besiegers of Londonderry upon the Windmill Hill, 5th/6th May, halted further immediate onslaught on the city. Hamilton regrouped his forces, moving the main body from St Johnstown to Bely-ugry (Balloughry) Hill, two miles south-west of the city, at the same time consolidating a camp at Pennyburn to northward, with a third immediately across the river to eastward by Strong's orchard. Close invested, the besieged found hazardous their access to the three St Columba Wells just outside the south-west walls; pasture denied, they were no longer able to forage their horses – which they killed to supplement their meted rations; communication with the outside world could no longer be sustained. With desultory bombardment by the Jacobites from across the Foyle and sallies by the garrison the month of May wore on. No sails appeared.[1]

Then, on 3rd June, twenty-eight large bombs[2] crashed into the streets from 'six pièces de gros canon'[3] which had just arrived from Dublin – not by sea! This preluded the second battle on the Windmill Hill, which, under the direction of General Bouchan,[4] began early on 4th June. Impetuous armed cavalry with infantry of uncertain morale found the defenders' river and southern, bogside out-works impracticable; and, at close of day, several hundreds of horse and foot lay dead on the field. Colours and spoil were taken into the city. 'You see here [observes Plunket] as you have seen all along that the tradesmen of Londonderry have more skill in their defence than the great officers of the Irish army in their attacks.'[5] Lacking, at this stage, the ability to carry the out-works, let alone the walls of the city, by storm, Hamilton could only maintain, from the orchard across the Foyle, the intensified bombardment he had begun and trust that an 'estocade', which he had allowed de Pointis to throw across the Foyle river, would hold against weather and tide or trial by any English vessel heading temerariously to succour the garrison. Unless siege mortars, scaling material, general supplies and spirited reinforcements reached him, the general had no choice but to leave hunger to effect the capitulation.

de Pointis was proud of his work. Reporting to Seignelay he began, on the 13th/3rd June, '*enfin malgré La disette où L'on est icy de toutes choses j'ay achevé L'estocade*'. A week earlier, so he said, it had not been begun. Now he had produced a float of squared beams roughly socketed at the ends, the ends iron hooked, the whole cross-cabled. A steadying rope, five or six inches thick, ran through cramps the entire length of the boom–but under water to make cutting difficult. Forts at the ends of the 'estocade' and shelter for troops placed to enfilade the barrier were being provided. de Pointis said that he intended to add another 'estocade' 'above the first'. He would not be happy till the English attempted his achievement. For, borne on a following wind, a vessel or vessels must strike the impediment, come under fire, fail to place any intended landing party, and, unable, against the wind to put about, inevitably be destroyed! Whilst he was writing, a report that the English were embarked '*poursecourir cette place par la rivière*' had, he said, reached the camp. It was time to redouble attention to the 'estocades'; wounded though he was he would be at his post. A second letter, 17th/7th June, repeated information contained in the earlier and dealt very fully with the besiegers' dispositions before Londonderry; it revealed that bombardment was now concentrated from the south-west and landward side of the river, Hamilton's cannon fronting the cannon of the besieged. This communication shows de Pointis prepared immediately '*mettre la main à la seconde estocade*' presumably nearer Londonderry.[6]

To de Pointis' own description certain data can be added: 'They made this Boom first of Oak but that would not float and was soon broke by the force of the water: Then they made one of Firr beams which answered their purpose better.' Thus Walker; and Mackenzie writes similarly. The boom was about two hundred yards long and five or six feet across. Its left-bank extremity was secured by a frame-like device to a rock, its right-bank end fixed under a huge heap of stones; it lay not directly athwart the flow of the Foyle but with its western end retracted to allow for the thrust of the flood and perhaps with calculation that boom, bank, following wind and inflowing tide would provide a fatal pocket for any challenging vessel. The boom was placed near Brookhall roughly half-way between Londonderry and Culmore which were about three miles apart. Culmore Fort, though with only 'two or three pieces of cannon', commanded from the western shore the restricted sailing channel from the Lough into the river and could be regarded by de Pointis as advance protection to his work; on the same side toward the boom was a 'battery of two small guns . . . called New Fort'. The main gun protection to the boom was provided by Charles Fort just beyond the float on the steep left bank (Londonderry side of the boom), and by Grange Fort opposite across the river.[7]

The complete blockage of the River Foyle could of course have been secured by sinking a vessel or vessels in the fairway. It is believed James forbade a device which might have rendered the port unusable for an incalculable period.[8]

The squadron with which, on the 4th May, Captain George Rooke bore away from Admiral Herbert into the St George's Channel (see pp. 141, 143 *ante*)–the three fourths, *Deptford*, *Antelope*, *Portland*, the fifth *Dartmouth* and the *Henrietta* yacht–lay, on the 11th May,[9] in Greenock, 'Since mine to your Lordship on the 5th of May off Kinsaile', Rooke wrote to Nottingham, 'I have bin rainging on the coast of Ireland from that place to Knock-fargus in hopes of meeting with the rest of the fregats to joine with me'. Not finding them, he had put into the Scottish port to gain intelligence, reassure the Duke of Hamilton[10] by his appearance and have opportunity to stop *Deptford*'s Bantry leaks. As information suggested that the frigates were at Chester,[11] he had dispatched the *Dartmouth* to order them to join him off Cape Kintyre and, as soon as they arrived, he promised to 'atempt whatever [might] be advisable with safetie to their Majesty's shipps for the reliefe of Londonderry which [was] agreed on by all to be in great distresse'. A comment on the 'verry weak condition' of 'Carrack-fergus'–Rooke on the way up had ridden one night before that place–would, for reasons which will appear later, be welcome news to Nottingham and the King.

Rooke reported again on 1st June.[12] His 'cruissing between Scotland and Ireland mostly on the Irish coast between Carrick-fergus and Londonderry' had enabled him to burn a provision ship in Carrickfergus Lough, 'assist Capt. Yongue, commandant of their Majesties forces in Kintire' to drive out 'a body of Scotts rebells . . . gott togeather in the iland Geiga'[13] and, on the 29th May, to meet 'the *Greyhound*, *Fisher* ketch and another ketch bound for London Derry' and pass them, under care of the *Portland*, into the Lough. At the time of writing he was returning to his station to meet 'the ships coming with Major Gen. Kirke'. He, Rooke, would cover the landing of the relief regiments. He warned Nottingham that his provisions were running very short!

It will be recalled (see p. 153 *ante*) that the sixth rate *Greyhound* (Captain Gwillam), *Kingfisher* ketch (Captain Boyce) and the merchant ketch *Edward and James* (Master–Mr Meers) now sent into the Lough had sailed from Hoylake on the 13th May, a miniature expedition whose leader, Captain Jacob Richards, with his four French officers, gunners and miners, had authority to prospect for batteries beside, or a boom across, the river Foyle, and proceed as far as Londonderry if that would not endanger the *Greyhound*. It was no fault of Captain Gwillam that the contest between sail and weather in the Irish sea had, from the 13th May, till, on the 29th, he fired a salute of nine to Rooke, gone against him; no blame attaches to Gwillam that, from the 1st June, on which day he made a two hours' run from Greencastle (starboard at the Lough entry) to Redcastle (starboard less than half way along the Lough) there had ruled for a week 'always contrary winds with great storms of rain and hail'. On the 7th Gwillam did, however, by dint of 'kedging and warping',[14] bring the *Greyhound* past Whitecastle (also to starboard and within three miles of Culmore), where, from the west bank folk presumably, information could be gleaned. That a boom existed at Brookhall all informants agreed; about its construction they differed. Richards, the French officers and Captain Gwillam concurring, decided to sail up.

Saturday 8th June began with 'a handsome gale at N.W.–a very fit wind for . . . enterprize'. Hammocks made up, quarter-deck barricaded against small shot, yards slung, trunks and chests stowed in the holds 'with everything not of use in the conjuncture', Gwillam, shortly after 8 a.m. weighed and cast anchor within cannon shot of Fort Culmore. The enemy were numerous 'hammering a great gun'; that and one other were all they appeared to possess. When *Greyhound* opened with her broadside, of perhaps half a dozen ordnance, Culmore replied with a gun that split. Richards' cheerful record puts it, 'we lay pelting them for above three quarters of an hour!' after which it was apparently safe for Richards to climb to the maintop whence his 'perspective glass' showed him 'over against Charlesfort, a little above Brook-hall, something that extended from side to side [of the Foyle] and several boats at a small distance from one another lay just by it as if they buoyed it up'. Cannon were being brought up to the boom ends:

> Wherefore [Richards enters in his *Diary*] having seen what I could & found we were not of sufficient force to attempt the breaking or cutting of the Boom, we weighed anchor with design to go & anchor again where we were this morning . . . and report by the *Fisher* ketch to Kirke.

At that juncture the fortune of the day changed. The *Greyhound*, 'not fitting time enough with the narrowness of the channel' as she endeavoured to head into the full Lough, went ashore, stem northward, starboard side to the bank! The ebb 'laid [her] almost dry' and heeling to such an extent that she could not make use of a single starboard broadside gun. There was no choice but to wait for return of the tide; and, in the next eight hours, eleven guns (some twenty-four pounders, some eight pounders, some three pounders) brought up chiefly on the east side as near as possible to the exposed starboard hull, worked severe damage–seventeen shots struck under the water line and four or five feet of water filled the hold. Three or four battalions of Irish foot gathered but were held off by a heavy fire of small arms from the *Greyhound*'s decks. Soldiers from the ketch were called on to add to the *Greyhound*'s numbers and, when Captain Gwillam, hit in several places, became incapable of command, Boyce of the *Kingfisher* was summoned aboard to replace him. He too was hurt, shot in the belly; but the total loss to the crew was small—two killed and fourteen wounded. Boyce and the warrant officers affirmed that the *Greyhound* could not be saved and they resolved to fire her. Those who were not her crew were ordered off. Richards left with them—doubtless unhappily reflecting that the ship he was bidden not to hazard at Londonderry would soon (though through no fault of his own) be ablaze. But *Greyhound* was not for burning! From a distance of scarce a quarter of a mile, Richards saw with wonder the sails of *Greyhound* spread and trimmed. Someone had been quick to note a sudden shift of wind to S.S.E., a wind blowing straight at the starboard side. Every sail was made to draw—the ship righted on fortuitous breeze and filling tide! Though Boyce was forced at the end of the next half hour to let *Greyhound* again go ashore—to avoid a sinking in deep water—the ship was not again attacked; and, under protection of the short summer night, shot holes were temporarily stopped, masts catted and rigging spliced. *Greyhound* was refloated on the morning tide. For Captain Richards, who, with his three French officer companions went aboard the *Portland*, the 9th June long remained an evil memory; he had lost belongings worth £300 and was not likely to be comforted by the knowledge that the wounded Gwillam's lockers had also been rifled, the Captain's glass money-case broken and robbed!

*Greyhound* departed on the 9th for Greenock 'in a great & breaking sea which so much worked [her] that she was in great danger of foundering', but she made harbour.[15]

Viewed plainly from Londonderry the arrival of Richards' three ships, the *Greyhound*'s challenge, her ill-luck and escape had aroused varying emotions.[16] For Hamilton the circumstance that the warship had, apparently deliberately, desisted from attempt to pass beyond Culmore had a military significance. According to de Pointis, writing to his correspondent (Seignelay) again on 22nd/12th June, the general doubted *'leur dessein . . . d'entrer par la rivière*' and countermanded work on a second estocade. de Pointis represents Hamilton '*tournant toute son attention*' from the place at which he, de Pointis, believes the English will attack and contrariwise, insisting that descent will be made on the Innishaven-Culmore side where will be found countryfolk ready to join with the landed forces.[17] *Portland*, Captain Richards aboard, on the 10th, headed for Carrickfergus to look for Kirke, hailed two provision ships working up from Bristol to Londonderry, doubled back towards Islay on the 11th and learned, from the *Henrietta* yacht, that the Major-General had at last arrived and lay under Rooke's protection by Innishowen at the Foyle Lough head. To Kirke Captain Richards, the leader of the exploratory venture, on the 12th, reported.[18]

It is necessary to recall that Major-General Kirke had arrived in Liverpool on the 5th May (see p. 153 *ante*) and that Shrewsbury addressed to him in sharp reprimand, dated the 13th May, expression of the King's 'no little concern' that the commander of forces designed for speedy relief of Londonderry was 'still on this side of the water'. Such a rebuke might have been expected to raise Kirke's anchors! But it may well be argued that, only when the wind blew from below west or east, would Kirke be navally advised to seek egress with his convoy through the intricacies of the outfall sands of Dee and Mersey; and it is fortunate for the general's reputation at this stage that the well-kept (Master's) log of the *Bonadventure* has been preserved.[19] At no time from the 5th May to the morning of the 21st did the wind offer – and then but for an hour or so – encouraging something of a false start. The rest of the 21st and the next day 'Small Gales all Round the Compass' and more tentative weighing and enforced mooring. The mid-day sentence for Thursday 23rd records: 'The Fleet all sailed out of high Lake this morning.' The wind was west-south-west. The corresponding entry for Friday, the 24th, tells, 'This morning ye Fleet put Back for High Lake'. The wind had moved more to the west and 'very fresh gales' blew. And in the wrong half of the card the winds sat for another week.

The crossing now to be accomplished began at half-past three in the afternoon of Thursday the 30th May.[20] The *Swallow*

(Cornwall–with Kirke aboard), *Bonadventure* (Hobson) and *Dart-mouth* (Leake), convoying twenty-four merchantmen, 'on which the Forces and all Provisions were embarqued'[21] filled, amid showers, to moderate gales from the south, their sails. Kirke's own 'Lambs', with Sir John Hanmer's regiment and that of the dismissed Cunningham, under the command of Colonel William Steuart constituted the forces of about two thousand men.[22] By mid-day of Friday the 31st 'Arne's Head'[23] lay six leagues to south-westward. Next noon, Saturday the 1st June–Ramsey Bay. And there, though the winds, in direction and strength, consistently offered voyage, till Wednesday 5th, Kirke lay. The log of the Master of the *Bonadventure* is now less exculpatory of the Major-General's delay. His ship spent Saturday afternoon veering away in anticipation of Sunday morning's service; service ended, she hove back into the Bay. Monday morning, the 3rd, broke wet and, for a few hours, a little boisterous; in the evening, aboard *Bonadventure* 'our Short Service', which, duly concluded, the frigate 'Veered away' for 'Morning Service' of Tuesday. All the forenoon watch of that Tuesday, the 4th, was occupied in letting out the reefs of the topsails and drying the rest of the suits of sails. The concluding entry at mid-day Wednesday the 5th 'Now at Noone we Weighed' does not suggest urgency! Still–the expedition was clear of the Point of Ayr the same night and up with 'the Meads'[24] by Thursday morning, the 6th. Anchors went down in Red Bay, north of Garron Point, early on Friday the 7th.[25] There, understandably, Kirke waited to be picked up by Rooke, who came in from Kintyre to shepherd the relief force under Rathlin Island to safety in 9½ fathoms in 'Flemings Bay' in Lough Foyle. So, on the 12th, under or near Innishowen Head, lay the *Swallow* and her convoy, Rooke's own fourth the *Deptford*, with the fourths *Antelope*, *Portland* and *Bonadventure*, the fifth *Dartmouth* and the *Henrietta* yacht–these last two under orders to fetch water from Islay–and the *Kingfisher* ketch. Rooke at once allocated to the Major-General (in the *Swallow*) the *Kingfisher* ketch, together with the *Dartmouth* and *Henrietta* yacht, as soon as they should return from Islay, and promised the *Greyhound*, when repaired, from Greenock. By the 15th the water had been fetched, victuallers from Bristol were coming in and Kirke's expedition had moved to lie off Redcastle.[62]

H

With *Dartmouth* back in the Lough, Kirke asked Leake on Saturday the 15th to prospect. He 'sailed within a large mile of Culmore' grounding, for an hour, on the way up. There was now much talk of pilotage, activity in sounding the Lough (17½ feet at most at high), mounting debate about breaking the boom—debate which led on the 19th to formal deliberation. 'All the Colonels and Lieutenant Colonels and Sea Captains were present this day at a Council of War'. Thus Captain Richards in his *Diary*; and he quite faithfully summarizes the decision they reached. But in view of the great significance of the finding, it is desirable to print in detail from a copy of the minute of the proceedings of the Council-of-War sent to the Duke of Hamilton.[27]

A Court Martiall held on board his Majesties ship
the Suallow June the 19, 1689

| | |
|---|---|
| Major General Kirk president | Major Rowe |
| Coll. Stuart | Major Tiffin |
| Coll. Sir John Hanmer | Major Carville |
| Lt. Coll. St. Johns | Mr Richards, engineer |
| Lt. Coll. Woolseley | |
| Lt. Coll. Dompiere | Capt. Cornwall, comander of the |
| Lt. Coll. Mainvilliers | Suallow fregate |
| Lt. Coll. De le Barte | Capt. Leake, commander of the |
| Lt. Coll. Lundini | Dartmouth |
| | Captane Gillam, Comander of the |
| | Greyhound |
| | Capt. Sanders, Comander of the |
| | Henrietta Yacht |
| | Capt. Boys, Comander of the |
| | Kings Fisher ketch. |

That by all we can see or hear it is positively beleived that ther is a Boume cross the River a litle above Brookhall at a place called Charles's Fort, wher one end of this Boume is fixed, the other extending to the opposite point. The Boume is said to consist of a chain and severall cables, floated also with timbers, at each end of quhich are redoubts with heavy canon. The sides of the River are entrenched and lined with Musketeers, Besides this obstacle in the river, severall intimations have also been given of boats sunk, stockadoes drove with great iron spikes, bot in what maner we could never perfectly learn, but its certain that they nether want boats, timbers &c. to effect any thing of this kind

The accident that hapned on Saturday the 8th instant to the *Greyhound Fregate* is evident proof that they are in a capacity to bring doun canon any wher they should be opposed; so that, should any thing be attempted in goeing up this streight channell and miscary therin by several accidents as may happen, as the shifting of a wind, striking ashoare, or damages receaved by ther great guns an ther is very litle reasone or hopes left to think to sett off. And if no other opposition should be then the Boume, which, if not broke by our attempt the breadth of the river is so narrow as that the ship will certanly run ashoare. This loss, tho great to his Majestie, would be of much more and of greater consequence in the leaving the enemie possessors of so many great guns with our stores of war and victualls, which, if they had, they wo[uld] certainly make a more formall attaque wpon the toun of Londonderie,–thich to this time they have not attempted. We suppose for noe other reasone, then for the want of artillery enouch, Besides the miscariage wold so disharten the toun and encourage the enemy as to be of extreame consequence. Besides since the *Greyhound* and the rest of the Fleets being heir, we never have receaved any intelligence from Londondery, which gives us great reasone and some assurence that they are not extreamly pressed by the enemy or want of ammunition or provisions of mouth.

All this being considered its the opinion of us now sitting at this Counsell, that it will be more prudent and for his Majesties service, to stay here, till a greater force joine us so that we may be a sufficient number to make a descent and force the enemy to raise the siege by which means the town will be succoured, or that the toun should have sent us advice of every particular relating to this affair by which we may with safety take other measures.

(Subscribed)

Ed. Boys
Tho. Gillam
Wm. Sanderson

La Barthelhomas
De Mainvilliers
Isaac De Dompierre

John Leake
W. Cornwall
G. Richards
Will. Carville
Lach. Tiffin
Henry Rowe
Londigny

Wm. Wolseley
Tho. St. John
John Hanmer
William Stewart
R. Kirke

It was probably earlier on the same day that Kirke wrote Hamilton saying that he could give no 'account of the condition of the Town' and that though he had 'sent severall messengers' he had had 'no return'.[28] A copy of the Council-of-War finding was sent to Schomberg.[29]

It is important to remark that 'all the Sea-Captains' are reported to have been present at the Council of War. As the boom could only be broken by naval means one must assume that the advice of the 'Sea Captains' would be especially solicited and valued. Amongst the signatories were Woolfran Cornwall of the *Swallow*, John Leake of the *Dartmouth* and William Sanderson of the *Henrietta* yacht; also Thomas Gwillam of the *Greyhound* and Edward Boyce of the *Kingfisher* ketch. Cornwall, commissioned by Herbert lieutenant in the *Tyger*, in 1681/2 may be supposed to have seen Algerine fighting. He had commanded first the *Dartmouth* and then the *Constant Warwick* in Lord Dartmouth's fleet of 1688 and played a significant part in strengthening William's faction in the fleet. Transferred at the end of the year to the *Swallow* he had shepherded Cunningham's earlier expedition to Londonderry—and back to Liverpool. He was clearly not without reasonable experience and enjoyed trust. John Leake, son of the Master Gunner of England, had begun his sea career at the age of seventeen as a Midshipman in the *Royal Prince*, taken part in the memorable sea-fight against the Dutch in August 1673, seen service in a merchant vessel and as a gunner in the *Neptune*. His presence at the battle of Bantry Bay and promotion to this present command has already been noticed. Leake, at the age of thirty-three, was an officer with by no means negligible experience—and if the *Fire Drake* at Bantry is to be given the credit for causing the explosion in Coetlogon's *le Diamant*, of outstanding bravery. Of Sir William Saunderson it can only be recorded that he had in

1688 captained the *Isabella* yacht and now commanded the *Henrietta*. We do not know whether any one of these captains at this stage held the opinion that the boom *could probably be broken*. It would appear that none held the view so strongly as to consider it a matter of professional importance that the opinion, if he held it, should go on record.[30]

Kirke took opportunity next day, the 20th, to go aboard the *Dartmouth* 'it being the advance ship' from which Richards maintained continuous look-out, to see easily for himself, 'from the maintop' the 'rippling of the Boom', the boom's bulk, just lifting upon the face of the water, several boats stern and stern alongside to float it up. In the distance—the day fair and clear—Derry, firing and being fired at, its house-tops shattered, the pavements taken up; and, clustered constrictingly around the city, as well as in pockets along the river banks toward the Lough, the Irish forces, showing now no sign of the disquiet with which the arrival of warships and convoy had filled them. Evidence the perspective glass supplied did nothing to cause the Major-General to change his notion of the hindrance the boom presented; it no doubt assisted him to check his estimates of enemy strength and dispositions; it should have shaken the previous day's 'great assurance' that the inhabitants of Londonderry were 'not pressed much by their enemies'. On the 22nd, a 'spy', sent out by Kirke to make contact with the citizens, returned—unsuccessful. Presumably the reason why no intelligences from the city had reached the ships began to be made plain.[31]

By the 18th, the *Greyhound*, patched up in Greenock, the wounded Captain Gwillam still in command, escorted by the *Kingfisher* ketch, the hurt Captain Boys equally on duty, had come into the Lough from Galloway and, on the 20th, joined *Swallow*, *Dartmouth* and *Henrietta* yacht preparatory to the next move. *Deptford*, *Antelope* and *Bonadventure* all lay at anchor 'without ye Tunnes' preparatory to the next move.[32]

Kirke did not rest content at the failure of several attempts to send a man to Londonderry. Two sailors, Roch, an Irishman, and Cromie, a Scot,[33] were put ashore in the late evening of the 24th to make their way through the investing forces, Roch completing the hazard by swimming to the walls in the early hours of the

following morning, while Cromie fell into the hands of the besiegers. The Major-General's emissary could and did assure the
Governors Walker and Michelburne (the latter now acting for
Baker, who was ill), the leading officers, and so the citizenry, of
the presence of Rooke's squadron in the North Channel, of the
warships and merchantmen with Kirke in the Lough–ships thirty
in all–of the three regiments, their colonels, their strengths; he
could talk of Bristol wheat, of Glasgow meal loaded for the forthcoming relief; and, to prove his good faith, ask for a discharge of
four guns next noon from the cathedral tower, a signal which was
to be duly answered from beyond Culmore. Being under arrangement to return to the Lough, Roch faithfully attempted the
exploit; but, confronted by enemy vigilance, he swam back to
safety with the garrison. A boat, sent to the place at which Roch
and Cromie had been put ashore on the 24th, waited, on the
night of the 26th, in vain to retrieve them.

It will not be thought that the Governors and officers of
Londonderry had not, previous to Roch's arrival, made strenuous
efforts to communicate with Kirke. They had. And, during the
night of the 26th, one McGimpsey, a shot-weighted bladder
containing three letters for Kirke tied round his neck, volunteered
to swim all the way to the fleet.

One of the letters was from Governor Walker. Mention of Roch
was followed at once by information that the enemy had 'this
day seventh' [instant?] offered terms which had been 'absolute
refused'; yet, should relief not come within 'a few days not
exceeding Six . . . Worse the[n] now is offered' would have to be
accepted. Walker sharply linked an assertion that 'the bumbs
Cross the River [were] certainly broken' to expectation of
provision; and he promised, if that provision were likely to come,
'to hold out' against the enemy. To leave Kirke under no illusion
he concluded, 'soe yt we presume to tell you that if for want of
that [provision] we be forced to Yield it will be none of Our
faults'.

A letter, signed by Adam Murray, John Kirnes [Cairnes] and
Ja Gbrastanes [Gladstanes] was less minatory. Again a reference
to Roch, who durst not risk the way back by land, and to the
bearer Mc Gimpsey bold 'to adventure all hazards to swim all the

way to carry these lines'. The city was said to be in 'deplorable case'; horseflesh was giving out, sickness spreading, mortality increasing. There were alas desertions and clandestine moves afoot. The appeal, 'wee beseech and obtest you, honoured S$^r$, in the Bowells of our Lord Jesus Christ that ye faile not to hasten to our reliefe with provisions at least–takeing your own way to do it and [providing] a person or persons to be Governors or Commanders in chiefe here', was of unmistakable urgency and modesty. As the trenches of the enemy pushed nearer the walls and the danger of mining threatened, they would trust God, who had preserved them 'wonderfully', and not further 'presse [a] case [which called] for help, help, help from God and [Kirke]'.

The remaining letter, over the names of Geo. Walker, Hen. Baker and Jno. Michelburne, together with those of Chr. Fortescue, Ja. Morrison, Ja. Strong and Edw. Davys, ran to length. It recounted the joy the city had at the first appearance of Kirke's ships, the effect on the enemy, who were said to have fallen into 'so great an Astonishm$^t$ that they Resolved to Raise the Siege ... tooke down their Tents, removed towards ffin Water their Morter peeces, Bombs and Artillerie', but since had advanced from bombardment to a design of mining. Eight or ten days' provisions only remained–after 'foure months'–for upwards of 20,000 soules' in the city. They of Londonderry (as of Enniskillen) were surely worth saving to the cause of 'King W$^m$ and Queene Mary theire Interest in this Kingdom'. So, let Kirke send 'a small Vessell or two loaden with Provisions ... Biskett, Cheese and buttur', for there was 'no fireing left to dresse meate'. The letter then talked of the insignificance of the Culmore guns, the military achievements of the garrison, and firmly insisted that every attempt had been made to 'send ... Expresses but Could not gett it done'. Flags put out at Kirke's ship's maintop and guns fired at eleven on the morrow would tell whether success had favoured this latest attempt.

Beneath the signatures a set of postscripts!

Wee will answr yr Gunns by our Gunns on the Church Steeple If you doe not send us reliefe we must Surrender ye Garrison W$^{th}$in six or seaven dayes

We understand that the bum is Certainly broke so that you may Come up w$^{th}$ Ease[34]

No flags were hung at the maintop of *Dartmouth* or *Swallow*, no guns boomed at 11 o'clock, on the 27th for the besieged to answer. Hamilton's offer of free pardon, religious liberty, restitution of property – even of cattle – would Londonderry but surrender, resolved against on the 26th (as Walker in his letter to Kirke had intimated) was formally rejected on the 27th. Twilight of the 28th saw begun Clancarty's superstition-inspired 'knocking' at the Butcher's Gate. The assault was repulsed; but the long night vigil of 'the great Baker', Walker's soldier colleague in the governorship, upon the walls, cost the fever-stricken man his life. At the close of Sunday the 30th Baker lay dead; across the river Mc Gimpsey's proclaimed body dangled on a gallows; de Rosen, not Kirke, had read the letters from the shot-weighted bladder that the swimmer had not been able to sink; and rumour of the special barbarity de Rosen would apply to constrain capitulation should it be withheld beyond 6 p.m. the next day, spread through the mourning, rain-soaked city. That no quarter would be granted, no respect shown for age or sex, should the city fall, few doubted.

Marshal General de Rosen had come north early in June and had been more concerned in watching Kirke than in intervening before Londonderry. The steps which, as the month drew on, he decided to take, in order to end a military stalemate in 'Palatinate style', are notorious – 'Protections' to be ignored and Protestant men, women and children, from thirty miles around Londonderry, to be driven, in hundreds, in the first days of July, literally at sabre point, to the defiant walls, there to be admitted or refused as the city choose. The first victims were indeed driven within the defences on the evening of 2nd July. Equally well known is the garrison's threat (should the barbarity develop) to hang at the Royal Bastion their score Irish prisoners. Hamilton's grudging co-operation with de Rosen, and the clear command of James to de Rosen ended the barbarity. But the effect of de Rosen's method of warfare on the morale of the besieged cannot be too strongly emphasized. Walker and Michelburne made tart reply to the proposals which Hamilton had submitted to Londonderry on the 29th June. No offer of terms which might be thought to depend in any way on the word or guarantee of de Rosen could ever be considered! And were not the powers held by Hamilton himself suspect? Was not his commission dated the 1st May; and had not the Parliament in Dublin on the 14th May proscribed all Protestant 'rebels'?[35] James might order de Rosen to abandon his uncivilized devices[36] and instruct Hamilton that he 'positively refuse obedience' to the Marshal's inhuman orders[37] but, as Dwyer shrewdly observes, 'the chicanery and savagery of de Rosen proved an antidote to the surrender of Derry ... worth to William and his cause almost not less than the army Schomberg was fetching over', and for which Kirke was waiting.[38]

The decision of the Council of War of the 19th June not to essay relief of Londonderry by going up the river but to continue in Lough Foyle till more forces should arrive from England posed for the Major-General obvious problems. How long could he keep penned on shipboard two thousand men? Where should the landing 'to raise the siege' be made?

Evidently, before the 21st, Kirke must have consulted Rooke, for Captain Hobson in *Bonadventure*, *Greyhound* and *Kingfisher* ketch in company, weighed, early on the 22nd, on a mission. The ships were in Culdaff Bay that evening, in Lough Swilly from the 24th to 26th, and *Bonadventure* was back off the Foyle Lough at sunrise on the 28th. Captain Hobson could tell that he had sent ashore on the island of Inch in Lough Swilly his lieutenant, who had encountered an Irish quartermaster busy commandeering supplies. Clearly the enemy attached importance to Inch. To land troops on the island would begin to solve Kirke's need to keep his soldiers fit, create a diversion six miles north-west of Londonderry in the rear of part of the besieging army—a base from which possibly to relieve the city? Additional reasons for its occupation lay in the fact that the enemy would be robbed of an area for foraging and, so Hobson was informed, several hundred Protestants of those parts would find a rallying point. It may be that, at this same time, Captain Henry Hunter, who had been lucky to escape with his life from the 'Break of Killyleagh', crossed over from exile in Scotland and urged on Kirke the value of Inch. On this occasion, a Council of War, held after dinner in the *Swallow*, the 2nd July (all the Field Officers and Sea Captains were there), acted promptly. Six hundred men should be sent to Inch.

The troops for Inch were taken off the merchant ships on Friday the 5th July. A west wind blew next day and Rooke's *Deptford* and the *Portland*, each loading a hundred soldiers, prepared to lead out *Greyhound*, Steuart and Richards aboard, with *Kingfisher* ketch and a flyboat in which two also were soldiers. *Antelope* had been sent to Liverpool to fetch provisions. At this point an Irish boy produced a strange contretemps! Had he not seen from the tops of the hills a fleet of forty ships in Lough Swilly? Kirke's (or Rooke's?) incredulity did not out-run caution. *Henrietta* yacht was sent to investigate while the ships worked out 'between the main and Innistrahull island'. They were borne by the current into Culdaff Bay; to which, hard on the wind, came in *Henrietta* to report nothing whatever in Swilly! Wandering in the ups and downs of Innishowen mountains the boy had evidently lost all sense of direction, seen Kirke's ships where they were not— Lough Foyle had become his Lough Swilly![39]

While troop selection was put in train, rumours and partial reports from the shore reached Kirke. A man and his wife walked from time to time along the west bank by the *Swallow*; if the woman wore a white mantle that was signal that a letter would be found under a certain stone. Then, a Mr Hamilton, 'who, "the day before" was driven among the rest of the Protestants under the walls of Derry', sought out Kirke and represented that, though the enemy made 'very advantageous terms' to the besieged, 'they would not hearken to them saying they have provisions enough for one month more, before which time they were well assured to be delivered or [they would] live on dogs and cats'. Read against the presentation of conditions of near extremity, upon which, in their letters of less than a week previous, Walker and the other chief officers of Londonderry insisted (two of the letters, it will be recalled, setting a six day limit to continuance of resources) Hamilton's evidence as reported in Richards' *Diary* may cause surprise. It should not do so. The 'antidote' to surrender, de Rosen's barbarity, worked potently! The difficult question of the extent at any one time of the besieged city's food supplies, the management of the common store from which exiguous rationing for the populace, with larger allowance for the fighting defenders, was provided, and into which not yet had all stocks been brought.

cannot here be fully investigated. It is sufficient to say that Kirke had not seen the three letters and to him Hamilton would rank as a credible enough reporter of conditions inside Londonderry—conditions which he, Kirke, might, on such evidence, regard as still militarily endurable. It was probably because of Hamilton's report of de Rosen's inhumanity that Kirke (not unwillingly?) indulged in petty reprisal. Two boatloads of his men made a landing, plundered and took off forty poor persons who were afterwards sent to Scotland.

Landing was made on Inch on the 9th and 10th July by Steuart, opposite Rathmullen across the water to the west, by Richards, on the coast opposite Burt Castle on the Innishowen mainland. Two purposes were pursued, the 'rustling' of as many Donegal cattle as possible (some beasts were sent to the Foyle) and the preparation of a redoubt on the mile-long strand fronting the fordable water towards Burt. In spite of the lack of co-operation of Lieutenant Colonel St John with Richards, the redoubt with a battery was sufficiently established by the 13th to justify the firing of a salvo of thirteen guns to inform the Major-General that the detachment was 'well settled' in Inch. What is more, Londonderry was now aware that the troops were there. For, writes Richards on the 12th, 'This day we sent three several messengers into Derry by three ways to let them know we were landed here and that we expected every fair wind an English army'. And, next day, the 13th, Richards could record:

about three o'clock two of our [three] messengers sent into Derry returned safe. They both agreed in their relations of that place: the one brought a letter from Doctor Walker the Governor which imported that he wondered we had not all that time relieved him. Their provisions were now very short and could not hold out longer than fourteen days more: that the enemies had offered them very honourable terms & hoped that before this time would be expired we would think of some way to relieve them: otherwise they will be forced to accept their enemies' offers.[40]

The expression 'fourteen days' is precise. Lieutenant General Hamilton had received from James a new commission, dated the 5th July, and, similarly dated, warrant for exercise of plenary discretion in treating with the 'rebels'.[41] He had lost no time in

officially acquainting the governors of Londonderry of the new
commission and of his continued willingness to offer terms;
moreover, lest the common folk should be hoodwinked by their
officers and fail to see copies of the appeal which had been
smuggled into the city, Hamilton had fired the bomb which,
bursting, disclosed the message still to be read in the porch of the
cathedral. '. . . If any chuse to leave the Kingdom they shall have
passes. You shall be restored to your estates & livings & have free
liberty of Religion whatsoever it be . . .' And on the 11th, because
James's Lieutenant General had demanded answer to his proposals, it had been the rulers of the city who had thought it
advisable to appoint Commissioners to meet Commissioners of
their enemy. Dated the 11th July,[42] nineteen demands represented Londonderry's almost arrogant conditions for surrender.
Conditions agreed, capitulation should take place on the 26th July
–but then only if an army should not have relieved them in the
meantime! Till the 26th July Londonderry required a truce to
allow time for confirmation of the articles by an Act of Parliament
or, at least, impress of the Great Seal of Ireland, appointment of
Commissioners to insure performance of the articles, delivery of
hostages by both parties–the Irish hostages to be placed on
Kirke's ships. The joint Commissioners were, on the afternoon of
the 13th on which the two messengers got back to the camp at
Inch, in session, the Irish demanding capitulation by the 15th.

It was during that period of absence of the city's Commissioners
that, according to Mackenzie, '. . . Colonel Walker received a
letter from Lieutenant David Mitchell out of the ships by a little
boy and transcribed it' with, so Mackenzie asserts, invented
specification of the numbers of horse and foot at Inch, 4,000 and
9,000 respectively. Ash recorded for the 13th, 'This day a boy
came with a letter from one Mitchell in the fleet to Governor
Walker which gave us an account (whether true or false I know
not) that 12,000 men are landed at Lough Swilly and that 2,000
horse are gone round to land there also'. For the 14th Ash added,
'Mitchell's letter desired us to give the usual signals; accordingly
seven guns were shot from the steeple . . . and about twelve
o'clock at night three more; a lantern was set on the pole which
bears the flag.'

Who Mitchell was or in what capacity he wrote is not clear; but should not one identify him with the officer of whom, on the 10th May, Mackenzie wrote, 'Lieutenant Mitchel went away also and came again with Major-General Kirk into the Lough'. Walker's statement, 'We received further intelligence in July by a little boy that with great ingenuity made two dispatches to us from the Major-General at Inch', and his account of the manner in which the lad successfully took back the first, but ate rather than surrender the second answer, lends probability to the view that the boy was one of the three messengers sent out by Steuart from Inch on the 12th, one of the two who returned on the 13th, the bearer who 'brought a letter from Dr Walker' upbraiding in tone but announcing the intention of holding out the 'fourteen days'. Had the presence of the troops at Inch influenced that critical decision? Though the sound of great guns in Lough Swilly had been heard in Londonderry on the 9th there is nothing to show that Londonderry knew before the 12th or 13th that warships had cast anchors in Lough Swilly on the 9th or that troops were ashore upon Inch on the 10th.[43] Grant that ignorance, accept as one must Nairne's and Mackenzie's dating of the conditions sent to Hamilton– the 11th–and the resolution of the city registers its finest hour.[44]

Captain Hobson, in *Bonadventure*, had weighed on the 29th June from Lough Foyle for Killeybegs near Ballyshannon reaching it on the 3rd July and staying a week to deliver powder and ball for the Williamites in that Enniskillen neighbourhood. He had worked back to the Foyle by the afternoon of the 12th. On board were gentlemen of Donegal anxious to put to Kirke their proposals for relieving Londonderry. Given arms and officers they would undertake to provide 8,000 foot and 1,200 good horse–enough to make a dragoon regiment. Hobson, ordered for a few hours to Swilly 14th/15th, handed on his 'Enniskillen' news and was no doubt told that Inch had just received 'certain advice that the [Foyle] boom was broken in several pieces and the great guns drawn off'. A messenger was sent over Innishowen to acquaint the Major-General of this report. The messenger returned next day unable to find Kirke who was believed to be at sea.

It was midnight on Friday the 19th when the *Swallow*, firing thirteen guns, hove into Lough Swilly. The 'battery' on Inch

answered with nine. 'His Excellency' Major-General Kirke had
arrived.[45] Kirke on the 16th[46] had written a letter to Walker—
without doubt that which is printed, undated, in Walker's *Diary*
immediately after his mention of the 'little boy that with great
Ingenuity made two dispatches to us from the Major General at
Inch'. Kirke is represented as acknowledging a communication
from Walker by the way of Inch; and affirming that he had written
Walker on Sunday last. He would 'endeavour all means Imaginable' to effect the relief which he found 'impossible by the River'.
He had, he said, sent 'a party to Inch' and intended going there
himself to try if he could 'beat off [Hamilton's] Camp or divert
them so that they [should] not press [the city]'. For encouragement Walker was informed that Enniskillen had received substantial reinforcements ('Officers, Ammunition, Arms great guns')
and led to believe that, whilst '3000 Foot and 1500 Horse and a
Regiment of Dragoons' in Donegal would operate to relieve
Enniskillen, Kirke would attack from Inch. '6000 Men' were
'every minute' expected from England and 'stores & victuals'
were laden ready for the resolved relief; England and Scotland
were 'in good posture'. The advice, 'be good Husbands of your
Victuals, and by God's help we shall overcome these Barbarous
people Let me hear from you as often as you can and the Messenger
shall have what reward he will', must surely have been regarded
by Walker as superfluous! To the assertion 'the Duke of Barwick'
is beaten, he could apply no check.

This, it must be supposed, was the second of the two missives
successfully carried by the 'little boy', Walker's answer to which
was undelivered. But, before Kirke had been twenty-four hours
in the Island, watching the putting ashore of the additional
troops he had just brought and sending on two small vessels with
'500 fuzees' and 'some officers' (see p 254 *infra*) for 'friends at
Enniskillen', a further communication from Walker did reach
Inch reflecting a state of desperation in the city and *inter alia* a
reiteration of the report that the boom was broken and the guns
guarding it drawn away.[47]

The substance of the letter is briefly indicated by Richards but
a text which would operate to cancel the consequences of the
finding of the Council-of-War of the 19th June must stand in full.[48]

Sir

Yours of the 16th wee received and in short must tell you to our grief this garrison hath lived upon catts, dogs and horse flesh this three days, and now there remains no victualls of any kind in the garrison to live on then three ——— of salt hides, one pound of tallow and one pint of meale a man which wee compute will not keep us alive any longer than next Wednesday. Above 5000 of our men are dead already for want of meat and those that survive are so weak that they can scarce creep to the walls, where many of them dye every night at their post. Wee are afraid wee shall loose our outworks every minute, and then wee shall be all cut off. There miners are come with their lines close to our walls, but hitherto their sinking under ground is prevented. Wee are offered very honourable terms from the enemy which we still rejected in hopes of relief, and now no expectation of aid during the time of our victualls. God knows what will become of us, for they vow not to spare age nor sex. A great many admire such a Fleet as a Fleet as yours should lie so long before us and send us no victualls, whereas the wind presented fair many times. Trust none of the enemies desertors for wee have been often deceived by such people. There came two battering guns here last night which plyes us all day and broke our curtains and shattered our Gates. The enemies gunns are brought up from Kilmore and that Boume which is cross the River is broke so that a small ship with provisions might easily pass up hither without hazard. The Enemies Regiment of Fuzaleers are marched up to Dublin and tis certain their Regiment of Guards marches in a day or two. The rest of their Army consists most part of Rabble.

Wee are, sir

Your very humble servants

GEO. WALKER

London Derry July 19th 1689.  JNO. MICHELBURNE

Richards tells us that, immediately on reading,

the Major General, with a great deal of privacy, ordered three ships laden with provisions with forty musketeers in each & this night [the 20th] went on board the *Swallow* & sailed with the three ships for Derry Lough with resolution to relieve that place or lie by it.

Meanwhile Rooke, in *Deptford*, Hobson in *Bonadventure*, Lee in *Portland*, Leake in *Dartmouth*, were gone after three French (or Irish) men of war which had seized, so Kirke told the Inch officers, the *James of Derry*, a vessel sent by him to Scotland to buy supplies including wine for the fleet![49]

A not inconsiderable commotion had been in progress in the Isles. As David Cairnes (here met with once again) recounted in a very long letter of the 11th July, to the Duke of Argyle, from Campbelltown in Mull,[50] he had an order 'from Edinburgh' to Captain Hamilton to be accepted aboard Hamilton's frigate and taken to Lough Foyle.[51] He embarked on Saturday the 6th July, at Greenock but, on the 10th, had, by reason of cross winds, got no further than the Mull of Kintyre when they on Hamilton's frigate saw, approaching them from Lough Ryan, '3 little vessels'. Hamilton bore up. One of the three had been sent by Kirke to fetch provisions and letters from Greenock and was returning to the Foyle.[52] Almost at once three *larger* vessels were seen approaching the three small. Hamilton desired Cairnes to 'go on board the little vessel with the packet bound for Derry' in order that he, Hamilton and Captain Brown, now first mentioned as commanding an accompanying small vessel, 'might goe & meet those [large] vessels & know who they were'. From 'a pretty distance' Cairnes heard the guns speak, two of the newcomers attacking Hamilton, one Brown. Brown first, then Hamilton was forced to surrender. The little ones next became prey to the 'French' (thus identified) and the craft to which Cairnes had betaken himself, lagging hindmost, was forced to run ashore 'under the great rocks of the utmost end of the Mull . . . 2 hogsheads of wine in her and some brandy etc.' But she broke away from mooring and was seized. Of the two other little ships one, containing fifty tons of provisions from Chester, was captured; the other got away. The three French ships with the two little vessels were last seen heading for Ila [Islay]; Hamilton's and Brown's frigates appeared to be left behind. And all this by the French sailing under English flags. The picture can be filled in.

First the background. When the Scottish Convention Parliament met on the 14th March 1689 Scotland had no Navy.

Within a week measures were taken to put to sea a token fleet. In Glasgow two ships were hired–*Pelican* and *Janet*; and, on the 13th April, Captain William Hamilton and Captain John Brown were commissioned. They had been told to acquire ordnance wherever it could conveniently be had; and a captain and his company of foot were sent to strengthen the seamen. Orders were given to the captains to fight and sink all ships belonging to James anywhere between Cornwall and Skye; but fitting out hampered immediate obedience–whether to assist the shipping of refugees from London-derry or break and burn boats off Carrickfergus. On the 7th and 18th May it was held more important that Hamilton and Brown give attention to destroying the 'birlines'[53] in the creeks between Mull and the back of Kintyre. It was thought likely that contact with Rooke might be made. And, opportunely, a 'French ship', crossing from Ireland to Kintyre with persons of quality, had been caught by the laird of Loup; supplemented by Glasgow biscuits, its beef came in handy.[54] So *Pelican* and *Janet* cruised and did small services.[55] Meanwhile, to William Burnsyde Master of the *Dogarvine* of Londonderry and John Woodsyde Master of the ————(?) and Andrew Douglas, Master of the *Phoenix*, a born Scotsman but 'of Coleraine in Ireland', Hamilton and the 'remanent Lords' of the Privy Council for Scotland, issued letters of marque, so adding three privateers to the miniature Navy.[56]

It is obviously possible to supply the names, not given in Cairnes's letter, of Hamilton's and Brown's vessels, guard boats to the Scottish Isles. They were *Pelican* and *Janet*. Turning to a broadsheet published in London on 2nd August, one gathers that *Pelican* carried '18 guns and 120 men', *Janet* '12 guns and 80 men' as against the 36, 30 and 34 of their three opponents. The broadsheet states that, at first, two of the Frenchmen fell on Brown and one on Hamilton and that, when Brown's vessel surrendered–its captain dead, lieutenant wounded and of the fourteen men left alive eight disabled–all three French ships fought Hamilton who, about to blow up the *Pelican*, was also slain–thirty only of his men left alive at the boarding.[57] The little craft to which Cairnes trans-ferred was surely the *James of Derry* (see p. 242 *infra*)? The three 'French' ships were the fifty-gun frigates lent by Louis to James, here led by du Quesne Mosnier, in *La Lutine*, with Captains Nagle and Booth (both late Royal Navy) commanding respectively *La Jolie* and *La Tempête*.[58] James's frigates went indeed beyond Ila! The pursuing Rooke lamented in a letter to the Duke of Hamilton, on the 20th, that 400 men of Colonel Purcell's regiment 'were landed in Lough Quaber [Lochaber] on the 17th in the morning in smale boates', and that he had not been able to fetch out of the mountains of Mull, to which they had escaped, thirty-six officers-names separately supplied with this letter. Evidently to ease pressure of space in du Quesne Mosnier's three frigates there had been transfer of officers and men to the two little vessels acquired after the Kintyre fight; for, out of them, upon recapture, Rooke took saddles, clothes, officers' commissions and lists and—some deserters. Hence the catalogue provided. The first six names in the catalogue stand thus:

| Coll. Cannon–Brigadere | Coll. Sir William Wallis |
|---|---|
| Coll. Lord Frendrick | Coll. Sir Charles Barkley |
| Coll. Lord Bohan | Coll. Purcell |

to which add the names of as many lieutenant colonels, two majors, nine captains, seven lieutenants, four coronets and two quarter-masters.[59] It is unsafe to speculate how many of the listed officers were at that moment on Mull. Buchan was certainly still in Ireland.[60] d'Avaux would in due course report to Seignelay, '*M. Duquesne a debarqué tout son monde en Ecosse*',[61] soldiery intended as a reinforcement to Dundee; but the day before Purcell's battalion was landed by du Quesne Mosnier in Lochaber or the officers of rank scrambled with soldiery among the mountains of Mull, Dundee, though victorious against Mackay, had fallen in the twilight in the Pass of Killiecrankie. Though some Dutch horse and English foot were ordered for Scotland William saw no need greatly to reinforce his general.[62]

It was *Bonadventure* which fetched out what her log calls the two prizes, probably Kirke's *James of Derry* and the Chester provision ship; for Rooke says he 'retook two smale vessels' and *James of Derry* is shortly to be greeted as a recaptured ship! (see p. 244 infra). *Bonadventure*, and no doubt the two other fourths, shot at 'Castle Docar' [Dewart]. Afterwards she began cleaning. She had only one side scrubbed when the commander weighed for his base. Rooke reached Islay on the 20th, Lough Foyle on the 21st.[63]

As for du Quesne Mosnier's three *La Lutine*, *La Jolie*, *La Tempête*, they had disappeared before Rooke got to Mull, en route for Kinsale.[64] But no chances were taken with the prizes they had acquired, described as '*un armateur Anglais de seize pieces de canon et "un" flutte de quatorze*', taken on the day on which du Quesne Mosnier set out from Carrickfergus with troops for Scotland. They were sent into Dublin harbour. In spite of the fact that Cairnes states that the three French warships 'left the 2 Scots frigats in the Channell behinde',[65] and another correspondent, the Duke of Argyll to Hamilton, says that Rooke retook Brown's ship and 'a ketch that was with them',[66] it is impossible to believe that the two prizes were not in fact the *Pelican* and *Janet*. They were, d'Avaux tells Louis, sailed into Dublin by the 'enseigne' of *La Tempête*, and, bringing them in, the officer had captured a packet boat bound from London bearing 'lettres de Mareschal de Schomberg à Kirk', one of which bore date, '29 Juin, vieux stile, avec un apostile de trois Juillet'. d'Avaux informed Louis that what the letters principally revealed was that the Count de Solms was under orders to land in Ireland in a fortnight with 12,500 men, infantry, cavalry, dragoons! The Lord Dover, James's Chancellor, was about to depart for France, to solicit 'un secours pour passer en Angleterre'. He would show Louis the captured letters. But the request for troops to facilitate a descent on England, 'the best place to land in is Beaumoris . . . in the middle of our Friends of Cheshire, Lanrshire &c or at Milford Haven where there is admirable poste for the Ships',[67] would have to be changed. Faced with imminent threat from Solms, James (so d'Avaux conveyed to his master) was persuaded that the bare maintenance of his cause in Ireland required trained French troops in the island. And the news from Londonderrry being what it was the ambassador had no hesitation in adding, '*si le Roy d'Angleterre n'y songe bien serieusement, toute son armée sera detruite avant que le Comte de Solms mette pied à terre!*' But d'Avaux could be practical as well as pessimistic and pressed James to put the captured prizes to use; whereupon James proposed turning two of them into fireships and sending them against the colliers assembled at Bristol for the transport of Solm's horses. To d'Avaux the thought occurred to dispatch such fireships on a good wind amongst Kirke's vessels in

Lough Foyle. James said he would confer with Chevalier Strickland on that.[68] A letter from d'Avaux to Seignelay, written on the
same day as that to Louis, covers the same ground (incidentally
giving the name of the 'enseigne' as Gabaret) and reveals d'Avaux
proud of having suggested to James the idea of sending fireships
into the Foyle. With any luck 'Dery se rendroit un quart d'heure
apres'. James decided in favour of a venture toward Bristol.[69]

The prorogation of the Irish Parliament upon the 18th July had
indirect bearing upon James's maritime, if not naval, situation.
Though the records of that Parliament have suffered official
destruction, it is known that the Irish Commons, defying the
English Navigation Acts, approved export of home-grown wool to
France. None the less, James – English exile in Ireland – unwilling
to concede to the Irish or French anything that might alienate
English Jacobite opinion or prejudice him at restoration, did little
to further 'l'affaire des laines' so dear to the heart of d'Avaux. In
any case Torrington's fleet held the Channel and even St Malo
corsairs took that fact into account.[70]

Back in Lough Foyle, Kirke had second thoughts about Inch.
He had seemed well pleased with what he had seen. Nevertheless,
the *James of Derry*, so happily recaptured, was ordered to Colonel
Steuart with a letter dated the 22nd, delivered on the 25th. 'Since
I have left you, I have had time to consider our island. I find it not
tenable if ever the enemy bring down cannon against it.' Such the
beginning. Preparations for evacuation, for 'a handsome retreat' in
case of need were to be made. The method to be followed was
indicated in detail – plans which involved placing most of the 'old
men' (the soldiers) aboard ships and leaving small companies of
'old men' to support the 'new men' (volunteers from among the
refugees) first to sustain any onslaught that might be made on the
Island. The lengthy letter concluded with a reference to the fact
that the cross winds had, at the time of writing, prevented getting
into Lough Foyle but that 'everything was in order' and that the
commanders of the three provision ships were very willing to go
up to Londonderry; they 'would either do it or lay by it'.

A council-of-war was called by Steuart. It decided not to put
Kirke's orders into effect before he, as commander-in-chief, had read

the council's reasons (drafted by Richards) for remaining in Inch.

Richards strongly stated a case, 'it is our opinion we had better continue as we are & that with more safety'. Insufficiently strengthened by the 'old men', the 'new men', if forced to retreat, would lose the guns before the 'old men' from the ships could reinforce them. The enemy would soon learn of the changed arrangements. And what of the twelve thousand folk who had taken refuge in the island? Carry out Kirke's plan and 'without doubt none will stick to say we basely secured ourselves in our ships & left the new raised men, their wives & children to be sacrificed'. Already Rathmullen, across on the western mainland, lay in ashes of revenge and, on the Innishowen side, an area at least two miles deep had been wantonly fired. But the council thought that, while Londonderry held, Berwick, his attention directed Enniskillen-wards, would not attack Inch. The council's views forwarded to Kirke and two messengers dispatched to inform Walker of the intention which Kirke had professed in the last paragraph of his letter to Steuart–to deal with the boom and send provisions up by the river–Steuart and Richards returned to their immediate duties. Soon their redoubt, facing Burt castle across the fordable strand, mounted twenty-two guns, the ford extremities strengthened by two ships lying dry in the sand and the guns of *George*, *Kingfisher* ketch and *Greyhound* ready to provide extra artillery.[71] Kirke received this memorial by the 29th and with Londonderry relieved was in no mood to discuss it adversely. News continued to pass from Londonderry to Inch.[72]

For the besieged, as July advanced, the situation, it is well known, daily became more desperate; discipline for the garrison was sharply tightened and from mid-July a court martial sat daily to deal with military defaults. Bombardment continued, lifting at times the dead from their graves and intensified–especially as Walker's letter (see p. 239 *ante*) stresses–against the Butcher's Gate and the Gunners' Bastion, for which purpose boom-head guns at Charlesfort were borrowed. Not that Hamilton expected success from bombardment. A Council-of-War held at this time, reported to James that the city would only fall by famine and James in Dublin was, on the 22nd, prepared to accept even the necessity to abandon the siege. Privation of food, decimating

plague, lack of shelter, stench, rain and misery, all were calculated
to induce surrender—all, but, above all, starvation! Tallow pan-
cakes in the first week of July, distribution of starch in the third,
then the slaughter of the last 'house-kept' cows and the sally to
capture some of the enemy's grazing cattle—the 'Battle of the
Cows'. Granted that money retained an ironic value to buy scraps
of horse-flesh, dog-carcase (fattened on eating Irish bodies), cat,
rat and mouse, tallow hides, horse-blood and the weeds of the
street, allowing that the garrison received to the end a differential
ration, it remains that, on Sunday the 28th July, Walker and
Michelburne were governors of a garrison which, states Walker
(looking back from the 30th), reckoned then on only two days of
life, 'nine lean Horses left and among [them] all but one Pint of meal
to each Man'. Of 7,500 men once regimented 'alive about 4,300
. . . one fourth unserviceable', of the population thousands dead.

That morning, of Sunday the 28th, the bloody flag on the
cathedral tower had, so Ash records, been:

> struck once or twice to let the fleet see once more [the city's]
> inevitable distress, as much as to say if they came not now, the
> wind blowing fair, they might stay away for ever. Beside the
> flag eight cannons were fired from the steeple . . . then the
> flag made a wave. The fleet returned . . . six great guns . . .
> which intimated that when the tide answered they would
> endeavour to relieve us . . .

'Hope deferred maketh the heart sick.' Walker, as he preached at
evensong in the cathedral of St Columb, could only point to 'the
several instances of Providence given them since they first came
into that place', and bid his hearers await the still unrevealed
event—would it be at the turn of tide?[73]

How best can the story of the relief be told? Kirke on Monday,
the 29th July, drafted a dispatch, copies of which, appropriately
introduced and subscribed, were sent to the King and the Duke
of Hamilton respectively. That to William is not extant, but the
material part of it, handed to the *London Gazette*, headed Hampton
Court the 4th August and turned to the third person appeared in
the issue 1st–5th August. To read the letter to the Duke of Hamilton is to have the dispatch in the first person and authenticated
by Kirke's own signature.[74]

'From on board the Swallow at Derry Lough July 29th 1689'
Your Grace will see that my going to the Island of Inch has been
with some reason, since it has weakened Culmore and the
River so much by drawing their forces that way, that wee have
in part releived Derry as your Grace will find by the following
account.

I . . . arrived at Lough Swilly the 19th at night the next morning
by break of day I landed all the soldiers . . . Colonel Stuart had
flung upp as good a work as either time or the small number of
tooles wee had would permit . . .

The enclosed [a reference to Walker's letter of the 19th received
by Kirke on the 20th *q.v. ante*] coming to me from Derry, I
thought it no time to delay, and that the running a risque in
hazarding some shipps[75] for the relief of those poor people and to
preserve a town might prove much more for his Majesties
service than to let it be surrendred made mee immediately to
leave Colonel Stuart and the troops in the Island and goe my
self to this Lough with the *Swallow* and three victuallers Capt.
Browning [*Mountjoy*] Capt. Pepwell [*Jerusalem*] and Capt.
Douglass [*Phoenix*].[76] I arrived at the mouth of it the 21st
[Sunday] where I met Capt. Lee in the *Portland* who told mee
Capt. Rooke was a cruising off of Carrick Fergus, I sent him
away presently[77] to desire Capt. Rooke to send mee the
*Dartmouth* [Leake].[78] The 22nd [Monday] I came into the
Lough and sent the 3 victuallers upp to Culmore Castle to lye
there.[79] The 25th [Thursday] the *Dartmouth* and Capt. Rooke
[*Deptford*] join'd mee. The *Dartmouth* was ordered to goe to the
victuallers at Culmore and lye there till the first opportunity of
wind should permit to carry them up the River. The wind did
not favour us till the 28th [Sunday]. At 6 a clock at night there
sprung up a moderate Gale at north north west, the *Dartmouth*
and the *Mountjoy* weighed,[80] the *Phoenix* had orders not to weigh
till the *Dartmouth* was engaged with the Castle and the *Mountjoy*
at the same time to goe up the River, the *Jerusalem* not to weigh
till a signall given from the *Dartmouth*, who was not to give her
the sign till one of the other shipps had past the Boume. With the
foremost ship was sent the *Swallow's* long boat[81] well barri-
cado'd and armed with seamen to cut the Boume in case there

was any; Capt. Leake Commander of the *Dartmouth* behaved himself so bravely and discreetly in this action, that I must beg your Grace to desire his Majestie to give him particular thanks, for at his going up to the Castle, hee neither fired great nor small shott (the both plyed him very hard) till he came on the inside of the Castle and there begun to batter, as the two victuallers might pass under the shelter of his gunns, then lay between the Castle and them within musket shott and came to an anchor.[82] The *Jerusalem* that was to have the sign to weigh at that instan the wind slackned, grew calm and came about to the south west. This did not hinder the *Mountjoy* that went first to goe to the Boume,[83] whether she cut it or broke it wee have not intelligence or whether it was not mended[84] as those of Derry tells us, but up she went and the *Phoenix* followed her. They were seen to fire and receive both great and small shott from the shore up to the Town, and soon after they fired from the town their great gunns as a sign given for the arrivall of the shipps. The *Dartmouth* lay still in her station by reason of the tyde, the Castle still saluting her and she returning 5 or 6 for one. She lay there till 8 a clcock this morning [29th Monday], then weighing came by the Castle again, who had gott much more small shott then before on both sides of the river,[85] but he plyed them so warmly with small and great shott that he received little or no damage only one soldier killed, one wounded and Mr Lee his purser has a contusion in his cods. This is so good a peice of service, that his Majestie I hope when he considers how well Capt. Leake has behaved himself Capt. Browning and Douglas thay have his favour and also the seamen and soldiers his bounty; I have promised more then I can think on, and do not question at least his Majesties approving of itt, for in my lifetime I never saw both officer, seamen and soldiers more willing nor zealous for his service then they are.

I am just under sail for Inch . . .

I have given you as just an account as I can in the little time I have, the messenger having been kept here this 8 days presses hard to goe.

Your Graces most humble and obedient servant<br>R. KIRKE

Kirke presumably observed from the maintop of the *Swallow;* but with Londonderry six miles or more south-westward, he was quite unable to tell what happened at the boom.

The[86] first movements of the three ships in the Lough, as they 'came swiftly to Culmore',[87] a league distant, were, it is implied, detected in the beleaguered, desperate city–possibly from the cathedral tower through perspectives. Culmore firing, a warship taking in sail in order to come to anchor just inside the river,[88] and thence, from a protective station, to pass on the two smaller ships –these were happenings also seen and reported to an anxious populace. At some point the two ships came into common, easy sight, 'plied with cannon and small shot from both sides of the river',[89] and expectation rose to 'a strange transport of joy'. One of the incoming pair would be noted to be twice the size of the other, though, to the knowledgeable, of scarce the tonnage of a small man-of-war. It would be seen to draw somewhat ahead and, on a shrinking wind under slackening way, approach the boom. But not come on! What, for the Londonderry watchers, took place at the boom? 'The smoke of the shot, both from the land and from the ship clouded her from . . . sight [and] the enemy, gathered in swarms to the waterside, raised a loud huzza . . . telling [the] ships were taken'.[90] The besieged witnessed Irish boats preparing to board the two trapped victuallers–for such the ships would be recognized to be. The 'dismal Prospect'[91] lasted, as it were, interminably! Suddenly–the crash of a ship's broadside, a confused scene resolving, and the larger of the two vessels emerging on a miniature tide-rush, clear of the parted timbers of the boom. The lesser vessel appeared. But the ordeal was seen not yet to be over! A dead calm had fallen and 'both [ships] sailed very slowly *by the tide*'.[92]

Along the shore hostile guns were hauled frantically from vantage point to vantage point. The enemy had more than a whole long river mile up which to harry what seemed the scarcely moving victuallers! It was 10 o'clock before the small *Phoenix of Coleraine* and then the *Mountjoy of Derry* moored at a familiar quay –the *Mountjoy* at a long-boat's tow–a circumstance which the Londonderry narrators must have seen but not thought worth mention! Word went round that, aboard *Mountjoy,* lay the dead

body of her commander, Micaill [Michael][93] Browning, a married
man some of them well knew, shot when his vessel had 'run
aground' after ramming the boom. The broadside which folk had
heard had, at the recoil, loosed (it was being said) the *Mountjoy*.
If any of the three diarists asked or discovered *how* the boom was
broken he did not record the answer. Sufficient for each that the
honour be given to the dead master of the *Mountjoy*. Yet to nine
seamen of the *Swallow*'s longboat, 'Robt Kells, Jeremy Vincent,
James Jamieson, J[no] Young, Alexand[r] Hunter, Henry Breman,
Will[m] Welcome, Jno ffield and Miles Tonge', sent (as Kirke
reported, see p. 247 *ante*) 'to cut the boume in case there were any'
and especially to one Shelly the 'boatswain's mate' who leaped
upon the boom hatchet in hand, led the party and was wounded—
receiving a splinter in the thigh—belongs the true glory of that
day.[94]

The *Phoenix*, commander Andrew Douglas of Glasgow, 'brought
from Dumbarton 800 bolls of meal' for which a petition had been
presented to the Scotch government.[95] The *Mountjoy*, capable of a
cargo of 135 tons, had sailed from England laden with 'beef, peas,
flour, biscuits etc all of the best kind'.[96] Unloading began as soon
as ever a blind of barrels filled with earth had been piled on the
quayside to protect willing labour from random shots out of
Hamilton's trenches. From the platform atop the cathedral tower
two shots boomed, signal of success to Leake at Culmore and
Kirke in *Swallow* up the Lough. At the pole the bloody flag hung
limp. The night was scarcely dark with a moon entering her last
quarter, the incoming tide lapping, till long past midnight, the
Quay. Soon dawn would break—the siege over.[97]

Kirke, according to Macaulay (and others have followed him),
unpardonably delayed the relief of Londonderry and needed
official spur to prick the sides of long delayed intent.

Just at this time Kirke received a despatch from England, which
contained positive orders that Londonderry should be relieved.
He accordingly determined to make an attempt, which, as far
as appears, he might have made, with at least an equally fair
prospect of success, six weeks earlier.

Macaulay indicates his authority for the dispatch. He annotates,

'A copy of it is among the Nairne papers in the Bodleian Library'.[98] The 'copy' referred to does indeed exist.[99] Dated the
29th June, Schomberg to Kirke, it acknowledges the receipt of the
finding of the Council of War of the 19th June, which had been
laid before the King. The inaction decided upon on the 19th June,
was, in the royal view, 'no otherwayes grounded than upon
supposition . . . whether the Boom and chain that are said to be
laid cross the River can be broken'. Therefore the command ran
that Kirke:

> use all meanes to know the truth of these things by sending
> intelligent persons to view the places; and to get the best light
> they can of the matter and to consult for that purpose the Sea
> Officiers whether it may not be possible to break the boom and
> chain and to passe with the Ships and that you attempt the
> doing of it for the reliefe of the Towne.

Just possibly, 'the Passage [might] be found altogether impossible'. His Majesty must, in that contingency, be informed of what
horse and foot are necessary for Kirke to maintain his foothold;
and Kirke must report to Schomberg 'a true information of the
condition of the Town and what may be fitt to be further done
for the Reliefe of the Town which is a matter of so great a consequence'. A postscript is added. It bears date 3rd July:

> Since the writing of this letter his Ma$^{ty}$ is resolved to send a
> considerable reinforcement of Horse and foot to your assistance
> which will speedily find you either at Derry Lough or at
> LondonDerry your letter of the 12th of last month came safe to
> my hands and was communicated to his Ma$^{ty}$.

A copy implies an original. The original was that 'lettre . . . du 29
Juin, vieux style, avec un apostile du trois Juillet', among those to
which d'Avaux refers as taken from the English packet boat
captured by the 'enseigne' bringing in du Quesne Mosnier's
prizes to Dublin (see p. 243 ante). It would not (for the copy does
not, in its postscript just quoted, go beyond general mention of
reinforcements of horse and foot for Kirke) name Solms as
commander or specify troop strengths. Other letters of the intercepted batch supplied those details. Schomberg's famous order for
Kirke and those other letters were handed to Lord Dover–then
about to depart for France–for delivery to the French King.[100]

Macaulay may be pardoned for missing the elucidating reference in the seven hundred and fifty pages of d'Avaux; but surely he should have sensed that Nairne's possession of a copy pointed to interception of the original and not to the delivery of the order to Kirke!

Schomberg's letter had, no doubt, at once been given to a courier. To whom? Not to David Cairnes who himself sent a letter from Campbelltown on the 4th July. And to whomsoever delivered, never, it is safe to conclude, to be handed to Kirke.

Aickin's *Londerias*, published ten years after the siege, contains the passage:

> . . . this was our last sally
> For Councillor Cairnes arrived immediately
> And brought an express from his Majesty
> Commanding Kirk for to relieve the town
> To guard some transports from the fort and
>                         boom

The last sally 'the battle of the Cows' was on the 25th July. Cairnes, in Edinburgh on the 4th July, shipwrecked on Mull and writing from Campbelltown on the 11th July, carried, as has been shown, orders for Kirke–but certainly none from Schomberg bearing date the 3rd July. If Cairnes did manage somehow to reach Kirke by the 25th–he did so six days later than the day on which Kirke had taken his decision and sailed with his relief vessels from Inch and on the very day on which the *Dartmouth* was moved up to Culmore where the victuallers already waited the wind![101]

Lieutenant General Hamilton did not pursue the siege of Londonderry further than to direct desultory fire from the trenches. By the 31st, firing their own camp and surrounding property, the Irish army departed towards Strabane. And Major-General Kirke's amphibious operations were almost ended. He sailed in *Swallow* to Inch on the last day of the month. There the fact of the relief of Londonderry had already been confirmed–but with differing tales as to how the ships reached the city. The most picturesque recorded a 'boat with a house upon it'–from which 'a-sudden a man (a witch they say!) [leaped] struck three strokes with a hatchet upon the Boom and cut it asunder'. Another emphasized that 'the man of war laid within Culmore' and had battered down 'all the upper part' of the castle wall. Steuart at Kirke's arrival had just raided as far as Burt Castle. No mounted enemy sentries rode the hill-tops on 1st August; fires marked the routes of Irish retreat. The memorial of the Council of War of the 25th had presumably ceased to have significance. Richards doesn't mention the matter. 'Extraordinary windy and rainy weather' prevented that night the return of grateful messengers from Walker to Kirke; but, next morning, they with Richards were early away and, at nightfall, on the 2nd August, reported to Kirke upon preliminary repair of the freed city. By Saturday the 3rd the besiegers had fallen back to Strabane. Presumably the *Jerusalem*, the third and small victualler which had not sailed to the London-derry quay on the 28th was sent thither from the Lough. The Major-General could survey his 'campaign'; he was, apparently not dissatisfied. He desired abstracts from Richards' *Diary* 'since our being at Inch' to be sent to the King and detailed Captain Henry Withers to sail in the *Dartmouth* to Liverpool to report to King and Parliament.

Sunday the 4th August ranked a memorable occasion in the maiden city. Detachments of troops from Inch were detailed to prepare on Windmill Hill a general camp. At 11 a.m. the Major-General reached the walls and was met by Walker and Michel-burne, the sword and mace of the city borne before them. The keys were offered and returned. Cannon saluted. The procession wound its way between lines of soldiers and the survivors of the hundred fateful days; the 'very sick', remarks Richards, 'of which there were many' greeted their deliverer. Kirke occupied his time in a practical manner and was ready to depart for Inch at six. To crown his day, just as he was leaving, came three horsemen from the Governors of Enniskillen and, to quote Richards, reported:

Col. Wolseley & Lt. Col. Tiffin [that the Major General sent to Enniskillen 20th July last to command those forces, see p. 238] having advice that Major General McCarthy was marching with about 6000 men towards the garrison & that Colonel Sarsfield at Donegal was coming to join them. Wherefore on

Thursday [1st August] Wolsey with 2000 horse & dragoons & 3000 folk marched & met Major General McCarthy between Lisnakea & Wattle Bridge where the enemy drew up to all the advantage with eight pieces of cannon . . .

The upshot of the engagement, the fight over 'a pass' with bog to right and left is common knowledge. Kirke cannot have failed to reflect that it was he who had (admittedly with the assistance of Rooke) sent Hobson in *Bonadventure* in the first fortnight of July with military supplies to Ballyshannon and in the third week, Wolsey and Tiffen and other officers and yet more ammunition for Enniskillen. Was not the break out from Enniskillen to Newton Butler, the raising of the western siege his victory also?

That day Kirke once more wrote to the King and Duke of Hamilton. Captain Withers delivered at Hampton Court by the 8th, the dispatch; and the *London Gazette*, 8th–12th August, gave the public the benefit of additional information concerning the relief. Again the archives of the Duke supply the first person statement.

The second letter 'From the Isle of Inch August the 4th 1689' supplies information not available when the first was written.

. . . Capt. Browning's shipp stopt at the Boume, where he was killed. The boatswain's mate of the *Swallow* who commanded her long boat cut the boume, so that the weight of the ship broke it and the shipps went up but so little wind that the long boat towed her all the way to the town. The enemy had four guns or thereabouts at the boume and 2000 small shott upon the river Wee lost but 5 or 6 soldiers. Lieutenant Leys of Sir John Hanmers Regiment wounded and the boatswain's mate shott with a splinter in the thigh; Capt. Brownings widow I have beg'd may be taken care of and for the rest I will endeavour to reward for the present with some of his Majesties money which I hope he will not think ill bestowed.

The enemy blew up Culmore Castle burnt Red Castle and all the houses down the river, . . .[102]

The letter concluded with a commendation of Captain Douglas –'I refer him to his Majestie and your Grace' and an intimation that he, Kirke, had given Douglas's crew 'something to drink the King's health'. It was subscribed and signed as its fore-runner.

Douglas was not overlooked by the King. On the 25th October Shrewsbury was ordered to ask the Admiralty to find him suitable employ. That same day the Board received the request but decided to defer consideration to an occasion when Torrington should be present.[103]

The names of the nine men of the long-boat have already been given. Rewarded by Captain Cornwall with a guinea apiece they could hope for more to come. Cornwall forgot neither his Boat-swain John Shelley nor the men. On the 8th October he wrote on their behalf to the Admiralty. A record of the Lord Treasurer's Remembrancer reads: 'a reward to them at the rate of X$^{li}$ Each abating a Guiney paid to each of em by Capt. Cornwall they being the Boats Crew that cutt the Boome at the carying the Victualling Ships to Releif of London Derry    xx.      s.    d.'[104]

iiij    vj   vj

On the 18th August the King had observed to Halifax that he would 'remember Shelly who cut the chain at Londonderry'.[105] To the five guineas was promotion ever added?

On the widow of Captain Browning William bestowed a 'diamond' chain and a pension which was irregularly paid.[106] Captain Withers also brought 'An Abstract of what passed at the Isle of Inch', the 7th July to the 2nd August, that summarized version of Richards' *Diary* which Kirke had desired should be available to the King. It contained no reference to Kirke's letter to Steuart, of the 25th July, suggesting withdrawal from Inch!

Kirke dined Walker 'and several of his Officers' at Inch, on Monday the 5th, and used the occasion to suggest to Walker he 'return to his own profession'! A letter to Hamilton recorded the Major-General's verdict on the siege.

I was in Derry yesterday to order a place to Encamp; since I was born I never saw a town of so little Strength to Rout an Army with so many Generals against it. The walls and Outwork are not touched the Houses are generally broke down by the Bombs; there have been five hundred and ninety one shot into the town.

It remained now to shift the whole main body of Inch soldiery to Londonderry, their supplies a sea and river operation, to parade them, regulate the town, pay thanksgiving, Thursday the 8th August, and spare a day for general rejoicings.[107]

Months later, one, Major George Holmes, who had endured and fought throughout the siege, looked back on the great deliverance. How suddenly, how strangely the enemy had vanished–bag and baggage, tent, gun and standard: 'After the ships came in with provision to us our enimies thought it was in vain to stay any longer, so on Lammas day they left us the wide fields to walk in.'[108] The relief of Londonderry and the carnage of Newton Butler settled that, in the fortnight following, the valleys and mountains of almost all Ulster–broadly, the territory north of Sligo and of the triangle Carrickfergus, Charlemont, Newry–should, without further fighting be lost to James.

Rooke had not stayed to see the operation of relief; for 'the wind not presenting' he had sailed on the 25th to Carrickfergus, expectant of three fourth rates to be added to his squadron.[109] He reported to Nottingham and Hamilton, on the 2nd August[110] by express, 'the siege of Londonderry is raised'. He told of the information Kirke had received upon visiting Inch concerning the desperate state of the besieged; their statement that cannon had been moved from the boom; of the Major General's decision to attempt a 'river' relief and his appeal for use of the *Dartmouth*. Rooke hands on the observation that the relief ships were 'opposed by cannon both at Kilmore and the place Where the boombe was which had been broke away by ill weather'. Nottingham might 'hourely expect a more particular account' from Kirke himself. A postscript added, 'I leave it to the Major Generall to doe the Captain of the *Dartmouth* justice in this service, tho' I can't but say he has beene always forward in it.' In a simultaneous communication to Hamilton Rooke reveals an undisguised sympathy for 'those brave poor people' and, of the operation of relief comments, 'contrary to the Major General's information they [the ships] had some prejudice from [enemy] cannon in passing Culmore & the place where the boom had been'. d'Avaux, telling his King of the relief of Londonderry declared:

> en effet l'estacade estoit si mal faite, qu'elle n'a pas resisté aux chaloupes qui remorquoient les deux petits bastimens que portoient des vivres et nous avions desja sceu plus d'une fois que cette estacade se rompoit souvent par le vent et par la seule force de la marée.[111]

Allowance must be made for overstatement by d'Avaux and for

some simplification by Rooke. But a floated dam of baulks of 'Firr beams', however skilfully socketed and bound together, subjected for a couple of months to the disintegrating stresses of twice daily tides and winds would require a degree of maintenance which it is likely this 'estocade' did not receive. For de Pointis was all that time a sick man[112] and one may suspect that Hamilton, who prevented the construction of a secondary boom and did not expect relief by the river, was not particularly interested in the project (see p. 223 *ante*). Damage the boom suffered; it remained too strong for a 135-ton ship to ram and break and scatter.

To the Duke of Hamilton Rooke wrote on the 9th introducing the bearer Governor Walker, now on his way to England with an address of thanks to the King. William in turn would issue (16th August) his letter to the Governors praising (how justly!) the 'eminent and extraordinary service' given in that 'resolute and unparalleled defence'.

Rooke continued to exercise his minor control of the Irish Sea and the Scottish waters to northward. He had no particular news for Nottingham or for Hamilton, only the wish, expressed to the latter, upon the 9th 'God send our fleete a good wind from Leverpoole'.[113]

Duke Schomberg appointed, on the 16th July, to conduct the campaign in Ireland with the Count de Solms as second in command,[114] had been at Chester since the 20th July. He had, on the 21st, deemed it proper to tell William of his intent to cross with the Count de Solms to Ireland and disembark at Carrick-fergus and Strangford to be within reach of Londonderry and so placed as to be able to march to make junction with Kirke and the Enniskilleners.[115] That communication had been followed by another next day giving an account of the condition in which he found his soldiers and waiting ships; with it he forwarded a packet from Kirke (it arrived opened from Scotland) in which the notion of relief of Enniskillen by sea *via* 'Belchanan' (Ballyshannon) and Lough Erne was outlined.[116] Schomberg on the 24th was worried because only the *Antelope* lay at hand. To wait until the Admiralty sent vessels from London would take too long–a plain hint to the King to act.[117] William did, issuing two orders in Dutch from

I

58 IN IRELAND

Hampton Court, on the 26th, addressed respectively to Captains
Van der Gijsen and Van der Zaan to take their ships to Chester.
Van der Gijsen [in *Damiate*] and Van der Zaan [in          ] had
called some days earlier and were gone out. So Mr Addis, Ply-
mouth Resident Commissioner, could not deliver the instructions.
What is interesting about the orders is the fact that, superscribed
William R, countersigned Huggens, they were issued under the
Great Seal.[118] Writing again on the 26th, Schomberg indicated
uncertainty as to Kirke's whereabouts; he believed the Major-
General to be at Inch; but if Kirke *'qui est un homme capricieux'* were
following orders [a reference to the King's instructions of the 3rd
July?], all should be well. None the less Schomberg had remained
fearful for the fate of Londonderry.[119] On the 27th the Duke
again addressed the King, full of complaint, which he said the
letters of Solms would underline. The Admiralty he held to lack
energy; and the fear that the French might molest his passage was
(as on the 22nd) with him.[120] Probably it was at this time or a
little earlier that a plan for taking Captain Sir Clowdisley Shovell
from Torrington's fleet and placing him in command of fifteen
men-of-war to cruise between Scilly and Ireland—two of the light
frigates to be detached from the fifteen for intelligence of any move
by the French fleet—was devised. The draft, undated, is endorsed
by Nottingham 'Proposals for Shovell—not ordered'. The document
shows on the part of the person or persons who inspired it—no
doubt Schomberg and the King—little confidence in the Grand
Fleet and small knowledge of the principles of naval strategy.[121]

When *Bonadventure* arrived on the 2nd August at Hoylake, having
left Rooke off Kintyre after noon of the 30th July,[122] Captain
Hobson could only give for latest news an uncertain report that
the boom was broken.[123] Hobson found *Antelope* and many ships
at anchor; *Mary Galley*, *Charles Galley*, *Saudadoes*, *Princess Anne of
Denmark* and other vessels joined on the 3rd. The troops were now
moving from Chester toward the sea to two[124] separate camps,
French and English-Dutch, and the arrival, on the 5th, of the
Earl of Portland, special emissary of the King, gave opportunity
for an inspection of the degree of preparedness of the expedition.[125]
Written complaints about the Ordnance Office and Mr Harboard
(Paymaster General) or rather his *'homme d'affaires'* Sir Joshua

Allen, had already gone to the King.[126] Here on the spot Portland '*favori d'un grand Roi*'[127] could weigh the force of those grumblings but above all, '*il étoit venu pour diligenter encore les choses, s'il eut été possible de les presser plus que le Duc faisoit*'. It was whilst Portland was with Schomberg that firm news of the relief of Londonderry got through (on the 6th) to Hoylake. The report arriving was probably that committed by Kirke to Captain Withers in Inch on the 3rd August. Portland, with the officer who brought it (Withers?), hastened to the King–only to find that William already knew; for, as has been noted (see p. 246 *ante*) the *London Gazette* of 1st–5th August, had published on the 4th August, a third person narrative emanating from Hampton Court. Schomberg swiftly put aboard the troops of ten regiments, all infantry; also his artillery and gun horses. When regimental officers 'à tout moment' represented that their men had no bread, beer or water,[128] Schomberg's mounting dissatisfaction with Commissary-General Shales found expression in charge to the King of general mismanagement and deceit.[129] On the 9th the Duke went aboard the *Cleaveland* yacht[130] ready for the first auspicious wind; and, till it blew, assiduous to visit ship after ship of the expedition. At nine at night on Sunday the 11th the wind swung to a favourable quarter.[131] In a last letter to the King before sailing, Schomberg returned to his castigation of Shales.[132]

A night sailing was not to be thought of; but, before it was light on Monday the 12th August, *Bonadventure* (Captain Hobson) had got up her best bower anchor and, less than an hour after sunrise, weighed on a moderate gale from E.S.E. With her the fourths *Antelope* and *Princess Anne of Denmark*, the *Monmouth* yacht, the *Cleaveland* yacht, shepherded between the East and West Hoyle Banks from the Hoyle-lake into Liverpool Bay[133] eighty hired transports, with perhaps 6,000 men, and immediately needed stores aboard. Another forty troop transports, store, artillery and ammunition, ships, and horse boats, left behind at this dawn departure, were expected to work out, under their assigned naval escort, with the least possible delay. Schomberg would wait for them in Ramsey Bay. But on a following wind Schomberg sailed fast; his convoy held well together; and, by three in the afternoon, he was off the Island. It would have been foolish to bear up. A small barque was ordered back with the information that the Duke had decided to stand on course set for Carrickfergus.[134] Although, in a letter to Duke Hamilton, written on this day of sailing, Schomberg professed that his landing place was undecided (he hoped that, wherever it might be, his presence would keep James from disturbing Scotland and allow Hamilton to send help to Ireland) it is fairly certain that the place for disembarkation was settled before sailing.[135] For some military reasons the Duke would have wished it to be Carlingford Lough, nearer to Dublin; but he also saw advantage in landing at a place which promised facilities for speedy rendezvous with the Londonderry and Enniskillen victors. What had no doubt settled the matter was the firm advice of the naval men and the pilots as to the merits of the more northern water.[136]

At 7 o'clock next morning, for Hobson and Schomberg the Isle lay four leagues astern. Rooke in *Deptford*, the *Portland* and *Henrietta* yacht and another vessel with him, waited opposite in 'Dunacade' (Donaghadee) Bay. He had played a merry preparatory tune on entering that Bay at just about the time Schomberg was leaving Hoylake: 'We [got] one smale shippe off, four others we burn't and broake aboute twenty boates'.[137] Rooke – exactly when is not certain – received formal orders from the Admiralty to accept the instructions of Schomberg and that, he presumed, would excuse communication with the Secretary of State unless he should find himself separated from Schomberg's oversight.[138] On sighting the incoming warships and convoy, Rooke stood out, fired thirty-eight guns, went aboard the *Cleaveland*, and technically, though scarcely professionally, came under the Duke's command. He told Schomberg of the Enniskilleners' great victory.[139] At noon anchors dropped in seven fathoms in 'Bangwell' (Bangor) Bay south at the entry to Carrickfergus Lough and opposite Carrickfergus town and castle.[140] For the Duke, entourage and soldiery regular and raw levies it had been '*le plus beau tems & le meilleur vent qu'on eut pu souhaiter*'. Voyage time? Thirty-one and a half hours for the seventy miles.[141] The *Portland* was sent to Ramsey to acquaint such ships as might be there of the Duke's safe arrival. Landing of the men, munitions and stores at once began. It was unopposed. A not inconsiderable body of James's forces, under

Brigadier Maxwell, which might well have contested the disembarkation, retired southward on Belfast and Lisburn *en route* for Newry where lay the scanty battalions of Berwick apprehensively guarding the road to Dublin. Isolated, McCarthy More, commanding Carrickfergus, burnt his suburbs and made fast his gates. On the 14th the *Monmouth* and *Cleaveland* yachts looked in on the village and wharf of Belfast. Next day, when a regiment took possession, the *Cleaveland* left for Londonderry. The *Princess Anne of Denmark* was by that time on her way back to Hoylake with empty transports. *Kingfisher* yacht was returned to Kirke on the 16th, the *Antelope* ordered to cruise for four days off the Isle of Man. The 17th saw the army marching to Belfast. In came *Portland* on the 18th; she and *Antelope* had found and brought from Ramsey Bay the rest of Schomberg's transports to which the *Charles Galley*, a fourth, the *Supply* and *Pearl*(?) fifths, and that maid of all work *Saudadoes*, a sixth, were acting as escort. This convoy had got away from Hoylake within three hours of Schomberg's departure but had not received a message before *Antelope* found it in Ramsey Bay. The welcome reinforcement received from Rooke a salute of twenty-seven guns.

Certain of the ships could now fulfil a different rôle. The guns of Carrickfergus were a menace to the massed shipping; and, in any case, the Jacobite stronghold could not be disregarded. So, as soon as the recently arrived troops, foot and horse and the necessary guns, had got ashore at Bangor, *en route* for Belfast, Schomberg invested Carrickfergus and selected ships began a bombardment which was not as effective as Rooke could have wished; consequently he lent some of his lower tier guns to supplement land batteries. It took six days (to the 27th August) to secure the fall of Carrickfergus.

Comings and goings of ships a-plenty had filled the interim of siege. Fifty-two merchantmen were escorted out of Hoylake on the 22nd. Thirty-four vessels delivered horses on the 26th; again a 'fleet of ships' with horses on the 30th. On the last day of August three fourths—the *Archangel*, the *Samson* and *Sceptre* and a fifth, the *Smyrna Merchant*, arrived in the Lough after having made their passage thither round the North of Scotland.[142] The time of the year was coming, so Rooke wrote Hamilton, when, unfortunately, he would not be able to venture too far northward. And indeed 'because of the approaching season of the year & provisions' he had, he told Hamilton, already sought Admiralty permission to return homeward.[143] Scotland, almost without a Navy, but on its dignity, had just declared War on France (6th August). The particular 'casus belli'? Louis had 'sent ships to bring Irish forces for the invasion of Scotland'.[144]

At the fall of Carrickfergus Schomberg had surveyed with content his supply of warships and stated to the King that he would send some of the larger rates to cruise off Dublin, Cork and Kinsale.[145] He had almost certainly received by this time a communication superscribed William R, penned at Hampton Court 11th August, the day before he, Schomberg, sailed. For two days before the 11th the palace vanes had pointed south-east and the King realized (and no doubt hoped) that his letter might be too late for delivery at Hoylake. None the less he was constrained to write, '*J'espère que Vous serez sur Votre départ, car la saison s'abaisse extrêmement et il est absolument nécessaire, que Vous fassiez toute la diligence possible*'. He had been reflecting on '*le gros de l'affaire d'Irlande*' and was convinced that '*il sera d'une indispensable nécessité*' to secure before the winter a good port in the south of Ireland, '*comme Kinsale ou Cork*', from which English warships might 'hibernate' to prevent supplies from France being thrown to the enemy. Then the surprising sentence: '*Ainsi j'inclinerois assez que Vous alliez directement débarquer là*', followed by the qualification, '*Mais comme il y pourroit avoir presentement des difficultés à cause de la distance & autres Vous pourriez, ayant une fois pris porte à Calingford, y faire un détachement*'.[146] But, on the 3rd September Nottingham required, in the King's name, that certain of the ships with Schomberg, which were designed for the West Indies should not be detained in the Irish Seas but immediately ordered on to Plymouth. And, further—the rest of the men-of-war which Schomberg intended to send before Dublin and to the south of Ireland should be left with Rooke whose squadron would otherwise be too much weakened if the French fleet should come on the Irish coast.[147]

On the first day of September Duke Schomberg marched south from Belfast toward Newry where Berwick unconfidently barred the road to Dublin.[148]

## II

In surveying naval happenings from mid-May to the end of August in the area covered by Rooke's subsidiary command, interest inevitably centres less upon the Captain's duty to prevent a traffic of Jacobites between Ireland and Scotland than upon the relief of Londonderry, assistance of Enniskillen and oversight of the crossing of Schomberg to Bangor Bay. Rooke could only accomplish his several purposes by incessant cruising. A complete plotting of the courses of the ships of his squadron during the months in question would indicate how persistently he crossed and recrossed the waters 'Carrickfergus–Kintyre–Swilly–the Western Isles' and how professionally unfortunate he was not to have been at hand when the three French frigates attacked *Pelican* and *Janet*. Yet professional ill-luck may well have been a blessing in disguise. For, in any encounter of Rooke's three fourths and the fifth *Dartmouth* with du Quesne Mosnier's three light frigates, the accident of damage sustained in combat might have denied Rooke's ability to lend Leake and the *Dartmouth* to Kirke in the supremely critical last week of July. Hurt sustained in a frigate encounter could, no doubt, have been put right by repair or reinforcement soon enough to enable Schomberg's expeditionary passage. Setting speculation aside, what emerges is the fact that, for three whole months, so absolute was Torrington's major command of the Channel–command, confidently assumed by a powerful blockading–cruising fleet, inspiring fear and never called upon to fight, that the tiny ancillary squadron enjoyed a reflected immunity from challenge, and reaped through Torrington, and its own assiduity, spectacular–and classic–achievement. It may perhaps be observed that the degree to which a military man placed in charge of an expedition may consider himself in control of allotted or contingent naval assistance is a matter not neatly settled by the letter of the instructions the soldier has received. The relationship between Kirke and Rooke was amicable and might be held a model of what such co-operation should be.

It is doubtful whether, during the month of August, James could have made any use whatever of his exiguous naval resources, the three frigates *La Jolie*, *La Lutine*, *La Tempête*. *La Jolie* was old and in need of refitting, *La Lutine*, du Quesne Mosnier declared, would not stand four or five shot in its side; and he asked for replacement of both, the latter by a more powerful vessel such as *Le François*.[149] But in truth all Irish action was paralysed. The fear of Schomberg's impending descent, the news of the relief of Londonderry so depressed the court, that d'Avaux, who, 6 Aoust/30th July, had opened a letter to his master with the words, '*Il n'y a plus que Dieu et vostre Maiesté qui puisse empescher la ruine entiere du Roy d'Angleterre*',[150] necessarily revealed to Louvois, a little over a week later, that emergency schemes for possible evacuation of Dublin were planned and withdrawal to Athlone and the province of Connaught contemplated–though not without a lively realization of the need to hold on if possible to Munster with its ports of Kinsale and Waterford. For, ruefully d'Avaux observed, 'Galloway n'a point de port, ce n'est qu'une rade et la grande mer y est si violente quand il soufle un vent d'ouest, que les vaisseaux en hyver en pouroient bien estre incommodez'.[151] And for that reason James's orders to du Quesne Mosnier to station his frigates at Innisboffin[152] '*personne icy ne connoissant ce port là!*'[153] read, to say the least, ironically. du Quesne Mosnier had no reason to like James. Reporting his Scottish voyage, '*esgalement perilleuse et heureuse . . . envoyé en les endroits où jamais navire n'avoit paru*', he received no 'gratification' for prizes taken or expenses in travelling post from Kinsale to Dublin at James's command.[154] In Dublin right to the end of the month indecision prevailed. On the 20th, Melfort, bête noire of d'Avaux, Tyrconnel and the Irish-French party, discontentedly resigned his post of Secretary of State. He left on the night of the 25th August for Versailles.[155] Upon his going James acted at least to the extent of heading a small troop of horse northward towards Schomberg. French ships intermittently stole across to Kinsale for and with dispatches. But nothing of note disturbed Rooke's command.

Historians have presented Major-General Kirke as an unlovable character and been disinclined to 'give the devil his due'. The charge of procrastination before sailing from Hoylake is difficult to maintain–the winds were adverse; for short delay in Ramsey Bay he may be held accountable (see p. 225 *ante*). He arrived in Lough Foyle on the 12th June, received report of Captain

Richards' reconnaissance. A boom lay across the river; that much was established, but Kirke was unable before the 15th to secure the *Dartmouth* and order Leake on supplementary investigation. Messengers Kirke had sent out; but he had obtained no news from the beleagured city. Leake sailed 'a large mile of[f] Culmore' and duly reported. The all-important council-of-war, which concluded that the breaking of the boom was too hazardous to be justified, followed, without delay, on the 19th instant. Is Kirke to blame for accepting the professional advice of the four sea-officers of the validity of which, from the maintop of the *Dartmouth*, he next day sought to assure himself? Occupation of the island of Inch was an obviously sound military procedure, calculated to draw off forces from Londonderry and Enniskillen and to give to the besieged of the former, told that they could not be succoured from the river, hope yet of relief. Captain Hobson in *Bonadventure* completed by the 28th June, the naval probe that preceded the Inch landing. Could the descent of Steuart's six hundred men have been effected before the 10th July to the earlier encouragement of the hard pressed city? Kirke had, by the 12th July (thanks to the willing co-operation of Rooke who had placed Hobson's *Bonadventure* additionally at Kirke's disposal) been of more tangible help to Enniskillen (via Ballyshannon) than to Londonderry! And it was Kirke who, on arrival at Inch, 19th July, sent Enniskillen-wards two little ships with further supplies and Colonel Wolsey and officers destined to fame at Newton Butler. The fact is that appearances conspire against Kirke—not least his seeming willingness, 25th July, to evacuate Inch if seriously pressed.

Concerning the last phase at Londonderry this much is clear. On arrival at Inch on the 19th/20th July, Kirke received first the information Colonel Steuart possessed but had been unable to convey to his general—that the garrison had discussed with the enemy surrender in fourteen days counting from the 12th—i.e. upon the 26th—and, secondly, Steuart had thrust into his hands on the 20th the desperate letter of Friday the 19th signed by Walker and Michelburne fixing a nearer term for capitulation—Wednesday the 24th July (see p. 239 *ante*). Startled, Kirke realized that Londonderry was as good as lost to King and Protestantism unless he were prepared to gamble against the unanimous advice of a council of war–including its four naval officers. Everything was rushed to readiness; the three victuallers at their starting points on the 25th. Fortune tantalized, withholding for three days the necessary wind, favoured him in that the heroic besieged endured to Sunday the 28th four days beyond their own stated utmost limits.

Though there is evidence that the boom was damaged when the attempt came to be made, it is not credible that the massed guns were less dangerous on the 28th July than upon the 19th June. Let the layman continue to argue that the earlier attempt should have been made, the shade of Kirke, '*homme caprixieux*', will reply, ' I might so have earlier acted had not seamen have advised against it. Failure of such attempt, with a ship sunken and blocking the channel would probably have produced the immediate surrender of the city which pictured relief only by its waterway. I avoided the risk and worked at an alternative until no other course lay before me. I acted. I relieved Londonderry.'

It remains to observe that the return of Cunningham and Richards with their regiments from the Foyle as the last week in April began, the delay till the very end of May before a new expedition to Londonderry sailed, pricked the national conscience; and, on Saturday 1st June, the House of Commons appointed a Committee to enquire into

the Occasion of the Delays in sending Relief over into *Ireland* and particularly to *Londonderry*, that they make Inquiry what Default was, in relation to Provisions that went over with the soldiers for *Ireland*; And . . . into the Carriage of Colonel *Lundee*, Colonel *Richards*, and Colonel *Coningham*; and to know the Reason, why the Relief . . . was brought back again; And . . . into all other Miscarriages relating to *Ireland* & *Londonderry*.[156]

His Majesty was desired, on the 3rd, to make copies of commissions and instructions available and allow Lundy, prisoner in the Tower, to be brought before the Committee. On the 4th the Commons required that Anderton the Chester Customs officer (see p. 54) be (with his father) produced for questioning. This was merely the beginning of an investigation into which the Lords entered on the 15th and 18th to play their parallel part, asking at once, through certain lords 'with White Staves', allowance of scrutiny of the Minutes of the Privy Council Committee for Irish Affairs. The King would, the 19th, consider of that! By the 22nd the Commons were seeking access to the same particular Minutes and calling for copies of all proceedings and orders, which of course, included those of the Admiralty. On the 28th they were politely told that the Lords were doing the same! The 3rd July witnessed the Commons request repeated.[157] By the 5th Ireland was pictured: 'over-run by [His] Majesty's declared Enemies the *French*, in Conjunction with *Irish* Rebels, occasioned . . . by the Neglect or ill Conduct of some Persons employed in the Management of the Affairs relating to that Kingdom'. So a new address was made for the Minutes – and papers back to the 27th December. Still no royal response! Whereupon, the 13th, a motion was put asserting that those who had 'been the Occasion of delaying the sending Relief to *Ireland* and those Persons that advise the King to defer the giving of Leave for some Members of [the] House to inspect the Minute Books . . . [were] enemies to the King and Kingdom'. It was passed *nem con* and a debate for a further address to bring about the dismissal of Halifax and Caermarthen from the councils of the King was initiated. The 16th brought the royal and executive surrender and, by the 29th, examination was again well under way. The Lords had not dropped from the scene (they were keen on the 26th to see the 'Books of the Admiralty' and on the 29th, in effect all relevant papers 'since His Majesty's taking the Administration . . . upon Him'); but it was the Commons Committee, which, on the 12th August, reported.

That eight-columns-long report brings to light little that is not, in the main, to be established from many convergent sources; yet it supplies much detail and possesses the value of evidence elicited in formal enquiry in a contemporary hour. Captain James Hamilton, who had arrived in Londonderry on the 21st March to swear in and encourage Lundy with supplies and money, 'had given a good Account of himself'. Not so Lundy, 'several times examined'. He had retreated too soon from Cladyford, closed his gates to fugitives, dealt doubly both with the city authorities and with Cunningham, who had arrived on the 15th April with two regiments and stores for his assistance; he had pronounced

Londonderry indefensible and, execrated by the citizens, ordered
back help whence it came. Cunningham brought to the Committee
sworn statements that he had taken 'the Oaths & Test' and relied
on a contention of correctitude of conduct; he could not at the
request 'from the Rabble' take Lundy's place; and he had a good
opinion of the governor's loyalty. Richards understandably
stressed that he had warned a council-of-war that 'Quitting the
Town was quitting of a Kingdom'; he had been critical of
Cunningham but obeyed him as his superior. Of Captain Cornwall
of the *Swallow*, a military man alleged (certainly in Cornwall's
absence) that the captain convoying Cunningham's transports
back to England charged £4 per head for refugee passage, or
swords, watches or clothing in lieu–a barbarous procedure!
Matthew Anderton, the Chester Customs official who had acted
as agent to the Navy Board and the Victuallers, for provision of
shipping, victuals and money, faced no sympathetic questioning.
He could maintain that he had, as ordered, provided seven ships
for Cunningham's 1,500 men, secured an extra vessel of 150 tons
when the officers complained of being straightened in three; an
extra one for the horses he had not added. Satisfactory victualling
had obviously been beyond Anderton's power. To the gibe that the
biscuit was drawn from Chester Castle, put there during Monmouth Rebellion, Anderton replied it had been baked 'but in
December'. He was told the beer in casks was said to miss a foot
of the full and to be so bad, 'That the men chose rather to drink
salt water, or their own urine. To that he answered he had paid
the best rates as the receipts showed.' Nobody complained of the
Cheshire cheese. Anderton's payment of £595 to Hamilton and
Anderton's payments of £2,000 to Cunningham within three days
of receiving instructions, were provable; but the task of providing
Cunningham with a further £2,000 before he sailed had been
beyond Anderton's capability. The demand had since been met.
Anderton declared that both sums of £2,000 had been raised on
Anderton's father's credit. The report submitted, Littleton moved
the House that the King be addressed to bail Cunningham and
commit Lundy to stand trial for treason in Londonderry city. It
cannot be said that, with the copies of the Privy Council, Admiralty
and Navy Office books before them and with an array of persons

called, the Commons' Committee had caused new rabbits to bolt from their holes. Bad beer, bad biscuit had not delayed the March arrival of Hamilton in Londonderry or the April sailing of Cunningham's soldiery and stores–though one may from the evidence suspect that Colonel Cunningham lingered loth to depart without his second £2,000. What does emerge is the corroboration that two soldiers turned their backs on Londonderry–cowardice was matched with pusillanimity. Cunningham must share in Lundy's shame. Eight days after the entry of this report–presumably intended as interim–Parliament was prorogued till the 20th September, to meet again on the 19th October next.

## REFERENCES

1 The authorities for events inside Londonderry are, in general, those cited at the beginning of Ch. V. and Macpherson, J. *Original Papers . . . to which are prefixed Extracts from the Life of James II as written by himself*, Dublin, 2 V. 1775, I, pp. 201–220. Particular indications are added when necessary.
2 Walker's estimate.
3 Berwick, *op. cit.*, p. 343.
4 Buchan, Thomas, major-general, *v.* biography *D.N.B.*
5 *A Jacobite Narrative . . .* p. 77.
6 P.R.O. State Papers Ireland, William and Mary, 1689–1690. v. 352, pp. 7–19 or *S.P.Dom . . . 1689–90*, p. 154–161 for summaries, in English, wrongly dated. Part of de Pointis' correspondence is in cipher. At p. 13 a loss is indicated '. . . pendant qu'on saisit la duplicata de ma lettre du 13ᵉ de ce mois' – in which connection *v. S.P.Dom . . . 1689–90* Dr. John Wallis to Nottingham 10 Aug., p. 217.
7 Walker, 15th June; Mackenzie, 13th June. T. C. D. Neville, F. (Capt.) *A Description of the Enemy's Camp* with Map. Story, G. (Rev.) *An Impartial History of the Wars of Ireland, with a Continuation thereof. In Two Parts. From the Time that Duke Schomberg landed . . .*, 1693, contains (Continuation p. 5) 'A Ground Plat of London-Derry' by Captain Sam. Hobson which should be compared with Neville's map. *A Jacobite Narrative*, p. 64.
8 The author of *A Jacobite Narrative*, p. 66, scouts that idea. 'And we are moreover of opinion that a gabbard or bark sunk in the channel of Londonderry may be taken up and the bottom of that sea cleared because the place is shallow at low water.'
9 *H.M.C. Finch II*, p. 209.
10 President of the Council of Estates. From this date the Duke of Hamilton's MSS become important. *v.* Authorities for significance of 'Lennoxlove'. Lennoxlove, 11th May.
11 They were *Bonadventure, Swallow, Jersey, Greyhound, Fisher* ketch. Logs of *Bonadventure*, P.R.O. Adm. 52/9 (Ezekias Gage, Master) and *Jersey*, P.R.O. Adm. 51/4228 (Lt Hammond). *Jersey* would not be joining Rooke. Having

'heeled ship & scrubbed both sides yesterday afternon', the 11th, she was bound for Plymouth.

12 *Ibid.* p. 213.

13 Bodleian. Carte 181 (Nairne's papers 1689–1701) fol. 292 is 'An Acct. of the Engagements that happened between the King's Partie and the Rebells in Scotland since May 1689.' It early refers to a descent of Rooke upon Sir Alex^r Maclaine who was moving some 400 men in small boats—reinforcements intended for Dundee—near Giga. They were bombarded and harried from 8 a.m. to 8 p.m.

14 i.e. Moving a vessel by running out a hawser to a fixed point, securing the end at that point and then heaving in.

15 From 'It will be recalled' to this point Richards' *Diary of the Fleet.*

16 Walker's *Diary*, 7th June.

17 State Papers Ireland . . . 1689–90, v. 352, p. 19.

18 Richards' *Diary of the Fleet.*

19 P.R.O. Adm. 52/9 Ezekias Gage, Master.

20 Log *Bonadventure* (*v.* entry 31st).

21 *A Particular Journal of Major General Kirk's Voyage from Leverpoole to his Safe Arrival at London-Derry*, Printed for Meade, G. 1689. This tract begins 'Notwithstanding the many Rumours & Insinuations etc . . . And because the Curious have much enquired into the reason of Coll. Kirk's being so long retain'd on his Voyage . . .'

22 Story, *op. cit.* Part I, p. 96. Strengths at review at Finglass, 7th & 8th July 1690.

Kirk's regiment   666 ⎫
Stuart's   ,,      660 ⎬ 1919
Hanmer's  ,,       593 ⎭

23 The Great Orme.

24 The Maids or Maidens, off Larne.

25 Log of *Bonadventure*, from 'filled amid showers . . . their sails.

26 Logs *Bonadventure* and *Deptford* (Captain's), P.R.O. Adm. 51/4180.

27 Lennoxlove [*H.M.C. XI*, vi, p. 185].

28 Lennoxlove, 19th June [*H.M.C. XI*, vi, p. 184] which also notes the arrival of three provision ships and names the *Phoenix* of Glasgow as one (*v.* p. 247 *infra.*).

29 Richards' *Diary.*

30 Charnock, J. *Biographia Navalis*, 6 v. 1794–8, Pepys 'Sea Commission Officers' *Naval Manuscripts in the Pepysian Library* (v. Authorities) Powley, *op. cit.* pp. 68f, 90, 137f, 141 (for Cornwall). For Leake *v.* Martin Leake, ed. Callender, *op. cit.*

31 Richards' *Diary.*

32 Logs *Bonadventure*, *Deptford*. ('Tunnes'–at the head of Lough Foyle, opposite Innishowen.) Lennoxlove [*H.M.C. XI*, vi, p. 185] Rooke to Hamilton on the 20th looking back at the *Greyhound*'s adventure writes 'the *Greyhound* unhappily attempting to goe by the Castle at Kilmore with a scant wind . . .' which suggests she essayed to go past the Castle into the River. Rooke says the *Portland*'s boats helped to refloat her–presumably after she had been purposely run ashore to avoid sinking (*v.* p. 223 *ante*).

33 Kirke was using the best spies available. Of Cromie: 'A man of good sense and speaks French perfectly well; he is likewise of a good family and possesses, it is said, an income of 500 guineas a year in this country . . .' Macpherson, *op. cit.* I, p. 204, translating a letter by Rosen 27th June on sending James the result of examination of Cromie. For the examination, Carte 181, fol. 220. James Roch, 17th Sept. (*v.* Petition Entry Book 2, p. 132 and *S.P.Dom* . . . *1689–1690*, p. 259) is found requesting relief and command of a small frigate–a request sent on to the Admiralty. Roch, said to have lost the use of his limbs, was to be granted £40 out of the customs of Kinsale–when taken. Meanwhile, the charge lay on the Secret Service with £20 in advance. Shaw *op. cit.*, vol. IX, Pt 1, 30th Oct. 1689, p. 61. In 1701 his claims for recognition were under consideration of the Commons and were referred to the Trustees for Irish Forfeitures, *Journals . . . H. of C.*, 19th May, p. 558. The name of another of Kirke's spies is known, that of William Irwin; but how and on what occasion he was employed is not ascertainable. On 31st March 1690, his petition (Petition Entry Book 2, p. 206) was referred to the Committee for Irish Affairs–*S. P. Dom* . . . *1689–1690*, p. 533.

34 Carte 181, ff. 222, 224, 225. These letters are reproduced by Dwyer, *op. cit.* pp. 88–93.

35 Carte 181, f.232, 2nd July.

36 *Ibid.* f.234.

37 *Ibid.* f.236, 3rd July.

38 Authorities for Londonderry and Richards' *Diary*. Dwyer, *op. cit.* p. 192.

39 The logs of *Bonadventure* and *Deptford*, Richards' *Diary* and, for Hunter, *Ulster Journal of Archaeology*, 1898, vol. IV, p. 184.

40 Richards' *Diary*.

41 Carte 181, f.240, 5th July. Wee Doe therefore Authorize and Impower you to Treat with Our said subjects now in Arms against us for ye rendring up of Our Citty of Derry into Our hands or that of Inniskillin or any other Towns or Castles . . . upon such Termes as you shall think fitt for our Service which shall be Ratifyed by us without Exception whatever they may be notwithstanding of any ffault or Treason Committed by any of ye Said Persons . . . and notwithstanding of any Law or Act of Parliament, made or to be made. Melfort.

42 Carte 181, f.244, gives the official version in 18 numbered (really 19) paragraphs. They are printed in Mackenzie among Addenda (*v.* Hempton, *op. cit.* p. 272).

43 Ash (1792 edition) records, 11th July, gunfire for 'the last three days' and the reports of landings as reaching them on the 13th.

44 Londonderry authorities as before with Richards' *Diary*.

45 Log *Bonadventure* and Richards' *Diary*.

46 See letter by Walker 19th July (p. 239).

47 Richards' *Diary*.

48 Lennoxlove [*H.M.C. XI*, vi, p. 185].

49 Richards' *Diary*, logs *Bonadventure*, *Deptford*.

50 Lennoxlove [*H.M.C. XI*, vi, p. 182].

51 Cairnes on 4th July was in Edinburgh receiving a warrant from 'His Majesty's High Commissioner and Lords of the Council' to press two

horses and a vessel 'for transporting of him . . . to Ireland with all expedition'. And a letter subscribed by Crauford, Lord President of the Scots Parliament, to Captain Hamilton of the *Pelican* which ordered him to put Cairnes on the

> next Irish coast or on any frigates near the Lough of Derry he [should] desire

Grant, J. *The Old Scots Navy from 1689–1710*, Navy Records Society, 1914, p. 15.

52 'a vessell Major Generall Kirke had sent over lately to Greenock for some provisions and intelligence and she on her returne having some letters back to him'.

53 Birline—a long-oared boat of the largest size, often with six, sometimes eight oars, generally used by chieftains in the Western Isles. It seldom had sails. Gaelic—*birlinn* (Grant).

54 Grant, *op. cit.*, p. 23.

55 *London Gazette*, No. 2641—capture of 50 Highlanders.

56 Grant, J. *op. cit.* pp. 7–24.

57 *A Full and True Relation of the Remarkable Fight betwixt Captain Hamilton and Captain Brown, Commanders of the Two Scots Frigates and Three French Men of War* . . . [2nd Aug. 1689, J. Fraser]. This is printed in full by Grant, J. *op. cit.* p. 26. For petitions for assistance to dependents and for fate of prisoners taken to Kinsale, see Grant *op. cit.* There are also accounts in the Nairne papers. (1) 'A Journall of What has Passed since his Ma^{tles} Arrivall in Ireland . . .' for 10th July, Carte 181, f.96. (2) An untitled single folio *ibid.* 133. For mention by d'Avaux *v. Négociations* . . . *d'Avaux*, pp. 319, 327.

58 *Négociations* . . . *d'Avaux*, p. 327, d'Avaux-Seignelay, 26th/16th July; p. 370, 9th August/30th July; p. 397, 19th/9th August for *La Lutine*.
d'Quincy, *op. cit.* p. 230.

59 Lennoxlove [*H.M.C. XI*, vi, p. 185]. The letter is in Rooke's own hand, the catalogue is not but follows the words 'I doe enclose . . .'
It may be of interest to military historians to have the rest:

| Lt. Colonels | Majors | Lieutenants | Qr Masters |
|---|---|---|---|
| Fountaine | Scott | Craford | Bradshaw |
| Douglas | Gordon | Smith | Law |
| Blare | | Grant | |
| Chartress, Senr | *Captains* | Steward | |
| Gordon | Maxwell | Johnson | |
| Chartres, Junr | Napper | Hickford | |
| | Witherington | Mackcullugh | |
| | Fitts Simmons | | |
| | Grant | *Coronets* | |
| | Dobbins | Frazer | |
| | Poque | Simple | |
| | Lupe | Grimes | |
| | Macklane | Gordon | |

Mackay, H. (Major Gen.) *Memoirs of the Wars in Scotland and Ireland*, MDCLXXXIX–MDCXCI. . . Edinburgh 1833 (Bannatyne Club), p. 46.

60 Macpherson, *op. cit.* p. 218, note. On 30th July Buchan concludes a letter 'I think I can do the King more service in Scotland than here' [Ireland].

61 *Négociations . . . d'Avaux* p. 370 9th Aug./30th July.

62 Lennoxlove [*H.M.C. XI* vi, p. 190] Melville to Hamilton.

Dalrymple, *op. cit.* p. 358, remarks that William, advised to send reinforcements, said that 'It was needless, the war ended with Dundee's life'.

63 Log *Bonadventure*. Argyll reported to Hamilton, 20th July, that Rooke ships 'fyred five hundred cannon shot at the house of Dewart' (Rooke's three fourths, *Deptford*, *Bonadventure* and *Portland* had some 130 guns of all sorts between them; the *Dartmouth* less than 30.

Lennoxlove [*H.M.C. XI*, vi, p. 183].

64 As note (61).

65 Lennoxlove [*H.M.C. XI*, vi, p. 182] Cairnes–Argyll, 11th July.

66 *Ibid.* [p. 183] 20th July.

67 The interpolated quotation is from Dover's first instructions, Carte 181, fol. 252, which are followed by further remarks in a different hand, fol. 258.

68 *Négociations . . . d'Avaux* p. 319, d'Avaux-Louis, 26 Juillet/16th July, Carte 181, fol. 96 (in 'A Journall of what has Passed since his Mat^les Arrivall in Ireland').

69 *Ibid.* p. 327, 26 Juillet/16th July and p. 338 two days later. Strickland– Vice Admiral James' fleet in the Nore, summer 1688, superseded by Dartmouth, 24th Sept. 1688 (Powley, *op. cit.* p. 25).

70 *Ibid.* p. 340, d'Avaux-Louis, 6 Aoust/27th July . . . et cela auroit esté necessaire pour guerir l'imagination de plusiers matelots qui ne veulent pas servir dans les bastimens qui transportent des laines en France, les matelots d'un navire de St Malo m'ayant refusé de le faire.

71 Richards' *Diary*. Kirke issued at this time, 24th July, from Inch, a warning, in the names of Their Majesties King William and Queen Mary, to the General Officers of the Irish Army before Londonderry; 'violence . . . against the Protestants in any part of Ireland' would force their Majesties 'to return it in the same manner upon all Roman Catholics . . . found in England' *H.M.C. Duke of Hamilton, XI*, vi, p. 185.

72 As note (71).

73 Londonderry authorities.

74 Lennoxlove [*H.M.C. XI*, vi, p. 185].

75 This is one of the reasons given by the Council of War of 19th June for hesitancy.

76 Captain Browning was a Londonderry man and the *Mountjoy* laden with a cargo of 135 tons, was of Londonderry, *v.* note (80) *infra*.

Captain Pettwell had sailed from Bristol with two other ships in company –at least such is a statement in *An Exact and Faithful Account Brought to a Person of Quality on the raising of the Siege of Londonderry by the Protestants and Garrison*, one of a number of broadsheets on Londonderry and not alone in descriptively announcing 'relief' before it happened. Date of licence 12th June 1689!

For Captain Andrew Douglas and the *Phoenix v.* p. 241 *ante*.

77 presently=immediately.

78 The career of Leake has already been noted (*v.* p. 228 *ante*). What sort of warship was the *Dartmouth*? In the small beautifully hand-written book which Edward Battine, an official at Portsmouth presented to Pepys, 20th December 1684, elaborate specifications for hull, masts, rigging, guns

etc. of the *Dartmouth* are set out—she being selected as a typical example of a fifth rate warship. See also Pepys's Register of Ships, Naval Manuscripts in the Pepysian Library (*v.* Authorities), Dartmouth.

*Dartmouth* was built at Portsmouth in 1665 by Sir John Tippets. Her hull cost £1693. She was 81 ft long, 25 ft beam, 10 ft deep in the hold and drew 12 ft of water. Her burden was 266 tons. Her guns were mounted on her lower, upper and quarter deck

| Lower deck Demiculverins | | Upper deck Sakers | | Quarter deck 3 pounders | |
|---|---|---|---|---|---|
| No. | Tons weight | No. | Tons weight | No. | Tons weight |
| 16 | 23 | 8 | 6 | 4 | $1\frac{1}{2}$ |

If therefore (leaving Battine's account and Pepys's Register of Ships) it be assumed that a demiculverin (4 in. bore) fired a 10 lb. shot, a saker ($3\frac{1}{2}$ in. bore) a 6 lb. shot, a three-pounder a 3 lb. shot, it would follow that a broadside would loose $(8 \times 10)+(4 \times 6)+(2 \times 3)$ lbs weight, 110 lbs—which is less than a hundredweight!

79 The anchorage at which for three days these three ships lay was, one supposes, just beyond gunshot of Culmore.

80 It had been High Water at Culmore at 12.15 that day and at 6 o'clock at the rendezvous of *Dartmouth* and the three victuallers, the tide of ebb must have been very far spent. It would be Low Water at Culmore at 6.40 that evening. Therefore *Dartmouth* and *Mountjoy* may be supposed to have approached the River entry at the slack or turning tide, the water at its neap height—for the moon was due to enter her last quarter at 6 a.m. on the morrow. Captain Samuel Hobson's 'Ground Plat of London Derry' (in Story, *op. cit.*) shows the depth of Low Water Culmore at springs as 11 fathoms—which is more than it is today. Low Water neap would be somewhat higher. There is no suggestion that *Dartmouth* or *Mountjoy* experienced any difficulty in working in. Any pilotage difficulty would occur nearer the city. But to Captain Browning the soundings and tidal sets in the River all the way to Londonderry would be thoroughly familiar and *Mountjoy*, as it were, knew her way home! Captain Douglass 'of Coleraine in Ireland' can also be credited with knowledge of the Foyle? Leake would certainly not be stinted of local pilotage information.

81 Longboat—probably about 30 ft long rowed by a crew of nine, four one side, five the other, a boatswain or boatswain's mate in charge.

82 When Leake 'began to batter' it was not, one may be sure, with a broadside (for it would be an appreciable time to re-load after firing) but with a succession of shots calculated to distract the attention of the fort from the victuallers as they passed ahead. To 'lay between the castle and them within musket shott' of the castle and provide protection as they, *Mountjoy* and *Phoenix*, went up toward the boom, Leake must have 'rounded' Culmore Point and laid himself at the very edge of the shore sand shelf before anchoring.

83 The victuallers would be going up wind or no wind, on a $\frac{3}{4}$ knot Culmore $\frac{1}{2}$ knot Londonderry tide, a tide building up to High Water at Londonderry at just after 1 a.m.

84 That would be learned and reported later (*v.* p. 257 *infra*).

85 The expression 'came by the castle again' confirming the view that
*Dartmouth*'s bombarding anchorage was round the Point and the mention of
8 o'clock [29th] indicated she waited the morning flood tide which had then
just begun (L. W. Culmore 7.20 a.m.). Recalling the disaster to the smaller
*Greyhound*, of 184 tons and drawing only 8 ft 6 inches, one is more inclined
to praise Leake's daring and seamanship than his high rate of firing; for
with 28 guns, though he couldn't perhaps till the morning boast he had
used all of them, his rate could easily be higher than that of the very many
fewer guns of the fort.

86 Londonderry authorities to 'the siege over' (with special indications where
necessary).

87 Ash. He places the hour at 'About five o'clock'. Mackenzie makes the time
they were first observed 'About seven o'clock'.

88 Ash 'the first to come by the Castle was a man-of-war . . . When she came
*above* she drew in her sails and cast anchor'.

89 Mackenzie.

90 As note (86).

91 Walker.

92 Ash.

93 Milligan, C. D., *The Relief of Derry*, 1946, Chapters VII–X for the Christian
name and much else concerning Browning and his wife.

94 See notes (102) and (104) *infra*.

95 Grant, *op. cit.* p. 16.

96 Ash.

97 For the age of the moon 28th and 29th July Pond, *An Almanack for the year
of our Lord God, 1689*, Cambridge and Coley, H. *Nuncius Sydereus or the
Starry Messenger . . . for 1689.*

I am indebted and most grateful to the Hydrographer of the Royal Navy,
Rear Admiral E. G. Irving, O.B.E., for tide calculations which have made
possible certain comments in the preceding notes and for the opportunity
of discussion of chart matters.

98 Macaulay, T. B. (Baron), *The History of England from the Accession of James II*,
5 v. 1856– v. III, p. 235 or ed. Firth, C. H. (Sir) 1914, 6 v. (illustrated)
Ch. xii, p. 1519.

Firth in *A Commentary on Macaulay's History of England*, 1938, p. 218,
having stated that Macaulay cites Martin-Leake, S. *Life of Sir John Leake*,
1750, as one of his authorities, comments 'it is remarkable that in the most
important point he [Macaulay] sets aside the very definite story of the
breaking of the boom' which that work records. The Leake account goes
beyond fact in speaking of more than one boat's crew at the boom. Firth
could have added that it is equally strange that Macaulay ignores parallel
evidence before him concerning the boat's crew, that of the *London Gazette*,
8th–12th August.

99 Carte 181, fol. 238. Dwyer, p. 208, reproduces in full.

100 *Négociations . . . d'Avaux*, p. 319, d'Avaux-Louis, 26 Juillet/16th July, 'ce
qu'elles contiennent de principal est que le comte de Solms doit venir icy,
etc.'

Carte 181, fol. 133 referred to p. 272 *ante* note 57.

'L'officier francois qui commandoit les deux prises fit encore une autre

en s'en revenant a Dublin d'une barque qui portoit des lettres de Schomberg a Kirke *et plusieurs autres* par les quelles en decouvre le dessein que le
P. d'Orange a d'envoyer faire une descente dans ce royaume avec 12000
hommes sous le commandement du Comte de Solms . . .'

There is also mention in Carte 181, fol. 96 verso (previously referred to)
of the capture of this 'small barque employed to carry letters from
Schomberg to Kirke . . . by which was discovered the Prince of Orange's
design to send 12,000 men commanded by Comte Solms'.

101 Cairnes petitioned to be Collector of Customs at Dublin, P.C. 6/2, 26th
May 1690, a fact overlooked in Lawlor, H. C., *A History of the Family of
Cairnes or Cairns and its connections*, 1906.

102 Lennoxlove [*H.M.C. XI*, vi, p. 186].

103 *S.P. Dom. 1689–90*, p. 303. P.R.O. Adm. 3/2 under date. The matter
came up again on 4th Dec. after Dr Walker had visited the Board on
28th Nov. But it is not apparent whether anything was decided. *Ibid.*
under date.

104 P.R.O. Adm. 3/2, 25th Nov.

Capt. Cornwall late Command$^r$ of the *Swallow* makeing Applycation
to the Board by Letter for Reward to Mr John Shelley who Com̄anded
his Long boate and the Boats Crew, who cutt ye Bomb at ye Carrying
Victualing Ships to the Releife of London Derry, and Signifying alsoe
by his Letter of the 8th Instant that the Said Mr Shelly was payd five
Guineys on Acct of this Service, and the rest of the Men which Served
in the Said Boate received each a Guiney–Resolved that the Navy
Board doe cause Such of the Said men of the boats Crew who Shall
appeare to receive it, to have the Money already paid them made up
Tenn Pounds each.

An entry occurs P.R.O. Adm. 3/2, 8th Jan. 1690 empowering the Navy
Board to pay 'unto Mr Tho. Jackson of London what money is due to
Miles Tounge for his service in cutting the Boomb at London Derry, the
said Tho. Jackson appearing to be empowr'd to receive the said money by
letter of attorney from Mary Toungue Wife of the Said Miles Toungue'.

P.R.O. Records of the Exchequer (L.T.R.), Declared Accounts Pipe
Office Series E.351/2333, 17, dorso. This entry was first noticed by
Oppenheim who communicated his discovery to the *Athenaeum* of 13th
Jan. 1889.

105 Foxcroft, *op. cit.* II, p. 231.

106 *v.* note (93), p. 275 *ante.*

107 Richards' *Diary* and Londonderry authorities with Lennoxlove [*H.M.C.
XI*, vi, p. 186].

108 *H.M.C. XII*, vii, *Le Fleming MSS*, p. 265, 16th Nov. 1689, to W. Fleming of
Coniston.

109 Lennoxlove [*H.M.C. XI*, vi, p. 186].

110 H.M.C. Finch II, p. 233; Lennoxlove [*H.M.C. XI*, vi, p. 186].

111 *Négociations . . . d'Avaux*, p. 375, 14th/4th Aug.

112 *Ibid.* p. 370 d'Avaux-Seignelay, 9th Aug./30th July.

'M. de Pointis se porte mieux; le devoyement qu'il avoit est arresté. Sa
playe va assez bien; ainsy on doit esperer sa guerison avec un peu de
temps.'

113 Lennoxlove [*H.M.C. XII*, vi, p. 186] Walker, *A Vindication of the True Account of the Siege of Derry in Ireland*, 1689, pp. 28–9 for royal letter.

114 *S.P. Dom. . . . 1689–90*, p. 188.
Tagebuch des Irlandischen Feldzugs vom Jahr 1689.
Kazner, J. F. A.
*Leben Friederichs von Schomberg oder Schoenburg*, 2B, Mannheim, 1789, ii, p. 282 et seq.

115 *S.P.Dom. . . . 1689–90*, p. 193. Solms also wrote the King concerning deficiency of boats and supplies.

116 *Ibid.* p. 194.

117 *H.M.C. Finch II*, p. 230.

118 *Ibid.* p. 498.

119 *S.P.Dom. . . . 1689–90*, p. 199.

120 *S.P.Dom. . . . 1689–90*, p. 201 [and p. 194].

121 *H.M.C. Finch II*, p. 498.

122 Log *Bonadventure*.

123 *S.P.Dom. . . . 1689–90*, p. 208.

124 Log *Bonadventure*.

125 Kazner *op. cit.*, p. 286.

126 21st July, *S.P.Dom. . . . 1689–90*, p. 194.

127 William Bentinck, groom of the stole, first gentleman of the bedchamber and privy councillor, described by Clark as William's 'closest friend the soldier statesman' (Clark *The Later Stuarts*, p. 173) and again (*ibid.* p. 180) as 'the one human being besides his wife with whom William was intimate'.

128 Kazner, *op. cit.* 'Le 7' p. 287.

129 *S.P.Dom. . . . 1689–90*, p. 215, 9th Aug. Schomberg to King, and Kazner *op. cit.* p. 288.

130 Lennoxlove, Schomberg to Hamilton [*H.M.C. XI*, vi, p. 186].

131 Kazner, *op. cit.* p. 289.

132 *S.P.Dom. . . . 1689–90*, p. 219.

133 Log *Bonadventure*.

134 Schomberg tells the King, 16th Aug. that he has not 6,000 infantry with him, *S.P.Dom. . . . 1689–90*, p. 222.
A B.M. Tract (*Political and Historical Ireland* 714/1/8) gives 154/21 'A list of Regiments that sailed with Schomberg *being all Foot*' and a list of the 'Second Reinforcement'. Story *op. cit.* p. 6, gives 'Not Ten Thousand Foot and Horse'; Kazner *op. cit.* p. 289; Log *Bonadventure*.

135 Log *Bonadventure*.

136 Kazner *op. cit.* p. 289.

137 Lennoxlove Rooke to Hamilton 13th Aug. [*H.M.C. XI*, vi, p. 186]; Log *Deptford*.

138 *H.M.C. Finch II*, p. 235, dated 26th Aug.

139 *Ibid.* Kazner *op. cit.* p. 290.

140 Log *Bonadventure*.

141 Kazner *op. cit.* p. 290; *S.P.Dom. . . . 1689–90*, Schomberg to King, 13th Aug., p. 220. Reporting to Hamilton Schomberg expresses the hope that his presence in Ireland will keep Scotland free from trouble. Lennoxlove, 13th Aug.

142 Ship movements and details about bombardment–Logs *Deptford* and *Bonadventure*. P.R.O. Adm. 8/2, 1st Aug. 1689. Letters Schomberg–King, 16th, 22nd, 26th, 27th Aug. *S.P.Dom.* . . . *1689–90*, p. 222, 226, 231. Kazner, *op. cit.* pp. 290–9. For orders to *Archangel* and company to go north-about, P.R.O. Adm. 3/1, 26th July.

143 Lennoxlove, 26th Aug. [*H.M.C. XI*, vi, p. 186].

144 *Tudor and Stuart Proclamations*; Grant *op. cit.*, p. 53.

145 *S.P.Dom.* . . . *1689–90*, p. 231.

146 Kazner, *op. cit.* p. 317.

147 *S.P.Dom.* . . . *1689–90*, p. 240.

148 Kazner, *op. cit.*, p. 299.

149 *Négociations . . . d'Avaux*, p. 397. d'Avaux-Seignelay.

150 *Ibid.* p. 350.

151 *Ibid.* p. 388, d'Avaux–Louvois.

152 As Note (149). Innisboffin Island is due West of the southern approach to the small deep Bay of Killary. Had James remembered it because it had been a penal settlement after the Cromwellian subjugation of Ireland? It was as remote as any refuge for vessels could possibly be.

153 As note (151).

154 As note (149).

155 *Négociations . . . d'Avaux*, p. 424, d'Avaux-Louis, 30 Aoust/20th August; p. 433, 4th Sept./25th Aug.

156 To the close of p. 295 see *Journals . . . H. of C.* and of *The H. of L.* under date with Grey, A. *Debates of the House of Commons . . . 1667 . . . 1694 . . .*, 1769, v. ix, p. 355.

157 It is interesting to observe that another quarry was being chased by the Commons on 3rd July–a move to enquire why the Dutch fleet were out no sooner to join Torrington's fleet; why Dartmouth's fleet had been laid up; and why there had been delay in setting out Torrington's fleet in the Spring. *Journals . . . Commons*, 3rd July.

CHAPTER X

# Grand Fleet returns – Winter Plans

## 1st September – Mid-October

*ARGUMENT*

*The Anglo-Dutch fleet in Torbay. The English ships much disabled by sickness attributed by the crews to bad provisions. Torrington considers that the fleet (the French gone behind Belle Isle) should not be sent again to sea – The King disagrees – Nottingham writes confidentially to Russell – A Council-of-War advises reconditioning at Spithead – Russell, like Torrington, against taking the fleet to sea but sees no reason why, at Spithead, the effective squadron should not be ready 'in less than four days' – William 'resolved the fleet [should] go again to sea with all speed' from Torbay – Captain Priestman of the Navy Board investigates the fleet's condition and reports – on victuals, on what ships could be spared for the Mediterranean and whether Torrington was prepared to cover an attack on Kinsale – Torrington asked to advise on the carriage of the newly married Queen of Spain from Rotterdam to Santander – Russell gathers that he, in the second-rate Duke with a small squadron is selected for the honour of conveying Her Majesty but demurs thereat, recommending Sir John Ashby – 15th September Torrington ordered reconnoitre before Brest – Russell's fears for the fleet's safety – Torrington clears Torbay on the 19th; is blown back on the 21st; by the 28th, receives the King's permission (the French withdrawn to Brest) to sail for Spithead – Torrington, on the 29th, detaching a squadron of 14 English and Dutch ships under Lord Berkeley, to westward, weighs from Torbay – Torrington is in London on 5th October.*

*The various steps that led to the drafting of a Winter scheme for Mediterranean and Channel squadrons (English and Dutch) and West Indies and North [Sea] squadrons (English only) – The ships allotted to those squadrons – Earlier neglect to watch the coast of Southern Ireland not to be repeated – The sailing of the Mediterranean squadron and trade a matter of concern with the King.*

*Rooke now heading homeward – Schomberg reinforced and supported from the sea.*

*The breakdown of victualling – Naval finance.*

*Russell fetches the Queen of Spain from Flushing to the Downs – He receives his final instructions and sails to Spithead arriving on 25th January 1690.*

*Wright, with the West Indies squadron and gathering merchant ships, Killigrew, with squadron and trade for the Mediterranean, wait for Russell, encountering difficulties of victualling, manning and with seamen's pay.*

*Lord Berkeley's detached operations in the Channel approaches (in the course of which the design against Kinsale was set in train and then abandoned) from 23rd September to the end of the year. The significance of Berkeley's cruising.*

*Melfort's mission at the court of Louis and the admissions of that King.*

*Anglo-Dutch command of the area, North Sea to the Soundings, as exercised, September to December, in trade protection, the interception of French commerce and, from the middle of August, in attempt to impose the conditions of the Treaty of 22nd/12th August concerning neutral trade with France – Winter sailings; allied losses, especially from privateers; difficulties with neutrals; damage done to French trade direct or through hindrance of neutral traffic; English privateering; Miscellaneous 'prize' matters, including a further Anglo-Dutch Treaty relating to captor claims at the re-taking of an enemy-captured ship.*

*Wear and tear to the matériel of the Navy and courts-martial subsequent on losses.*

*The resignation of Torrington from the Board of Admiralty and the design for the 'Grand Fleet' of 1690—which are connected topics.*

*The attitude of Parliament and King, at the close of 1689, towards the Royal Navy.*

---

IT WAS on the last day but one of August that Nottingham wrote to the commander-in-chief of the Anglo-Dutch fleet concerning contraband trade carried on by Lübeck and Dunkirk vessels—some fifty of them—plying through the Danish Sound to France. Such vessels ought, so contended the Lord Mayor of London who supplied the information, to be seized by the King of Denmark and made prize. Not in a position to dictate to the Danish King, William could at least order Torrington to give directions for the interception and arrest of such vessels. The King did so. And, Nottingham concluded, 'He commands me to say that he would have you write by every convenience, though you have nothing to say but where you are, it being a great while since any letters have come from you'.[1] Torrington's two letters of the 24th and 29th August[2] reached Whitehall next day. Nottingham headed for Hampton Court. On Sunday, the 1st September, King and minister considered the naval situation.

The letter of the 24th had been written while the fleet was N.N.W. from Scilly eighteen leagues, its commander-in-chief persuaded that, since the August winds had been suitable to bring out the French who, though reported W.S.W. of Ushant, had not appeared, talk of 'theyr coming to sea' could be dismissed as 'a fanfare'. Danger from the enemy thus scouted, the Admiral had 'less regret' in heading for Torbay, for 'want of beer and water'; moreover, the onset of a killing sickness had already 'almost disabled' several of the ships. The surgeons, he said, could not agree upon the cause of the distemper; the men declared their meat poisoned; for himself he did not know 'whether refreshings would have prevented this misfortune but it [was] certayne fresh provisions [always proved] cheaper to the King then salt'. Torrington had heard that the Admiralty intended to victual the fleet till the 1st December. Victualling would take time and the season be then too late for going to sea. Indeed 'without urgent necessity' the Anglo-Dutch fleet should remain in harbour to recuperate. At the close of that letter, Nottingham was given the news of the capture of the *Portsmouth* by a superior French force; but Torrington stated that 'when the captain [George St Loo] saw there was no remedy he threw the packet of letters he had for me overboard. The French say that he behaved himself bravely and that he is shot through the body and arm'.[3] Was the *Portsmouth* carrying in mid-August dispatches to Nottingham and King? If so, the ignorance of King and minister of the doings of the fleet has ready explanation.[4] The second of the two letters on the Hampton Court table, that of the 29th August, came from Torbay. It stated that the fleet was being watered, but not in expectation of being sent 'any more out this year'; it gave firm news, derived from a captured Brest vessel, that the French lay at Belle Isle (proof in Torrington's eyes of French preoccupation in guarding the home coast) and, finally, stated that the men so convincedly attributed their plight to the badness of the provisions that a strict enquiry should be made.

Answer was penned immediately. Torrington was told that the King, much troubled concerning the sickness, promised strict investigation. William would not, however, accept his Admiral's opinion that the French were at harmless rendezvous by Belle Isle; they would be out at first opportunity—especially when they learned that the English fleet was in port! Let the fleet be put in readiness for sea. And, while that proceeded, if Torrington should wish to come to London, he, but no other officers, might do so. Nottingham's letter maintained 'convenance'. The King was angry.[5] To Admiral Russell also a letter was sent.[6] Representing the King as 'much surprised' that the fleet should be in Torbay and remarking that lack of provisions and sickness seemed 'not very good reasons' (since the fleet's provisions were at Plymouth not Torbay and because at Plymouth the sick could better be cared for), Nottingham underlined the King's central fear that, with a fleet 'come so farr into the Channell', it could not 'possibly prevent' a French move towards Ireland. Genuinely perturbed and puzzled, he continued:

Tis more than three weeks . . . till yesterday . . . we know not what you have been doing. I pray you to send me some account

of your proceedings and the reason for them and of the state of
the fleet; that such measures may be taken as are most for his
Majesty's service. For which reason only I ask this of you–and
you may be assured I shall not make use of your letter to your
disadvantage and I hope what I write to you you will keep to
yourself.

The move to ingratiation had come from the Secretary–not the
Admiral!

Nottingham's letter of the 1st reached Torrington by the 3rd
and, next day, he called a Council-of-War of English officers only;
for the Dutch admirals alleged that their ships lacked only beer
and that their men were fit for sea. Not so the English!

> upon owr arrivall here [wrote Torrington to Secretary Notting-
> ham][7] toock an account of the sick and dead in the fleet since
> owr sayling from Spithead and found it amount to 530 dead and
> 2,327 sick. I have taken a new account this day and finde that
> it is increased to 599 dead and 2,588 sick and this at anchor . . .

261 new cases in five days; in five days 69 deaths. The fleet off
Ushant had borne just over 12,000 men.[8] One in twenty was dead;
of the remainder more than one in four sick. The figures were
sufficiently alarming; but it was not simply, nor primarily, the
condition of certain crews (the distemper had not affected all ships
equally) that argued in Torrington's mind the case for harbour.
The Dutch admirals might boast their crews robust; it was no less
a fact that, 'in the fayrest weather that could bee', four of their
ships had been 'forced by their deffects to leave the fleet' and their
admirals might well have 'some reason to be doubtfull of the rest'.
Anyway, Torrington had. And since, so he firmly stated, 'it is
generally agreed that the season is too far spent for a fleet of this
consideration to cruise in the sea', it followed that, for him to put
into the Channel in autumn weather would be tantamount to
risking the ability to provide from the fleet, in due course,
the customary winter squadron. But, time-honoured formula, the
commander-in-chief would 'submitt to better judgments'. The
remark would have come with more grace if, in the next sentence,
Torrington, thanking the King for the offer of leave for which he
had not asked, had not revealed his suspicion that the King might
be desirous of receiving his resignation!

The minutes of the council-of-war corroborated the text of the Admiral's dispatch. The whole fleet could not, at that place, Torbay, be put into immediate service, because the sick were too many to dispose of or cure in Torbay and because many of the ships were 'too infectious'; other vessels needed repair. Part of the fleet could, while in Torbay, be put into service; but all could be done 'with more speed and less danger' at Spithead. The signatures of Torrington, Admiral of the Fleet, Russell, Admiral [of the Blue], Vice-Admirals Davies [Red] and Killigrew [Blue], Rear-Admirals Lord Berkeley [Red] and Sir John Ashby [Blue], as well as that of Torrington's Flag Captain Mitchell, were all appended.

Torrington had spread himself the length and breadth of four pages. Russell, the same day, at the bidding of Nottingham to be frank, wrote no less.[9] Yet there was not a sentence of the letter which did not justify Torrington. Straightway Russell declared himself 'by no means a freind att [that] season of the yeare to Tor Bay', but he 'must conclude' it a better place than Plymouth for a 'fleat of great shipps'–there existed 'in many places foule ground' and there a ship that 'should . . . goe into Catt Watter' could not work out on the wind 'proper to carrey . . . to the enemy'. Provisioning could more easily be effected in Torbay than the Sound. With a fleet 'extream sickly', 500 buried over the side, 2,000 sick still aboard (Russell's figures are slightly less than Torrington's), and 'neather Plymouth or Dartmouth' able or willing 'to receive abouth 300 sick' Torbay was the right choice. He, Russell, did not 'greatly fear the French coming out'; the season was 'farr advanced', the French were 'not the boldest seamen!'[10] His Majesty could conveniently keep thirty ships to sea (English and Dutch) for the September month–that should suffice. Six or seven of the present fleet in any case must be subtracted from the present English total; infected and foul, their ballast must be put ashore and thorough cleaning undertaken. Their 'well men' might of course 'be turned over'. Admiral Russell took up Nottingham's remark (of the 1st) that it was 'more than three weeks' since Whitehall 'had any account of the fleet'. He simply expressed himself as 'surprised'–because Lord Torrington had told him that he gave 'from time to time' account of their proceedings. Russell then outlined what had taken place in the three weeks in question and clinched with the statement, 'We have kept the sea longer than any sea man I believe remembers a fleet to have don. I have bin ten weeks without ever leting go my anchor.' It was inevitable that somewhere in the letter there should be detailed remarks on the provisions. The beef was 'full of gaules' and, though Russell did not believe there was 'any harme in itt', the men of the *Duke* did; several had thrown their provisions overboard and ate only when hunger finally compelled them. As for the beer, 'noe longer agoe then yesterday, in several of the buts . . . great heapes of stuff . . . not unlike to mens' guts which . . . alarmed the sea men to a stronge degree'. Bad victualling might not be 'occasioned wilfoley—it must be neglegence'; but the result was the same in either case. The service suffered. Rounding off this letter Russell left no doubt that he stood side by side with Torrington and his brother admirals in the choice of Spithead as 'the properest place' for refitting. He saw no reason why from that road, especially if Sir Richard Haddock, with his special knowledge of Navy Board and Victualling office affairs could be sent down to assist, 'in less than four days' the thirty ships to which he had referred, English and Dutch vessels, should not be at sea. But the selected ships must not be above third rating. In the winter months it was difficult to keep more than seven thirds together! So much for the immediate future. As for the campaign concluded —and students of naval strategy would do well to note Russell's judgment: 'Wee have don as good servis in not fiting as if we had, since wee have hindred the French desines—unless our strength had bin soe great that we mought a proposed distroying them . . .' What was really a postscript followed:

> I will only add that my Amarall is jellous anuff of the King's not caring for him, tho I doe my week indevor to make him of a nobler opinion, and you sending him leave to come upp without he asking for itt makes no small incress. If I have done amiss in wrighting so freely my thoughts, I hope you will pardon it.

Nottingham would no doubt welcome the news and opinion he had elicited.

Quite clearly, when the postscript just quoted was written, Admiral Russell had no knowledge of the contents of a further

letter, dated the 2nd September, sent at the King's orders from
Nottingham to the Commander-in-chief.[11] It cannot have been
delivered before the flag officers were piped aboard *Elizabeth* on
the morning of the 4th September. Torrington was told that his
Majesty was 'resolved the fleet [should] go again to sea with all
speed', and, since the Admiral's absence from Torbay 'might
occasion delays', the King had changed his mind and would have
Torrington stay with the fleet. Captain Priestman would shortly
be with him to receive 'account of all matters relating thereto';
the preparations for sailing must 'be dispatched with all diligence'.
Captain Henry Priestman would be known to Torrington as the
Comptroller of the Storekepeer's Account appointed earlier in the
year to that office.[12] Presumably a copy of the instructions now
handed to Priestman[13] was enclosed with the letter of the 2nd
September to the Admiral. Priestman would examine the state of
the provisions, look into their defects and assess whether the
prevalent sickness could be attributed to the alleged cause; he
would tabulate the numbers of dead, sick and wanting of each
ship's crew. But the Commissioner had not been sent merely to
talk of victuals and sickness! Torrington must inform him what
ships could be spared for Mediterranean convoy duty and when
they could sail; whether he, the Admiral, considered himself
able to make an attempt on Kinsale with the help of the three
regiments already sent to Plymouth for that service;[14] and, lastly,
what ships should be designated 'to keep in the Irish seas for the
winter'.

Priestman arrived, saw, reported to Lord Nottingham on the
same day, the 7th. From Torrington he had secured the required
lists of the dead, the sick, the able, ship and ship. The dead now
totalled 638, the sick 2,895. Though the Admiral would not,
Priestman wrote, absolutely impute the distemper to the victualling, he held it to have been bad – the beer, butter and cheese
especially unsatisfactory. Moreover, 'many galls [had] been found
in the beefe caskes throughout the fleet and, in some caskes of
porke, galls thrust into the flesh'. This was more than enough to
make the sailors believe 'the papists [had] found means to poyson
them'! If (in spite of the warning his lordship was understood to
have given against sending out again the fleet) the King insisted

on that requirement, six ships only could be spared for the
Mediterranean convoy; but, if the fleet as a whole were not
ordered out, many more ships could be provided. At present the
Dutch ships were readiest. Priestman gathered that Torrington
was of opinion that one fourth, two fifths, three sixths, one yacht
and six or eight hoys and ketches should be left for duties Tuskar
Rock to Londonderry and that attempt on Kinsale should be
delayed till a winter squadron replaced the main fleet. He
Priestman would leave Torbay next day.[15] There can be little
doubt the unnamed killing sickness was scurvy.

Whilst Priestman drafted his report, Torrington called Admiral
Russell to discuss with him the problem which yet another letter,
just arrived from Hampton Court, and dated the 4th September,
provided—a by-product of Williamite diplomacy which, apart
from major desire to see Spain ranged permanently against Louis
hoped for 'full and free liberty of the Spanish ports', especially of
Cadiz and Gibraltar—gateways to the 'Streights' and all beyond.
This letter began:

> The Queen of Spain will be at Rotterdam on the 9th instant in
> order to be transported in his Majesty's ships to St Andera
> [Santander]. The King is very desirous to comply with his
> engagement to the Emperor but will not resolve on the method
> of it till he has your advice . . .

Anna Maria of Neubourg, married in her father's Palatinate town
by proxy of the King of Hungary to Charles II, King of Spain,
whose country had been forced into war by declaration from
Louis in April last, could reach Madrid only by sea. The States
General would bring her on from Düsseldorf to Rotterdam by
yacht; conveyance and convoy thence had been promised by the
English King. Maria was 'reine actuelle' and the seven men of war
originally intended, might, Nottingham thought, with the French
fleet cruising off Belle Isle, prove too few for royal safety. Yet seven
would be a number 'too considerable to be separated from the
fleet'. What would Torrington propose? He could count on the
'West India ships now in the Irish Sea'[16] joining him shortly at
Plymouth and on six additional third rates reported set to sea.
Would such additions help enable solution of the diplomatic problem? 'I pretend not to give but to ask your advice,' Nottingham

concluded; but it could not come too soon, for the King would be
loth to 'disappoint the expectations of the Emperor'.[17]

Santander is the port nearest Madrid; but the two Admirals
(Torrington wrote in the first person plural for them both),[18]
consulting on the 7th, only saw it as lying far inside the Bay and
more dangerous of winter approach than Corunna—to all English
seamen 'The Groyne'. Choose the Groyne and the warships of the
outgoing joint Mediterranean and West Indies convoy could add,
that far, additional protection to Majesty. But,

> We think [wrote Torrington] a second-rate very improper for
> the winter season, either in the Bay of Biscay or our own
> Channel . . . a third-rate . . . fitter to transport the Queen, if
> she can resolve to prefer her safety to a little more state.

Whenever His Majesty pleased, four thirds and three fourths
(seven warships had been mentioned in Nottingham's letter of the
4th) could be drafted from the fleet for this special purpose; for
(the plural maintained) Torrington and Russell saw 'no likelihood
that the fleet in a body [could] go to sea again [that] year without
terrible inconveniences'. Reports of 'the French fleet being joined
and at Belle Isle' left the two unmoved, because 'all sea-faring
men' concluded that, if the French ships were not already in
Brest, they soon would be. It was the present plight of the ships
that mattered to Torrington. In spite of the resolve of the King,
expressed unequivocally in the letter of the 2nd, that the fleet
must go again to sea, 'with all speed', he, for the second time in
this same letter, demurs. 'Since [he says] the state of the fleet is
such that we cannot think of going to sea with the whole', (just
as if the King had not spoken!) the attempt on Kinsale should wait.
In the last three days forty more men had died and 200 more gone
sick. Nothing less than 'changing all theyr ballast' could clear the
ships of the infection.

The proposal to offer a second-rate for the conveyance of the
Queen touched Russell on the raw![19] So it was to be the *Duke*? At
least he heard so! That might well prove of 'ill consequence'. The
*Duke* was a 'very improper ship to go so deepe into the bay as St
Andero is'. Of course he saw it as 'a great honour to carry the
Queen'—but not with the small force that could be spared. With
it, Russell suggested he might risk meeting 'an enemy that would

overpower him and "put him upon the running part"'. He would
not wish that 'to fall to his lot'. But in this matter 'as in all other
things', he was ready to obey command.

Russell, finishing his personal protest on the 7th, had left himself insufficient time to comment on the general situation. In the
light of Nottingham's invitation of the 1st and the letter to
Torrington dated the 2nd, Russell may well have thought that
observation would be expected from him. So, on the 8th, he began
by telling Nottingham[20] 'the distemper increases', then fixed upon
the circumstance that Priestman had stressed that the King
'would have the fleate for some few dayes put to sea againe'.
Well—there were eight ships which couldn't possibly go out;
Priestman had their names—and there were others! It didn't enter
his head, wrote Russell, that the French would 'venter with thire
whole fleate out againe this winter', and, suppose they did,
Torrington depleted would be unwise to engage them. If the King
should think it 'absolutely necessary for the fleet to go out again'
then he should order Torrington to that effect, 'but with the
condition [that] he and the officers think it possible [and to be]
don with safety'. True—and this was a 'least incouridgment' to
their situation, 'the lite moune . . . now in hand [might] produce
fair weather'. Yet, commonly, the wind sat westward in September and that would mean that the French couldn't get out of
Brest, or the Anglo-Dutch fleet go west to meet them. Perhaps—
and here Russell advances a modification of the Spithead plan—
it would be worth while to stay in Torbay till positive news be
received that the French were really back in Brest, in the meanwhile
making 'the usiall showes of sayling' and spreading rumours of
intended weighing for sea. The prejudice to that course would be
the unavoidable delay in putting out the winter guard. Russell
could rest content he had put the pros and cons fairly and ventured
his advice with perceptible firmness. That done, might not the
personal matter of 'carrying the Queen of Spain' be excusably
allowed a further airing? Nottingham was solicited to believe it
was not pride that made his correspondent say, ''tis not a squadron
[seven ships] fitt for a flag att the maine topmast hed [a full
admiral] to appear with, in time of warr espetialy'. And, 'if [he]
mought take the liberty' he would recommend a man who would

do it 'with great care and prudence' and one who might be thought to 'stand in neede of such an advantage as will atend this voyadge'. Sir John Ashby, Rear-Admiral of the Blue, had been from the first 'very zelouss' for their Majesties. It would be a mark of favour and–it happened that Ashby's ship [*Berwick*] was 'very fitt for the service'. Then, back to national concerns. When the fleet is finally called in, Russell urged, do not lay up any ship which can be regarded as serviceable, 'the charge will be greater than desined but . . . the reputation itt will give abroad that wee have a fleate all winter redey to sayle upon any occasion will answer any other inconveniency.'

Torrington and Russell had had their say–twice each–and Priestman had reported. On the 15th William 'cut short all intermission'. Instructions were drafted for Torrington:

to send any ships not fit for sea to Portsmouth or some other port to be refitted or the men transferred to others; to dispose of the sick men in Plymouth or elsewhere as he sees fit; and to sail with the fleet before Brest. If the French fleet be gone into Brest he is to return to the Spithead; but if it is at sea is to do what he shall judge best, with due regard to the season of the year . . .

The commanders of four of the ships designed for Newfoundland, of six of the 'West India squadron' still cruising off Ireland and of the *Harwich* and *Exeter*, thirds, were under Admiralty orders to join him.[21] Three days later, the 18th, the Admiral acknowledged the receipt of these instructions saying that he would sail as soon as the weather allowed. A fair wind was blowing; but the Dutch were riding 'so far in' that, till there was less of it, they could hardly weigh.[22]

Another letter, Russell to Nottingham, was to be expected.[23] It bore date, the 19th September.

I am realy under the greatest aprehension imaginable of our sucksess, the time of the yeare being so uncertin, long nights and a dark moune comming uppon ous, which are dredfull things att sea, att this time of the yeare. Besides, wee goe out when all sea faring men expect a storme; itt has bin very seldom knowne that Mickellmas ever came without itt and our shipps are very ill provided to receive such a guest; and if wee happen to be on

K

the French coast and a north west wind comes upp, you may
very reasonably expect the news of som part of your fleatt lost
and the rest drove where they cannot be supleyed with provisions; of which wee have no more then is absolutely necesary to
carrey ous into port. God send I doe not prove a profitt, but I
much feare it, and if my advice may be taken, sending this
fleate to sea now should be the last thing I would doe. I never
was of the opinion twas a very feazable thing unles unavoidable
occasion, but what mought a bin don tenn dayes since, is not
to be don now with near the safety.

I have nothing more to add but that I think itt woud be extreamly for there Majesties service wee ware otherwis ordred.
Besides, my lord, a positive order such as my lord Torington
has, puts him uppon no consideration of ships, weather or any
thing but going before Brest, which is not a good one in the
sumer, and I leave your Lordshipp to judg what may provably
be the isseu. The wind came last night westerly, which hindred
ous from sayling.

Reading the above with recollection of Russell's letter of the 8th,
does one encounter contradiction? The Admiral's 'lite moune now
in hand' had already spent her 'tenn dayes' for a 'dark moune
comming'–a moon at the full as he wrote his letter.[24] His 'old
style' Thursday the 19th September, would sidereally, be later
in the year than the date immediately suggests–indeed 'new style'
the 29th September or Michaelmas Day itself as we should calendar. And anyone who has read a ship's log of Russell's century and
noted the incessant 'took in topsails', 'hoisted top sails' entries,
when but the winds of summer blew, can sense the apprehension
wakened at the bare thought of equinoctial gales. Russell had
never proposed an unequivocal order to his commander-in-chief.
That is what Torrington had received.

Torrington 'rid fast' till 10 on the morning of the 19th, unmoored but did not clear the Bay. At two in the morning of the
20th he weighed on a N.E. wind in fair weather; was off Ramhead
in the evening 'about 70 Saile of good Shipps'. But the wind swept
round and he was in Torbay before nightfall of the 21st[25] whence
he reported to Nottingham telling in few words of his efforts and
their negative result, affirming his willingness to obey His Majesty's

commands, 'whatever the consequences might be', but opining
that it was likely to be some time before the wind got back to
east.[26]

As a weather prophet Torrington proved right; no east wind
blew. Eight 'infected' men-of-war turned up at Portsmouth from
the fleet.[27] A week passed, during which the Admiral had opportunity to consider papers forwarded by the Admiralty—copies of
the minutes of the Board,[28] complaints that lay against the commanders of the *Yorke*, *Centurion* and *St David* for tampering with
prizes before sending them in[29] and requests such as that handed
on from the Sheriff of London (following a protest at the losses
suffered from St Malo privateers) that the fleet look out for very
considerable merchantmen inbound from Smyrna and Barbados.[30] On the 14th the *Lion* and the *Reserve*, both of Russell's
Blue squadron, had been detached to take '35 Sayle . . . from ye
West Indies' safely up Channel to the Downs. They had brought
all their charge as far as Spithead by the 19th.[31] The Admiralty
did much to respond to such requests.[32] It was fast getting late in
the year for Atlantic passages. A group of London merchants who
discussed with the Board on the 12th September whether it would
be wise to allow the wind-bound Newfoundland ships, long waiting
at Plymouth, to stand convoyed to sea, remarked that merchants
set Michaelmas Day as the normal date for last arrivals and
departures.[33]

By the 28th, Torrington received a new communication from
the Secretary[34] which informed that the King accepted that the
French had gone into Brest. It also stated that the King had just
heard that Kinsale was defended by only one regiment, news
which strengthened his determination to attack it with three
regiments shortly mustering under Colonel Trelawny at Plymouth.
Torrington should therefore detach ships to watch the Channel
and be available to transport Trelawny, come with the main fleet
to Spithead and report in London, where he might assist deliberations about the winter guard and other squadrons. (He must not,
Nottingham tactfully observed, misinterpret the call to town. It
was for the sole purpose of professional deliberation!) Placing his
Rear-Admiral of the Red, Lord Berkeley, in charge of a detachment of fourteen English and Dutch ships, ordered westward,

Torrington with them and the rest of the fleet, on the 29th, cleared
Torbay. He reached Spithead on the 1st October.[35] There he
handed responsibility to his Admiral of the Blue.[36] Russell, who
had not scrupled, just before weighing from Torbay on the 29th,
to write Nottingham to suggest that he too might be granted leave
to visit town, took the opportunity the letter provided to rub in his
opinion of the unsuitability of the *Duke* to go 'to the bottom of the
Bay' in winter and the eminent fitness of Ashby, man and ship
for the Spanish undertaking.[37]

Torrington, arrived in London by the 5th October, attended that
day at the Admiralty Board. The King was at Newmarket and
Nottingham was wondering whether, at the impending discussion
on squadronal arrangements, it would be wise to have present
Russell and the Dutch admiral. Nottingham had before him three
outline schemes for assigning ships to the Channel, Mediterranean,
Irish, West Indies and other groupings—one which he had obtained on the 23rd September from the Board of Admiralty,
another which he had himself forwarded on the 26th for Torrington's consideration and Torrington's own plan—not yet given him
by the Admiral but privately forwarded by Russell, to whom it
had obviously been shown by its author. Sufficiently sure of his
own importance as acting commander-in-chief, Russell on the 6th,
wrote to say how thoroughly he was putting the fleet 'in the best
posture', how wise it would be that 'a good squadron' be maintained all through the winter in this 'the best Rode in England'
with 'a prudent man . . . keept att the head of them' and how
'very glad' he would be if the King's service did not 'require his
going to the Straits'. He was less concerned about leave. But he
was not left in Spithead. Called to London, he arrived late on the
9th or early on the 10th, and Vice-Admiral Davies took command[38]
unaware that an express was about to post to Portsmouth to tell
him the French fleet, or some part of it, was at sea! For, on the
morning of Thursday the 10th, the Board of Admiralty listened
to letters, delivered at York Building the night before, from
Captains Tyrell of the *Mordaunt* and Jones of the *Foresight*, fourth
rates, which recounted how they, with the *Lively Prize*, rated a
fifth, had run into a French squadron with the consequent loss of

the *Lively*. Torrington had been informed by the Secretary as soon as the letters came and Nottingham was now being asked to tell Torrington 'what hee shall think further necessary for their Mats Service'.[39] Although Nottingham, handing on the information to Shrewsbury for transmission to the King, due to reach Hampton Court the next day, Friday 11th, painted a threatening picture of danger to Schomberg's troop transports in the Irish Sea, to Berkeley's squadron in the Soundings and perhaps to the fleet itself at Spithead (Vice-Admiral Davies in command) nothing startling was done[40]–almost certainly because Torrington saw the incident as an ill-conducted minor action in the Soundings–upon which a court martial should follow![41] . . . The King reached Hampton Court on Friday the 11th. The naval conference must have been held the same night; for Torrington reported to the Board of Admiralty next morning the upshot of the deliberations upon the divergent disposition schemes and, in the minutes of the Board, but without the names of the twenty-four Dutch vessels, a detailed statement appears. Omitting the names of the Dutch rates, a tabulation can be presented overleaf.[42]

This winter squadronal project, decided upon 11th October and announced (as has been said) next morning to the Admiralty by Torrington for the King, squared well with the proposals which the Board had tendered at Nottingham's request. Across in Brest lay, great and small, seventy ships of the line. It was assumed that thirty-four men-of-war (twenty-five English and nine Dutch) or forty if the Irish squadron (six English) were added, could deal with any adventurous break-out from Brest toward Ireland. Meanwhile the Mediterranean squadron of thirty (fifteen English, fifteen Dutch)–a few of which would sail with the Queen of Spain ('collected' from Holland) as far only as the Groyne or Santander and then return to Plymouth–would, with reasonable safety, hulling far westward of Brest, take out the varied and valuable Streights trade, show the flag, fulfil William's diplomatic aim to 'impress the Turk, strengthen the friendship of Genoa and Venice', assist the favourable posture of affairs with Tripoli, Tunis and Algiers, and return as soon as possible with gathered trade to home waters. At this stage it was taken for granted that this Mediterranean squadron would sail as a 'Blue', Russell, Killigrew and Ashby retaining in it their recent blue squadronal Summer Allied Fleet ranking. The West Indies squadron and trade (to be under the command of Captain Lawrence Wright) could, times and convenience fitting, leave the home shores in company with the Mediterranean strength. It may be said that in the Autumn of 1689, William, while still determined that seasonal presence in the Mediterranean should be on a significant scale, was not repeating

| Mediterranean | | Channel | | West Indies | |
|---|---|---|---|---|---|
| 2 *Duke | 1 | 3 *Hampton Court | | 3 Mary | 1 |
| | | Essex | | | |
| 3 Exeter | | Monmouth | | 4 Bristol | |
| *Berwick | | Harwich | | Foresight | |
| Eagle | | Swiftsure | | Assistance | |
| Expedition | | *Henrietta | | *St David | |
| N'humberland | | *Yorke | | *Hampshire | |
| Burford | | *Rupert | | *Jersey | |
| *Montague | | *Suffolk | | *Tyger-Prize | 7 |
| Hope | | *Plymouth | 10 | | |
| *Resolution | 9 | | | 5 Guernsey | |
| | | 4 *Mordaunt | | Swan | 2 |
| 4 *Woolwich | | *Centurion | | Rates | 10 |
| *Greenwich | | Kings Fisher | | | |
| *Happy Returne | | Deptford | | f.s. St Paul | |
| Newcastle | | Portland | | Richard & John | |
| *Oxford | 5 | Bonadventure | | | |
| | | Anthelope | | Irish Squadron | |
| Cadiz Merchant | | Swallow | | | |
| f.s. Half-Moon | | Ruby | | 3 Monck | 1 |
| Thomas & Elizh | | Nonsuch | | | |
| | | Phoenix | | 4 *St Albans | |
| 3 Ketches as | | James Galley | | *Dover | |
| tenders | | Mary Galley | | *Advice | |
| | | Constant Warwick | | Dartmouth | |
| Rates | 15 | Tyger | 15 | Sapphire | 5 |
| Dutch quota | 15 | | | Rates | 6 |
| Total | 30 | Rates | 25 | | |
| | | Dutch quota | 9 | North Convoys | |
| | | Total | 34 | | |
| | | | | 4 Assurance | |
| | | | | Sweepstake | |
| | | | | Guardland | |
| | | | | Pearle | 4 |
| | | | | Rates | 4 |

*Ships which had sailed in the recent Grand Fleet—making 23 of that Fleet's 34.

outright the mistake of the preceding January. The southern Irish coast was not to be left unwatched all through the winter, an attack on Kinsale was definitely purposed–planned to the stage at which troops were already in readiness at or moving towards Portsmouth and Plymouth for embarkation. The Channel fleet would, when the 'Queen of Spain ships' got back from the Groyne to strengthen it, be twice as large as the squadron entering the Mediterranean. One consideration must have been obvious to all concerned, the over-riding need for the Mediterranean squadron to get early away and early return–that is to say before next year's 'fighting season' in the Channel could begin. The ability to match the probable size of a fleet drawn from Tourville's seventy men-of-war and over 100 fireships would depend on the return of the Streights warships.

Friday night, the 11th October, the conference; Saturday the announcement to the Admiralty of the project; Monday, the 14th, William, through Nottingham, demanding of the Board an answer, to be delivered by five next afternoon to the question– When would the Mediterranean and West Indies squadrons be ready to sail?[43] From the Navy Office Nottingham received, on the 15th, answer for the King: '... the squadron for the Mediterranean may be fitted by the middle of next month and that for the West Indies between the middle and end of the said month; but such ships as are out should be ordered into port to refit.'[44]

It will be recalled that, following the surrender of Carrickfergus, the 27th August, Schomberg informed the King of his intention of sending some of Rooke's larger rates 'to cruise off Dublin, Cork and Kinsale', a proposal which, on the 3rd September, he was told through Nottingham to modify and keep Rooke near at hand (see p. 262 *ante*). None the less, Rooke was sent southward. He weighed from Carrickfergus on the 13th September, with, so it is credibly stated,[45] the *Deptford, Bonadventure, Swallow, Portland, Antelope, Mary Galley* (fourths), *Dartmouth* (fifth), *Greyhound* (sixth), *Henrietta* (yacht) and the *Anne, Kingfisher, Unity* and *Richard and Martha* (ketches) with the *Archangel, Samson, Sceptre, Princess Anne, Supply* and *Smyrna Merchant* in company. That left with Schomberg the *Pearle* (fifth), *Saudadoes* and *Fan-fan* (sixths), the *Navy, Monmouth* and *Cleaveland* (yachts), *Dragon* (sloop), the *Charity* and *Prosperous* (ketches), *Seaventure* and *Edward and Susan* (hoys) and the *St Malo Merchant*.[46] Rooke, as a long dispatch, the 24th September,[47] indicates, in the mistaken belief that Schomberg was advancing on Drogheda, had struck first at the Skerries, ten miles further down the coast. Though the 200 landed were called back at the appearance of the enemy in strength, a fine staving and burning of small vessels and fisher boats had taken place. Dublin's quays had been marked out by Rooke for attack from small ships led by himself; but, a storm blowing hard out of the bay, the design had been rendered impracticable. Cork harbour was, however, on the 18th September penetrated by four of Rooke's ketches; and, in spite of fourteen or fifteen cannon, the sailors had 'possest themselves of the greate Iland', taken what cattle they pleased, looked in on the town and brought out a pink with casks of brown sugar. Rooke in his letter lamented the absence of a few trained soldiers to stiffen sailor discipline–always, he said, uncertain in withdrawal . . . So much for what had happened on the cruise! *Swallow*, *Henrietta* yacht and *Kingfisher* ketch were now so foul that he must send them home–with the letters. He would stay on his present station–till relieved–or, at latest, another fortnight, the 10th or 12th October. But Rooke arrived in the Downs on the 13th October after having lost, on the Irish coast, company with all his ships save the *Pottland*.[48]

It is common knowledge that Duke Schomberg, after the fall of Carrickfergus, passed swiftly on to Dundalk, looked toward Drogheda and Dublin, stayed his march and went into quarters. The light naval force remaining with him sufficed to insure convoy of the transports which brought to Carlingford Lough or the inner Dundalk Bay victuals and forage, ordnance and ammunition, general stores and reinforcements of foot and horse. On the 13th September Colonel Villiers' regiment of Horse, which had lost a hundred of its animals, disembarked. Twenty-seven ships were counted at anchor by the town shore on the 1st October. By the 9th, Sir John Lanier's, Colonel Langston's Horse, Colonel Hefford's Dragoons, and Colonel Hasting's Foot arrived from Scotland. The number of hired merchantmen required in the service of sustaining and reinforcing Schomberg's army, the paper strength of which was approaching 2,000 horse and 12,000 foot, was indeed considerable. When the Privy ·Council, desirous to take off an embargo resting on all ports from Padstow to Carlisle, asked the opinion of the Admiralty as to the wisdom of action, the Board replied that the step should only be taken if Schomberg would return '250 saile of ships' taken up at London, Bristol, Barnstaple, and other ports and make them available for transport of the expected Danes! By the end of the second week of October for many of the merchantmen at Schomberg's disposal a new sad use was perforce found–they became improvised hospital ships. In Carlingford Lough on 13th October lay 105 ships and at Dundalk many others.[49]

As the group of ships which Schomberg and Rooke had been ordered to return for West Indies service had been duly sent on by Rooke (they had turned up at Plymouth on the 22nd September[50] and were to be retained in hired employ but for changed unspeci-fied purposes), as Rooke himself was, by mid-October,[51] anchored in the Downs, and, since any wanted ship on convoy duty could readily be called in and substituted, there was now little risk that any ships named for Mediterranean and West Indies duties could not be brought to the yards for refit and revictual. Yet, considering what the Commissioners of the Navy knew of their own affairs and those of the Commissioners of Victualling, they must have recog-nized that their answer of the 15th to Nottingham for the King (see p. 295 *ante*) had been given in hope lacking conviction. In any case they could count on it having been received with royal impatience.

## REFERENCES

1 *H.M.C. Finch II*, p. 236.

2 *v.* p. 186 *ante*.

3 *v.* p. 185 *ante*. It would be interesting to know how Torrington learned of the jettisoning of the packet.

4 *v.* p. 189, note (102) *ante*.

5 *H.M.C. Finch II*, p. 236. See also Foxcroft, *op. cit.* II *Spenser House Journals* 'The K said [to Halifax] he had been struck as if he had been thrust to the heart when he heard Herbert was come in to Torbay. Said that men talk'd of Impeachments but he was sure Lord Torrington deserved to be impeach'd as much as any man ever did.'

'Said the Dutch Officers were in awe of him at present because they were strict in obeying orders, but in a little time they would tell all.' Foxcroft, *op. cit.* II, p. 238.

6  *H.M.C. Finch II*, p. 236.

7  *Ibid.* p. 238.

8  *v.* pp. 182, 183 *ante*. A note on the Admiralty's own list for 1st Sept. puts it at 13847 for 52 ships technically under Torrington's command. P.R.O. Adm. 8/2.

9  *H.M.C. Finch II*, pp. 240–1.

10  'I cannot fancey they will attempt what wee sea faring men think hazardous anuff.' Greenville Collins, *op. cit.*, writes of Torbay 'Here the Royal Navy rides in safety'.

11  *H.M.C. Finch II*, p. 237.

12  *v.* p. 184 *ante*.

13  *H.M.C. Finch II*, p. 237.

14  Orders which Torrington would require to present to the regiments to take their place on ship-board were sent him on the 3rd. *Ibid.* p. 238.

15  *H.M.C. Finch II*, pp. 242–4. Priestman had passed through Exeter on the 6th where he received complaints from some of the men of the *Portsmouth* who said that they 'were set sick ashoar at Plimouth', had been ill-used by the surgeon and given no conduct money at discharge.

The ship by ship figures are not printed in *H.M.C. Finch II*. They can be seen in the *MS.* Keevil, *op. cit.*, p. 173, notices this disastrous outbreak.

The vessels Torrington suggested be allotted to the St George's Channel–Irish Sea area were *Hampshire* (4), *Pearl* and *Sapphire* (5), *Greyhound* and *Saudadoes* (6) and *Charlotte* (yacht). The Tuskar Rock is off Carnsore Point below Wexford.

16  *v.* p. 262 *ante*.

17  *H.M.C. Finch II*, p. 238, Nottingham to Torrington; Count Mansfield–Nottingham [24th Aug./3rd Sept.].

For an excellent brief biographical notice of the Spanish King Carlos II (1661–1700) see *Ency. Brit.* XIth edn; for Maria Ana ó Mariana de Baviera Neuburg (1667–1740) second wife of Carlos II, see *Ency. Universal Illustrada* . . . and the references to her in the notice upon Carlos II in the same work. If the view 'al contrario de la reina francesa no fué sympática ni al peublo ni á los cortisanos, por su carácter altanero y despótico' be accepted, the officer destined to take 'reine actuelle', of twenty, aboard would scarcely make acquaintance with the romantic figure Victor Hugo portrays in *Ruy Blas*. There is a lengthy notice, Mariana de Neoburgo, *Dicionario de Historia de España*, Madrid, 1952.

18  *H.M.C. Finch II*, p. 242–3.

19  *Ibid.* Russell to Nottingham, 7th Sept., p. 243.

20  *H.M.C. Finch II*, p. 244.

21  *H.M.C. Finch II*, p. 247. The *Exeter* joined on the 17th. Log of *Yorke*.

22  *Ibid.*

23  *Ibid.* pp. 247–9.

24  At 5.47 a.m. 19th Sept.–Pond *op. cit.* and *Nuncius Syderius*.

25  Log of *Yorke*.

26  *H.M.C. Finch II*, p. 248.

27 *Ibid.* p. 248. They included *Montague, Plymouth, Defiance, Woolwich.* Log of *Yorke,* 19th Sept., and possibly *Cambridge* and *Warspight.* H.M.C. Finch II, p. 255. Russell to Nottingham, 6th Oct. P.R.O. Adm. 3/2 7th Oct. would add *Breda, Portsmouth, Lyon* to the list of 'sick ships' making 9 in all.

28 They were sent from time to time, e.g. P.R.O. Adm. 3/2, 8th Sept.

29 *Ibid.* 17th Sept.

30 *Ibid.* 18th Sept.

31 Log of *Yorke* for detachment. *London Gazette* (19th–23rd Sept.], Portsmouth 19th Sept.

32 P.R.O. Adm. 3/2 passim.

33 *Ibid.* under date.

34 *H.M.C. Finch II,* p. 249, 26th Sept. The time taken for transmission of a dispatch was less than might be supposed. One finds, for example, Mr Addis, Navy Board Agent at Plymouth, complaining to the Admiralty that a letter recently sent him by the Board, express, had taken 44 hours to deliver. Mr Wildman (Postmaster General) was told 'to prevent the like in future'. P.R.O. Adm. 3/2, 20th Sept.

35 Log of *Yorke.*

36 *H.M.C. Finch II,* p. 255, Russell to Nottingham, 6th Oct.

37 *H.M.C. Finch II,* p. 250.

38 *Ibid.* Nottingham–Torrington 3rd Oct., p. 252; Nottingham–Shrewsbury, 5th Oct., p. 254; Shrewsbury–Nottingham, 5th Oct., *ibid.*; Russell–Nottingham, 6th Oct., p. 255; Nottingham–Russell, 7th Oct., pp. 256–7. P.R.O. Adm. 3/2, 23rd Sept., 5th Oct.

P.R.O. Adm. 2/3, 20th Oct.

Warnsinck, *op. cit.* p. 53, implies that both Evertsen and van Almonde were called to the conference.

39 P.R.O. Adm. 3/2. For an account of the incident see *London Gazette* (10th–14th Oct.), Plymouth 8th Oct.

40 *H.M.C. Finch II,* p. 257.

41 P.R.O. Adm. 3/2, 15th Oct.

42 *Ibid.* 12th Oct.

43 P.R.O. Adm. 3/2. P.R.O. Adm. 3559. f. 497/8.

44 H.M.C. Finch II, p. 249.

45 *The Life and Glorious Actions . . . Rooke,* p. 9.

46 *Ibid.*

47 *H.M.C. Finch II,* pp. 248–9.

48 *The Life and Glorious Actions . . . Rooke,* p. 11. Burchett, *op. cit.,* p. 34.

49 Story, *op. cit.* pp. 14–29, 41 and, for P.C. and Admiralty. P.R.O. Adm. 3/2, 15th Sept.

50 *London Gazette* (23rd–26th Sept.).

51 *H.M.C. Finch II,* p. 258, Rooke–Nottingham (17th October) and Note (48) *ante.*

52 P.R.O. Adm. 3/2.

53 *Ibid.*

# CHAPTER XI

# Berkeley's Cruise — Russell's Voyage

## *Mid-October – January 1689/90*

*ARGUMENT*

*Lord Berkeley's detached operations in the Channel approaches (in the course of which the design against Kinsale was set in train and then abandoned) from 23rd September to the end of the year. The significance of Berkeley's cruising.*

*Melfort's mission at the court of Louis and the admissions of that King.*

*Wear and tear to the matériel of the Navy and courts-martial subsequent on losses.*

*Attempt to estimate the extent to which Allied trade suffered, September–December 1689. Determination to impose on neutrals the conditions of the Anglo-Dutch Treaty of 22nd/12th August concerning trade with France – in the case of Denmark and Sweden a particularly difficult undertaking. Miscellaneous 'prize' matters, including a further Anglo-Dutch Treaty relating to captor claims at the re-taking of an enemy-captured ship. Probable extent of damage to French trade by capture of enemy ships or interception of neutrals carrying contraband.*

*Naval debt and the breakdown and re-organization of Victualling – Parliament asked to vote supply for the charges of the War in 1690. The Commons, in Grand Committee, decide to debate the State of the Nation and conduct a naval inquest.*

*The resignation of Torrington from the Board of Admiralty (to the King's annoy) and the continued design for the 'Grand Fleet' of 1690.*

*Russell fetches the Queen of Spain from Flushing to the Downes – He receives his final instructions and sails to Spithead arriving on 25th January 1690. Wright, with the West Indies squadron and gathering merchant ships, and Killigrew, with his squadron and trade for the Mediterranean, wait for Russell, encountering difficulties of victualling, manning and with seamen's pay.*

*Russell's comment on Torrington's resignation. Reconstitution of the Board of Admiralty.*

---

THE MIXED Anglo-Dutch squadron, sentinel of the Channel approaches, under Rear-Admiral Lord Berkeley of the Red squadron of the Allied summer fleet, detached by Torrington on leaving Torbay on the 29th September for Spithead, headed for the Soundings, whence, on the 10th October, Berkeley reported to Nottingham. Eleven English men of war and two fireships were with him; but he wondered why 'three other English ships . . . pretty good saylors', which Torrington had led him to believe 'were in those waters', could nowhere be seen.[1] The missing vessels were, of course, *Foresight* and *Mordaunt* and the lost *Lively* for whose captains, 'being off station', courts-martial were threatened (see p. 293 *ante*). Unfortunately it is not possible to name with certainty the English components of Berkeley's squadron. His flagship was the *Hampton Court* (3); the *Essex* (3), *Monmouth* (3) and *Harwich* (3) were probably with him;[2] *St. Albans* (4) and *Dover* (4) joined him on 10th October; the *Foresight* and *Mordaunt* on the 12th.[3] The Dutch ships with the Rear-Admiral are said to have been seven in number:[4]

| | | | |
|---|---|---|---|
| *Tijer* | 52 | Kap. | Teding van Berchout |
| *Eendracht* | 70 | ,, | Snellen |
| *Schattershoeff* | 46 | ,, | van der Eves |
| *Provincie Utrecht* | 56 | ,, | Decker |
| *Elswout* | 50 | ,, | van der Nieuburg |
| *Europa* | 48 | ,, | Hidde de Vries |
| *Veere* | 60 | ,, | Mosselman |

The cruise ended by the 18th when Berkeley put into Plymouth, telling Nottingham how he (Berkeley) had led in an East Indiaman and a Hudson Bay pink richly laden with furs. All the time he had been out, the Dutch had been the 'greatest strength' which left him 'out of countenance', considering the operation had been solely for protection of English coasts.[5] The Rear-Admiral's presence in the Soundings, though he may not have known it, had provided additional safety to forty or more merchantmen outward-bound, the 12th October, from Plymouth, vessels which were being set on their way for fifty or sixty leagues into the Atlantic by the large fourth-rate *Coronation* (Captain Raines) and four hired vessels.[6] Whilst Berkeley stayed in Plymouth, provisioning with difficulty, arrangements operated for at least two ships to cruise in the vacated Soundings.[7] These, to begin with, were the fourths *St. Albans* (Captain Leighton) and *Dover* (Captain Byng). Out till the 31st October and chasing every day, the captains secured but one good prize. Afterwards, engaging two Frenchmen, they took the smaller of the two, laden with arms and powder 'for King James's service' and learned from their prisoners that, in the warship that got away, Lord Dover (James's Chancellor returning from the mission to Louis undertaken in July (see p. 243 *ante*)) the Marquis d'Albeville 'and gentlemen with money to pay some French ships' in Ireland, had escaped them! d'Avaux reported to Louis Lord Dover's arrival at Kinsale, the 16th/6th November and what had happened '*à trente lieües par le travers des Sorlingues*'.[8]

Apart from desire to prevent French landings on the Irish coast
King William still nursed the notion of capture of a southern
Irish port, the obvious choice being Kinsale (see p. 291 *ante*).
Troops had been moved to Portsmouth (Talmash's regiment) and
to Plymouth (Trelawny's); the Duke of Bolton's regiment waited
at Milford. On the 31st October the King learned that Torrington
had not given the necessary orders for the transport of Talmash's
men and stores from Portsmouth to Plymouth; he desired immediate compliance with his wishes;[9] and on the 3rd November,
Nottingham asked Torrington to arrange for the passage of
Bolton's regiment from Milford to the Devon port.[10] By the 10th
Berkeley professed to Nottingham that the soldiers gathered in
Plymouth wanted 'nothing now but their arms to be ready to
embark'. Therefore, as soon as Sir Clowdisley Shovell came in
with Talmash's regiment from Portsmouth, a move toward
Ireland could be made.[11] Sir Richard Haddock at Portsmouth
reported to Nottingham on the 10th that twelve companies of
troops had been put aboard the *Monck*, *Advice*, *Exeter* and *Yorke* and
that he had never seen 'soldiers goe more willingly and cheerfully
in his life, saying they hoped shortly to take their winter quarters
in Kinsale'.[12] Shovell in *Monck*, with the *Henrietta*, *Yorke* and
*Advice* and five tenders reached the Sound on the 11th,[13] the
*Exeter* on the 14th;[14] and the Rear-Admiral expected to have all
the soldiers waiting in Plymouth (except some of the Duke of
Bolton's men who were marching from Bideford) aboard by the
16th. He would, so he told Nottingham, 'Sayl with the first
opportunity of wind'.[15] On the 16th the Plymouth folk saw enter
the Sound six Dutch warships[16] the largest in tow, her main and
mizzen masts gone, the *Voorzichtigheed*, a 74, flagship of Schout-by-
nacht Jan van Brakel. Near the damaged vessel lay the *Hon-
selaardijk* (50), *Phoenix* (26), *Damiate* (36), *Alida* (52) and *Cortgene*
(50). Brakel, consequent on the orders of William to Evertsen to
send Brakel to strengthen Berkeley, had sailed from Portsmouth on
the 5th/15th[17] and run into a prolonged storm which Shovell had
fortunately avoided. Brakel's reinforcement, in spite of the loss of its
most powerful unit, would do much to make up for the 'two [English]
men of war and four fireships' which Berkeley otherwise expected.
Attempt on Kinsale appeared imminent. Events ran oppositely

Nov. 26

From *Wensday ye 13 to tuesday the 26* we lay in Plym⁰ Sound w^th little wind but this day it blew very hard at SW and SWBW so that we were forct to lett goe our Sheete Anchor and so rid by him and the best Bower we have had very much rain all this day

Nov. 27

This day the wind Dullors . . . SWBN to ye S and SSW . . .

Nov. 28

Rid fast, very hard gale S and SSW. At 8 this morning ye wind came to ye SWBS and blew a great Storme we lett goe our Sheet Anchor againe . . . about 10 a Clock this morning our Cable broke . . . got up our spare Anchor and bent ye Cable readie to fall to it but ye Cable broke at a 3^d of ye Cable

Nov. 29

. . . wind SWBS–SSW . . . we coud hardly Ride it out then we let fall another Anchor . . . the Storme continu'd till 6 at night then it began to Duller[18]

Side by side one places another record[19] – that of Captain Byng of the *Dover* – who had returned a fortnight earlier, disappointed, from the Soundings to the Sound. He found himself on the 29th 'in great danger from a violent storm of wind which blew [Lord Berkeley's squadron] from their anchors on a sunken rock about 2 cables length from the Citadel'. After the *Dover* had struck and beaten on the rock several times, Byng 'cut his cables and stood into les water swinging there athwart a fireships cables, who was just got in before. They being cut, she [the fireship] drove upon the rocks and in less than half an hour sunk'. The *Dover* was secured with 'great difficulty' but 'Lord Berkeley's ship that lay in Catwater did likewise brake from her cables and, falling on board the *Dover* did her some damage'. First a long spell of 'little wind', next 'violent storm', then, one must suppose, a measure of harbour confusion. On the 2nd December it was 'still blowing fresh'; but, by the 3rd, the wind dropped, veered S.E. and brought in the *Centurion* and *Kingfisher* from Torbay. A quick departure promised. With winter light on the morning of the 5th, Berkeley weighed; an hour later, 'fir'd a gun, hoisted up his mizentopsaile w^th ye Clulines up, w^ch was a Signall for ye Fleete to moore againe he having *an order to put all ye Souldiers ashore out of ye Fleete*'.

Another day was taken up putting ashore the soldiers' arms. Then, early on the 7th, Lord Berkeley, in the *Hampton Court*, signalled to unmoor. At 11 o'clock two of his captains were called on to dispose, rope and yard arm, of unpleasant duty: '2 men hanged on board ye *Monmouth* and a Doctor hanged on board the Fireship'.[20] The squadron, *Hampton Court* (3), *Monck* (3), *Centurion* (4), *Monmouth* (3), *Advice* (4), *Henrietta* (3), *Exeter* (3), *St Albans* (4), *Yorke* (3), *Harwich* (?) (3), *Dover* (4), two ketches, the fireships *Salamander*[21] and *Owner's Love*, together with Dutch warships available from those which van Berckhout and Brakel had brought to Plymouth, was, soon after mid-day, under sail, with a fresh gale blowing from N.E. Rame Head faded in the early afternoon light, the Scillies were passed in the next night's darkness. Shovell, in *Monck*, with *Centurion*, *Monmouth* and *Advice*, parted north-west to look in on the coast of Southern Ireland. The Rear-Admiral picked up his own cruising ground on the 9th at latitude 49.50 and longitude 00.40 west (i.e. of the meridian of Land's End). For a fortnight, increscent to decrescent moon, he zigzagged as low as 49.17 as far west as 02.14. Till the 21st the weather was indifferent; but, on the 22nd, the wind hardened with rain squalls that blotted out the Dutch ships, as the squadron, rejoined by Shovell, began returning, passing the familiar landmarks St Mary's, the Lizard, the Rame to the Mew. Berkeley worked into the Sound at mid-day of the 23rd.[22] No landing at Kinsale had been ventured. But if, on the morning of Christmas Eve, the gale (to use the picturesque expression of the Master of the *Yorke*) 'dullered', it gathered again that night and, after once more moderating with false promise at the break of Christmas Day, built up a fury of tempest long after remembered.

The 25th inst., in the night, arose a very violent Storm of Wind at S.W. blowing by Gusts, and often shifting, which forced the *Henrietta* Frigat from her anchoring in the *Sound*; she first struck on St Nicholas Island and afterwards on Fisher's Nose under the Cittadel and then drove into Cat-Water, where she sunk, but all her men, except about 80, were saved. At the same time went likewise from her anchor a Dutch man of war called the *Unity* who, falling foul upon the *Centurion* frigat, they were both driven ashore and staved under *Mount Batton* within the *Sound*; of the former there were lost about 150 and of the later 12 men. There

were likewise cast away the French privateer lately taken by the
*Dover*; and 2 other French prizes. And the Merchant Ships
received some damage, especially the Dutch, which lay very
close together in Cat-Water.

Thus the *London Gazette*.[23] The day after the ships moved into the
Hamoaze.[24] The disaster must have strengthened the already
indicated purpose of the authorities to provide full facilities of
supply and repair at Plymouth, there being nothing of substantial
dock kind west of Portsmouth.[25]

In a letter to Nottingham, written while entering harbour on
the 24th, Berkeley expressed himself content that, apart from
privateers of which 'the sea is full', there was nothing to be feared
from the French. He suggested that the men aboard the privateers
were the very ones who would ordinarily be employed in regular
naval vessels – further proof that the French royal units would not
soon be seen in the Channel. But privateers could be made 'weary
of their trade' if 'clean ships' were sent out 'two and two' to deal
with them 'for' (one must let the Rear-Admiral voice his English
mariner view) 'the French are not prime saylors'. The crews of the
squadron, Berkeley reported, were very sickly.[26] The Admiralty,
on the 27th, accepted the suggestion made by Berkeley for dealing
with the privateer plague and ordered that four ships be kept –
two on station, two ready to replace – constantly cruising. Berkeley brought his squadron to Spithead on the 16th January.[27]

When 'writing off' William's projected but unattempted seizure
of Kinsale – no small set-back – not for a moment must there be a
lessening of recognition of the manner in which Berkeley's scouting
and Anglo-Dutch cruising had operated to maintain the all-
important subsidiary command of St George's Channel, the Irish
Sea and of the North Channel beyond, the visible sign of which
was nothing but a weak miscellany of vessels which gave to
Schomberg a sense of safety and a limited notion of personal
maritime control. Troops had reached him; supplies sustained
him (see p. 296 *ante*). On that command hung the promise of the
future. In mid-November a Danish admiral, transporting 6,000
Danish foot and 1,000 horse and steering for Leith, his warships
and troop-carrying ships totalling eighty sail, had met with bad
weather off 'the west-end of the Dogger' and received permission

to disembark his charge at Kingston-upon-Hull.[28] Hull – Carrickfergus! The last stage of the route was possible only so long as
watch was kept by a Berkeley, or those who might succeed him,
in the tempestuous Soundings, '30 leagues S.W. by W. of Scilly'.[29]

The state of alertness on the part of William, Nottingham,
Torrington and the Lords of Admiralty throughout the last three
months of the year towards the possibility of French assistance to
James in Ireland stands to their common credit. It is true that
James expected, during the shortening days, reinforcements as well
as military supplies and money. In a letter to his ambassador at
the court of St Germains, Lord Waldegrave,[30] he wrote that he
could 'hold out till November, the time designed for our succours'.
It was aid for which Lord Dover had been sent to plead.[31] Lord
Melfort, who had followed Dover (see p. 264 *ante*), was charged to
emphasize expectation and urgency and, specifically, to turn the
existing request to one of polite demand for intervention in
England.[32] Melfort's dealings with Louvois are known in detail.
Men? Louvois saw no great difficulty; horses would be a different
matter. Moreover, the English fleet barred the way! Melfort was
sure that the English would not 'keep out their great ships this
winter' the timber of many of them 'green'. He advanced the
consideration that, as some French warships would, in any case, be
needed for the protection of the transport to Ireland of 'the 6000
already condescended upon' a small addition of fighting vessels
would be enough to safeguard a rather larger expedition to the
west coast of England. Louvois countered that dragoons were
asked for, dragoons and horses needed many boats; many transports made a convoy vulnerable even to an armed few. Melfort
retorted that vulnerability did not prove a hindrance to William's
armada. Louvois shifted ground. The real difficulty would lie in
the absence of a port for landing. Melfort of course replied that the
quays of any English harbour would be open the moment a French
fleet appeared! ... There, till Louvois had talked to Louis and Louis
to Melfort matters rested[33] – though, in the interim, Melfort met
Seignelay and found him averse from hazarding the fleet.[34] Louis
professed great desire to help. But, he is represented as saying,
    if, by accident he came to lose his fleet the affairs [of Melfort's

royal master] would be desperate ... Some years it would have been looked on as extravagant to say France could have coped with any of the two sea powers ... now both powers were united against him.

He, Louis, knew he was blamed for not fighting this last Summer; but – facts were facts. The 6,000 troops would be sent; they were being gathered at Brest and James should have all that didn't run away.[35] After that Melfort could only advise James to write to Louis.[36]

Than the futility of Melfort's mission and the admissions of Louvois, Seignelay and Louis, what stronger evidence of the fact of an established Anglo-Dutch command from the late Spring to mid-Winter, for military purposes at least, of the Channel and adjoining seas?

The damage suffered by Dartmouth's fleet, that incidental to the activities of Torrington's fleet, the casualties to the matériel of squadrons, Rooke's and now – not least – Berkeley's, have received their degree of attention. The record of wear and tear could obviously be extended. The *Pendennis* (Captain Churchill), shortly after convoying trade from Western harbours was, on her way from the Downs to Chatham, lost on the 26th October upon the Kentish Knock; the Admiralty ordered the *Mary*, a hired ship of Margate, the *Providence* hoy and *Dragon* sloop to salvage her stores and report to Deale.[37] At a court-martial, the 20th December, before Vice-Admiral Davies and eight captains, the pilot Thomas Whitherow pleaded he steered a true course by a faulty compass. It was held he had on 'too presse of sail' and was over-anxious to reach the Naze(?) before night. A sentence of imprisonment during Their Majesties' pleasure was passed.[38] Captain Austin Birch faced the same tribunal on charge of disobeying the orders of Captain Churchill of the *Pendennis*, in that, being under Churchill's command, he had refused to work up to the sinking *Pendennis* to help save her crew. Dismissed the service, he also was sent to prison. Earlier, on the 29th November, charged with oversetting the *St David* in Portsmouth Harbour, Captain Graydon, the eldest lieutenant, carpenter and gunner of the ship, had faced, aboard *Eagle* a formidable court – Vice-Admiral Killigrew and fifteen captains – with (except for Graydon) consequence of loss of pay and pension and 'dismissal for ever'.[39] On the 23rd

November, Thomas Adams, a pilot, faced Vice-Admiral Davies
and a court, charged with grounding the *Sapphire* on the Whiting
Bank, below Orford Ness. Adams protested it wasn't the Whiting
but the Middle Ground south of the Ness and that there wasn't
sand a year ago where the *Sapphire* stuck. Specious plea! But
Adams was fortunate with a verdict of 'guilty in ignorance', loss
of Trinity House status and of all his accrued pay to the Chatham
Chest. If a court-martial could ever be amusing (for the court!)
possibly the case following on provided the rarity. Pilot Stephen
Harland listened to the charge that he had put the *Assurance*
aground on the Spell. That he admitted; but offered to prove that
the buoys were wrongly laid, the black where the white should be
– and one buoy missing. In support of his contention he submitted
a statement, bearing the signatures of some seventy persons, prepared to swear that other ships with pilots aboard were sent
aground in manner like to his misfortune. Acquitted![40] A pilot's
lot was not a happy one![41]

On the 17th October the Navy Board had been required by the
Admiralty to report the condition of each ship in its care;[42] by the
19th November the provision of twelve fireships of 350 tons had
been approved by the King;[43] and, on the 13th December, the
matter of building, equipping for sea (furnishing with boatswains'
and carpenters' stores for eight months) of the twelve fireships and
also of four fifth rates reached a stage at which costs were tabled
and a decision taken to ask the Treasury for the money.[44] Wear
and tear apparently justified supply to the master of Torrington's
barge of a new 'gang of oares' and 'all things also necessary',[45]
whilst the Admiral of Zeeland, Evertsen, was to have choice of a
'Trim Oard Barge very well Adorn'd with gilt carved worke and
fitted in all respects with Sailes, Oares etc.'. Normally, Dutch ships
were supplied by the yards with the assistance and stores they
required, the cost entered in an account borne against the States
General. This barge was to be a gift.[46]

How far, as the Autumn of 1689 wore on into Winter, was the
trade of the Allies suffering from the enemy? While groups of
convoyed ships sailed out and the coasters received protection,[47]
ocean going vessels, singly or in company, were continuously
homing to their English or Dutch ports;[48] and some, especially if

expected, would have the good fortune to be sighted and brought by escort to their desired havens.[49] Neither on the English nor Dutch side exists a complete and systematic record of losses; such as are extant are not for 1689 but for other periods of the war. Larousse, citing Raynal, informs the reader that, in the course of the war, Dunkirk alone sent out 792 corsairs and that *'seulement dans le cours de guerre de 1689 les Anglais ne perdirent pas moins de 4200 navires par le fait de nos courses'*.[50] Raynal, it appears, borrows from St Croix, who fixes the value at 750 million *'livres tournois'*, which T. E. White his translator puts (in 1802) at 'nearly thirty millions'.[51] The exhaustive analysis of such data as is available for guessing the answer for the *whole war, 1689–1697*, leads Sir George Clark to a very different conclusion:

> We do not know the relative sizes of the Dutch and English merchant fleets, nor whether their proportionate losses were unequal; but, supposing the number lost to have been fairly evenly divided between the two nations . . . an annual average loss of well under a hundred vessels to each.[52]

At this time the losses were not likely to be below the average.

It was during the last four months of the year 1689 while Berkeley complained of the privateers that England determined to enter vigorously the trade. The grants to the end of August had been few – seven only (see p. 193 *ante*). But, between the 1st September and the 31st December, fifty-six letters of marque were issued out of the High Court. Add the seven grants already made and a total of sixty-three represents an impressive beginning to English determination not to be outdone in this wide-ranging field. And here it is well to warn against the common error of picturing the private warship as small of tonnage. The following tabulation[53] for the sixty-three English privateers registered July–December 1689 should dispel that notion.

| | | |
|---|---|---|
| Of 600 tons | 1 | comparable with a large 4th rate |
| 500–600 tons | 0 | |
| 400–500 tons | 7 | comparable with a small 4th rate |
| 300–400 tons | 17 | comparable with a large 5th rate |
| 200–300 tons | 17 | comparable with a small 5th rate |
| 100–200 tons | 17 | comparable with a large 6th rate |
| Under 100 tons | 4 | |

Privateering invited abuses. Letters of marque were revocable.
A case in point – on the 23rd October Shrewsbury required the
Admiralty to call in a grant to Captain Powell for making himself
'serviceable to some persons discovered to have designs against the
Government'.[54] The Admiralty, on the 25th September, instructed
Doctors' Commons to inform grantees that they might not 'wear
the King's Jack'. It was found necessary to watch and repeat that
prohibition.[55]

The determination of William to bring to a halt neutral aid to
France through the enforcement of the treaty of 12th/22nd
August (see pp. 195–197 *ante*)[56] entered, in the September of 1689,
on its first period of test. Sir George Clark writes:

> The States General, awaiting the ratifying of the Convention
> [the treaty 12th/22nd August] by the States of Zeeland do not
> seem to have enforced it seriously during the Autumn of 1689
> while the Danish and Swedish ships arrested by the English in
> the summer were restored to their owners after the enemy and
> allied goods, other than contraband, were taken out of them.
> Nor, though neither of them accepted it explicitly, did the
> northern powers promptly and decidedly oppose the principle
> of the Convention.[57]

Undoubtedly to the year's end the situation, *vis-à-vis* the two chief
neutrals, was highly confused. One sets the King's orders of the
30th August to Torrington (see p. 280 *ante*) to seize, if possible,
fifty ships believed emerging from the Sound, because of the
unwillingness of the King of Denmark to co-operate against
France beside the fact that a Danish admiral could, in November,
convoy hired Danish troops to England for William's use against
the French King. A report from Hamburg, 16th/6th September,
might be thought to place Sweden at the very door of the Grand
Alliance: 'The Swedish fleet returned the 28th past to Carelecrone
where the squadron which is sent to assist Holland is fitting out
with all possible speed.'[58] Yet, on the 15th November, Nottingham
penned a dispatch to Duncomb, the English minister in Stock-
holm:

> I believe it will be impossible to exempt Sweden from the
> prohibition of Trade with France without breaking the whole
> project . . . they cannot well refuse if they really intend, as I do

not doubt, to enter the Treaty of Alliance with us which . . . must end in rupture with France.[59]

In spite of the disclaimer 'I do not doubt', one senses hope of concerted alliance wilting away. The purpose of William, in the case of both Denmark and Sweden was to cajole and, by stimulating them to partial assistance to his cause, involve them, in the long run, in war with France. Continued cajolery became more difficult to practise as enforcement of the treaty against the merchant subjects of those states applied. But, at the year's end, the states in question had not decided to convoy with warships their subjects' trade and, till that happened, or the states refused to sell to their tormentors essential naval supplies, stalemate would continue.

Many devices were being practised by neutral merchants with the connivance of their governments in hope to deceive the Allies. To take an example. On the 5th December the Admiralty instructed Russell, on his way to Holland (see p. 326), diligently 'to look out for a convoy of Danish vessels emerging from the Sound', bound ostensibly for Portugal but in fact en route for France. They were to be seized and sent in as prize.[60] And the fact that the *Tobias of Hamburg* caught in September at presumed trading with the enemy was, in November, under Admiralty arrest as prize, provides a typical instance to indicate that not only neutrals but Allies were prepared for gain to steer crooked courses.[61] Hamburg was a particularly bad offender!

A Commission of Appeals for Prizes was established on the 25th October. For that the Marquis of Carmarthen and many others were named.[62]

During the Autumn, 26th October/5th November, yet another treaty was concluded between William and the Seigneurs of the Estates General of the United Provinces *'au sujet de vaisseaux pris et repris'*. It was designed to avoid disputes which might arise concerning the measure of reward rightly claimable by an English or Dutch captain, who, at the sight of a ship belonging to his ally in course of being carried off by the enemy but not yet taken *intra praesidia*, should succeed in retaking that ship.[63]

Any attempt to indicate the number of French ships being captured or neutrals arrested, searched and restored (less their allegedly contraband cargoes) towards the end of 1689 or any subsequent period of the War faces difficulties like to those encountered in seeking to fix a figure for Anglo-Dutch losses. Sir George Clark makes it clear that the greater part of the Dutch privateering 'industry' (for such it may be called), was monopolized by Zeeland;[64] and he shows that, by the time the Treaty of Ryswick was reached, the Admiralty courts of England and Zeeland had each issued some 700 sentences. The *English* record is one of 483 seized vessels sold, presumably all French, an average of over fifty annually for nine years. Of 399 quantities of goods auctioned 225 were goods taken from neutral vessels an average of twenty-five annually.[65] This implies that 708 vessels came under official English arrest – which total is stated by Sir George 'to be almost exactly equal to that of Zeeland'.

> Assuming [he writes] as seems probable . . . that the proportion
> of enemy ships to cargoes taken from neutrals is about the same
> in the *Dutch* statistics as in the English, we reach a total between
> nine hundred and a thousand French vessels of all sorts and
> sizes [actually 966] captured in the War [1688–1697] about a
> hundred each year.

And what of neutrals intercepted? Presumably one doubles the English figure of 225 – to come to rest on 450 interferences – an average of fifty or more each year? Sir George firmly concludes that by the end of the War: 'the French must have suffered in proportion to the size of their mercantile marine by far the most heavily of the three nations,'[66] and it would not be wise to attempt for this early or indeed for any stage of the conflict particularization.

It was the custom for the Admiralty to maintain close contact with the Principal Officers and Commissioners of the Navy and to summon them to consultation frequently. Their impecunious plight was known. On the last day of September[67] they had been asked to supply a plain statement of the money needed 'for all the purposes' of the Navy. On the 7th October[68] they had done so, together with their own suggestions for supply, which, accepted, would, they held, tide them over current difficulties. It was not a scheme for spectacularly reducing the whole naval debt standing at over £567,542 and concerning which an Abstract was possibly at the same time submitted.[69] In simple terms the proposal can be presented thus:

| To: | Amount | | | Request |
|---|---|---|---|---|
| | £ | s. | d. | |
| Bills for Stores, Workmanship, hemp | 65,470 | 19 | 4 | £9,000 0 0 Weekly to clear |
| Tickets – seamen's wages | ? | | | £2,000 0 0 Weekly to clear |
| Yards – Deptford, Woolwich, Portsmouth with deficits going back to Lady Day 1686 | 14,857 | 3 | 9 | £9,189 3 9 This week £5,676 0 0 Next week |
| Monthly hire of ships for transport of Army to Ireland | 12,207 | 10 | 0 | £4,000 0 0 Weekly to clear |

At the same meeting the Admiralty was asked to take cognizance of the fact that the Victualling Commissioners carried a debt £95,000 plus £4,444 for soldiers transported to various places. The Victuallers confessed themselves 'incapable to proceed with victualling the Fleet, having neither money nor Credit'. On the 8th, a little item the Commissioners had overlooked the day before was minuted. Let the Treasury be informed that two months' pay had been promised by 'their Mats. late Declaration' to such as had served six months from the 1st May and that the 1st November was near at hand![70]

Obviously the victualling situation was one for the attention of the King and Council, if for no other reason than that the Victualling Commissioners supplied other than naval needs and were not wholly subordinate to the Admiralty. The Admiralty, on the 23rd October, minuted to move Sir George Treby, Attorney General, to prepare a bill for the King's signature for the appointment of Simon Maine, John Agarr, Humphrey Ayles and James How as Commissioners of Victualling – which suggests that the existing Commissioners of Victualling, Sir Richard Haddock, Sir John Parsons, Mr Anthony Sturt and Mr Nicholas Fenn were already regarded as on their way out![71] On the 25th, the Admiralty, the Navy Board attending (Admiral Russell their Treasurer

present), had before them a new figure of the Victuallers' debts –
£97,000 – together with a statement from the Victuallers that
such and such were the ships which they, the Victuallers, had been
ordered to supply but that they could do nothing about it! The
Commissioners of the Navy were – the usual routine – told to sue
for money from the Treasury 'a speedy and Considerable Supply
for . . . the service of Victualling'.[72] On the 26th the King in
Council debated whether to resort to contract with merchants
rather than continue victualling through Commissioners.[73] Summoned to appear before the Council, on the 23rd November, the
unfortunate Victualling Commissioners managed to put themselves almost completely in the wrong. They could give little
account of their stocks. At least the mystery of the 'gauls' in the
summer fleet provisions was cleared up. One, William Parsons,
coming from Spain, took in salt for ballast and loaded a number
of sacks of oak galls. Rats ate through the bags; galls and salt got
mixed. In salting the fleet's beef and pork 'one lare of victuals
they throw in a shovel full of salt', galls went in with the barrelled
meat. When the barrels were opened the melted salt would bring
the galls to the top. 'But', said Sir John Parsons (not, one may be
sure, very acceptably!), 'those Gauls are not poyson'.[74] Nottingham now took a hand. He made a special appeal to Sir Richard
Haddock whose dual rôle – as a Commissioner of the Navy and a
Commissioner of Victualling – gave him a special standing and
influence. Nottingham was sure Haddock needed not to be told of
'the necessity of getting to sea with all possible speed the fleets
for the Mediterranean, West Indies and [ships for] service in the
Channel'. It would do much to recommend him in the King's
favour if he could anyway expedite these matters. When, in fact,
*would* the ships at Portsmouth and Spithead be ready to rendezvous? What provisions did they still need? And how could such
be obtained?[75] Sir Richard, two days later, gave the best answer
he could and, ironically, told the Secretary of State that he had
been summoned to London to answer a House of Commons
enquiry into the 'miscarriages of Victualling the Navy'. But he
would risk staying where he was, in Portsmouth, and do his utmost
to hasten the ships.[76] In the King's presence, on the 5th November,
contract was again discussed.[77] Then, on the 14th,[78] the Lords

Privy Seal and President of the Council, both Secretaries of State, the Lords of the Treasury and Admiralty and the Treasurer of the Navy met to vote a new Commission. To the head of the list came the King's nominee, Thomas Papillon. Yet another week elapsed – to the 21st November – before Lowther, straight from attendance on the King, announced to the Admiralty that the former Commissioners had been dismissed and that Mr Papillon with the four gentlemen already known to the Admiralty would take office. The Admiralty should solicit the Attorney General to prepare a warrant under the Great Seal for the Commissioners' appointment.[79] Actually, Papillon, accompanied by his colleague Agarr, had consulted with the Board of Admiralty and the Naval Commissioners the day previously. He had put forward a 'proposal' for dealing with immediate difficulties and, in pursuance of an Order in Council of the 7th instant, consideration was given to a comprehensive design that, in the coming year, 30,000 men should be victualled for seven months and 16,000 for six months.[80] The Navy Board, on the 23rd November, informed the Admiralty that the cost of the victuals would be £306,000 and the wages, wear and tear for the men £918,000. The ratio one to three is instructive. The Board shortly recommended in what ports the victuals should be stored and in what proportions distributed.[81]

By what reasoning the King and Council had been led to fix upon the numbers and times specified is not clear, but the victualling design can have caused the Admiralty no surprise; for, on the 26th October, nearly a month previous to this November date, Torrington had entered the boardroom to inform that it was His Majesty's pleasure 'a Project be made for the next year's Service'[82] – in other words that thought be given to the number and rates for the Spring and Summer armaments. And though nothing in this respect was settled before the very end of December rough working notions no doubt were in mind.

A digression is necessary.

At this date, William and Mary's first Parliament had been for just over a month in second session. In a speech from the King (he is said to have composed it himself) passed to the Speaker of the Commons, Henry Powle, to read on the 19th October, William had asked, 'That what they thought fit to give towards the

Charges of the War for the next year might be done without delay'. This he especially desired because, in a month's time, there would be 'at the *Hague* a general Meeting of the Ministers of all the Princes and States concerned in the War against *France* in order to concert the Measures for the next Campaign'.[83]

The Commons had responded, on the 2nd November, by voting a 'Supply . . . not exceeding . . . two millions to be added to the Public Revenue',[84] and the Land Tax Bill represented a move by the House to give some substance to their undertaking. But to vote was not yet to provide! On the 13th November, the House, sitting in Grand Committee, began to debate 'The State of the Nation' – in effect to criticize, and that with acrimony, the conduct of recent, and not so recent, naval affairs.

The onslaught had begun on Wednesday the 13th November when Sir Robert Clayton (very much the Londoner) presented a petition of certain merchants of London who went so far as to allege that the masters of English merchantmen were hiring Dutch privateers to lead them up Channel! While the Speaker was sought, Sir Thomas Clarges used the interval to indulge a violent outburst. He pointed to 'a great Fleet' in Harbour, obviously Torrington's Anglo-Dutch fleet under Davies's command at Spithead, consuming its victuals, giving 'no account of its service', the men debauched, the captains rioting in London, never having gone on cruise. There had been lack of merchant convoy, pressing from merchant ships. England was 'over-reached in Treaties' – Clarges spoke disparagingly of the Dutch. The command of the main fleet he held should, as in 'usurpation' times (neat loyal phrase from an old Scottish Commonwealth man) be committed to three conjoined admirals . . . The Speaker arrived. Sir Robert Clayton presented the petition, which declared a loss of 100 sail worth £600,000, as merchantmen from the Streights and West Indies came into the Channel and French capers fell upon them. Those that escaped had run for West of England ports seeking convoy; and the petitioners averred that naval captains had sought 'convoy money' for that service. Evidence being demanded, Captain George Churchill of the *Pendennis* (see p. 307) was named. Sir Patience Ward, M.P. London, attacked Captain Churchill; Garroway wanted to know if Churchill's case stood alone. Hawles, the lawyer, drew a distinction between the 'ordinary' giving of a gratuity, service performed, and a bargain made before hand. Sir Edward Seymour, sometime Treasurer of the Navy, sometime Speaker, wanted a widened enquiry into all 'neglect of guarding the sea'. Garroway interposed on the wording of an appropriate motion. Sir Thomas Lee, both member of Parliament and a Lord Commissioner of Admiralty, weighed in with: 'If merchants will go Ship by Ship and not by Company all the Fleet cannot protect them,' which remark brought Admiral Russell, like Lee a member of the House, and Treasurer of the Navy, to his feet. ''Tis impossible to guard all places; but if your Merchants venture, they cannot be guarded.' And Russell (not unnaturally!) thought 'the Question better left alone'. Sir Samuel Dashwood would not agree. Why – he would 'justify it by Persons that the Sugar-Fleet lost seven Ships', that the Admiralty when 'acquainted that the Fleet was in danger' did order Berkeley to protect the ships then 'commanded Berkeley home'. Was not that a clear case of 'want of Convoy'. Lee changed his quasi-official ground of defence. He was prepared 'to agree with the Gentleman in what he said' but Berkeley, on the King's orders, had been brought in to embark troops for Ireland. Papillon (who the next morning would find himself 'chief' Victualler and inside the Admiralty camp) asked why 'provision was not made for *both* Trade preserved and Ireland guarded'. Lee answered with a frank 'it could not'. Ships were being subtracted from the main fleet to refit for the Streights and Indies squadrons. Berkeley, he had shown, was but temporarily called in – to Plymouth. 'I think, [he concluded] the Admiralty not much asleep in the Service'.

Next day, Thursday the 14th, the debate had been resumed by Howe ('Jack How'), who returned to the subject of merchant losses, wanted to discover 'how the *Toulon* Fleet came to join the *Brest* Fleet [and] how K James got into Ireland'. Sir Thomas Clarges followed with the motion, 'That not guarding the Seas is an obstruction of Trade and a Grievance to the Nation'. Sir Joseph Tredenham was anxious to 'satisfy the People' that they might 'pay Taxes more easily'. When Clarges again rose, Sir Thomas Littleton thought it time to apply moderation with the

plea 'find out persons' do not 'pick holes in the Government'.
But neither Sir John Guise, nor the yet more outspoken Colonel
Birch (of Civil War repute) was for moderation:

We all agree that one Such a Year's War will make an end of
you. In short from one end to the other, there is no part of
what we have done this Year that will serve our turn the next
Year . . . Part with your Money and wait better luck. That
eighteen or twenty French Ships should come from *Toulon* to
*Brest* and nobody hear of them! . . . We must have the hands
next Year else the game is up – had you other hands I would
give my consent to hang good numbers. . . . Had we Tar-
paulins to commend, we should, next Year have 'something for
something'.

That was more than Admiral Russell could be expected to take
calmly – yet his retort reads as a model of restraint:

I know not well where to begin. I had the honour to be long in
the Navy which seems [now] charged with Ignorance, Cowardice, or Corruption . . . 'Tis said 'When the *French* came out we
ran away' . . . We lay on the *French* Coast six weeks & I
believe for the most part, not three leagues from *Ushant*. We lay
there as long as the Weather would permit. We are accused of
letting the *Toulon* Squadron join the *Brest*. We had no way to
know it but by Scouts. There are foggy nights, weather, and
winds, that carry us eight or ten leagues from thence. Nobody
that served in the Fleet but was as desirous to prevent this as
any Gentleman here. I attribute this to misfortune only. Unless
we should pull the *French* out of Port by the ears. I know not
how to have fought. I do aver this, that fifteen days after we left
*Brest*, no Ship came in there. I desire that either these things
may be proved and these reflections laid aside.

After a plea from Hampden, typical of the man who could refuse
reward from William, to avoid 'personal reflection' and a return
to the attack – by Colonel Austen – Sir John Trevor advised
adjournment. Lee ventured an amendment, 'That which is done
could not be helped – I move That you appoint a Committee to
search the Admiralty books for their Orders and numbers of
Ships and see the State of the Ships and then give your Judgment'.
No use! Elwell and Sir Edward Seymour revived the prevailing

militancy and it was not the amendment but Clarges' motion which was carried: 'That the want of a Guard, or Convoys, for the Merchants, for the last year, hath been an obstruction to Trade and an occasion of great losses to the Nation'.

So had ended a debate which stands as the classic precedent for many a later call upon the Admiralty to defend, in the House and to the nation, the policy of placing exercise of command for military purposes before its use in the protection of trade.[85]

Of course Captain George Churchill, M.P. for St Albans, whose professional rectitude had been called in question (see p. 316 *ante*) could scarcely expect that he personally had heard the last of the accusation. In his place in the House he listened as 'several Masters of Ships' gave evidence at the Bar that he had extorted money as a condition of convoy and had pressed the crews of those masters who would not proffer. Churchill admitted convoying 'twenty-two of twenty-four', receiving 150 guineas as a voluntary gift. He denied compelling any man. It was Lee who closed the long debate, moving committal to the Tower rather than abasement at the Bar. There should be no 'over-doing' of punishment: 'This Gentleman would rather [Lee believed] fight three battles with the French than one with the House of Commons.' Churchill was sent to the Tower. He petitioned and obtained release fourteen days later.[86] Shipwreck, the *Pendennis* lost in course of convoy, the Tower – and no enviable standing at the court-martial of pilot Witherow ahead! But George Churchill is not a character on whom to waste sympathy.[87]

The House continuing, with intermissions, its inquest, on the 23rd was presented with a new stick with which to beat the Navy.

And it is here that the digression (begun on p. 315) swings back to relate with the day to day affairs of the Naval Board and the Victualling Commissioners.

One, Rice, had received a letter from his son in Plymouth, telling of the 'abuses discovered in the victuals and beer provided for the Fleet'. This had been passed to Sir Robert Napier, M.P. Weymouth, who asked that it be considered. Rice at the Bar owned it and the House moved simply, after formality over the presence of the Speaker, to the question of bringing up in custody the 'old' Victuallers Sir John Parsons, Sir Richard Haddock,

Alderman Sturt, Mr Nicholas Fenn to answer their shortcomings. Papillon told his fellow members that, a week since, the King had imposed on him the duty of a Victualler and not even Lee could do much to excuse the fiasco. The general willingness to assume that anyway Haddock, 'an able Seaman and a good Protestant . . . a man who had commanded a squadron at sea', would not be found culpable was the single satisfaction the Naval Administration could extract from a sorry scandal.[88] Arrested, the 'old' Victuallers obtained bail after the 5th December.[89]

All storms spend themselves. As the month of November wore on, the intensity of criticism of the Navy eased. The House voted, on the 26th, His Majesty be moved that 'Mr John Shales, Commissary General of the Provisions' for Duke Schomberg, be taken into custody. It learned, on the 27th, that the King had anticipated its wish and, on the 30th,[90] that a request, made on the 11th,[91] that 'some fit Persons go over into *Ireland* to take an Account of the Number of the Army there and the State and Condition of it', was acceptable to the King. The 2nd December brought discussion of the royal message.[92] A week later, a debate proceeding on the voluminous Land Tax Bill suddenly assumed importance for the Navy, for Mr. Sacheverell introduced, on the 9th, an 'appropriating clause' 'for money to the Seamen'.[93] The 16th December saw the Land Tax Bill an Act.[94] Mr Sacheverell and the Attorney General had assured – as far as appropriating clauses written into an Act of Parliament could do so, an allocation of £400,000 to naval indigency – £200,000 of it for the speedy payment of the sailors, £100,000 for the victualling and £100,000 for stores. Mr Ehrman has pointed out that, constitutionally 'The relevant articles are worth some examination; for they set the pattern for all future Parliamentary appropriations during the war.'[95]

Grants from the £400,000 then firmly voted were not destined to reach the Navy or Victualling Commissioners smoothly before late in the first quarter of the coming 1690 year. From various sources in the last quarter of 1689 the Navy Board and the Victuallers, the 'old' before demise, the 'new' on appointment did draw working sums. It would be found, when the accounts for the year came to be made up,[96] that, in this closing quarter of

1689 £142,740 passed to the Navy Board from the Treasury, £79,564 of which was earmarked for use of the Victuallers. But, because, all the while, expenditure so greatly outran income, it would also emerge that the naval debt increased in the same period by £215,428, moving from £567,542 (see p. 313, note (69) to stand at £782,970 on the 31st December.[97] A naval accountant subtracting £200,000 as a round estimate of the state of the naval debt on the 1st January 1689[98] and writing down £582,970 as the sum by which the debt had grown in the year ended the 31st December 1689, might well have been struck by the fact that the increase roughly equalled another cast which the books revealed – £581,685, the total of the moneys received from the Exchequer in the same twelve months interval. The inference? A naval expenditure in 1689 of £1,164,655 and for every pound drawn from the Exchequer two spent!

To complete the Parliamentary story. Who could expect the House, on the 21st,[99] after all the commotion, to desist from rounding off the ordinary work of the preceding weeks by a long address to the King on 'Miscarriages'? Of several paragraphs one accusingly began: 'The Miscarriages in reference to the Fleet have been as destructive to your Majesty's and your People's Interest as those in the Army . . .' The necessary references to want of convoy, avaricious officers, unnecessary pressing of men, discouraged trade, diminished Customs, loyal subjects impoverished, sailors fed on corrupted provisions, were all worked in; but, somehow, the Admiralty and admirals were left uncensured![100]

One side issue of Parliamentary interest in Admiralty affairs is difficult to follow. Lee, on the 14th November, when the attack on the Navy had raged fiercest, had closed his remarks with the suggestion that, if members were unconvinced by the case for the Admiralty (see p. 317 *ante*), 'a Committee search the Admiralty books for their Orders and numbers of Ships . . . etc.'[101] It would appear that a Committee under Sir John Guise prosecuted, or at least set out to pursue, an enquiry far wider than mere reference to Admiralty journals proper. For, on the 29th,[102] an order was issued by the Admiralty to Russell in the Downs enclosing an order of the House of Commons that:

all ye Flagg Officers, Captains, Chief Mates, Pursers, Gunners,

L

Masters, Carpenters and Boatswains and all other Officers whatsoever that Serv'd in their Mat⁵ Ffleet ye last Sumer do bring or Send in their Journalls and Acc⁵ to Sʳ John Guise Chairman of the Said Committee at the Speaker's Chamber at Westminster.[103]

How many officers obeyed? And where are the journals of the obedient?

Earlier in this chapter it was noted that the King had deputed Torrington, on the 26th October, to desire of the Admiralty 'A Project be made for next yeares Service' (see p. 315 *ante*).

On the 1st December, the Admiralty Board (Torrington, Carbery, Lee, Lowther) waiting upon the King, Nottingham and Halifax in the Robes Chamber, heard the demand again made – the project to be 'forthwith prepared'. Torrington constructively suggested the name of one, Barret of Shoreham, as a fireship builder; the King settled that twelve fireships already ordered be constructed here and not abroad. And Torrington advanced the notion of re-rating ships for guns and complements and putting 4,000 landsmen to sea. On the 8th, 15th, 22nd and 29th further attendance at the Robes. For the 29th the Board's minutes recorded that the 'Grand Fleet' (so denominated) would consist of two first rates, six seconds, twenty-five thirds, seven fourths [40], with lesser rates and fireships in numbers to be settled later. Nottingham's own list for the 22nd showed four firsts, nine seconds, twenty-five thirds, six fourths [44], two fifths, four sixths and seventeen fireships. William's later personal file – of the 5th January – gave four firsts, nine seconds, thirty-two thirds and eleven fourths [56], four lesser vessels, a yacht, a bomber and two hospital ships; it also indicated the three admirals selected for flags and captains and lieutenants proposed for the rated ships. All the Grand Fleet lists contained the names of eight or nine ships belonging to the Russell-Killigrew or Groyne-Mediterranean squadron, which, not having yet performed its Winter allocated work of royal and trade convoy, could only be of Summer use in the Grand Fleet if back in time. In number the ships in commission in the Summer of 1690 – Grand Fleet, Mediterranean and West Indies squadrons, with those required for the Irish Sea and for other duties abroad and in home waters – would, in the King's expectation, total between 90 and 100. They were to be manned by 33,000 men. It was, of course, taken for granted that the Dutch contribution, Channel and Mediterranean, would accrue in the ratio three to five.[104] Nottingham tabulated the Dutch contribution as fifty-seven; nine first or second rates, eighteen thirds, nine fourths, six fifths, fifteen sixths and twelve fireships – of which whole quota seven rates and one fireship were for service in the Mediterranean and the rest 'remained to be sent'. On such official arithmetic, King William could expect, in the Summer of 1690, 150 ships wearing English or various Dutch flags at sea.

Admiral and Commander-in-chief of the 1689 Anglo-Dutch fleet Torrington, from the day on which he arrived in London, on the 5th October, had been well placed to resume his earlier rôle of professional naval adviser to the King. But his stock was low (see p. 281 *ante*). He may be found irregularly attending the almost daily meetings of the Board of Admiralty, a dozen times in October, rather less frequently in November, once only in the first week of December, followed by three occasions on which he joined the Board to meet the King with the selected councillors in the Robes Chamber.[105] Go-between 'twixt King, administration and Admiralty, there is only limited evidence that Torrington played initiatory or markedly advisory part in these naval deliberations. He was not present at the fourth conference in the Robes, on the 29th December, and, intimating to William a desire to resign from the Board of Admiralty, was allowed to do so.[106] Conversing with Halifax, the King is reported: 'said he beleeved nothing but meer lazinesse was the cause of Lord Torrington's quitting'.[107] Torrington still remained Vice-Admiral of England.

Had Torrington been able to accept, on the 29th December, that even seventy rated ships English and Dutch would really be available in a Grand Fleet in the coming Spring, he could scarcely have withdrawn; but, knowing full well the battered state of the ships putting in from cruising with Lord Berkeley, doubting the ability of the yards to fit, rig and store, or the Ordnance at the Tower, to gun, the Victuallers to provision or the Admiralty to man the ships new-called into commission, unable to count on a timed return of the eight or nine Mediterranean ships allocated

to the 1690 Grand Fleet service or to feel sure of rendezvous by
the Dutch, Torrington feared, grumbled and argued. Conference
with Nottingham is attested.[108] Nor was Torrington the only one
to grumble. His alarm as will be seen was shared by Russell. Yet
what could Nottingham have done? The fact that the King had
kept his first Anglo-Dutch fleet unnecessarily late at sea had
lessened the margin of time for the 1690 reconditioning. Then too,
from early September he had desired the fetching of the Queen of
Spain from Holland, her conveyance to her new home. This was
a diplomatic undertaking reasonable if initiated with immediacy
and performed to a fast time-table. Royal punctilio over dis-
patching a large second rate to Flushing, Russell's dilatoriness to
undertake a mission he disliked, above all the Victualling Office
chaos, which might as readily have been resolved in October as
November, had incredibly delayed the Groyne-Mediterranean
sailing, a sailing which, as this narrative will in due course show,
had only completed its initial stage and appeared likely to throw
out of gear the whole wheel of William's naval preparation for
1690. Recognition of this likelihood was at the root of Torrington's
vexation. The question resolves – should Torrington, enduring
frustration, yet have stayed at a post of circumscribed usefulness?
Papillon the King had commanded; Torrington he ignored and
the royal resentment went deep. William was quite prepared for
Torrington and the Earl of Pembroke each to raise a regiment of
'blue' Marines; but he would do nothing to hinder Torrington's
departure from the Commission of Admiralty and, apparently,
intended to deny the Vice-Admiral of England and Commander-
in-chief of the 1689 Allied Fleet a further flag at sea. From the
list, filed in King William's Chest, of ships and officers, admirals,
captains, lieutenants for the Grand Fleet of 1690 the name of
Torrington is missing; that of Russell is entered as Admiral of the
1690 Grand Fleet.[109]

The watch-dog cruising of Berkeley to and from the Soundings
his vessels drawn from the Winter Channel and Irish allocations,
a strong Dutch contingent also following his flag, the protection
and supply of Schomberg's base in Carrickfergus, the harassing of
French trade, the constant convoy work up and down and across

the North Sea and along the Channel to counter the plague of Dunkirk and St Malo privateers – these represent the naval achievement of Autumn and the turning year. In contrast, the triple combined diplomatic and trade operation – finally planned on the 11th October in the royal presence – Russell to fetch from Holland a Queen for speedy conveyance to Spain; Russell, passing through the Channel, to collect Vice-Admiral Killigrew's squadron (with supporting Dutch warships) and the Mediterranean-bound merchantmen; Russell, with Killigrew, to shepherd well clear of the Channel Captain Wright and his West Indian trade – all that considerable operation, presented a picture of belated disarray.

The 24th November was reached before orders were drafted for Russell, in the second rate *Duke*, lying in the Downs, to proceed with the thirds *Berwick*, *Montague*, *Suffolk* and *Rupert* (the two latter borrowed from the Channel squadron), the fourths *Happy Return* and *Newcastle*, and the yachts *Mary* and *Phubbs* to sail 'on the first oppertunity of Wind and Weather . . . before Vlushing in Zealand and there receive on board her Ma^tie the Queen of Spain and her retinue and Equipage . . . her Ma^tie . . . on board the *Duke* . . .' The Admiral (of the Blue, his recent Allied Fleet rank) was authorized 'upon her Ma^tie coming on bd to hoyst the Union fflagg at the Maintopmast head' and instructed, on landing the Queen, 'to strike ye Union fflagg and weare ye blew fflagg according as . . . empowered [on the] 30th May last'. Details of salute at embarkation and disembarkation by the Queen were left to Russell's discretion; his ships would fire 'a number of Ordnance in . . . manner . . . suitable to the Extraodyness of the Occasion'. The order forbade waiting in the Downes for any of the ships that ought to accompany the Admiral but might not be ready to sail; it indicated that, on return, he could expect further instructions at Spithead. The signatures of Torrington, Carbery, Sir Thomas Lee, Sir John Chicheley, Sir John Lowther were appended to the order, which Secretary Bowles sent 'under cover to the Postmaster at Deale by Express at ½ an hour past 7 at night'.[110] It produced no immediate obedience. Russell was convinced of the danger of taking the *Duke* among the Dutch sands. And it would appear that their Lordships of Admiralty, on the 2nd December, first sanctioned instructions permitting their Admiral to leave the *Duke* in the Downs and fetch the Spanish Queen in some lesser vessel, countermanded their decision, upon orders from the King, and then, also by royal desire, reversed the countermand![111] Russell, hesitating off the North Foreland on the 4th December, made a last protest to Nottingham that the pilots thought the *Duke* too big to take on the coast of Zealand at that time of the year 'the weather being very uncertain and often thick'. Indeed the pilots were 'almost dead with fear'. If the King pleased, he, Russell, would take smaller ships and the yachts and bring the Queen to the Downs. A loss of a 'big ship' would not be 'easily repaired'.[112] Another letter next day, the 5th, reiterated the pilots' apprehension. 'And (setting aside the grandure of the business) the Queen of Spain would [remarked Russell] come over in a yacht with more safety, having frigats to attend her.' Moreover, that procedure would prevent delay; for, even with a favourable wind, no one would dare to sail the *Duke* to Holland 'till the tides fall out in the day time'.[113] Professional opinion and common-sense won. Ordered by the Admiralty on the 5th December[114] and, on the 6th December, more sharply spurred on 'by the King's command to make all the haste possible to Flushing . . . his Majesty very uneasy to think how long this voyage [had been] delayed'.[115] Russell, in the *Phubbs* yacht with the three fourths *Newcastle*, *Assistance* and *Hampshire*, the fifth *Guernsey* (the last three named borrowed hurriedly from Wright), the sixth *Saudadoes* and the *Mary* yacht cleared the Downs on the 10th.[116] He arrived off Flushing on the 12th.[117] On the 16th, in a yacht of Middleburg, near which town the *Mary* yacht anchored, he went out to meet the Queen, approaching with an escort of ten Dutch yachts. The guns of all the English ships (assisted by an East Indiaman at anchor) boomed salute![118] But the Queen did not come aboard till the 18th/28th.[119] Ill weather and great storms followed, the English ships riding it out 'a league off at the Rammekins'.[120] On the 2nd January Russell unburthened himself to Nottingham.

I have been in daly hopes of a favourable wind . . . but my patience and expectations being att an end, I send this to acquaint your lordshipp that I have had the Quene on board thire Majesties yautche this sixten dayes, and have as well as I could, disposed of a numerous begerly traine a board the severall men of ware. They are about 220 persons, all very proud, few cloaths and no mony. The Quene has but six hundrid pistolls, and no more creditt in this part of the world ... They all lieve att the King's charge, and I take all imaginable care to have them served with reputation to my master, and rather chuse to under goe any hardshipp myself then show the least uneasines to them, though truly I have a great deall with in myself, besides the trouble the croud gives me. I have leived thre weeks under watter and in a hole in the yautch but a yard long and not two yards broad; it is soe great a burden to me that I am weary of leving, and shall be soe, till I am blessed with a safe returne from the Groine to England. If I have or shall be able in the voyadg to do the King any servis I shall be extreamly pleased, but ware itt in my own choyse, the price of a kingdom would not tempt me to pass a winter as I am like too do this; t'is not to be imagined what I undergoe, but I hope this, as all other things, will have an end, that I may goe to my poore dwelling in the country, thank God for my delivarance and never soe much as loock towards salt watter againe. The weather has bin extreamly tempestus and I have often bin under no small frights about the frigets, the Rode being very bad, and the ground wors. God be praysed as yett we have recived no prejudice, but tis more by mericle then anything else.

Enclosed with the letter was a list of the Queen's retinue and their disposition on board the ships:

Lady of Honour, Mother of the Maids, two Maids of Honour, a Bedchamber woman, dwarf, butler, the Queen's cook and her husband, Master of the horse, confessor, physician, chirugeon, laundress, wardrobe keeper, guard of the plate, abbot, two friars and a priest, with the servants attending upon the various members of the household; also the Queen's brother, with twenty-seven gentlemen and servants; and a numerous train of noble men and gentlemen with their attendants.

In all – 212 persons!

Russell's next communication, of the 7th, reported Count Mansfeld's fears that seven French men-of-war would emerge from Dunkirk for interception of the squadron: 'I had as live be

in the Bastele as heare! Pray my lord by your prayers to God for
a fair wind . . . forward my deliverance from this eternall trouble'.
The 9th – more to the same effect lest that of the 7th should
miscarry. On the 16th, after a gibe at Mansfeld, whose seven
threatening warships turn out to be 'three small privateers',
and an expression of relief that in spite of the 'great extremity
of bad weather' the warships float safe, Russell recounted the
shattering rumour of a hundred ships ashore in the Downs.
That, 'aded to the afliction [he] ley under' made him, he declared,
'of all mankind the unesiest . . . The trouble the Quene and her
retinew has given [him] the brutality . . . among the Zelanders
and the life [he] have bin forced to leive, has made [him] pass the
bounds of a good Christian.' With the Admiral – amused commiseration! For the 'inland' German and her immediate entourage (her first experience at sea high price for her kingdom?)
sympathy also.[121] Anchor was dropped in the Downs on the
18th.[122] There her Majesty could be transferred to the more
spacious second rate, *Duke*, the captain's cabin made ready for
her reception with hangings brought from the Great Wardrobe
and a silver brazier from the Queen of England's withdrawing-
room. Grenadiers guarded her.[123]

Whilst Russell was tossing off the Rammekins his final orders
had been drawn and dated the 23rd December. They reached him
as soon as he appeared off Deale.[124] The Queen transferred to the
*Duke*, Russell, with the waiting vessels of his fleet and the traders
collected in the Downs, was required to head for his rendezvous
Spithead, where he would find his Vice-Admiral Killigrew with
the rest of the English ships and Captain Wright with his West
Indies squadron. Wright should be hastened, particularly in
taking aboard a regiment at Plymouth. (Russell would, without
specific indication, understand that Dutch warships would join
him – under his command.) On leaving Spithead, frigates should
be sent westward to round up any intending Streights traders.
With the *Duke*, *Berwick*, *Montague*, *Suffolk*, *Eagle* and *Rupert*,
Russell, accompanied by his Rear-Admiral Ashby, would put in
at the Groyne, his Vice-Admiral standing on with the trade to
Cadiz and beyond. The Queen landed and the *Duke*, *Berwick* and
*Montague* dispatched to join Killigrew, Russell, with the *Suffolk*,

*Eagle* and *Rupert* would be expected to await the Queen's pleasure at the Groyne, take on certain persons and make for home. Killigrew and Wright must put their crews on reduced rationing, 'six to four' on sailing and out of contingent money, pay what is due to them when put on 'short allowance'. The usual provision empowering the Admiral to fill vacancies occurring among the officers was included in the orders. Lastly, the ships 'borrowed' by Russell from the West Indies squadron for the voyage to Holland just completed, must be provisioned at Portsmouth for eight months before rejoining Wright.

On the 20th January Admiral Russell left the Downs for Spithead,[125] accompanied by Rear-Admiral Ashby who had been waiting there for him.[126] He, no doubt, had with him (apart from the borrowed West Indies ships *Assistance* (fourth), *Hampshire* (fourth), and *Guernsey* (sixth)) the originally allotted 'Mediterranean' *Duke* (second), *Berwick* (third), *Montague* (third), *Happy Return* (fourth), *Newcastle* (fourth) and *Eagle* (third), with the *Rupert* (third) and *Suffolk* (third) and possibly *Portland* (fourth) all three taken from the October 'Channel' allotment as replacements (see p. 294 *ante*), and probably one or two smaller vessels and with trade going that way. On the 22nd a human drama, enacted in the *Duke* as the squadron swept past Beachy, found record in Captain Edward Stanley's log. 'The Queene of Spain Desyred of our Adm[ll] ye life and Liberty of one Mackins a Mallifactor Who had deserted our Shipp'.[127] One assumes her wish was granted. Two days later the *Duke* entered St Helens Road[128] and, on the morrow, the 25th, reached Spithead. There Killigrew, in *Resolution* (third) with *Oxford* (fourth), *Burford* (third) and *Greenwich* (third) and other craft awaited and the Dutch Vice-Admiral Van Almonde in *Gelderland* with his contributory contingent of fourteen lay. There too Captain Wright in the third rate, the *Mary*, with half a dozen fourths of the West Indies squadron; there also units of Vice-Admiral Davies's Channel squadron, Berkeley's *Hampton Court*, *Monmouth*, *Essex* and *Exeter*,[129] and laden merchantmen, at least two hundred in number, swinging at their moorings. Suddenly, as the *Duke*, Queen aboard and union at the main, looked visible through the haze and rainfall, the guns of all the warships in the Road, of the forts of Portsmouth and of the far from insignificant armoury of the 'omnium gatherum' of the impatient victual-consuming traders, saluted the *Duke*.[130]

In preparing for the West Indies 'expedition' and readiness to sail in company with Russell and Killigrew on the first part of the voyage, Captain Laurence Wright [131] had experienced vexation – interference with the quota of ships allotted him in mid-October, ranging from the loss of the fourth rate *St David*, overset in Portsmouth harbour[132] to the borrowing by Russell just referred to. To contend with the demands of prospective colonial governors – Colonel Kendall bound for Barbados, asking space for 40 tons of household stuff and two coaches, accommodation for ten horses and twenty-six servants[133] and Lord Inchiquin, appointed to Jamaica, putting the weight of his belongings at 100 tons, his other demands corresponding, taxed Wright's patience.[134] Moreover Wright was understandably anxious that his command at sea should not be interfered with by these governors.[135] An Admiralty order that plain Mr James Read be given passage to Barbados, 'hee being appointed by his Ma^ty for Improving Plants in that and other Plantations and sending them home for the King's Garden',[136] was not a troublesome request. Official advertisement that Wright was 'almost ready to sail' had gone out as far back as the 11th November and the Instructions of the Lords Commissioners for Trade and the Plantations sought.[137] It was the 21st December before meticulously phrased orders for Wright were drafted by the Admiralty.[138]

Upon alarm in London that forty sail of Frenchmen would break into the Channel to carry troops to Ireland, Killigrew was ordered, on the 5th December, with all available ships, to the assistance of Lord Berkeley in the Soundings – indeed, told to take Berkeley under his command for twenty days, which service completed, he would leave Berkeley on station and himself make for Plymouth or Torbay. Actually, though the winds were many days easterly,[139] and though it was believed in Portsmouth on the 10th that ships in Spithead[140] would sail westward 'this day or tomorrow', Killigrew did not weigh and his orders were revoked on the 12th December.[141] He received his final orders as commander-in-chief of the Mediterranean squadron (that is to say after Russell should cast off near the Groyne) on the 28th December.[142]

It will surprise none to learn that Wright and Killigrew had faced continuous difficulties in preparing their squadrons for sea. The only chance for Wright and Killigrew at Spithead, Ashby in the Downs, to make good their provisioning deficiencies had been to find what they lacked for their squadrons' ships in the depleted stores of Portsmouth or Dover (Plymouth could do little to help), or to acquire the content of some victualler en route to them from the Thames. Two days before Russell's arrival at Spithead individual ships of both Wright's and Killigrew's squadrons were still unsupplied and storeships to attend the warships on their voyage were 'undispatched'. For defective manning the securing of 'turned over' men the application of the press on the strength of warrants (commonly granted by the Admiralty specifically to this or that ship's lieutenant to search in and around the ports) provided the usual solution; and from the 3rd January onwards the merchant ships were 'officially' searched for what investigating captains might consider excess complement.[143] In respect of pay the situation in which Torrington had found himself (see p. 108 *ante*) in the Spring repeated itself. It was imperative that payments should be made. A party of horse arrived in Portsmouth on the 28th December with money for the ships;[144] and though, on the 8th January, the Admiralty minuted that the Navy Board declared that it could not hold out much longer without money and that soon 'the whole affairs of the Navy [would] inevitably be at a stand', somehow some money was obtained and some payment of wages proceeded. On that same January day the Admiralty instructed Killigrew that, 'When the Ships of the Mediterranean and West Indies squadrons have received their two months pay hee send one of the g$^d$ Ships round to the Downes with the remainder of the money and Clerkes for paying the Ships which are there of those Squadrons'.[145] More surprisingly the Navy Office on the 22nd was asking the Admiralty to sanction the retention of £5,000 and £20,000 (just secured) for redemption of pay tickets in the office, since there was 'enough money at Portsmouth at present'![146] Such a temporary alleviation was too good to be true! The Admiralty agreed. A Commissioner of the Navy went down to Portsmouth to assist the Resident Commissioner in the necessarily slow process of payment of the men of the

two squadrons and Killigrew was required to ensure that the crews
of the *Hampton Court*, *Essex*, *Exeter* and *Monmouth*, which Lord
Berkeley had just brought in from the West were treating them as
though they were Mediterranean ships to be prepared for service
in that sea.[147] It was at this stage, and with three fourths which
Russell now returned to Wright requiring their three months
victualling, that matters West Indian and Mediterranean stood
when, on the 25th January Russell arrived at Spithead – to the
King's qualified satisfaction. The Admiralty Minutes indicate royal
questioning on the 18th January; some necessary last minute
instructions on the 25th, concerning delivery of presents to the
rulers of Algiers, Tunis and Tripoli; and at last, on the 27th firm
orders to Russell to sail without the West Indies squadron and
convoy if by that change the voyage to Spain could be hastened.[148]
It could not be expedited while the wind blew hard into Spithead
and Portsmouth Harbour!

A letter en route from Russell to Nottingham crossed with the
passage of the orders – a letter less remarkable for chagrin at
compelled inaction than for alarm at naval unpreparedness in
general.

> For Godsake my Lord cast your eye sometimes towards the next
> summer's fleet. I dread the French being out before us . . . the
> matters relating to the Navy goe on soe slowly that I am in
> amaze. I hope Lord Torrington designes to make up by his
> diligence this summer what disservice the King has sustained
> by his quitting at soe unseasonable a time, at least I think so.[149]

True, in the course of the month, a reconstitution of the Board of
Admiralty had taken place.[150] With Torrington, Wharton and
Sacheverell had been dropped, the two latter, as Mr Ehrman
points out, for political rather than professional reasons.[151] Herbert, earl of Pembroke, the single new appointee, back from
ambassadorship at the Hague, would be expected to prove useful
in discussion with Hiob de Wildt, this year, as last (see p. 35 *ante*),
the visiting States envoy for naval co-operation – coming with a
willingness to add more ships to the Dutch quota?[152] A change in
the Admiralty secretariat had also occurred – James Sotherne,
formerly Clerk of the Acts, had replaced, on the 16th January,

Phineas Bowles, Torrington's obsequious protégé, and Charles Sergison succeeded to Sotherne's old post.[153] But changes of this sort counted for little so long as no regular financial supply flowed from the Treasury to the Navy Board in Seething Lane, to the Victuallers at Tower Hill, the Ordnance at the Tower and Berkeley's fear would be proved only too well founded.

## REFERENCES

1 *H.M.C. Finch II*, p. 257 Berkeley-Nottingham.
2 Log of *Hampton Court* (Master's). P.R.O. Adm. 52/46.
3 *London Gazette* (14th–17th Oct.). Falmouth 10th Oct., and Plymouth 12th Oct.
4 Warnsinck, *op. cit.* p. 52 (Evertsen aan S. G. dd 11th Oct. 1689 Lias Adm.).
5 *H.M.C. Finch II*, p. 499; Log *Hampton Court, London Gazette* (21st–24th Oct.). Plymouth 18th Oct.
6 P.R.O. Adm. 3/2, 12th Oct.; *London Gazette* (14th–17th Oct.). Plymouth 12th Oct.
7 P.R.O. Adm. 3/2, 8th Oct.
8 *Memoirs . . . Torrington*, p. 41; and d'Avaux *op. cit.*, p. 543. Supplemented by *H.M.C. Finch II*, p. 499 Berkeley–Nottingham. Also *London Gazette* (11th–14th Nov.). Portsmouth 7th Nov. The Admiralty later questioned whether Leighton had not been too concerned with the 'powder prize' and Byng negligent of pursuit. P.R.O. Adm. 3/2 1st Dec. It is perhaps of interest that d'Avaux has earlier (*v.* p. 304) singled out 'le Chevalier [Duc?] de St. Simon' as among the best of couriers to and from France. His 'petit bastiment . . . peut aisement tourner de coup de vent'.
9 *H.M.C. Finch II*, p. 253.
10 *Ibid.* p. 259.
11 *Ibid.* p. 499.
12 *Ibid.* p. 260.
13 *London Gazette* (14th–18th Nov.). Plymouth 12th Nov.
14 *Ibid.* (18th–21st Nov.). Plymouth 15th Nov.
15 *H.M.C. Finch II*, p. 260, 15th Nov.
16 As note (14). Plymouth 17th Nov.
17 Warsinck, *op. cit.* p. 53 with authority cited–P.R.O. Adm. XI, 20; en Journael gehouden op't Lans fregat de *Vogel Phenix*. P.R.O. Adm. 1097.
18 Log of *Yorke*.
19 *Memoirs . . . Torrington*, p. 41.
20 Log of *Yorke*. Berkeley had received court-martial authority 21st Oct. (P.R.O. Adm. 3/2). Trials–12th Nov. of Dorrington, the surgeon of the fireship *Owner's Love* who assaulted his commander (in drink!) and 14th Nov. of Richard Stone and William Dawson who attempted desert and 'fell at courts' feet'. P.R.O. Adm. I 5253. There was correspondence with the Admiralty, Berkeley asking a pardon for Dorrington (P.R.O. Adm. 3/2, 16th Nov.) and the men(?). The Admiralty agreed to 'move' the King 19th Nov.; but, 24th Nov., King and Board refused clemency. *Ibid.*

21  *Ibid.* and Log of *Hampton Court.* P.R.O. Adm. 52/46 (Master's).

22  Log of *Hampton Court.*

23  (30th Dec–2nd Jan.). Plymouth 27th Dec.

24  Log of *Yorke.* The Admiralty required Berkeley to provide seamen to assist raise the *Henrietta.* P.R.O. Adm. 3/2, 3rd Jan.

25  For intention P.R.O. Adm. 3/1, 22nd June 1689; the dock matter was discussed at the Admiralty 22nd Jan. (for Cattewater). *Ibid.* For the topic generally *v.* Ehrman *op. cit.* p. 416–.

26  *H.M.C. Finch II.*

27  P.R.O. Adm. 3/2. P.R.O. Adm. 2/5, 29th Dec., *Dover* and *St Albans* sent.

28  *H.M.C. Finch II.* p. 260. 22nd/12th Nov., Danish Admiral to Prince George of Denmark, *London Gazette* (11th–14th Nov.). Hull 10th Nov. The ships were badly scattered–some put in at Leith, Shields, Peterhead. *Ibid.* various dates.

29  P.R.O. Adm. 3/2, 16th Oct. There the Soundings are so defined.

30  Bodleian Nairne Papers, vol. 1, fol. No. 42, p. 315. After 6th Sept.

31  *Ibid.* fol. No. 9, p. 300.

32  *Ibid.* fol. 74, p. 320.

33  *Ibid.* p. 323.

34  *Ibid.* p. 324.

35  *Ibid.* p. 325.

36  *Ibid.* p. 326.

37  P.R.O. Adm. 3/2, 31st Oct., 5th Nov.

38  P.R.O. Adm. I 5253. The Naze? Whiteness–n. of N. Foreland? Foreness further inside the Thames Estuary?

A very human entry in Admiralty Minutes (P.R.O. Adm. 3/2, 17th Dec.) may be of interest. Elizabeth Colvin, widow of James Colvin, wounded at Bantry 'which wounds not being Cured was the Occasion of his being drowned in the *Pendennis*' (this certified by Captain Churchill) prays bounty, she being 'in very great distress with two children'.

A minute, 4th Dec., indicates that the survivors of *Pendennis* were to be 'turned over', 6 months' pay required for them.

39  P.R.O. Adm. I 5253. For attempt to weigh P.R.O. Adm. 3/2, 24th April 1690. The cause of disaster was 'manning the yards' after the guns had been 'run over' . . . 'Extraordinary negligence'!

40  *Ibid.* Spell. 'The "Middle" and "Spile" are the names of a drying patch about 7 miles north of Warden Point, Sheppey', *North Sea Pilot,* III, p. 306.

41  *v.* p. 326 *ante* and Russell's reference to pilots 'almost dead with fear'.

42  P.R.O. Adm. 3/2.

43  *Ibid.* under date.

44  *Ibid.* under date.

45  *Ibid.* 24th Oct.

46  *Ibid.* 17th Oct. for gift; 24th Aug. Nottingham–Admiralty for authority to repair and charge.

47  *London Gazette* (18th–21st Nov.). Newcastle, 15th Nov. Yesterday sailed 200 laden colliers with convoy. Yarmouth, 15th Nov. Yesterday sailed 7 or 8 merchant ships under *Phoenix* convoy for Holland. This day about 200 laden colliers are come into the Road.

48  *Ibid.* (21st–24th Oct.). Portsmouth 19th Oct. Yesterday arrived at Caves
the *Deering* (one of the Hudson Bay ships . . . from Port Nelson, in the
northwest parts of America where he departed 3rd September).
     *Ibid.* (7th–11th Nov.). Falmouth 3rd Nov. Yesterday arrived the *Friends
Adventure* laden with sugars from Surinam . . . [she] parted about ten days
ago with a Dutch East India ship homeward bound which intended *to go
about Northwards.*
     *Ibid.* (28th Nov.–2nd Dec.). Barnstaple 26th Nov. Here is likewise
arrived the *Terra Nova* of this place from New-found-land.
     *Ibid.* (2nd–6th Jan.). Falmouth 30th Dec. Yesterday arrived the *James* of
Boston, in 9 weeks from Jamaica bound for London.
     N.B. The foregoing references are typical not exhaustive.

49  *Ibid.* (16th–19th Dec.). Plymouth 15th Dec. Yesterday arrived here . . .
*Yorke* and *Kings Fisher* from Berkeley's squadron which they left last
Thursday [12th] about 30 leagues W. of Scilly. They came to convoy the
*Elizabeth* of London, from Jamaica, the *Turkey Merchant*, from Virginia, and
a Dutch merchantman from Surinam. These three ships had not heard of
war till they fell in with our squadron. Last night arrived here *Providence* of
London, from the Canaries.

50  Article La Cour. I have not been able to trace this estimate *in* Raynal who,
presumably, borrowed from the earlier Sainte Croix quoted by Monentheuil, A., *Essai sur La Course, son histoire, sa réglementation, son abolition,* Paris
1898, p. 66. Monentheuil's reference to St Croix is *Histoire des progrès de la
puissance navale de l'Angleterre* t. II, p. 15. A work by White, T. E., *History
of the Rise and Progress of the Naval Power of England,* . . . is apparently a
translation of St Croix. [St Croix is not obtainable in the B.M., the Bodleian or the University Library, Cambridge, nor, for that matter, in the
Bibliothèque Nationale. The three main English libraries have no copy of
White; but there is one at the Admiralty.] For the Monentheuil reference
I am indebted to Clark, p. 126.

51  White, *op. cit.* p. 192.

52  Clark, *op. cit.* p. 127.

53  P.R.O. H.C.A. 26/1 Declarations. Letters of Marque. . . .

54  *S.P.Dom.* . . . *1688–1690* under date.

55  P.R.O. Adm. 3/2. 25th Sept. and *passim.*

56  P.R.O. Patent Rolls 1–14 William III (66/3326).

57  *Op. cit.* p. 106.

58  *London Gazette* (9th–12th Sept.).

59  P.R.O. State Papers, Foreign Entry Book, 1679–1704, S.P. 104/153 (cited
by Clark, p. 106).
     As William saw the matter:
          'The Trade of Sweden to France is generally in such comoditys as are
     necessary to their Fleet and for that reason altho we made no Treaty of
     Prohibition it cañot be expected we should allow it while we are at Warr
     with France . . . Their trade cheifly from France is of Wine and Salt and
     are the things they most complain of the want of. But since they can have
     better from Portugal and Spain . . .'
     Nottingham-Duncomb, 17th Jan. 1689/90.

60  P.R.O. Adm. 3/2.

61 *S.P.Dom.* . . . *1689–90*, pp. 273, 341.

62 *P.R.O.* Patent Rolls 1–14, William III (66/3326).

63 *du Mont, op. cit.* VII, pt ii, p. 301, Clark, *op. cit.* p. 36, states that the date given in du Mont, 22nd Oct., is incorrect and his emendation is followed.
   For a case in point see *S.P.Dom.* . . . *1688–90*, p. 388. Wm. Boghill of Glasgow, partner and freighter of the ship *Concord*, bound from Madras to Amsterdam, on 11th July 1689, was captured by two Frenchmen then retaken. Capt. John Layton of the *St Albans* considered *Concord* prize and plundered to the value of £2,605 as prize. Boghill petitions Parliament.

64 Clark, *op. cit.* p. 52.

65 *Ibid.* p. 61. For example of an official notice of sale see *London Gazette* (2nd–5th Dec.).

66 *Ibid.* p. 62.

67 P.R.O. Adm. 3/2.

68 *Ibid.*

69 An Abstract of the Estimates of the Debt of their Ma[ts] Navy as by the Severall Accoupts hereafter appeares Between the 1st of January 1671 & 30th of September 1689 viz

|  | £ | s. | d. |
|---|---:|---:|---:|
| On Bills for Stores & Wages to Ships & Yards Between the 1st of January 1671 & 24th March 1685 | 68,818 | 13 | 5 |
| On Bills for Stores &c. Between the 25th of March 1686 & 30th September 1689 | 16,226 | 5 | 8 |
| To Ticketts for seamen Discharg[d] for Service Between the 25th March 1686 & 30th September 1689 | 5,500 | – | – |
| To Wages to their Ma[ts] Ships Between the 25th March 1686 & the 30th September 1689 | 321,637 | 1 | 4 |
| To Wages Due to the severall yards Between the 25th March 1686 & 30th September 1689 | 75,736 | – | 7 |
| To the Freight of Ships Hyred into their Ma[ts] service to serve as Men of Warr & Tenders to the Fleets from the time of their first entring into the Service to the 30th September 1689 | 17,067 | 6 | 3 |
|  | 504,985 | 7 | 3 |
| Abate for Seamens Tickets in the Office as in 3[d] Article of this Accoupt that Summ being included in the Estimate due to the Ships | 5,500 | – | – |
|  | 499,485 | 7 | 3 |
| Whereunto is to be added y[e] Debt for the Victualling | 68,057 | 11 | 8 |
|  | 567,542 | 18 | 11 |

Beneath the document the signatures of Sir Richard Haddock (Comptroller), Sir John Tippetts (Surveyor), Sir John Berry (Comptroller of the Victualling Accounts), and James Sotherne (Clerk of the Acts).
   Entered in P.R.O. Adm. 49/173, f. 10 undated.

70 P.R.O. Adm. 3/2.

71 *Ibid.* For Sir George Treby, see *D.N.B.*

72  *Ibid.*

73  Shaw, *op. cit.*, v, IX, Pt 1, p. 61.

74  *Ibid.* p. 62.

75  *H.M.C. Finch II*, p. 259.

76  *Ibid.*

77  Shaw, *op. cit.* p. 63.

78  *Ibid.* p. 65. How well Thomas Papillon (1623–1702), Merchant of London, M.P. for Dover, deserved of William's government may be gathered from the *D.N.B.* notices of Papillon and Sir John Maynard (1602–1690). See also Papillon, A. F. W., *Memoirs of Thomas Papillon of London, Merchant*, 1887.

79  P.R.O. Adm. 3/2. For the text of the warrant, defining rights and duties, 21st Nov., see P.R.O. Adm. 2/4, p. 462, partly unreadable through ink smears, but apparently identical with the earlier 23rd/24th October draft, q.v. The *Patent Roll* endorsement reference is 1–14 Wm III, anno 2, dorso, 20th May.

80  *Ibid.* 20th Nov. For abstract of Order in Council, P.R.O. Adm. I 5139.

81  *Ibid.* 23rd and 27th Nov. London, Portsmouth, Plymouth, Dover, Liverpool, Milford, Harwich were the home ports selected.

82  P.R.O. Adm. 3/2.

83  Grey, A. *op. cit.*, p. 387–8.

84  *Ibid.* p. 394.

85  *Journals . . . H. of C.* 13th, 14th Nov. Grey, *op. cit.* pp. 411–421. There are *D.N.B.* notices of Powle, Clayton, Clarges, Ward, Howe, Littleton, Seymour, Birch, Hampden, Sacheverell. The History of Parliament Trust has yet to publish notices of M.P.s of this period.

86  *Journals . . . H. of C.* 18th Nov. Grey, *op. cit.* pp. 430–436.

87  *v.* p. 307. For biography and later career of this brother of the first Duke of Marlborough see *D.N.B.*

88  *Journals . . . H. of C.* 23rd Nov. Grey, *op. cit.* pp. 441–446.

89  *Ibid.* 5th Dec.

90  *Ibid.* under date and so throughout this section to . . . the admirals were left uncensured. Grey, *op. cit.* pp. 446–466.

91  Grey, *op. cit.* p. 406.

92  *Ibid.* p. 466.

93  *Ibid.* p. 473. William, 19th October, had asked the Commons to decide 'what they thought fit to give towards the Charges of the War for the next year'. The Commons had responded, 2nd November, by voting that up to £2,000,000 be added to the further revenue and the Land Tax bill represented an attempt to give substance to the undertaking.

94  *Journals . . . H. of C.* under date.
  *An Act for the Grant to the Majestyes of an Ayd of Two Shillings in the Pound for One Year* . . . William & Mary, 2 C. 1.
  *Statutes of the Realm*, v. VI, pp. 104–142–p. 141 for appropriation.

95  Ehrman, *op. cit.* pp. 338–9. The comments will repay attention.

96  Totals of Payments made by the Exchequer to the Navy 1689

| Period | £ | s. | d. | Purpose | £ | s. | d. |
|---|---|---|---|---|---|---|---|
| Jan. 14 | 22,821 | 0 | 0 | Current service | | | |
| to | 18,736 | 0 | 0 | Yards, ships | 111,557 | 18 | 3 |
| Mar. 7 | 70,000 | 0 | 0 | Victualling | | | |

| Mar. 16 | 123,216 | 14 | 0 | Current service | | | |
| to | 108,471 | 2 | 2 | Yards, ships | 327,387 | 16 | 2 |
| Sept. 30 | 95,700 | 0 | 0 | Victualling | | | |
| Oct. 1 | 39,320 | 0 | 0 | Current service | | | |
| to | 23,855 | 19 | 0 | Yards, ships | 142,740 | 5 | 6 |
| Dec. 31 | 79,564 | 6 | 6 | Victualling | | | |

£581,685 19 11

This table is based on easily identified lists in P.R.O. Adm. 49/173 and Shaw, *op. cit.*, pp. 274–It will not be entirely correct–some payment was made by the Treasury direct to creditors. But the margin of difference is small.

97 P.R.O. Adm. 1/3560, f.497.

98 The debt at 1st Jan. £200,000 (approx.). (*v.* p. 71).

It should be noted that none of the proceeds of the appropriation of £400,000 made to the Navy by the Act referred to p. 320 produced income for the year 1689.

99 Grey, *op. cit.* pp. 504–5.

100 Action by naval commanders was not infrequently vexatious or high-handed and harmful to the merchant. Two examples described in full in the *Journals H. of C.*, 11th Dec. 1689 (following, at p. 315, the entry for the 20th) may serve.

101 *Ibid.* p. 420.

102 P.R.O. Adm. 3/2.

103 *Ibid.* 6th Dec.

104 P.R.O. Adm. 3/2, under dates. *H.M.C. Finch II*, p. 263.

William's list–King William's Chest 6, No. 86 to be seen in *S.P.Dom. . . . 1688–90*, 5th Jan. 1690.

105 P.R.O. Adm. 3/2 *passim* and 15th(?) and 22nd Dec. at the Robes Chamber.

106 *The Earle of Torrington's speech to the House of Commons in November 1690 . . .* 1710, p. 12.

. . . not seeing Matters go so well in the Admiralty as I thought the Service requir'd, & that it was not in my Power to prevent it, I humbly beg'd and obtain'd the King's Leave to be dismissed from the Commission and giving any further attendance at that Board . . .

That Board was replaced 20th January (*v.* p. 332).

107 Foxcroft, *op. cit. II*, 'Spenser House Journals', p. 200.

108 *Earl of Torrington's Speech . . .* p. 14.

. . . and I appeal to him [Nottingham] whether I did not tell him, when I had urg'd many Reasons for strengthening our Fleet, which he only answered with, *You will be strong enough for the French*, 'My Lord, I know my business, and will do my best with what I have; but pray remember it is not my fault the Fleet is no stronger. I own I am afraid now in Winter, whilst the Danger may be remedy'd; and you will be afraid in Summer when it is past remedy. I could say more upon this Subject.'

109 But not in the King's own hand. *S.P.Dom. . . . 1689–90*, 5th Jan., p. 395.

110 P.R.O. Adm. 2/4, p. 471.

111 P.R.O. Adm. 3/2. The King changed his view because of letters received. The *London Gazette* (28th Nov.–2nd Dec.) published news 26th November/

5th December from the Hague, telling how on 29th/19th November Vice-Admiral Van de Putten and Lieutenant Admiral Evertsen, entering the harbour at Flushing, the latter flagship *Walcheren*, carried on a fresh south wind and flood tide, struck the head of the haven, holed and sank. It is possible that a copy of the just printed *Gazette* was brought to the Admiralty board-room table.

It could also have happened that a communication from Evertsen for William his Admiral-General, dated 5th December [25th November] and transmitted through Portland had reached its destination and Nottingham and the Admiralty been made aware of its contents. Warnsinck, *op. cit.* pp. 57–61 quotes from the report of the 'Advocaat fiscaal' of the Admiralty of Zeeland, to which the ship belonged, narrates the happening and its consequences and concludes by printing Portland's reply, 3rd January, with its assurance of royal understanding and commiseration.

112 *H.M.C. Finch II*, p. 262.
113 *Ibid.* p. 263.
114 P.R.O. Adm. 3/2.
115 *H.M.C. Finch II*, p. 263. Nottingham–Russell.
116 *London Gazette* (12th–16th Dec.). Deale 11th Dec.
117 *Ibid.* (19th–23rd Dec.). Hague, 22nd/12th Dec.
118 *Ibid.* (26th–30th Dec.). *Mary* yacht, 29th/19th Dec.
119 *Ibid.* (9th–13th Jan.). Middleburg, 11th/1st Jan.
    *H.M.C. Finch II*, p. 267, Russell–Nottingham.
120 As *London Gazette*, Note (10), for anchorage; and for weather *London Gazette passim*.

If, before leaving the Downs, Russell had heard no rumour of the loss of the *Walcheren*, he would, on reaching Dutch waters, gather reports of the disaster and reasonably congratulate himself on his persistent opposition to taking the *Duke* on the Dutch coast. It was (*v.* Warnsinck, *op. cit.* p. 57) in endeavouring to approach Flushing through the Spleet, past the Elleboog that, victim of gale and tide, Evertsen's flagship had got out of control.

The Rammekins was a well known fort on the east side of Flushing.

121 'their Majesties yautche' to which Russell refers, the *Mary*, was of 166 tons burden with a keel of 66 ft (the length of a cricket pitch!) beam of 21 ft, depth of hold less than 9 ft and draught of 7½ ft. She carried a crew of 20 to 30 and mounted 6 to 8 guns. 'Pepys's Register of Ships', Naval Manuscripts in the Pepysian Library (*v.* Authorities). Appreciation of the congestion and conditions aboard must be left to the imagination.
    For Russell's letters *H.M.C. Finch II*, pp. 267, 268(bis), 269, under dates.

122 *London Gazette*, (16th–20th Jan.). Deale, 18th Jan.
    *H.M.C. Finch II*, p. 269, Russell–Nottingham–with derogatory remarks upon 'this crowd'!

123 P.R.O. Adm. 3/2, 18th Nov., 12th Dec. *H.M.C. Finch II*, 5th Dec., p. 263.
124 P.R.O. Adm. 2/5. *London Gazette*, 20th–23rd Jan. Deale, 21st Jan.
125 *Ibid.* (20th–23rd Jan.). Deale, 21st Jan. Russell wrote to Nottingham from the Downs on the 20th asking what he should do with Danish soldiers whom he 'took in' in Zealand. *H.M.C. Finch II*, p. 269.

126  P.R.O. Adm. 3/3. Ashby received orders there on 14th Jan.

127  P.R.O. Adm. 51/4174.

128  *London Gazette* (27th–30th Jan.). Portsmouth, 28th Jan.

129  P.R.O. Adm. 3/2 and 8/1. 1st Feb. 1690. Ship List.

130  *London Gazette* (27th–30th Jan.). Portsmouth 28th Jan.

131  For biography see *D.N.B.*

132  P.R.O. Adm. 3/2. 17th Nov.

133  *Ibid.* 24th Sept. and later.

134  *Ibid.* 28th Sept. and later. For Inchiquin see *D.N.B.*

135  *Ibid.* 20th Dec. He appealed to the Admiralty and was told his Instructions should prove satisfactory.

136  *Ibid.* 3/2.

137  *Ibid.* under date.

138  P.R.O. Adm. 2/5.

139  For winds: Russell had been held at the North Foreland by easterly winds on the 3rd. *London Gazette* (2nd–5th Dec.). Deale 5th. Berkeley himself sailed from Plymouth westward on the 7th.
      *Ibid.* (9th–12th Dec.). Plymouth 8th, etc.

140  *London Gazette* (9th–12th Dec.). Portsmouth 10th Dec.

141  P.R.O. Adm. 3/2.

142  P.R.O. Adm. 2/5. Fully summarized in Burchett, pp. 36–8.

143  P.R.O. Adm. 3/3. 3rd, 9th and 14th Jan. for Admiralty orders. The crews of outgoing merchantmen would normally carry 'protections' granted by the Admiralty. 'Illegal' taking of sailors from ordinary vessels was always a temptation to a naval captain with a reduced crew and the Admiralty Minutes contain numerous entries of censure of a practice which could produce undesired results, e.g. certain ships of Topsham were left in the Downs disabled because the captains of the *Cadiz Merchant* and *Sampson* (fireships) had taken out men. Rear-Admiral Ashby, 23rd December, was ordered to redress.

144  28th December *London Gazette* (30th Dec.–2nd Jan.). Portsmouth 31st Dec. This in consequence of an order of the 26th by the Admiralty to the Navy Board?

145  P.R.O. Adm. 3/2.

146  P.R.O. Adm. 3/3.

147  *Ibid.* 22nd Jan.

148  *Ibid.* 11th Jan. for orders to Ashby, Killigrew, Berkeley, concerning merchantmen attempting to sail and *London Gazette* (20th–24th Feb.), Portsmouth 21st Feb., for the numbers of waiting merchantmen. The Admiralty Minutes referred to are in P.R.O. Adm. 3/3.

149  *H.M.C. Finch II*, p. 269.

150  *S.P.Dom. . . . 1688–90*, 6th Jan., p. 398 for revocation; for reconstitution, 20th Jan. Patent Rolls. For Herbert see *D.N.B.*

151  Ehrman, *op. cit.* p. 322.

152  *H.M.C. Finch II*, p. 275.

153  P.R.O. Adm. 3/2 under date. Charles Sergison who acted from 26th Dec. 1689. Patent 6th Feb. 1690.

# CHAPTER XII

# Russell – d'Amfréville
# The King – Torrington

## *1st February 1689/90 – 14th June 1690*

---

### ARGUMENT

*Russell (Queen of Spain aboard, moody and ill-disposed to accept the offered command of the Blue Squadron of the 1690 Fleet), with Van Almonde, Killigrew and the Streights trade, clears Spithead 14th February, St Helens 20th February, seeks the shelter of Torbay 23rd February and is there at the month's end.*

*William, who would have preferred a descent on France, hastens preparations for crossing to Ireland – Parliament dissolved; fast days instituted; supplication enjoined for the royal safety, the prosperity of arms in Ireland and of the 'naval forces'.*

*Torrington to command the Allied Fleet – A searching questionnaire on fleet preparedness addressed to the Navy Board, the Victuallers and the Ordnance Office to be answered by the 26th – the Navy Board to be especially assistant to a new Committee for 'Transporting the Army to Ireland'.*

*No squadron, January to March, replaces Berkeley in the Channel approaches – 17th/7th March, d'Amfréville, with 27 warships convoying from Brest reinforcements for James, reaches Cork unhindered 22nd/12th March – Simultaneously Russell, Killigrew and Van Almonde work out from Torbay with 400 merchantmen – Killigrew and Van Almonde stand on with the trade – Russell reaches Coruña (the Groyne) 16th March and on the 27th, disembarks the Spanish Queen – Wright's West Indies squadron and trade leave Plymouth 9th March – Deepening Naval Debt and its consequences.*

*d'Amfréville with l'échange convenu, five raw Irish regiments, has returned to France, 19th/9th April (Chateaurenault's Bantry exploit repeated but without the battle!) Shovell active in Dublin Bay – Russell, the 25th, back in Plymouth – Killigrew and Van Almonde storm-battered in Cadiz, where they will be found well into May.*

*Gossip and fact concerning tardy acceptance by Torrington of his commission as commander-in-chief – He hoists his flag at the Nore, 10th May, returns to London, rejoins his flagship in the Downs 30th May, too early to learn the names of those appointed, 2nd June, as an advisory 'cabinet' to the Queen (in the King's absence) or details of interlocking nominations to the Board of Admiralty – Torrington's strength 28 rates, 12 fireships, 17 Dutch warships and 3 fireships – Instructions reach him – He is, perforce, content with royal assurance of the extent of his authority over officers of the Marines he is taking aboard – With his men in health and the odds not too great he hopes for success.*

*Irish waters – logistic matters – the King's passage, convoyed by Shovell, Hoylake to Carrickfergus 11th–14th June – Shovell and his ships to be sent at once to the Main Fleet.*

*Torrington off St Helens 14th June – His adversary Tourville, out of Brest the day before with 70 Vaisseaux en ligne, 5 frégates légères, 18 brûlots and other ships.*

*Killigrew and Van Almonde, alerted on 9th May, head south to Gibraltar and Tetuan Bay to intercept Chateaurenault who, out from Toulon intent to pass the Streights and join Tourville in Brest, outsails them – They, 20th May, return to Cadiz to forward remaining trade–14th June, the admirals, with 12 sail of men-of-war, fireships, tenders and merchantmen are distant from the Lizard a round thousand miles and will not sight it for another 28 days!*

*So the ships of Killigrew, Admiral designate of the Blue Squadron of Torrington's Grand Fleet, the vessels with Shovell, Rear-Admiral designate of that squadron are destined to be absent when, shortly, issue is joined between Torrington and Tourville off Beachy Head!*

---

ON THE 9th February – another fortnight gone – Russell again to Nottingham:[1]

> Least by my long stay heare your lordshipp should belive I am faulen in love with the Quene or Spitthed I trouble you with . . . my ill fortune, a contrary wind; that, and the trouble I have undergon, has allmost broake my heart . . . whether I shall ever recover my quandom strength God knows.

Russell was in a thoroughly bad mood. A letter from the Admiralty, sent by express on the 3rd February, with request for reply by express, lay on his table; now in his hand another, of the 7th, express also, enclosing a copy of the former and like request for express reply. He was offered the command of Blue Squadron of the Summer Fleet. Whom would he desire for captain? Sir John Ashby would be his Rear Admiral.[2] Russell brings himself to the point:

> The King desines me for the sea next summer . . . a litell hard to goe into a shipp which I am seure will not be man'd, but indede I have the same feare of the whole fleate . . . I heare Sir John Perrey [Berry] is ordred Vice Admirall of the Red, which I supos he will not except on, but my post mought tempt him . . . I belive he woud do the King as good if not better servis than myself without ralary. If I could be dispenced with this summer att sea . . . I should be very glad off itt, for besides my health is not in soe good a condition as I could wish, my one affaires in England is in much wors, but though I shall be glad to be excused I shall never desier itt when my servis may be of any consequence to his Majesty and my country. I must desier your lordshipp to recommend me to some of the Sea Ports to be chose a member for this parliment, I have troubled you a nuff.

'The [Admiral] doth protest too much methinks!' Is not the critic of Torrington's 'disservice' (see p. 332 *ante*) an admiral disappointed of supreme command? Away back in December (see

p. 324 *ante*) the name of Russell had appeared in the royal list as
that of Admiral designate of the 1690 Allied Fleet. The time taken,
and likely yet to be spent in performance of the mission to Spain,
must, in any case, have proved fatal to Russell's prospects. It was
St Valentine's Day before the Admiral, with Killigrew and Van
Almonde, marshalling 150–200 merchantmen, could work out of
Spithead – only to be at once penned in St Helens Bay! There,
till the 20th February they remained. Down Channel, Russell was
compelled on the 23rd to seek shelter of Torbay. Again he swung
embayed – for another fortnight. The ill wind gave more than
ample time for the West Country traders assembled at Plymouth
to join him.[3]

King William had long tended to run away from his Irish
problem:

| | |
|---|---|
| May 27th 1689 | Said if he would be rightly understood he would land in France to save Ireland |
| June 2nd | Said there was but one reason to appoint the Rendezvous at Milford and that was not to be told *viz* more convenient to go from thence into France. He hath such a mind to France that it would incline one to think hee tooke England onely in his way. |
| June 6th | Said he had a great mind to land in France and that was the best way to save Ireland – Still this ran in his mind. |
| June 24th | If he could bring people to it going to France was the only thing to be done. I asked him whether it was because he had a mind to command the army in France – he said nothing but he did not deny it. |

These remarks to Halifax are evidence as valid of William's mind
and purpose as any other entries in the 'Spenser House Journals'.[4]
A second Henry V? To us the notion is quixotic and before
January 1690 William himself had recognized there could be no
détour from destiny. He must to Ireland! London learned the
news in the first week of the year. In early February citizens
gossiped that Sir Christopher Wren had 'compleated the itinerant
house' for the King 'to carry into Ireland to lye in'; learned, the

7th February, of Parliament dissolved, a new one to be called for the 20th March; gathered, from the posted Proclamation of the 20th that general fast-days were fixed for the 12th March and each third Wednesday of the month as long as the War should last – penitence enjoined and supplication for the safety of His Majesty's person abroad, for prosperity to his arms in Ireland and the 'naval forces'. Newsletters of the 27th confirmed renewed military activity in Ireland – the burning of Cavan.[5]

In the quickening pace of the King's Irish and wider preparations the Admiralty with its subsidiaries was caught up. The minute-book for 13th February received a surprising entry:

A letter to be written to my Lord Torrington to acquaint him y$^t$ the Commission is signd to comand their Mats ffleet for this Expedition and desier to know when his Lord$^p$ will come hither to receive the same and take the Oathes . . . an order is sent to the Navy Board for his pay to the date of his Commission.

One must presume that the King, without whose knowledge this step could not have been taken, preferred to put practicality before pique. Promotions were made – on the 13th Delavall, at Portsmouth, to the rank of Rear-Admiral of the Red; on the 17th, Killigrew and Ashby (who were with Russell in St Helen's Bay) each to that of Vice Admiral of the Red, the latter after one day as Vice Admiral of the Blue.[6] Admirals first – ships to follow?

On Sunday the 23rd February, the Admiralty Commissioners left conference with the King and councillors at the Robes Chamber, charged to present to the Navy Board, the Victuallers and Ordnance Office searching questionnaires; the Navy Board to report on the material condition and manning of each ship designed for service in the Main Fleet; the Victuallers to state how soon the said ships could be provisioned (and what money would be required for the purpose); the Ordnance to indicate the measure of its degree of ability to supply gunners' stores. All returns to be in the King's hands via the Admiralty the following Wednesday, the 26th, by the evening! And the morning of that day the Admiralty, minuting that the Irish Committee of the Privy Council had appointed Commissioners Sir Peter Rich, Mr Joseph Carpenter, Mr Robert Henley and Mr Bayle to act with

Captains Henry Greenhill, Atkinson, Ackerman and Nicholls, 'to undertake the whole care in takeing up prepareing &c the Shiping for Transporting the Army to Ireland', directed the Navy Board to secure co-operation of its captains and agents already at the task.

The Navy Board, with reason to be well satisfied, though Schomberg seldom was, with the transport achievements of Captains Greenhill and Atkinson, whether operating from Glasgow, Liverpool, Hoylake or Chester or the opposite shore could welcome the appointment of Sir Peter Rich and his colleagues. It could be confident that Duke Wurtemberg and 3,000 more Danes would be safely shipped from the Dee or Mersey in the next fortnight. This Board's troubles were much nearer home. Its scrupulously detailed answer to the questionnaire, punctually on its way to the King, would not reassure His Majesty.

What steps could be taken to stimulate manning? Answer—
'Wee are mightily at a loss to know what answer to make thereunto'. The 'Great fleet' of merchantmen recently 'suffered to go out' had taken the seamen. But there were over forty small ships, each attached to ships designate for the fleet (details given) cruising the coasts to pounce on likely seafolk. The Board could only recapitulate for royal choice the measures resorted to in previous Wars. One possible move King and Council had already anticipated. A Proclamation would appear on the morrow morning:

Whereas divers seamen and mariners have lately . . . removed themselves into . . . obscure place in the Inland Countries . . . to escape the press . . . their Majesties, by advice of their Privy Council . . . do hereby straitly charge . . . all seamen and mariners that they forthwith render themselves . . .

As for the readiness of ships (in hulls, masts rigging, boatswains' and carpenters' stores) passing through the yards to take their place in the Grand Fleet, tabulation, so the Board stated, would show that of thirty-four larger rates (first to fourth) only five were complete and the rest would not be ready till well into March. The twelve new fireships building would not be available till May. And none of this programme could be promised if £50,000 a week for a fortnight and £10,000 a week afterwards

could not be guaranteed to the Commissioners. A note of expostu-
lation, though necessarily subdued, is unmistakable. The returns
made by the Victuallers and the Ordnance were not likely to be
more committal.[7]

The Admiralty's Ship Distribution List of the 1st March,[8]
under a quill flourish heading 'Maine Fleete in the Channell',
first listed the thirty-four rates just referred to then added eight
thirds and eight fourths at sea. Of those, seven thirds and one
fourth would be away till Russell's mission was complete; one
third and two fourths were under Sir Clowdisley Shovell moving for
long service into the Irish Sea; two fourths were cruising between
Land's End and Scilly, one fourth leaving the Nore, one convoy
for Newcastle, one for Jersey. No move to rendezvous had begun.

From the time Berkeley brought in his Anglo-Dutch squadron,
on the 24th December (see p. 305 *ante*), fourth rates 'two and two'
sailed to the Soundings on anti-privateer patrol. To guard the
Channel approaches and, by implication, bar the back door to
Ireland, no squadron had replaced him. Strategy which the King
had held essential October to December, more necessary than ever
since the purposed capture of Kinsale had not been achieved,
was not pursued as the days lengthened. The 1st March – Torrington a commander-in-chief designate without flagship, fleet, rendezvous or orders; Russell slave to his queen and huge, ill-
conglomerating flock of merchantmen; no single English warship
nearer to the littoral of Munster than the Isles of Scilly – 180
nautical miles! And already, on the 28th February, Shovell, in
*Monck*, anchored in Plymouth had been warned by a ship re-
patriating prisoners from St. Malo of unusual activity in Brest[9]
and pushed on to his command, of quite negligible force, in the
Irish Sea;[10] three days hence Russell from Torbay would tell
Nottingham he believed a strong French force at sea and attack on
Plymouth 'feazable'.[11]

On Friday, 7th/17th March d'Amfréville cleared Brest and
Russell got out of Torbay – the moves of each unknown to the
other!

The force which the Lieutenant Général took to sea to convoy
and convey le comte de Lauzun and his troops, listed as 6,511 men,

351 officers in 115 companies of the regiments Zurlanbert, Mérode, Tamichon, Forest, La Marche, Tournaisis, consisted of twenty-seven warships and the auxiliaries.[12] It therefore exceeded by three the combatant squadron Châteaurenault commanded at Bantry and included seventeen of the twenty-four then under his flag. Mounting some 1,500 guns, d'Amfréville's was, in fact, the more powerful armament. To particularize – the asterisks denoting participation at Bantry – *L'Ardent* (66)*, *L'Arrogant* (58)*, *L'Emporté* (42)*, *Le Vermandois* (60)*, *Le Content* (66), *Le Prince* (58), *Le Neptune* (46)*, *Le Diamant* (54)*, *Le Français* (48)*, *L'Entre-prenant* (56)*, *Le Saint-Michel* (56)*, *Le Trident* (44), *Le Furieux* (64)*, *L'Esclatant* (70), *Le Fort* (66)*, *Le Léger* (44)*, *Le Sérieux* (64)*, *L'Apollon* (58)*, *Le Bon* (?), *Le Modéré* (50)*, *Le Glorieux* (62), *Le Marquis* (58), *Le Sans-Pareil* (60), *Le Brave* (58), *L'Arc-en-Ciel* (44)*, *Le Courageux* (56)*, *Le Mauré* (44), d'Amfréville held a course that took him southerly and westerly right across but clear of the path Russell must follow to reach Spain. Two captains, de Relingues and Desnots de Champmeslin, intercepted stray English merchantmen.[13] On the 12th/22nd, St Patrick's Day (d'Avaux neatly observed to Louis that exactly a year previously James had reached Kinsale) d'Amfréville began to unship Lauzun's troops on the quays of Cork[14] – of Cork not of Limerick, which was where Louvois would have had them deposited.[15] To honour 'l'échange convenu', demanded by Louis of James, five raw Irish regiments, those of Montcassel, Butler, O'Bryen, Fielding and Dillon, were rounded up and put aboard.

The squadron was under orders for immediate return to France. d'Avaux, Louis' long suffering exemplary ambassador, now, with de Rosen, recalled to Paris, went aboard d'Amfréville's *L'Esclatant*. On 2nd/12th April he reported the winds continuously adverse to sailing.[16]

On the night of Saturday the 8th and during Sunday the 9th, Russell, off the Start, gained sea-room. The 'mighty train' (the phrase used by the correspondent of the *London Gazette* aboard the Admiral) the concourse of English and Netherland merchantmen (Danes, Swedes, Hamburgers and Lübeckers among them) now not less than 400 in number – 'very troublesome' – was shepherded between the warships. Russell in the *Duke*, with seven thirds *Berwick, Rupert, Suffolk, Expedition, Hope, Northumberland, Plymouth*, and a fourth the *Deptford* ranged ahead in line. Van Almonde in *Gelderland* (72) was assigned the port station with fourteen other warships *Ridderschap* (60), *Wapen van Hoorn* (52), *Noordholand* (70), *Holland* (70), *Elswout* (52), *Schattershoef* (46), *Haarlem* (64), *Amsterdam* (64), *Gaasterland* (52), *Vlaardingen* (46), *Vere* (60), *Zierikzee* (62), *Vrede* (52), *Vrijheid* (72). Killigrew in *Resolution* the starboard, with three thirds, *Eagle, Burford, Montague*, six fourths *Newcastle, Greenwich, Happy Return, Oxford, Portland, Tyger*, and smaller ships; the last four named of Russell's thirds had been picked up in Torbay and would as soon as they could be spared by him be sent to the Soundings.

Early on Monday the 10th a Dutch privateer from windward made contact with Russell and startled with report of '30 sail of men-of-war and 20 other ships about 20 leagues to westward', 'so that' writes our correspondent, 'must have been the French going for Ireland'. And surely a great relief to Russell, his Queen aboard, that the French were hulled-down and distant westerly rather than likely to be about to appear over the port horizon. On Tuesday the 11th, after a few Dutch ships had left for the West Indies and some for Bilbao, Killigrew and Almonde, in the afternoon, stood on for Cadiz and Russell with eight English and six Dutch ships parted for the Groyne. Aboard the *Duke* a fire, happily quickly extinguished, threatened the powder room! As the flagship approached Spain on the 14th − it was Good Friday − 'at 12 o'clock three artists made their observations and found . . . 34 leagues from Cape Ortegal and 43 from Cape Finisterre and the Groyne between them'. Saturday the 15th brought report of land; the nightfall a storm with wind 'extreme high [that] made the ship for all her greatness pitch and roll that there was no standing for anybody'. By this time, victims of the Bay, the condition of the crowded distinguished passengers must have beggared description.

On the 16th, Easter Sunday morning, so soon as the squadron was observed from La Coruña its governor sent out a pilot, who, for greater safety, steered his charge into the small northward neighbour port of El Ferol. Even so, as the storm built up, the great second rate *Duke* drave ashore − only by good fortune and much labour to be refloated. The union was dipped as Maria Anna, Queen of Spain, landed on the 27th March, seven months after quitting home and at the end of a voyage of three, during which time she had but once, through the kindness of Russell and Captain Stanley, the *Duke* riding in Torbay, been taken ashore.[17]

Wright's West Indies squadron – his convoy of a third, six or seven fourths, lesser vessels and considerable trade had weighed on the 5th March from Spithead, cleared Plymouth on the 9th, almost caught up with Russell at exit from the Channel and, far out beyond Scilly, run into the fury of the storm of the 16th. The *Jersey*, scared soldiers aboard, limped back dismasted to Portsmouth.[18]

To return to England. Money did reach the Navy Board – and Victuallers and Ordnance – after that alarm of the 26th February. It had never *not* 'spurted' to them before that particular date in the quarter – part from the ordinary revenue, part from the appropriated £400,000 (see p. 320 *ante*). Broadly, between the 1st January and the 31st March, £198,333 passed to the Navy of which £135,000 came from the appropriated money.[19] But though money trickled spasmodically it was never enough. The total naval debt deepened and that which stood on the 1st January at £782,000 totalled on the 31st March £867,203.3.3.[20] It would be difficult to overstress the human hardship caused by the irregularity of payment of wages to the yards and seamen. Mid-February had seen the whole yard at Deptford thirteen months in arrear and petitioning. Result? Referred to the Admiralty; passed to the Treasury![21] In mid-March the more militant wives of the unpaid workmen at Chatham forced their way inside the Admiralty board room and were placated only when 'tould the King would be moved therein'.[22] Yet workers stayed at the yards and at this time did, under stress and even in hunger, largely produce the repairs conditionally promised on the 26th. The sailor, volunteer or pressed, his pay quite commonly a year overdue, himself, once in the service liable to be 'turned over' from ship to ship without consent, his legal wife possibly penniless, had no remedy but desertion with the risk of the rope if betrayed or found. The inland press had by this time become intense. On the 17th March the

Yarmouth magistrates shut the gates and went from house to house to catch seamen;[23] on the 24th forty-one seamen from very inland Huntingdonshire were forwarded to Blackwall by Lord Manchester.[24]

In early April, false reports circulated that d'Amfréville's powerful squadron had returned to Brest. It would appear that it left Cork on the 17th April and, buffeted by contrary winds, reached Brest on the 4th May.[25] Its commander had been precluded by nature of his orders and responsibility for the five thousand exile soldiery in his care from temptation to attack Schomberg's flock of Irish Sea transports – which Shovell, as Torrington later pointed out, with *Monck* and four fourths and five or six 'little things' could scarce have protected. Bantry repeated – without the battle and without, as far as one can gather, knowledge in London of what was happening though Captain Byng of the *Dover*, cruising off the Saltees, on the 13th March, actually observed eighteen of d'Amfréville's ships in Cork Harbour and duly reported to Shovell at the end of the month.[26] On the 19th April Shovell achieved a picturesque venture into Dublin Bay hauling out the *Pelican* – already notable in these pages. His strength was augmented to three thirds, six fourths with more 'little things' before April ended and the work of military transport in all its aspects gathered uninterrupted momentum.[27]

Back from the Groyne, in *Suffolk*, blue ensign at the main, five other vessels in company *Rupert, Berwick, Deptford, Expedition* and a Dutch vessel (two left in the Soundings) Russell anchored off Plymouth on the 25th. He reached Portsmouth three days later and there saw the last of the 'persons of quality' who had attended the Queen from Holland.[28] There Russell would learn that a suggestion he had made to Shrewsbury (why not to Nottingham?) just before he [Russell] had left England, had indeed been acted upon embodied in an order to him as Admiral dated the 9th March, and personally signed by the King. Before it could be delivered, Russell had already cleared Torbay![29]

Killigrew's orders (see p. 330 *ante*) required him to send in the Lisbon ships and make for Cadiz, there to watch the movements of the French and, with various convoys and to a time table, dispatch to and collect from Malaga, Alicante, Genoa, Livorno, Naples, Messina, Zante, Gallipoli, Constantinople, Smirna, Scanderoon,[30] the now much delayed trade. There were other duties imposed – the delivery of presents to the rulers of Algiers and Tripoli, the collection of brimstone, and work at the rudimentary base, Gibraltar. The particular royal order just referred to – the fruit of Russell's suggestion – which had arrived too late for delivery to Russell at Torbay – required that Killigrew should send into the Mediterranean only the four fourths and two smaller vessels detailed to convoy the trade, cancel the rest of his programme of tracking French movements and delivering presents to corsair rulers and, with the fourteen English and Dutch large warships at his command, head for home to join the gathering Main Fleet. Redrafted in appropriate terms, the order, on the 14th March, was sent to Killigrew at Cadiz.[31] As it was, Killigrew and Van Almonde, more than Russell and Wright, had experienced the terror of the storm – Van Almonde, with Evertsen his subordinate, while skirting the Portugal coast, taking in the trade behind Ilha Berlenga (the Burlings) to Lisbon, Killigrew, while standing on to Cadiz. Van Almonde's flagship *Ridderschap* – sunk; *De Vreijheid* – mastless, abandoned; Killigrew's flagship *Resolution* – main mast over the side; ship on ship 'damnified' in sails and rigging; merchantmen in numbers had disappeared! It was well on in April before the body of the ships, convoy and merchantmen, could be found gathered in Cadiz Bay – the refloated *Duke* and other warships sent on by Russell from the Groyne not arriving till the 20th. Only after altercation could the admirals secure the facilities of Puntall, the inner harbour, for purposes of repair. Hamburg traders, which so far had enjoyed protection of the convoy, slipped away, abortively pursued, with suspected contraband for Toulon and Marseilles.[32]

It may be taken for granted that the letter which, on the 13th February last, the Secretary of the Admiralty was instructed to send to Lord Torrington, inviting him to attend to swear the oaths and receive his newly signed commission to command the 1690 Fleet, was not forwarded; no draft of the letter, no record of dispatch is extant. Though Torrington had, since the 13th February, been regarded as 'appointed', he was 'uncommissioned'.

Suddenly, in mid-April, the talk of the town: 'The Earl of Torrington is disgusted . . . he will not hold by commission from the lords of the Admiralty, unless he may have a particular commission from his Majestie constituting him admiral',[33] and Van Citters on 25th April/5 Meij reporting, but more precisely, to the States General – to give an English version of his Dutch:

> My Lords, After the rumour, however uncertain, had been in circulation for some days that Lord Torrington wished to resign his commission as Admiral and that he Torrington preferred not to be placed under the commissioners of the admiralty and take orders from it, but that, being at sea, he wished to act according to what he deemed to be in the best interests of *her* majesty, and during the expedition to fill all posts that would become vacant and such like, and that he wished in such matters to be subject simply and solely to his most eminent majesty, so did he last Tuesday, being unable to achieve his desire, lay down his charge and commission.

What else the diplomat had to say – concerning possible substitute admirals (Haddock likeliest) and analysis of an additional rumour (concerned with the City's lieutenancies) that Nottingham contemplated resignation – took time; and, before the ink was sanded, an interruption! 'While I write I hear that Lord Torrington on the receipt of some satisfaction has accepted his commission again.'[34] Had Torrington threatened resignation? And, if so, what had inspired his conduct? Prudence or presumption? Allowance must be made for the commander-in-chief of an Anglo-Dutch fleet who might – the times being what they were and the King shortly to go abroad, prospectively distrust a Queen's governance operating, as he would foresee, under the advice of a select council – a governance able in turn to influence the Admiralty. Were coming events indeed casting their shadows before? Or was there no more at the back of the gossip than Torrington's fear, and reaction to the fear, that, although any Admiralty commission to a commander-in-chief would (as Torrington well knew) adequately empower to fill naval vacancies and supplant for naval incompetence, such commission might not safeguard him, Torrington, in dealing with officers of the two Marine (quasi-soldier) regiments, ordered to be taken aboard ships of his Fleet? Companies of one regiment, that bearing his own name were to be shipped at the Downs; others, of Lord Pembroke's regiment, at Portsmouth. 'Some satisfaction' is mentioned. The cynic would point to calculated magnanimity of the King. On the last day of the month, the town talk was renewed: 'The earl of Torrington is now better satisfied and hath his commission as admiral to putt in and turn out any officers as he thinks fit and the King hath given him 3000 l per annum of the lands belonging to the late queen Mary.'[35] Those lands were the 'Ten Thousand Acres' known as the Peterborough and Bedford level – a gift clear of all liability for bank repair and sewerage.

Torrington's commission as admiral, quite customary in form, and his warrant to hold courts-martial, duplicates of the authorizations of the 15th March of the preceding year, issued out of the Admiralty on the 28th April over the signatures of Pembroke, Lee, Lowther and Chicheley. When recording the April documents in the great 'out-letter copybook' Sotherne's clerk, as the exceptional erasures and alterations reveal, had both a February dated commission and February dated warrant beside him.[36]

At the close of April, two firsts, six seconds and four thirds swung at the Buoy of the Nore; another third lay at Blackstakes; four more were in the Hope; there were waiting at Spithead or Portsmouth or in the Downs a second and perhaps ten thirds; a few fifths could be called on and a number of fireships were loading their fireworks. These components of the Main Fleet had at least left the yards – whether or not fully manned and stored, or the men paid, is another matter.[37] To the *Royal Soveraigne* at the Buoy of the Nore Captain Johnson of the *Phubbs* yacht conveyed the 'Admiral of their Majesties Fleet'.[38] Captain Neville received him, 'May 10 Faire wether w^th a small gale at E:N:E my lord Torrington came aboard & call'd a Councell of Warr wee fired 21 Gunns to answr ye Salutes of all ye Shipps'. And 21 more guns bellowed that evening from the Fleet flagship as Rooke ran up the red to the mizzen of the *Dutchess*.

Torrington went back to London on or before the 21st May leaving Rooke to take the Nore vessels in gale weather to the Downs, where he anchored on the 23rd, saluting, with eleven guns, the flag of Vice Admiral (of the Red) Ashby, spread at the foretop of the *Berwick*. A few days later, the 29th, Rear Admiral (of the Blue) Delavall hoisted his new flag of Vice Admiral (of the Blue) at the foretop of the *Coronation*(?) the occasion demanding nineteen guns; and, 'it being Restoration Day' twenty-one more were added. Not in the best of tempers – he had just been set upon in his coach by footpads and robbed[39] – Torrington was piped back at cloudy nightfall of the 30th to the quarter deck of *Royal Soveraigne* which answered a rowdy welcome with a final thirty-one.[40]

During his self-granted(?) leave in London Torrington would find the Board of Admiralty entering new premises, Judge Jeffries' old house in Duke Street Westminster. He would learn that a bill of the new Parliament authorizing administrative action by Her Majesty during His Majesty's absence from the Kingdom had received, on the 20th May, the King's assent, that three days later, His Majesty, attending Parliament had declared that he could no longer delay his departure for Ireland and desired the Houses to adjourn. But, till Torrington had been several days returned to shipboard, he would not know that the marquis Caermarthen, the earls Nottingham, Devonshire, Dorset, Marlborough, Monmouth and Pembroke, Sir John Lowther and Admiral Russell had been chosen, on the 2nd June, as an advisory 'cabinet'; nor would he be aware that the Board of Admiralty had been augmented. The resignation (or removal) of Sir John Chicheley had dropped the Admiralty Commissioners to four – the Earl of Pembroke, Sir John Lowther, the Earl of Carbery and Sir Thomas Lee; Admiral Russell, Sir John Onslow and Captain Henry Priestman had been called on to join them. So the Queen's Council and the Admiralty interlocked – with Nottingham already virtually a 'minister of marine' and Pembroke, Lowther and Russell on both Council and Board. Russell quickly decided not to go to sea. The official Ship Distribution List for the 1st June might show him Admiral of the Blue for Torrington's Grand Fleet, the first rate *St Andrew* his flagship; but that allocation was changed on 3rd June – and the absent Killigrew given the vacated rank, place and flag. Shovell at the same time became Rear Admiral of the Blue.[41] And at court an address of loyalty was presented to His Majesty on behalf of the Flag Captains and

Captains of the Fleet and Sir Ralph Delavall confirmed in the order of knighthood.[42]

On Saturday the 31st May aboard *Royal Soveraigne* was held the inevitable council of war and scouts were sent to cruise off Beachy. Torrington reported to Nottingham. Under his flag he could count twenty-eight rates (two first, six seconds, seventeen thirds, two fourths, one fifth) and twelve fireships as well as seventeen Dutch warships (named with guns, complements and captains) and three fireships. With the wind in the west he could not sail and would take aboard his own regiment of Marines – to the extent to which it reported at Deale and Dover. Clearly he was not at ease as to the limits of his authority over Marine officers and demanded, 'whether it was not the King's pleasure [he] should have further Instructions than those very lame ones . . . received from the Admiralty'.[43] (Bearing date the 26th May the Instructions were, as a matter of fact, cast in traditional of rather lengthy form and were entirely apposite to the needs of the hour. Ignored for the nonce by Torrington, consideration of their content can be set aside till the strategic aspects of the coming campaign come to be considered.)[44] In a letter, of the 1st June, crossing with Torrington's dispatch, the assertion, 'His Majesty allows of your placing and displacing such officers in the Marine regiments as you see cause for', plainly proves that the issue had been raised by Torrington before the 31st May.[45] It, Nottingham's reassurance, did not quieten the admiral who retorted, on the 4th June, 'placing & replacing Marine officers [I] must have a power from the King or [I] cannot do it'.[46] The 10th June brought Nottingham's last word – in effect the King's – 'And as he [the King] then gave you leave to displace and place officers in the Marine regiments, you need no particular authority . . . though your lordship's disposall of them must be confirmed by the King's commission when they come ashoar.' With that, on the 11th, Torrington expressed 'temporary' content, remarked that the *Warspight* and *Rupert* were 'almost manned' and that the manning of the *Exeter* and *Cambridge* would be completed – at Portsmouth. His concluding sentence ran, 'I wish we may meet the French whilst our men are in health, for if theyre ods are not very great I cannot doubt successe'.[47]

The logistics of William's whole military undertaking in Ireland from the advent of Schomberg to William's landing and later are essentially, though not entirely matter for the military historian; but at least the safety, during sea-crossing, of troops, horses, clothes, food, provender, artillery, small arms, ammunition waggons – and money – was a solely naval concern.[48]

Upon d'Amfréville's return to France, threat to Shovell's minor command receded and duty to protect the hired ships of the Commissioners for Transporting the Army to Ireland (see p. 345 *ante*) simplified. Shovell would have little to do with the heavily convoyed dispatches of muniments and stores from Channel ports or the Thames;[49] for the warships appointed as particular convoy shepherded their flocks straight into Carrickfergus Bay. The provision of convoy for the 'deliveries' (men, horses, matériel) and 'empties' shuttling incessantly between Hoylake and opposite Carrickfergus imposed a spectacular responsibility – four warships and 250 merchantmen rode in the Dee estuary on the 7th May;[50] and for the safe conduct of intermittent sailings from the West Coast ports, large and small, Appledore to Kirkcudbright Shovell's ships were on call. Early in May all embargo on coastal trade to Williamite Ireland was lifted. And there was shortly good land news – Charlemont had fallen.[51]

But now, that is to say at the beginning of the second week in June, Shovell's preoccupation was convoy of a very special kind. William had reached Chester on Sunday the 8th, attended a service in the cathedral, moved on to Gayton, received Shovell and, in the evening, visited the ships. Only a 'bare' wind offered on the 9th and 10th, and royal[52] impatience mounted: 'he would [a servant heard him say] think of going by Scotland if the wind should long oppose him.'[53] On Wednesday morning, the 11th, a letter William to Nottingham: 'Our pleasure is that the fleet be hastened forth with all possible expedition, & that you lett Lord Torrington know we shall, on our arrivall at Belfast send away Sir Cloudsley Shovell to join it'.[54] By noon that day Prince George of Denmark already aboard the *Henrietta* yacht (Captain Sanderson) the King, to a salute of thirty and one guns, embarked on the *Mary* yacht (its Captain – Greenville Collins, the royal Hydrographer). The *Monck* 'Hoysed ye blew fflagg at Mizzen topmast

head', and Rear Admiral Shovell with his seven yachts and six
rates put to sea. But fog settled; Shovell for a time lost sight of his
charge; and through the afternoon of Wednesday, through all
Thursday and Friday, the 12th and 13th, the expedition made
slow way. Friday night was passed in Ramsey Bay. Happily, on
the morning of Saturday, the 14th June, 'the wind grew high and
pushed [the ships] forward and so that at half an hour after one,
the King cast anchor'. About three in the afternoon, while thirty-
one guns again boomed from the squadron, William left the *Mary*
and betook him to Shovell's barge to be rowed to the quay.
Overspreading 'the spatious bay of Carig-fargus' His Majesty saw
(measure of the continuing task of convoy) 'three or four hundred
ships' which likewise 'all fired to express their joy'. At Belfast,
'fireworks & bonfires concluded the solemnity of the nigt . . . the
neighbouring hills & villages had their bonfires alsoe'.[55]

Torrington weighed from the Downs on the 12th June.[56] On
the 14th, when near St Helens, fuming over shore news that only
one company of Pembroke's marines had marched into Portsmouth for embarkation, he received from Nottingham a letter,
which, written the day before, told him the King had sailed on the
11th, after ordering that 'the fleet be hastened forth' and promising that Shovell's squadron should be sent at once from Belfast to
join it. Nottingham ventured the suggestion that perhaps the
admiral would care to appoint a rendezvous? He was 'glad the
fleet [was reported] in so good a condition'. And Nottingham had
positive news to add – from Madrid via Holland – to effect that
Killigrew had been engaged with the French. Might not an
engagement account for his non-arrival?

Replying on the 14th to Nottingham Torrington accepted and
interpreted the Killigrew news as 'so good success', begged 'for
God sake' that pressure be exerted on Lord Pembroke, promised
to send the *Crowne* and *Portsmouth* to lead Shovell into Plymouth
from 'Silly . . . a malencholy little station for foull ships'. He
asseverated – a little testily – 'I hope he [the King] believes that,
without being hastened, I will loose noe oportunity nor tyme.'[57]

Torrington, commanding his Anglo-Dutch forty-five warships
and fourteen fireships (the fifteenth the *Hopewell* had accidentally

been blown up), riding in the sunlight off St Helens, certainly did not know that, the day before, Friday, 13th/23rd June, his French adversary Tourville, with strength of seventy *'vaisseaux en ligne'*, five *fregates légères*, eighteen *brûlots* (and *galères*?) had stood from Brest to sea.[58]

What of the absent Killigrew? It is not clear when the Russell-inspired royal order of the 9th March, as redrafted for Killigrew, 14th March (see p. 351 *ante*), reached him. Anyway at nightfall of the 10th May (the day on which Torrington had assumed his command at the Nore) Killigrew, with van Almonde in company, was dropping anchor west of Cape Trafalgar four leagues. He had weighed – a dozen English and two States ships – at dawn from Cadiz, in consequence of receipt, the preceding day, of:

three several Expresses; one from the Consul at *Alicant* another from him who resided at *Malaga*, and the third from Captain *Skelton*, who was with part of the Squadron at *Gibraltar*. They all advised him that the *Thoulon* Squadron, commanded by Monsieur *Chateau Renault*, was seen from those Places, [it] consisted of 10 Sail, and three of them of 80 guns each.

Killigrew's continued activity – 4 a.m. 'up anchors' on the 11th and mid-day junction with Captain Skelton's ships in Gibraltar; a search of the 12th into Tetuan Bay; the vigorous but abortive pursuit of 'Chatternaw' (as the admiral called the Frenchman); the return on the 21st to Cadiz to forward, under convoy, the waiting merchantmen to their assigned Mediterranean ports are topics, which could, if use were made of the evidence hidden in the extant logs of the ships of Killigrew's squadron and Almonde's Dutchmen be pursued in detail. It must suffice to record that Chateaurenault escaped Killigrew and, emulating on a minor scale Tourville's exploit of the previous summer, reached Brest, to reinforce Tourville's fleet. Killigrew reported to Nottingham on 26th May. By that time the order of the 14th March had been read. On 14th June Killigrew (in the *Duke*) and van Almonde, with twelve sail of men-of-war, English and Dutch, two fireships, two tenders, two victuallers and trade were seven days out from Cadiz on course for England. Lookouts would not sight the Lizard for another twenty-eight days.[59]

So the curtain would rise on Beachy-Bévéziers with the Admiral and Rear Admiral designate of Lord Torrington's Blue squadron, Henry Killigrew and Sir Clowdisley Shovell with their ships, so essential to completion of strength of the Grand Fleet, distant in the wings – the wings Cadiz and Carrickfergus, the one a thousand, and the other half as many miles away. The battle will be fought before they can reach the stage!

## REFERENCES

1 *H.M.C. Finch II*, p. 270.
2 P.R.O. Adm. 3/3 under dates.
3 *H.M.C. Finch II*, Russell-Nottingham, 13th, 16th, 23rd Feb., 4th, 7th March, *London Gazette, passim*.
    On the 13th Russell alleged that combatant officers hearing that Captain Hill 'a man who has never served in the navey Royall' was likely to be made a Commissioner, were highly resentful. He, Russell would recommend Captain Aylmer, whose service to William 'before and att his arivall in England meretts a great deale' [see Powley *op. cit.* p. 143]. For postscript to the 13th 'tis feared Sir John Berrey [will not] leive till 12 a'clok'. Still recommending, the Admiral, on the 16th, advanced Sir Francis Wheeler's claims for Governorship of Deale Castle.
4 Foxcroft, *op. cit.* pp. 218–222. 'Milford Haven is certainly the best Harbour in the three Kingdoms', Greenville Collins, *op. cit.* p. 13.
5 Luttrell, *passim*.
6 P.R.O. Adm. 3/3 and Ehrman *op. cit.* Appendix X.
7 P.R.O. Adm. 3/3 Admiralty-Navy Board; P.R.O. Adm. 1 3560, ff.801, 807, Navy Board-Admiralty. *Handlist of Proclamations . . . 1509–1714*.
8 P.R.O. Adm. 8/1.
9 *London Gazette* under date.
10 P.R.O. Adm. 8/1.
11 *H.M.C. Finch II*, p. 271.
12 Sue, *op. cit.* p. 329.
13 Guerin, *op. cit.* t.iii, p. 448.
14 *Négociations . . . d'Avaux*, 14/4 Mars, p. 699.
15 *op. cit.* Louvois-d'Avaux, 11/1 Nov. 1689, p. 581.
16 *op. cit.* d'Avaux-de Croissy, p. 700.
17 Warnsinck, *op. cit.* h.10; Adm. 8/1. *S.P.Dom.* . . . *1689–90* (James Clarke–) 14th March, p. 511; *London Gazette* (31st March–3rd April). Log of *Duke* (Captain's). P.R.O. Adm. 51/4174.
18 *London Gazette passim*. Luttrell, p. 48. Late in May news that Inchiquin and Kendal had been installed governors respectively of Jamaica and Barbados reached London; but a score merchant ships and the *Guernsey* and *Quaker Ketch*, which were separated from the main body, were still unaccounted for.
19 P.R.O. Adm. 49/173.
20 *Ibid*.

21 *S.P. Dom.* . . . *1689–90*, 10th Feb., p. 454.

22 P.R.O. Adm. 3/3, 15th March.

23 *S.P.Dom.* . . . *1689–90*, p. 516.

24 P.R.O. Adm. 3/3.

25 *Gazette de Rotterdam.* No. 16. On 20 Avril 1690. Luttrell pp. 29, 33, 41.

26 P.R.O. Adm. 8/1. *Earl of Torrington's Speech* . . . p. 11. That we were not in a condition to prevent the Descent at Cork, or to destroy the *French* Fleet whilst it lay there, is it may be a very great Miscarriage . . . a very great *Misfortune* and might have been more fatal, for had they destroyed our Transport-Ships in those Seas, it is not likely his Majesty would have been able to have gone to *Ireland* this year . . . From which I think . . . *Ireland* wholly reduc'd if that Fleet had been destroy'd in *Cork* as surely it might, if we had had ships ready. The late Insult which some call Disgrace! For Byng and the *Dover Memoirs* . . . *Torrington*, p. 42; the Saltees are islands and rocks midway between Carnsore Point and the Hook.

27 *London Gazette* (24th–28th April). A full account from a correspondent aboard the *Monck.* Luttrell, p. 35. P.R.O. Adm. 8/1. For transport *London Gazette passim.*

28 *H.M.C. Finch II*, p. 276. Luttrell, p. 36. Burchett, *op. cit.* p. 36.

29 *H.M.C. Finch II*, p. 272 (originals consulted).

30 At N.E. corner of Levant sea.

31 *H.M.C. Finch II*, p. 276.

32 *op. cit.* p. 276. Killigrew–Nottingham, Warnsinck *op. cit.* h.11.

33 Luttrell II, p. 33.

34 B.M. Additional 17677. I am indebted to Mr P. King, Lecturer in Dutch in the University of Cambridge, for providing this version of Van Citter's Dutch.

35 Luttrell II, p. 36; H.M.C. XIII, App. 5, p. 86; *Cal. Treas. Books 1689–92*, pp. 595–9. The official reason for the gift was 'in consideration of his faithful services and for support of His Honour'. Local historians–of Huntingdon and Peterborough–may be interested in the itemising of tenancies and acreages.

36 P.R.O. Adm. 2/5.

37 P.R.O. Adm. 8/1.

38 P.R.O. Adm. 2/379 f.543.

39 Luttrell II, p. 45.

40 Log *Royal Soveraigne.*

41 P.R.O. Adm. 2/1728.

42 Luttrell II, p. 49.

43 *H.M.C. Finch II*, p. 283.

44 P.R.O. Adm. 2/1728.

45 *H.M.C. Finch II*, p. 284.

46 *Ibid.* p. 286.

47 *Ibid.* p. 292.

48 A broad notion of the size of the undertaking can be formed from the reports of military reviews. Story, Impartial History of the Wars in Ireland, Pt I, p. 95, shows, at Finglas, 7th–8th July, for 'private men' only. *Foot* Danish 4581+Dutch 4663+English 13335=22579: *Dragoons* 1870, *Horse* 5881.

49 e.g. Luttrell II, p. 42. 'There have been lately ship't away at the Tower some great mortars, several granado guns, and a great parcel of granado shells for the service of Ireland.'
50 e.g. *London Gazette*, Chester, 7th May.
51 *Ibid.* passim.
52 *H.M.C. Finch II*, Southwell to Nottingham, p. 292. Luttrell II, p. 55.
53 *Ibid.* Southwell–Nottingham p. 292.
54 *Ibid.* Southwell–Nottingham p. 296.
55 *Ibid.* Southwell–Nottingham p. 298; Log of the *Monck* (Master's) Adm. 52/72. Illustration in Greenville Collins *Great Britain's Coasting Pilot*, Map 32.
56 *Ibid.* p. 293.
57 *Ibid.* p. 296.
58 Delabre, *Tourville et le marin de son temps*, p. 167.
59 *H.M.C. Finch II*, p. 282. Burchett, pp. 41–3; Log of *Duke*.

N

# Appendices

## APPENDIX A

### On Strategic Command

A *command* of a given area of sea (for, always, one must speak of a definite and given extent of sea) may be defined as *the power to use and the ability to deny to the enemy the use of the waters of the area in question whether for military purposes or trade.* It is a condition which is only assured when no enemy fleet can operate in the area; hence it can only be set up after a battle decision between rival fleets has driven a defeated combatant out of the area; or so long as one fleet, blockading the other in harbour, keeps it from all intervention therein. Even so, a command is seldom or never absolute; and its duration may be long or short. Once secured, it may be enjoyed and exercised. Its exercise is, of course, seen in the few or many ways in which its possessor employs his power to use the waters in question for military purposes or trade and the deprivation of the similar facilities which he inflicts upon his enemy. The variety in exercise will depend on the strength of the belligerent and the particular purposes which he has in hand. But if, in theory, the exercise of command waits upon the establishing of the condition of command by battle decision or by blockade, practice often ignores logic; there is, in short, always a tendency on the part of a combatant to act as though possessed of a command which he has not yet made his own or which he may even know to have been definitely lost.

Two main courses are therefore open to a belligerent entering upon naval warfare. They may be called (1) the proper course of securing command by battle decision or by blockade, before attempting to exercise it; and (2) the assumption of an undecided or an adversely decided command in order to accomplish the purpose in hand–an assumption which may be either an *open* or a *concealed* procedure. These considerations, so well known to the modern naval officer, were not hidden from English and Dutch seamen of the later seventeenth century . . . no one who has studied the operations of the three Dutch Wars can remain in doubt that the modern cardinal doctrine of command was, at least as an implicit notion, part of the stock-in-trade of the admiral and naval adviser of 1688.

Powley, E. B., *The English Navy in the Revolution of 1688.* Cambridge, 1920, p. 39.

## APPENDIX B

[Ch. IV, p. 82, Note (12)]

*Would Pepys, if requested, have continued in office?*

Sir A. Bryant, *op. cit.* III, p. 384, decides against the probability; and J. R. Tanner, in *Mr Pepys*, 1925, which, as a compendium, is not likely to be superseded, writes, p. 267, 'his relations with James II were too intimate for the new government to leave him in office undisturbed' and adds that James was sitting to Kneller for a portrait commissioned by Pepys when the news arrived of the landing of the Prince of Orange in Torbay. None the less, Pepys's Puritan-Parliamentarian upbringing left, to the end, its mark on the man. His respect for Cromwell 'what brave things he did and made all the neighbour princes fear him (*Diary*, 4th Dec. 1660); his attitude to confession (1662), the surplice (26th Oct. 1662), the service in the Duke of York's chapel 'silly devotion, God knows' (15th April 1668) to Heylin's *Life of Laud* '[it] will do the Bishops . . . no great good but hurt; it pleads for so much Popish. (16th Sept. 1668) – These evidences and much else in the *Diary* should not be overlooked (*v.* Tanner *op. cit.* ch. xvi). Nor should it be forgotten that, just before retiring, Pepys was seeking entry into Parliament – for the borough of Harwich. Election would certainly have involved the taking of the new oaths. Further, Tanner (*op. cit.* p. 269), puts on record that:

On 8th February 1689/90, two days after the dissolution of the Convention Parliament he [Pepys] began to make interest with his friends to find him a 'berth' in the new Parliament which had been summoned for 20th March. He flattered himself that his 'being in this Parliament might not be wholly unuseful'.

Again – the oaths? Is it to be argued that Pepys, in January 1688/9 or, in February 1689/90, would have been prepared to swear an allegiance he did not intend to honour? If Daniel Finch could vote for regency and against declaring the throne vacant, yet come to accept the Revolution settlement, is it unthinkable that Pepys, had he been solicited, would have found like justification? He was not – doubtless to the satisfaction of Herbert and Russell and possibly as a consequence of their influence – invited.

Pepys was committed to the Gatehouse 25th June 1690 'on suspicion of being affected to King James' but released on 15th October of that year. The circumstance proves little either way. More to the point is the pronouncement of that expert in plot-detection James Vernon who, writing of Pepys to Matthew Prior in Paris 16th August 1689, declared:

I believe the old gentleman means fairly and hath sent no underhand compliments to his old master, having professed the contrary (H.M.C. XVI, MSS of the Marquess of Bath, III, p. 261; Tanner, *op. cit.* p. 270).

There we may leave the matter.

## APPENDIX C
[Ch. IV, p. 84, Note (38)]
*The duties and rights of the Commission of Admiralty*

The maintenance of ships already built, the construction of new, the fitting, arming, victualling of such ships and fleets as the Privy Council might command to be employed would be the Commission's care; the wages and rewards of all persons whom they might employ would be at their ordering; the obedience of all officers and Ministers of the Navy or Shipps and all others in their severall places, the Commission's expectation and due. And that their Majesties and the Privy Council might be better instructed how to perform the Great and Weighty Services required of them, a speedy survey should be made of all ships, tackle, stores and munitions, as well as of the method of 'managing, ordering and Governing the Navy' upon which report might well follow measures affecting wages and the reform of abuses. The Commission was enjoined to abate nothing of its claims in respect of wrecks, the hulls & goods of pirate vessels, its interests in prize, its divers Droits, Rights, Duties & Privileges; yet such assertion would in future be not to the Commissioners' benefit but rather to their Majesties' profit–their 'onely use and behoof and not otherwise'. The necessary authority of the Commission to give under the seal [they] would 'commonly' use,

> upon . . . accounts for tenths of Prizes and all other Duties & Droits & Profitts Whatsoever received by . . . Vice-admiralls [of counties] and other collectors authorized by the Court of Admiralty

was forthcoming; and exemplifications under the 'Great Seal of the Admiralty' were provided for. Of the 'divers offices, profits & places & employments' resting in the gift of the Lord Admiral and becoming vacant during the Commission's continuance, the Commission would dispose. The Commission itself would continue till the royal pleasure declared it void notwithstanding the same be not continued by Adjournment.

## APPENDIX D
[Ch. IV, p. 85, Note (43)]
*Declaration of War by United Provinces upon Louis XIV*

The *London Gazette* faithfully prints the 'Substance' of the preamble to the Declaration–a lengthy recitation of cumulative aggressions and persecutions, since 1676, by the French king, proceeds to the announcement of hostilities 'as well by land as by sea' and summarizes thus the thirteen concluding paragraphs of manifesto.

I.  That none of the Inhabitants of this State, nor any foreigner residing within their Territories, shall transport anything to France that's useful in War, or Correspond with the French to the prejudice of the State.

II.  That all Contraband Goods which shall be taken going to France shall be declared Prize.

III.  That good Security shall be given by all Persons carrying any Contraband Goods out of these Countries that they are not designed for France.

IV.  That all Ships laden with Contraband Goods, as shall be found on the French Coasts shall be taken for good Prize.

V.  That all Ships ought to have Lawful Passports.

VI.  The Men of War not to molest any Ships, having such Passports and not being bound with any Contraband Goods to any Ports in France.

VII.  That such as shall be found offending herein shall be punished with Confiscation of Ship and Goods.

VIII.  That the Commanders of the Ships of War shall punctually govern themselves in this Matter, according to the Treaty made in Relation thereunto with other Kings, Princes and States.

IX.  That the Admiralties have the Cognizance of these Offences.

X, XI, XII.  The Monies arising by such Confiscation shall be disposed of as has been heretofore practised in like Cases, and as to the Seizure, etc., former Placeats are to be observed.

XIII.  None of the Inhabitants of that State shall injure any French Ships or Goods or others bound to France on Forfeiture of the Sum insured. Given at the Hague the 9th March 1689.

## APPENDIX G

[Ch. VII, p. 164, Note (86)]

*King William's Declaration of War 7th May 1689*
*Resumé*

The Declaration condemns

The Methods the French King hath in late years taken to gratifie his ambition

He has invaded the Empire 'in amity with us'

We can do no less than Joyn with Our Allies in opposing the Designs of . . . the Disturber of the Peace & the Common Enemy of the Christian World

That obligation would be sufficient justification for war but the – many injuries done to us . . . [demand] Publick & Just Resentment – and must be particularized. The French no longer take out licences to fish in Newfoundland waters; they have invaded 'Our Charibee Islands' and, at the very time of negotiating here for 'Neutrality and good Correspondence in America' have barbarously possessed themselves of territory in the province of New York and by Hudson Bay. 'Proceedings against our subjects in Europe' are too 'notorious' to need enlargement. Privateering and the refusal to admit English trade into France are a threat to the

Navigation upon which the Wealth and Safety of this Nation very much depend

Moreover

The Right of the Flag inherent in the Crown of England hath been disputed by [Louis's] Orders in Violation of Our Sovereignty of the Narrow Seas which in all Ages has been Ascribed to Our Predecessors and [which] We are resolved to Maintain . . .

There has been persecution of 'Our English Protestant Subjects' in France to the extent of prison and the galleys; and, lastly,

## APPENDIX E

[Ch. VI, p. 128, Note (81)]

B.M. MS Additional 3650, p. 13, v°.

Signalls for Speaking wᵗʰ yᵉ Severall Commanders yᵉ Fleet under yᵉ Command of yᵉ Honᵇˡᵉ Admirall Herbert Esqʳ, Admirall of their Maᵗⁱᵉˢ Fleet on the Expeditⁿ to Ireland in April 1689 . . .

| The Places of Severˡˡ Pendants | | A Blew Flag on yᵉ Ensigne Stafe | | The Ensigne abroad | | | White Flagg } Miz Shroe / Redd Flagg } Miz Shroe | to Chase to Windˡᵈ: Give over Chase |
|---|---|---|---|---|---|---|---|---|
| | Rate | Shipps Name | Commander | Rate | Shipps | Commanders | | |
| Maintopgᵗ } Foretopgᵗ } Masthead  Mizontopmˢᵗ } | 3 | Defiance | C Jnᵒ Ashby | 4 | Bonadventure | C Tho Hopson | | |
| | 3 | Yorke | C Ralph Delavall | 4 | Portsmouth | C Geo Sᵗ Loe | | |
| | 3 | Plymouth | Capᵗ Rᵈ Carter | 4 | Ruby | Capᵗ Fred Froud | | |
| Starboard } Mᵗtopgᵗ } Yard | 3 | Pendennis | | 4 | Diamond | C Ben Walters | | |
| Larboard } Mᵗtopgᵗ } Arme | 3 | Cambridge | Capᵗ Jnᵒ Clement | 4 | Sᵗ Albans | C Jnᵒ Layton | | |
| Starboard } Foretopgᵗ } Yard | 3 | Edgar | Capᵗ Clow. Shovell | 4 | Advise | C Greenvell | | |
| Larboard } Foretopgᵗ } Arme | 3 | Mary | C Math Aylmer | 6 | Anthelope | | | |
| Starboard } Mᵗtopsa: } Yard | 3 | Dreadnought | C Anth Hastings | 6 | Saudadoes | Capᵗ Fran Wivell | | |
| Larboard } Mᵗtopsa: } Arme | 4 | Deptford | Cᵗ Tho Rooke | | Greyhound | Capᵗ Tho Gilliam | | |
| Starboard } Foretopsa } Yard | 4 | Greenwich | | | Halfemoon Fire/sp | Capt Bounty | | |
| Larboard } Foretopsa } Arme | 4 | Woolwich | C Ralph Saunders | | Salamander Keᵗʰ | | | |
| Starboard } Miztopsa } | 4 | Portland | C Geo Aylmer | | Fire Drake | Cᵗ Jnᵒ Leake | [Herbert in *Elizabeth* (3)] | |
| Larboard } Miztopsa } | 4 | St David | Capᵗ | | Kingfisher Keᵗʰ | Capᵗ Boyce | Captain David Mitchell] | |
| Starboard } Main Yard Arme  Larboard } | | Cadix Merchᵗ } Hospitall Shipp | | | Fubbs } Henrietta } Yaᵗˢ | Capᵗ Wm Saunderson | *Herbert's own signature | |

att Mizon Peake . . . All yᵉ Yachts Smacks and Ketch to bear under my Sterne

The Respective Signall & a White Flagg on yᵉ Mizon Shroud to Chase to Windwᵈ,
A Redd Flagg on yᵉ same place to Leewᵈ
If I Lowre my Topsaile and Fire two Gunns distinctly you are to give over Chase

Ar Herbert*

In Case of seperation if wee meet by day the Weathermost Shipps shall hawle up their Foresailes & lowr their Maintopsaile, those to Leeward shall answer, by Lowring their Foretopsaile and brayling up their Mizon If by night yᵉ Shipp that hayles shall aske what Shipp is That yᵉ Shipp hayled shall answer          The Protestant Religion

The other shall reply          The Liberties of England.

I will maintain

Then shee that first hayld shall answer—          - Ar Herbert*

When I would have all yᵉ Shipps in yᵉ Fleet Chase I will hoist a White Flagg att yᵉ Mizon Topmast head, when I would have all Chase Shipps that are not probable to come up with yᵉ Chase give Over chaseing I will take in the White Flagg and Fire a Gunn, yᵉ other Shipps are to continue Chaseing untill I make a Signⁿ appointed for a private Shipp to give over Chaseing

When I would have all yᵉ Barges & Pinnacs in yᵉ Fleet Chase I will hoist a White Flagg at yᵉ Mizon Peake and when all yᵉ Boats in yᵉ Fleet a Redd Flagg att yᵉ Mizon Peake when I would have them give Over chaseing I will make a Weft wᵗʰ yᵉ Flagg att yᵉ Maintopmast head and when all yᵉ Boats in yᵉ Fleet a Redd Flagg at Mizontopmast head

When I would have all yᵉ Barges and Pinnaces come on board me in yᵉ day (Armed) I will hoist a Blew Flagg at yᵉ Mizontopmast head and when all yᵉ Boats in yᵉ Fleet a Redd Flagg att yᵉ Mizontopmast head

When I would have all yᵉ Barges and pinnaces come on board me in yᵉ Day (Armed) I will hoist a Blew Flagg at yᵉ Mizontopmast head and when all yᵉ Boats in yᵉ Fleet a Redd Flagg att yᵉ Mizontopmast head

When I would have all yᵉ Barges and Pinnaces come on board me in yᵉ Night (Armed) I will putt a Light in yᵉ Fore Topp & when all yᵉ Boats in yᵉ Fleet I will putt a Light in each Topp allowing yᵉ Constant Light in yᵉ Maintopp for One

*Signature

# APPENDIX F

[Ch. VIII, p. 205, Note (33)]

B.M. MS Additional 3650, p. 16 v°

Signalls for Speaking we ye Severall Commands in their fleet under ye Command of Arthur Earle of Torrington Barron of Torbay and admll of their Mats Fleet on ye Expedicon off of Brest in ye Month of June & July 1689.

| The Places of Severall Pendants | | Captains of ye admll Division | | | Vice admll Division a Redd Flag at Foretopmst head downwd & Pen | | | Reere admll Division a Redd Flag at Mizn Topmsts head downwd | | |
|---|---|---|---|---|---|---|---|---|---|---|
| | | Rate | Shipp | Commanders | Rate | Shipps | Commaniders | Rate | Shipps | Commander |
| Maintopgalant } | Mast head | 3 | Edgar | Sr Clow Shovell | 3 | Yorke | C Cha Delavall | 3 | Lyon | C Char Shellton |
| Foretopgalant } | | 3 | Pendennis | C Geo Churchill | 3 | Plymouth | C Carter | 3 | Henrietta | C Jno Nevell |
| Mizontopmast head | | 3 | Rupert | Sr Fran Wheeler | 3 | Cambridge | C Clements | 3 | Mountague | C Tho Leighton |
| Starboard } Maintopgalt Yd arme | | 3 | Defiance | Capt Tho Allin | 3 | Warspight | C Botham | 4 | Mordaunt | C |
| Larboard } | | 4 | St Albans | C Jno Layton | 4 | Woolwich | C Goter | 4 | Jersey | |
| Starboard } Maintopsa Yard arme | | 4 | St David | | 4 | Diamond | C Ben Waters | 4 | Oxford | |
| Larboard } | | 4 | Advice | | 4 | Reserve | | 4 | Tyger Prize | |
| Starboard } Foretopgalt Yard arme | | 4 | Happy Returne | | 4 | Portsmouth | C Geo St Loe | 4 | Greenwch | |
| Larboard } | | 4 | Centurion | | 4 | Hampshire | C Robinson | 4 | Char Gally | |
| Starboard } Foretopsa Yard arme | | Fire Ships | Halfe moone / Alexander | | [6] | Salamander | C Jno Voteere | | Merline Yat | |
| Larboard } | | [6] | Fire Drake / Fubbs Yacht | | Fire Ships | Tho & Eliz / Owners Love / Char & Henry | | Fire Ships | Jno of Dublin / Charles | |
| Starboard } Mizontopsa Yard Arme | | Fire Ships | Cygnett / Cadiz Mercht | | | | | | Sophia | |
| Larboard } | | 3 | Berwick | | | | | | Rich & Jno | |
| Starboard } Main Yard arme | | | St Paule | | | | | 4 | Kingffisher | |
| Larboard } | | | | | | | | | | |
| Starboard } Fore Yard arme | | | | | | | | | | |
| Larboard } | | | | | | | | | | |
| Starboard Crosjack Yard arme | | | | | | | | | | |

Any Shipp Chase to Windwd ye Respective Signall for speaking wt a Redd Flagg on ye Mizon Shrouds . If to Leeward a White Flagg--A Pendt on ye Flagstaffe at Foretopgt Masthead & One Gun fired & send my Barge & Pinnace a Chaseing all ye Shipps to doe likewise Mand & armd w. Musts A Pendt on ye Flagstaffe at Miztopmhead & fire a Gunn & send my Longboat all ye Capts to send their Longboats armd w Musquetts, Bagnetts & hand Greds When I make ye above mencond Signall wthout sending my Boat to Chase all ye Boat in ye Fleet are to come on board me Mannd & armed accordingly When I would have any Shipp in ye Fleet call a Shipp I will make his Signall for Chaseing & fire a Gunn

Torrington

Actual invasion of Our Kingdom of Ireland
Therefore war against the French King 'by sea and land' will be vigorously prosecuted
    with the Concurrence and Assistance of Our Subjects . . . Our General of Our Forces, Our Commissioners for Executing the Office of High Admiral [who are] to do and execute all Acts of Hostility . . . against the French King with whom and whose subjects all 'Communication' is strictly forbid. Nevertheless
    all such of the French nation as shall demean themselves Dutifully towards Us . . . Shall be safe in their Persons and Estates & free from all Molestation & Trouble of any Kind.
Hampton Court 7th May 1689
    God save King William & Queen Mary
Printed by Charles Bell & Thomas Newconb, Printers to the King & Queen's Most Excellent Majesties, 1689.

## APPENDIX H

### [Ch. VII, p. 164, Note (87)]

*Treaty of the Concert of the Fleets of England and Holland,
or Anglo-Dutch Naval Convention 29th April 1689*

The Convention consisted of fifteen clauses:

I.   England to provide 50 large vessels (1 second, 17 thirds, 32 fourths) 15 frigates and 8 fireships, manned by 17,155 men.

II.  The United Provinces to send 30 large vessels 8 of 70–80 guns, 7 of 60–70, 15 of 50–60, 9 frigates, 4 fireships, manned by 10,572 men.

III. Junction to be made where the King of Great Britain might decide– the sooner the better.

IV.  Three squadrons (or as we should say–fleets) should be constituted– The first of 50 large 6 frigates & 8 fireships to be employed in the Mediterranean; the second of 30 large 8 frigates & 4 fireships in the Irish Sea and Channel–unless by common consent to be otherwise directed; the third of 10 frigates to be deployed between Calais–Dover and Yarmouth–Walcheren.

V.   The squadrons (or as we should say–fleets) were to be made up with both nationalities represented in ratio.

VI.  The Mediterranean squadron (fleet) was to be supplied for a year. What the ships could not carry to be stored at Port Mahon (Minorca) Porto Perrara (Elba) or elsewhere that the admiral & council of war should decide–the King of Spain, the Grand Duke of Tuscany, the Republic of Genoa to be required to give facilities. The two other squadrons (fleets) should be provided for a year also, or other suitable period.

VII. Command of the three (fleets) squadrons or detachments therefrom would devolve on English officers.

VIII. Councils of war were to be composed of flag officers. If in voting equality were reached the captains would be required to attend. The senior English officer would always preside. English officers would sit on his right the Dutch on his left. In all affairs of whatever nature, the majority vote should determine the issue & the council's decision be punctually in the prescribed manner executed.

IX. An English council of war would deal with any matter concerning only English officers or men, a Dutch council with Dutch officers & men.

X. Where both English & Dutch personnel of whatever rank or quality might be involved, a joint council must meet & punishments be awarded according to the laws instructions & customs of the state to which the offender belongs.

XI. All prizes shall be shared in proportion to the number of vessels in each fleet ⅝ English : ⅜ Dutch ; this ratio to be always observed even when the said prizes have been taken by the vessels of their Majesties without assistance of those of the Seigneurs of the States General and vice versa.

XII. Adjudication must take place in the court of the nationality of the captor and the proceeds shall be shared following the provisions of the preceding article; but the portion which will be delivered to the non-adjudicating Admiralty will not be charged with the actual fees for the officers of both parties but only with the necessary expenses.

XIII. If a prize be taken by more than one vessel the prize is to be adjudicated upon in the court of the nationality of the vessels of higher gun power.

XIV. Captains of British warships convoying merchant ships anywhere, or sailing to the West Indies, should be expressly instructed to protect Dutch merchant ships following the same route & desiring convoy. And expressly bid protect, if requested, Dutch West Indian possessions, present or to be acquired, as far as the state of English possessions would allow. The captains of Dutch warships must be likewise & similarly instructed.

XV. Ratification shall take place within six weeks unless a treaty of offence & defence be between the partners concluded in which case this treaty shall be included. Meanwhile the agreed provisions shall be mutually performed just as if the ratifications were already made.
Executed at Whitehall 29th April 1689. Nottingham, Carbery, Russel, N. Witsen, W. de Nassau, De Weede.

# APPENDIX I

[Ch. VIII, p. 212, Note (101)]

*Louis XIV – Au Marquis de Seignelai, Ministre de la Marine*
[*1 ou 2*] *Août 1689*

Si les ennemis vouloient faire une descente en Normandie, Picardie et Boulon-nois, en ce cas seul, je vous permets de faire entrer mes vaisseaux dans la Manche, pour les combattre et pour empêcher leur dessein à quelque prix que ce soit.

Mandez-moi souvent des nouvelles; quoi-qu'elles ne soient pas toutes importantes, elles ne laissent pas de me faire plaisir.

Si vous vous mettez en mer, envoyez-moi souvent des nouvelles par des barques qui pourront venir aux côtes voisines.

Faites tout avec prudence, patience et sagesse, et ne précipitez rien dont on puisse se repentir.

Montrez cette lettre à M. de Tourville, afin qu'il ne puisse douter de mes intentions, et que cela lui serve pour la conduite qu'il devra tenir, quand vous ne serez plus sur mes vaisseaux.

Demeurez tant que vous croirez être nécessaire, et sur-tout voyez ce qui se passera d'important, pour me rendre un compte exact de ce que chacun aura fait.

Vous n'avez rien à craindre de l'absence; soyez assuré que je suis très-content de vous, et que je compte plus les services que vous me rendez où vous êtes, que si vous étiez auprès de ma personne

(Réflexions) depuis avoir écrit.

C'est de bonne part que, si ma flotte ne sort point, et s'il n'y a point d'avan-tages sur elle, que les ennemis ne peuvent rien entreprendre de la campagne.

Que cela me fait croire qu'il vaut mieux changer de pensée, et qu'il n'y ait que Seignelai qui le sache, qui est de ne point sortir, mais de faire croire que l'on sortira aussitôt qu'on le pourra.

Donner ordre à Tourville de joindre par le raz, s'il a un vent bon pour cela, et qu'après la jonction, que l'on ne sorte point jusqu'à nouvel ordre, lequel dépendra de la manoeuvre des ennemis; c'est-à-dire, s'ils demeurent encore ou s'ils se séparent.

Qu'il est important que Seignelai demeure, faisant croire que les ordres sont toujours d'aller aux ennemis.

Mander à Tourville, que s'il ne peut venir joindre, que sur la moindre apparence que les ennemis puissent aller à lui, qu'il se retire dans les rades de la Rochelle, et même dans la Charente à Rochefort. Suivant cette conduite à l'égard de la mer, c'est se conduire avec le même esprit qui me fait agir sur la terre.

Que ne craignant point de descente, ma flotte pouvant sortir à tout moment, que cela me donne lieu de tirer des troupes que j'ai sur la Saare et du côté de Flandre, et d'en renvoyer en Guienne.

En un mot, c'est le plus sûr et le plus vraisemblable, pour nous faire penser à empêcher les ennemis de ne rien faire contre mon royaume de bien considér-able. Cela étant, c'est le parti le plus sage, le plus sûr, et celui que je dois prendre.

*Œuvres de Louis XIV*, ed. Grimond et Grouvelle, 6 v. Paris and Strasbourg, 1806, VI, pp. 18–19.

# Authorities

Only those authorities which have been laid under specific contribution – as indicated in the notes to the text of this work – are included in the following tables and lists.

(A) *PRIMARY*
    (i) MSS.
    (ii) Printed – Contemporary or containing contemporary material reproduced, tabulated or summarized.

(B) *SECONDARY*

(A)
Primary (i)

*Public Record Office*

| | | |
|---|---|---|
| King William's Chest | | Selected papers |
| Exchequer | E 351/2333–17 | L.T.R. Declared Accounts |
| | dorso | Pipe Office Series |
| Patent Rolls | 66/3326 | I–XIV William III |
| Privy Council | P.C. 2/73 | Register Feb. 1688–1690 |
| | P.C. 6/2 | Irish Affairs, 14th Feb. 1688 to 25th Sept. 1691 |
| State Papers, | | |
|   Ireland, 1689–90 | v. 352 pp. 7–19 | de Pointis to Seignelay |
| Admiralty Secretary | Adm. 1/4080 | Letters from Secretaries of State |
| | 1/3557<br>3561 | from Navy Board |
| | 1/5139 | Orders in Council (affecting Admiralty) Abstract, Index. |
| | Adm. 1/5253 | Reports, Courts Martial 1680–July 1698. |
| | 2/3<br>2/1743 | Orders and Instructions March 1688– |
| | 2/377 | Secretary's Out letters. |
| | 3/1–3 | Minutes of Board. |
| | 7/169 | Estimates |
| | 7/685 | Entry Book of Patents |
| | 8/1 | Disposition of Ships |
| Accountant General | 49/173 | Naval debts 1671– |
| | 51/— | Ship logs, Captains' |
| | 52/— | Ship logs, Masters' |
| High Court of | H.C.A. 26/18 | Instance and Prize, Letters of |
|   Admiralty | 34/15–21 | Marque, Declarations/Sentences |
| State Papers Foreign | S.P. 104/153 | Nottingham to Duncomb |
|   Entry Book, | | (Sweden) |
|   1679–1704 | | |

*Bodleian Library*

| Rawlinson MSS. | A 170, 186, 451 Pepysian matters |
| | C 198 Log *Swallow* |
| | 968 Log *Yorke* |
| | 969 Log *Cambridge* |
| Carte Papers | Carte v. 181 Nairne papers 1689– |
| Firth MSS. | Admiralty pay books |

*British Museum*

| Additional | 28042 | f 34, Danby–'Memorandums' |
| | 28084 | f 265, Torrington–contingent money |
| | 28053 | Leeds Correspondence (Ireland 1688/9) |
| | 3650 | Signals |
| | 18989 | Journal of Leonard Brown of the *Benjamin*. |
| | 19306 | Wood (G.), Killigrew's cruise, 1686 |
| | 17677 | Van Citters to States General |
| Egerton | 2621 | Correspondence Prince of Orange and Admiral Herbert |

Additional } 9324 } Tables of Flag Officers
Harleian } 6003 }

| Lansdowne | 849 f 79, Copy–order of William to Herbert |

National Maritime Museum &
Adm. L/G./188. Ship's log.

*Bibliotheca Pepysiana, Cambridge*

| 2862 | Pepys out letters v. XV |
| 2879 | Miscellanea | v. IX | Sovereignty of the Seas, Rights of the flag. Sailing Instructions. Signals. |

Miscellanea VI }
Miscellanea XI } Sick and wounded, dependents, prisoners.
2867 Naval Precedents }

977 Battine, E. 'The Method of Building . . . His Majesty's Ships of War,' 1684.

1608 Book of Paintings of Flags, 1686.

*City of London Archives*

| Misc. MSS. 133, 25. | Loan to King William |
| *College of Heralds* | Grants and exemplifications (Torrington) |

Primary (ii)

| Calendar of State Papers Domestic Series | 1689–1690 |
| (Petition Entry Book 2 not printed) | |
| Calendar of Treasury Books | 1685–1689 v. VIII, pt iv. |
| | 1689–1692 IX, pt i. |
| | 1731–1734 |
| | 1742–1745 |

*Parliament*

| *Journals of the House of Lords* . . . | v. XIV | 1688–1691 |
| *General Index* | v. XI–XIX | 1660–1714 |
| *Journals of the House of Commons* . . . | v. X | 1688–1693 |

# KING WILLIAM'S WAR 373

| | | | |
|---|---|---|---|
| General Index | | v. VIII, IX, X | |
| Statutes of the Realm | | v. IV, V, VI | |
| Members of Parliament, Pt I, Parliaments of England | | | 1213–1702 |
| Debates . . . see GREY, A. | | | |

*Historical Manuscripts Commission*

| | Report | | |
|---|---|---|---|
| Bath | 16 | III | |
| Buccleuch and Queensbury | 16 | II | |
| Dartmouth | 11 | V | } Originals often used |
| Finch | 19 | II | |
| Hamilton | 11 | VI | See note* |
| House of Lords | { 12 | VI | |
| | 14 | VI | |
| Le Fleming | 12 | VII | |
| Ormonde | 19 | VIII | |

*Lennoxlove

The Duke of Hamilton's MSS. have been calendared and documents relative to 1688/9 are noticed in the Report indicated above–but unequally. Through the courtesy of the Duke it has been possible to use originals now at Lennoxlove.

*Newspapers, Periodicals*
London Gazette 1688, 89. 90.
*Gazette, Recüeil des Nouvelles . . . l'année mil six cent quatre-vingt-neuf*, Paris.
[Répertoire historique et biographique de la *Gazette de France*.]
*Gazette de Rotterdam*, No. 16. Avril 1690.
*Ulster Journal of Archaeology*, 1898, v. IV.

*Pamphlets*
*Expedition of the Prince of Orange to England 1688*, signed N. N. [Burnet].
[Harleian Miscell. i, p. 449]
[Somers Tracts ix, p. 276]
*A Particular Journal of Major General Kirk's Voyage from Leverpoole to his Safe Arrival at London-Derry*
Printed for Meade, G. 1689.  [B.M. 816 M 23 (57)]
*A Full and True Relation of the Remarkable Fight betwixt Captain Hamilton and Captain Brown, Commanders of the Two Scots Frigates and Three French Men of War*
[Fraser, J.] 1689  [B.M. with *London Gazette* of 1689]
(Grant *op. cit.* infra p. 26 reprints)
*An Exact and Faithful Account Brought to a Person of Quality on the Raising of the Siege of Londonderry by the Protestants and Garrison*
June 12(!) 1689  [B.M. 807 f 36 (15)]
*A List of Regiments that sailed with Schomberg . . .*
[B.M. 714/1/8]
*A Full and True Account of the Landing and Reception of King James at Kinsale . . . in a letter from Bristol*, 1st April 1689  [B.M. 816/50 m 23]

*An Exact Relation of the Most Remarkable Transactions that happened lately in Ireland With an Account of a great Sea Fight between the English and French Fleets*
[B.M. 807 f 36, 12]

*A Full Relation of the Surrender of Kilmore*
[B.M. 807 f. 36, 13]
*An Impartial Enquiry into the Causes of the Present Fears and Dangers of the Government*
[Bodleian, Godwin 1789, No. 21]


*Charts and Maps*
SELLER, J., *The English Pilot*, 1672.
*L'Irlanda o'vero Hibernia distinta nelle sue Provincie e Contee* . . . dae, Molto, R. P.
Agostino Lubin . . . Geografo Ordinario di S.M. Christianissima Data in luce
da Gio Giacomo Rossi . . . Roma . . . 1689. This is to be seen in *Atlante Veneto*
. . . *Studio del Padre Maestro Coronelli* . . . Venetia, 1690.
*Hiberniae Deliniatio quoad Lactenus* licuit *Perfectissima Studio Guilielmi Petty* . . . 1690.

COLLINS, Greenville (Captain), *Great Britain's Coasting Pilot*, 1693.
*Le Neptune François ou Atlas Noveau des Cartes Marines–Levées et gravées par ordre
exprès du Roy pour l'usage de ses armées de Mer.* Reveu et mis en ordre par les
Sieurs Pene, Cassini et autres . . . Jaillot, H., Paris, 1693.

NEVILLE, Francis (Captain), *A Map of Londonderry as besieged in 1689*, in *A
Description of Londonderry* . . . 1689. In Trinity College, Dublin. [Engraved by
Edwin Sandys, Dublin and dedicated to Baron Capell of Tewkesbury–
presumably 1693. In three sections 19 in × 15½ in. with two sections of letter-
press. The version used is from G. W. Sampson, Statistical Survey of County
Londonderry, Dublin, 1802, p. 480.] For additional Londonderry matter
see B.M. Map Room Catalogue K54/33a.

HOBSON, S. (Captain), *A Ground Plat of Londonderry etc.* to be seen in Story,
G. (Rev.) *An Impartial History of the Wars of Ireland* . . . (v. Authorities).
Coloured 'charts' of the Harbours of Kinsale, Corke, Dublin (City & Bay)
Carrickfergus, Waterford, Londonderry, in *The Accounts of His Majestys
Revenue in Ireland* . . . *From the Landing of Duke Schomberg in August 1689 to
Christmas 1693*, B. M. Egerton 790, f.4. For Carrickfergus—*A small view. With
plan of Bay and Chart of the Irish Sea*, Ashmolean. Sutherland C.I.329:73 (329).

HUDDART, J., *The Coasting Pilot for Great Britain and Ireland*, Sayer, London,
1786–94.

ADMIRALTY, Charts Nos. 2 and 2424 and various '*Pilots*'.
*Actes et Mémoires des Négociations de la Paix de Nimègue* 4 t La Haye, 1697 (3° edn).


AICKIN, J., *Londerias or a Narrative, Siege of Londonderry . . . 1689*, Dublin, 1689.

AITZEMA, L. van, *Tweede Vervolg van Saken van Staat en Oorlog in en omtrent de
Vereenigde Nederlanden . . . 1687 . . . 1692 Boek 28*, Amsterdam, 1698.

ASH, T. (Captain), *A Circumstantial Journal of the Siege of Londonderry From a
Manuscript written on the Spot at the Time*, Londonderry, 1792.

AVAUX–see d'AVAUX.

BENNET, Joseph, *A True and Impartial Account of the Most Material Passages in Ireland since December 1688, with a Particular Relation of the Forces of Londonderry, Being taken from the Notes of a Gentleman who was Eyewitness to most of the Actions mention'd during his residing there. To which is added a Description and Map of Londonderry,* 1689.

BERWICK, James (duke of), *Mémoires du Maréchal de Berwick* in Collection des Mémoires relatifs à l'histoire de France depuis l'avénement de Henri IV jusqu'à . . . *1763*, ed. Petitot, A. et Monmerque, T., [t. LXV] Paris, 1828.

BOTELER, N. (Captain), *Boteler's Dialogues,* ed. Perrin, W. G., 1929 Navy Records Society.

BURCHETT, *Memoirs of Transactions at Sea, during the War with France 1688–1697,* 1703.

BURNET, Gilbert (Bishop of Salisbury), *Bishop Burnet's History of his Own Times (with Notes by the Earls of Dartmouth and Hardwick, etc.*), ed. Routh, M. J., 6 v. Oxford, 1833.

CALMON-MAISON, J. J. R. (Marquis de), *Le Maréchal de Chateau-Renault,* Paris, 1903.
   Reproduces from Archives de la Marine, Paris
     (B⁴12 f.60 Ship List, battle of Bantry Bay 1689.
     (B⁴12 f.404 Ship list, battle of Bévéziers 1690.
     (B²28 f.345 Reprimand of Chateaurenault.
     (B²68 f.111 Louis to Chateaurenault.

CAMPANA DI CAVELLI [Emilia] (Marchesa), *Les derniers Stuarts à Saint Germain-en-Laye,* 2 t, Paris, etc. 1871.
   Reproduces from
     Archives de Medici (Florence), d'Este (Modena) and those of the departments Guerre, Marine, Affaires Etrangères, Paris, concerning James II in France, de Pointis Mission 1689 to Ireland and James sailing thither.

CLEMENT, P., *L'Italie en 1671, Relation d'un Voyage du Marquis de Seignelay . . . précédée d'une Etude Historique,* Paris, 1867.
   Reproduces
     Letters Seignelay to Chateaurenault and de Pointis, 1689.

CLARKE, J., *The Life of James II, King of England, Collected out of Memoirs writ of his own hand . . .,* 2 v. 1816 [v. I].

CONVENT–see WARNSINCK.

DALRYMPLE, John (Sir), *Memoirs of Great Britain and Ireland from the Dissolution of the last Parliament of Charles II until the Sea-battle off La Hogue,* 2 v. London and Edinburgh, 1771–3 (2nd ed.)–prints original papers.

DALTON, C., *English Army Lists and Commission Registers 1661–1714,* 6 v. 1904 [v. III].

d'AVAUX, J-A de Mesmes (Comte), *Négociations de M. le Comte d'Avaux en Irlande 1689–90,* ed. Hogan, J., Dublin, 1934.

DAVENPORT, F. M. G., *European Treaties bearing on the History of the United States and its Dependencies 1648–1697*, 2 v. Washington, 1917–29, continued by Davenport in v. III to 1715, 1934; later further continued in v. IV by Paullin, C. O. to 1815, 1937 [v. II 1650–1697].

DELABRE, J., *Tourville et la Marine de son temps. Notes, lettres et documents 1642–1701*, Paris, 1889.

de la FAYETTE, M. M. (Comtesse), *Mémoires de la Cour de France pour les armées 1688 et 1689* in *Mémoires de Mme de la Fayette*, ed. Asse, E. Paris, 1890.

de la RONCIÈRE, C. B., *Histoire de la Marine Française*, Paris, 1932.

de QUINCY—see SEVIN de QUINCY.

DOUBLET, Jean, *Journal du Corsaire Jean Doublet de Honfleur, Lieutenant de Fregate sous Louis XIV*, publié d'après le Manuscrit autographe . . . ed. Bréard, C. Paris, 1883.

DU MONT, J. (baron de Carels-Croon), *J. Corps universel diplomatique du droit des gens*, 8 t. in 15 v., Amsterdam, 1726–31 [v. VII, ii].

DWYER, P., *The Siege of Londonderry in 1689* [reproducing Walker's *A True Account* . . . and *A Vindication of the True Account*], with other original material with Notes, etc., 1893.

EVELYN, J., *The Diary of John Evelyn, now first printed in full* . . ., ed. de Beer, E. S. 6 v., Oxford, 1955.

FORBIN, C. (Comte de), *Mémoires du Comte de Forbin, Chef-d'Escadre*, 2 v., Amsterdam, 1730.

FOXCROFT, H. C., *The Life and Letters of Sir John Savile, Bart., First Marquis of Halifax* . . . (includes *Spenser House Journals*), 2 v., 1898.

[GILBERT, J. T.] *A Jacobite Narrative of the War in Ireland 1688–1691*, Dublin 1892, ed. Gilbert, J. T. (ascribed to Plunket, N.).

GRANT, J., *The Old Scots Navy from 1689–1710*, 1914, Navy Records Society. Prints original papers and broadside concerning fight of two Scots frigates and three French ships of war, 1689.

GREY, A., Debates of the House of Commons From the Year 1667 to the year 1694 collected by the Honble Anchitell Grey, Esq. . . ., 10 v. [v. IX], 1769.

HALIFAX, George (Marquis), *A Rough Draft of a New Model at Sea*, 1694.

HEMPTON, J., *The Siege and History of Londonderry*, Londonderry, 1861. Contains, inter alia, in whole or somewhat abridged, AICKIN'S Londerias and the Diaries of WALKER, MACKENZIE and ASH.

HERBERT, Arthur, Earl of Torrington, *The Earl of Torrington's Speech to the House of Commons, November 1690*, 1710.

HOSTE, Paul (le Père), *L'Art des Armées Navales ou Traité des Evolutions Navales*, Lyon, 1697.
A Jacobite Narrative—see GILBERT, J. T.

KAZNER, *Leben Friederichs von Schomberg oder Schoenburg*, 2 b, Mannheim, 1789. contains 'Tagebuch des Irlandischen Feldzugs vom Jahr 1689'.

KENNETT, White (Bishop), *A Complete History of England . . .*, 2 edn., 1719.

KILLEN, W. D.–see MACKENZIE.

LEAKE, S. Martin (Sir), *The Life of Sir John Leake, rear admiral of Great Britain*, ed. Callender, G. (Sir), 2 v., 1920. Navy Records Society.

LOUIS XIV, *Œuvres de Louis XIV*, ed. Grimond et Grouvelle, 6 v., Paris and Strasbourg 1806. Reproduces Letter to Seignelay 1689.

LUTTRELL, N., *Brief Relation of State Affairs from September 1688 to April 1714*, 6 v., Oxford, 1857.

MACKAY, H. (Major General), *Memoirs of the Wars in Scotland and Ireland, MDCLXXXIX–MDCXCI*, Edinburgh, 1833, Bannatyne Club.

MACKENZIE, J. (Rev.), *A Narrative of the Siege of Londonderry . . . Faithfully Represented to Rectifie the Mistakes and supply the Omissions of Mr Walker's Account*, 1690. *Mackenzie's Memorials of the Siege of Derry, including his narrative and its vindication*. Introduction and Notes by Killen, W. D., Belfast, 1861.

MACPHERSON, J., *Original Papers; containing the Secret History of Great Britain from the Restoration to the Accession of the House of Hanover to which are prefixed Extracts from the Life of James II as written by himself*, 2 v., 1775.

MARSDEN, R. G., Documents relating to Law and Custom of the Sea, v. II, ed. 1916, Navy Records Society.

MARTIN LEAKE, S., *Life of Sir John Leake*, 1750.

MARVELL, Andrew (the younger), *The Character of Holland* (1681), (*The Poems and Letters of Andrew Marvell*, ed. Margoliouth, H. M., Oxford, 1952). *Memoirs relating to the Lord Torrington*, ed. Laughton, J. K. (Sir), Camden Society, 1889.

MONSON, W. (Sir), *The Naval Tracts of Sir William Monson in Six Books*, ed. Oppenheim, M. IV, 1913. Navy Records Society.

PEPYS, S., *Memoirs relating to the State of the Royal Navy of England for Ten Years determined December 1688*, 1690. See also TANNER, J. R.

POWLEY, E. B., *The English Navy in the Revolution of 1688*, Cambridge, 1920. Reproduces from Dartmouth and other MSS.

PLUNKET, N.–see GILBERT.

RAPIN de THOYRAS, *The History of England written in French . . .*, trans. (with Additional Notes) Tindal, N. 1757, 4th edn, corrected 13.

RERESBY, J. (Sir), *Memoirs of Sir John Reresby*, ed. Browning, A., Glasgow 1936.

RICHARDS, *Diary of the Fleet*–see WITHEROW.

RONCIÈRE–see de la RONCIÈRE.

SÉVIGNÉ, M. R-B. (Marquise de), *Lettres de Madame de Sévigné de sa famille et de ses amis*, ed. Monmerqué, M., 16 t., Paris, 1862-6 [t. viii].

SEVIN de QUINCY (Marquis), *Histoire Militaire du Règne de Louis le Grand . . . tant sur Terre que sur Mer* (Avec approbation et privilege du roy), 7 t., La Haye, 1726 [t. II].

STEVENS, J. *A Journall of my Travels since the Revolution . . .* edited as *The Journal of John Stevens, containing a brief account of the War in Ireland 1689–91*, Murray, R. H., Oxford, 1912.

STORY, G. (Dean of Limerick), *An Impartial History of the Wars of Ireland with a Continuation thereof. In Two Parts. From the Time that Duke Schomberg Landed . . . to the 23rd of March 1691–2 . . .*, 1693 (1691).

SUE, [M. J.] E., *Histoire de la Marine Française*, 5 t., Paris, 1835–7 (XVIIᵉ Siècle [t. iv, v.]).

Reproduces from Archives de la Marine, Paris
B⁴ 12 f. 69     Chateaurenault Gabaret and Forant to Seignelay–
                Bantry Bay, 1689.

B⁴ 12 f. 101
B² 70 f.  49     } Account by Selingue, joined to letter from d'Amblemont,
          61       of fight off Texel, July 1689.
          68
C⁴ 242   253

Sue does not supply the references to the Archives which as, de la Roncière accepts, he so fully transcribes. de la Roncière *op. cit.* pp. 47, 57 supplies.

TANNER, J. R., *A Descriptive Catalogue of the Naval Manuscripts in the Pepysian Library at Magdalene College, Cambridge*, v. i, 1903. Navy Records Society.

Reproduces
Pepys 'A Register of the Ships . . . 1660 . . . 1688' 'Sea-Commission Officers–My Naval Register . . .' covering the same period. *Mr Pepys*, 1925.

TEONGE, H., *The Diary of Henry Teonge, Chaplain on board H.M. Ships . . . 1675–1679*, ed. Manwaring, G. E., 1927.

TINDAL–see Rapin de Thoyras.

TORRINGTON–see HERBERT.

VILLETTE, Philippe de Valois (Marquis de), *Mémoires . . .*, ed. Monmerqué, M., Paris, 1844.

WALKER, George (Rev.), *A True Account of the Siege of Londonderry, 1689*, with *A Vindication of the True Account of the Siege of Londonderry*, 1689.

WARNSINCK, J. C. M., *De Vloot van den Koning Stadhouder*, Amsterdam, 1934. Contains tables and, edited, Convent, Johan van (Kapitein), *Journaal gehouden int's Lants Schïp genaemt Honslaardijck . . . in Zee Gezeijlt den 24 Meij 1689*.

WITHEROW, T., *Two Diaries of Derry in 1689*, being Richards' 'Diary of the Fleet', now first printed from the original MS and Ash's *Journal of the Siege* reprinted from the edition of 1792 with Introduction and Notes by Thomas Witherow. Printed by William Gailey, Waterloo Place, Londonderry, 1888.

# KING WILLIAM'S WAR

379

## (B)
### Secondary

ANDERSON, R. C., *English Flag Officers 1688–1713* (Mariners' Mirror, XXXV, 4).

BAGWELL, R., *Ireland under the Stuarts and during the Interregnum*, 1916.

BONNER-SMITH, D., *Samuel Pepys and York Buildings* (Mariners' Mirror, XXIV, 2).

BRYANT, A. (Sir), *Samuel Pepys . . .*, 3 v., 1933–8 unfinished [v. III].

CHAPMAN, W. R. (Captain), *The Corporation of Trinity House of Deptford Stroud from the year 1660*, 1952.

CLARK, G. N. (Sir), *The Dutch Alliance and the War against French Trade*, Manchester 1923. *The Later Stuarts 1660–1714*, Oxford, 1934.

CORBETT, J. S. (Sir), *Fighting Instructions 1530–1816. Signals and Instructions 1776–1794 with Addenda*, 1905 and 1909, Navy Records Society.

de JONGE, J. C., *Geschiedenis van het Nederlandsche Zeewezen*, 5 dln en Register (2 e druk), Haarlem, 1858–62.

EHRMAN, J., *The Navy in the War of William III, 1689–1697*, Cambridge 1953. 'The Official Papers transferred by Pepys to the Admiralty by July 12th 1689' in *Mariners' Mirror XXXIV*, 4.

FAUCONIER, P., *Description Historique de Dunkerkque*, Bruges, 1735.

FIRTH, C. H. (Sir), *A Commentary on Macaulay's History of England*, 1938. *Cromwell's Army. A History of the English Soldier during the Civil Wars, the Commonwealth and the Protectorate*, 1902.

GUÉRIN, L., *L'Histoire Maritime de France depuis la fondation de Marseille jusqu'à la prix de Nimégue*, 6 t. Paris Lagny, 1859–63, [t. III].

JACKSON, George (Sir), *Naval Commissioners . . . 12 Charles II–George III*, ed. Duckett, George F. (Sir), 1889.

JONGE–see de JONGE.

KEEVIL, J. J., *Medicine and the Navy, 1200–1900*, 3 v. Edinburgh and London, 1957–. v. ii, 1649–1714.

LAWLOR, H. C., *A History of the Family of Cairns and its Connections*, 1906.

MACAULAY, T. B. (Baron), *History of England from the Accession of James II*, 5 v. 1850–. (ed. Firth, C. H. (Sir), 6 v. 1914 (illustrated)).

MALO, H., *Les Corsaires; Les Corsaires dunquerquois et Jean Bart*, 2 v. Paris, 1914.

MAZURE, F. A. J., *Histoire de la Révolution de 1688 en Angleterre*, 3 t Paris, 1848.

MILLIGAN, C. D., *The Relief of Derry*, 1946. *History of the Siege of Londonderry*, Belfast, 1951.

MONENTHEUIL, A., *Essai sur la Course, son histoire, sa réglementation son abolition*, Paris, 1898.

MORPHEW–see R. J.

MURRAY, R. H., *Revolutionary Ireland and its Settlement*, 1911.

NORMAN, C. B., *The Corsairs of France*, 1887.

OPPENHEIM, M., *A History of the Administration of the Royal Navy and of Merchant Shipping in relation to the Navy from 1509–1660, with an Introduction dealing with the Preceding Period*, 1896. Letter, *Athenaeum*, Jan. 1889.

OVINGTON, J. (Chaplain to His Majesty), *A Voyage to Suratt in the year 1689*, 1696.

PAPILLON, A. F. W., *Memoirs of Thomas Papillon of London, Merchant*, 1887.

PERRIN, W. C., *British Flags–Their early history and their development at sea . . .*, Cambridge, 1922.

RAYNAL, G. T. F. (Abbé), *Histoire Philosophique et Politique des Etablissements et du Commerce des Européens dans les Deux Indes*, 12 t. and Atlas, Paris 1820 (t. 10).

R. J. (and sold by J. MORPHEW), *The Life and Glorious Actions of the Right Honourable Sir G. Rooke*, 1707.

TANNER, J. R., *Mr Pepys*, 1925.

TRAMOND, J., *Manuel d'Histoire Maritime de la France*, Paris, 1916.

TROUDE, O., *Batailles Navales de la France*, 4 v., Paris, 1867/8.

*Ulster Journal of Archaeology*, 1898, v. IV.

VANDEREST, *Histoire de Jean Bart . . .*, 1844.

WESTLAKE, J., *The Collected Papers of John Westlake on Public International Law*, Cambridge, 1914.

WOOD, A. C., *A History of the Levant Company*, Oxford, 1935. *Pilotage and Navigation*.

A new Chart of Lough Foyle . . . 1807    Admiralty
Part of Chart 2486 (Culmore)    Admiralty
Irish Coast Pilot, 1954    Admiralty
West Coast of England Pilot, 1948    Admiralty
The British Isles, 1960 (2)    Admiralty

WHITE, T. E., *History of the Rise and Progress of the Naval Power of England interspersed with various important notices relative to the French Marine . . . Observations on the Principal Articles of the Navigation Act . . .*, 1802.

REFERENCE
*A Naval Expositor*, *1750* (Admiralty library copy). Date unknown.

Bibliotheca Lindesiana, *Handlist of Proclamations . . . 1509–1714*, v. I, Aberdeen, 1893.

*Catalogue of Tudor and Stuart Proclamations*, v. i, Oxford, 1910.

CHAMBERLAYNE, E., *Angliae Notitia or the Present State of England*, 1687 issue.

CHARNOCK, J., *Biographia Navalis*, 6 v. 1794.

CHEYNEY, C. R., *Handbook of Dates for Students of English History*, Royal Historical Society 1945.

COKAYNE, (G. E. C.) *The Complete Peerage* . . ., 8 v., 1910.

COLEY, H., *Nuncius Syderius or The Starry Messenger for 1689*.

*Diccionario de Historia de España*, Madrid, 1952.

*Dictionary of National Biography*, Oxford, 1925–.

DUZOBRY, C., BACHELET, T., DARSY, M. E., *Dictionnaire Général Biographie et d'Histoire*, Paris (édition d'après guerre).

*Enciclopedia Universal Ilustrada Europeo Americana*, Madrid.

HOEFER, J. C. F., *Nouvelle biographie universelle depuis les temps les plus récules* . . ., 46 v. Paris, 1854–66.

JAL, A., *Glossaire Nautique–Répertoire polyglotte de termes de marine, anciens et modernes*, Paris, 1848.

*La Grande Encyclopédie* . . . *par une société de savants et gens de lettres*, Lamirault et Cie, Paris . . .

LAROUSSE, P., *Grand dictionnaire universel français* . . . 17 v. Paris, 1865–90.

LOON, G. Van, *Histoire Métallique des XVII Provinces des Pays Bas* . . ., v. IV, La Haye, 1736.

*Members of Parliament, Pt. 1. Parliaments of England, 1215–1702*, 1878.

*Metallic Illustrations of British History*, v. I, 1885. *Medallic Illustrations of the History of Great Britain and Ireland*, Plates LXXI–LXXX, Oxford, 1908 (for British Museum). See also LOON, G. Van.

*New English Dictionary*, Oxford, 1933–.

POND, *An Almanack for the Year of Our Lord God, 1689*, Cambridge.

# Index